Frederick Law Olmsted

Journeys and Explorations

in

the Cotton Kingdom of America

Volume II

Elibron Classics
www.elibron.com

Elibron Classics series.

ISBN 0-543-72152-3 (paperback)
ISBN 0-543-72151-5 (hardcover)

This Elibron Classics Replica Edition is an unabridged facsimile
of the edition published in 1861 by Sampson Low, Son & Co., London.

JOURNEYS AND EXPLORATIONS

IN

THE COTTON KINGDOM.

A TRAVELLER'S OBSERVATIONS ON COTTON AND SLAVERY
IN THE AMERICAN SLAVE STATES.

BASED UPON THREE FORMER VOLUMES OF JOURNEYS AND INVESTIGATIONS
BY THE SAME AUTHOR.

BY

FREDERICK LAW OLMSTED.

IN TWO VOLUMES.

VOL. II.

LONDON:
SAMPSON LOW, SON & CO., 47 LUDGATE HILL.
1861.

LONDON: PRINTED BY WILLIAM CLOWES AND SONS, STAMFORD STREET.

CONTENTS.

CHAPTER I.

CHAPTER II.

CHAPTER III.

CHAPTER IV.

CHAPTER V.

CHAPTER VI.

CHAPTER VII.

CHAPTER VIII.

CHAPTER IX.

APPENDIX (A.)

APPENDIX (B.)

APPENDIX (C.)

APPENDIX (D.)

COTTON AND SLAVERY.

CHAPTER I.

SOUTH-WESTERN LOUISIANA AND EASTERN TEXAS.

Nacogdoches.—In this town of 500 inhabitants, we found there was no flour. At San Augustine we had inquired in vain at all the stores for refined sugar. Not satisfied with some blankets that were shown us, we were politely recommended by the shopkeeper to try other stores. At each of the other stores we were told they had none: the only blankets in town we should find at ———'s, naming the one we had just quitted. The same thing occurred with several other articles.

Houston County.—This day's ride and the next were through a very poor country, clay or sand soil, bearing short oaks and black-jack. We passed one small meadow, or prairie, covered with coarse grass. Deserted plantations appeared again in greater numbers than the occupied. One farm, near which we stopped, was worked by eight field hands. The crop had been fifty bales; small, owing to a dry season. The corn had been exceedingly poor. The hands, we noticed, came in from the fields after eight o'clock.

The deserted houses, B. said, were built before the date of Texan Independence. After Annexation the owners had moved on to better lands in the West. One house he pointed out as having been the residence of one of a band of pirates who occupied the country thirty or forty years ago. They had all been gradually killed.

During the day we met two men on horseback, one upon wheels, and passed one emigrant family. This was all the motion upon the principal road of the district.

The second day's camp was a few miles beyond the town of Crockett, the shire-town of Houston County. Not being able to find corn for our horses, we returned to the village for it.

We obtained what we wanted for a day's rest, which we proposed for Sunday, the following day, and loaded it into our emptied hampers. We then looked about the town for current provisions for ourselves. We were rejoiced to find a German baker, but damped by finding he had only molasses-cakes and candies for sale. There was no flour in the town, except the little of which he made his cakes. He was from Hamburgh, and though he found a tolerable sale, to emigrants principally, he was very tired of Crockett, and intended to move to San Antonio among his countrymen. He offered us coffee, and said he had had beer, but on Christmas-day a mass of people called on him; he had "treated" them all, and they had finished his supply.

We inquired at seven stores, and at the two inns for butter, flour, or wheat-bread, and fresh meat. There was none in town. One innkeeper offered us salt beef, the only meat, except pork, in town. At the stores we found crackers, worth in New York 6 cents a pound, sold here at 20 cents; poor raisins, 30 cents; Manilla rope, half-inch, 30 cents a pound. When butter was to be had it came in firkins from New York, although an excellent grazing country is near the town.

Trinity Bottom.—On landing on the west side of the

Trinity, we entered a rich bottom, even in winter, of an almost tropical aspect. The road had been cut through a cane-brake, itself a sort of Brobdignag grass. Immense trees, of a great variety of kinds, interlaced their branches and reeled with their own rank growth. Many vines, especially huge grape-vines, ran hanging from tree to tree, adding to the luxuriant confusion. Spanish moss clung thick everywhere, supplying the shadows of a winter foliage.

These bottom lands bordering the Trinity are among the richest of rich Texas. They are not considered equal, in degree of fatness, to some parts of the Brazos, Colorado, and Guadaloupe bottoms, but are thought to have compensation in reliability for steady cropping.

We made our camp on the edge of the bottom, and for safety against our dirty persecutors, the hogs, pitched our tent *within* a large hog-yard, putting up the bars to exclude them. The trees within had been sparingly cut, and we easily found tent-poles and fuel at hand.

The plantation on which we were thus intruding had just been sold, we learned, at two dollars per acre. There were seven hundred acres, and the buildings, with a new gin-house, worth nearly one thousand dollars, were included in the price. With the land were sold eight prime field-hands. A quarter of the land was probably subject to overflow, and the limits extended over some unproductive upland.

When field-hands are sold in this way with the land, the family servants, who have usually been selected from the field-hands, must be detached to follow the fortunes of the seller. When, on the other hand, the land is sold simply, the whole body of slaves move away, leaving frequently wives and children on neighbouring plantations. Such a cause of separation must be exceedingly common among the restless, almost nomadic, small proprietors of the South.

But the very word "sale," applied to a slave, implies this cruelty, leaving, of course, the creature's whole happiness to his owner's discretion and humanity.

As if to give the lie to our reflections, however, the rascals here appeared to be particularly jolly, perhaps adopting Mark Tapley's good principles. They were astir half the night, talking, joking, and singing loud and merrily.

This plantation had made this year seven bales to the hand. The water for the house, we noticed, was brought upon heads a quarter of a mile, from a rain-pool, in which an old negress was washing.

At an old Settler's.—The room was fourteen feet square, with battens of split boards tacked on between the broader openings of the logs. Above, it was open to the rafters, and in many places the sky could be seen between the shingles of the roof. A rough board box, three feet square, with a shelf in it, contained the crockery-ware of the establishment; another similar box held the store of meal, coffee, sugar, and salt; a log crib at the horse-pen held the corn, from which the meal was daily ground, and a log smoke or store-house contained the store of pork. A canopy-bed filled one quarter of the room; a cradle, four chairs seated with untanned deer-hide, a table, a skillet or bake-kettle, a coffee-kettle, a frying-pan, and a rifle laid across two wooden pegs on the chimney, with a string of patches, powder-horn, pouch, and hunting-knife, completed the furniture of the house. We all sat with hats and overcoats on, and the woman cooked in bonnet and shawl. As I sat in the chimney-corner I could put both my hands out, one laid on the other, between the stones of the fire-place and the logs of the wall.

A pallet of quilts and blankets was spread for us in the

lean-to, just between the two doors. We slept in all our clothes, including overcoats, hats, and boots, and covered entirely with blankets. At seven in the morning, when we threw them off, the mercury in the thermometer in our saddle-bags, which we had used for a pillow, stood at 25° Fahrenheit.

We contrived to make cloaks and hoods from our blankets, and after going through with the fry, coffee and pone again, and paying one dollar each for the entertainment of ourselves and horses, we continued our journey.

Caldwell.—Late in the same evening we reached a hamlet, the "seat of justice" of Burleson County. We were obliged to leave our horses in a stable, made up of a roof, in which was a loft for the storage of provender, set upon posts, without side-boarding, so that the norther met with no obstruction. It was filled with horses, and ours alone were blanketed for the night. The mangers were very shallow and narrow, and as the corn was fed on the cob, a considerable proportion of it was thrown out by the horses in their efforts to detach the edible portion. With laudable economy, our landlord had twenty-five or thirty pigs running at large in the stable, to prevent this overflow from being wasted.

The "hotel" was an unusually large and fine one; the principal room had glass windows. Several panes of these were, however, broken, and the outside door could not be closed from without; and when closed, was generally pried open with a pocket-knife by those who wished to go out. A great part of the time it was left open. Supper was served in another room, in which there was no fire, and the outside door was left open for the convenience of the servants, in passing to and from the kitchen, which, as usual here at large houses, was in a detached building. Supper was, however, eaten with such rapidity that nothing had time to freeze on the table.

There were six Texans, planters and herdsmen, who had made harbour at the inn for the norther, two German shopkeepers and a young lawyer, who were boarders, besides our party of three, who had to be seated before the fire. We kept coats and hats on, and gained as much warmth, from the friendly manner in which we drew together, as possible. After ascertaining, by a not at all impertinent or inconsiderate method of inquiry, where we were from, which way we were going, what we thought of the country, what we thought of the weather, and what were the capacities and the cost of our fire-arms, we were considered as initiated members of the crowd, and "the conversation became general."

The matter of most interest came up in this wise: "The man made a white boy, fourteen or fifteen years old, get up and go out in the norther for wood, when there was a great, strong nigger fellow lying on the floor doing nothing. God! I had an appetite to give him a hundred, right there."

"Why, you wouldn't go out into the norther yourself, would you, if you were not obliged to?" inquired one, laughingly.

"I wouldn't have a nigger in my house that I was afraid to set to work, at anything I wanted him to do, at any time. They'd hired him out to go to a new place next Thursday, and they were afraid if they didn't treat him well, he'd run away. If I couldn't break a nigger of running away, I wouldn't have him any how."

"I can tell you how you can break a nigger of running away, certain," said another. "There was an old fellow I used to know in Georgia, that always cured his so. If a nigger ran away, when he caught him, he would bind his knee over a log, and fasten him so he couldn't stir; then he'd take a pair of pincers and pull one of his toe-nails out by the roots; and tell him that if he ever run away again, he would pull out two of them, and if he run away again after that, he told them he'd pull out four of them, and so on, doubling each time. He never had to do it more than twice—it always cured them."

One of the company then said that he was at the present time in pursuit of a negro. He had bought him of a relative in Mississippi, and had been told that he was a great runaway. He had, in fact, run away from his relative three times, and always when they caught him he was trying to *get back to Illinois*;* that was the reason he sold him. "He offered him to me cheap," he continued, "and I bought him because he was a first-rate nigger, and I thought perhaps I could break him of running away by bringing him down to this new country. I expect he's making for Mexico now. I am a-most sure I saw his tracks on the road about twelve miles back, where he was a-coming on this way. Night before last I engaged with a man who's got some first-rate nigger dogs to meet me here to-night; but I suppose the cold keeps him back." He then asked us to look out for him as we went on west, and gave us a minute description of him that we might recognize him. He was "a real black nigger," and carried off a double-barrelled gun with him. Another man, who was going on by another road westward, offered to look for him that way, and to advertise him. Would he be likely to defend himself with the gun if he should try to secure him? he asked. The owner said he had no doubt he would. He was as humble a nigger when he was at work as ever he had seen; but he was a mighty resolute nigger—there was no man had more resolution. "Couldn't I induce him to let me take the gun by pretend-

* Many freemen have been kidnapped in Illinois and sold into slavery.

ing I wanted to look at it, or something? I'd talk to him simple; make as if I was a stranger, and ask him about the road, and so on, and finally ask him what he had got for a gun, and to let me look at it." The owner didn't believe he'd let go of the gun; he was a "nigger of sense—as much sense as a white man; he was not one of your kinkey-headed niggers." The chances of catching him were discussed. Some thought they were good, and some that the owner might almost as well give it up, he'd got such a start. It was three hundred miles to the Mexican frontier, and he'd have to make fires to cook the game he would kill, and could travel only at night; but then every nigger or Mexican he could find would help him, and if he had so much sense, he'd manage to find out his way pretty straight, and yet not have white folks see him.

We slept in a large upper room, in a company of five, with a broken window at the head of our bed, and another at our side, offering a short cut to the norther across our heads.

We were greatly amused to see one of our bed-room companions gravely *spit* in the candle before jumping into bed, explaining to some one who made a remark, that he always did so, it gave him time to see what he was about before it went out.

The next morning the ground was covered with sleet, and the gale still continued (a pretty steady close-reefing breeze) during the day.

We wished to have a horse shod. The blacksmith, who was a white man, we found in his shop, cleaning a fowling-piece. It was too d——d cold to work, he said, and he was going to shoot some geese; he, at length, at our urgent request, consented to earn a dollar; but, after getting on his apron, he found that we had lost a shoe, and took it off again, refusing to make a shoe while this d——d norther lasted, for any man. As he had no shoes ready made, he absolutely turned us out of the shop, and obliged us to go seventy-five miles further, a great part of the way over a pebbly road, by which the beast lost three shoes before he could be shod.

This respect for the north wind is by no means singular here. The publication of the week's newspaper in Bastrop was interrupted by the norther, the editor mentioning, as a sufficient reason for the irregularity, the fact that his printing-office was in the north part of the house.

Austin.—Before leaving Eastern Texas behind us, I must add a random note or two, the dates of which it would have been uncivil to indicate.

We stopped one night at the house of a planter, now twenty years settled in Eastern Texas. He was a man of some education and natural intelligence, and had, he told us, an income, from the labour of his slaves, of some $4,000. His residence was one of the largest houses we had seen in Texas. It had a second story, two wings and a long gallery. Its windows had been once glazed, but now, out of eighty panes that originally filled the lower windows, thirty only remained unbroken. Not a door in the house had been ever furnished with a latch or even a string; when they were closed, it was necessary to *claw* or to ask some one inside to push open. (Yet we happened to hear a neighbour expressing serious admiration of the way these doors fitted.) The furniture was of the rudest description.

One of the family had just had a hæmorrhage of the lungs; while we were at supper, this person sat between the big fireplace and an open outside door, having a window, too, at his side, in which only three panes remained. A norther was blowing, and ice forming upon the gallery outside. Next day, at breakfast, the invalid was unable to appear on account of a "bad turn."

On our supper-table was nothing else than the eternal fry, pone and coffee. Butter, of dreadful odour, was here added by exception. Wheat flour they never used. It was "too much trouble."

We were waited upon by two negro girls, dressed in short-waisted, twilled-cotton gowns, once white, now looking as if they had been worn by chimney-sweeps. The water for the family was brought in tubs upon the heads of these two girls, from a creek, a quarter of a mile distant, this occupation filling nearly all their time.

This gentleman had thirty or forty negroes, and two legitimate sons. One was an idle young man. The other was, at eight years old, a swearing, tobacco-chewing bully and ruffian. We heard him whipping a puppy behind the house, and swearing between the blows, his father and mother being at hand. His language and tone was an evident imitation of his father's mode of dealing with his slaves.

"I've got an account to settle with you; I've let you go about long enough; I'll teach you who's your master; there, go now, God damn you, but I havn't got through with you yet."

"You stop that cursing," said his father, at length, "it isn't right for little boys to curse."

"What do *you* do when you get mad?" replied the boy; "reckon you cuss some; so now you'd better shut up."

In the whole journey through Eastern Texas, we did not see one of the inhabitants look into a newspaper or a book, although we spent days in houses where men were lounging about the fire without occupation. One evening I took up a paper which had been lying unopened upon the table of the inn where we were staying, and smiled to see how painfully news items dribbled into the Texas country papers, the loss of the tug-boat "Ajax," which occurred before we left New York, being here just given as the loss of the "splendid steamer Ocax."

A man who sat near said—

"Reckon you've read a good deal, hain't you?"

"Oh, yes; why?"

"Reckon'd you had."

"Why?"

"You look as though you liked to read. Well, it's a good thing. S'pose you take a pleasure in reading, don't you?"

"That depends, of course, on what I have to read. I suppose everybody likes to read when they find anything interesting to them, don't they?"

"No; it's damn tiresome to some folks, I reckon, any how, 'less you've got the habit of it. Well, it's a good thing; you can pass away your time so."

The sort of interest taken in foreign affairs is well enough illustrated by the views of a gentleman of property in Eastern Texas, who was sitting with us one night, "spitting in the fire," and talking about cotton. Bad luck he had had—only four bales to the hand; couldn't account for it—bad luck; and next year he didn't reckon nothing else but that there would be a general war in Europe, and then he'd be in a pretty fix, with cotton down to four cents a pound. Curse those Turks! If he thought there would be a general war, he would take every d——d nigger he'd got, right down to New Orleans, and sell them for what they'd bring. They'd never be so high again as they were now, and if there should come a general war they wouldn't be worth half as much next year. There always were infernal rascals somewhere in the world trying to prevent an honest man from getting a living.

Oh, if they got to fighting, he hoped they'd eat each other up. They just ought to be, all of them—Turks, and Russians, and Prussians, and Dutchmen, and Frenchmen—just be put in a bag together, and slung into hell. That's what he'd do with them.

Remarking, one day, at the house of a woman who was brought up at the North, that there was much more comfort at her house than any we had previously stopped at, she told us that the only reason the people didn't have any comfort here was, that they wouldn't *take any trouble* to get anything. Anything that their negroes could make they would eat; but they would take no pains to instruct them, or to get anything that didn't grow on the plantation. A neighbour of hers owned fifty cows, she supposed, but very rarely had any milk and scarcely ever any butter, simply because his people were too lazy to milk or churn, and he wouldn't take the trouble to make them.

This woman entirely sustained the assertion that Northern people, when they come to the South, have less feeling for the negroes than Southerners themselves usually have. We asked her (she lived in a village) whether she hired or owned her servants. They owned them all, she said. When they first came to Texas they hired servants, but it was very troublesome; they would take no interest in anything; and she couldn't get along with them. Then very often their owners, on some pretext (ill-treatment, perhaps), would take them away. Then they bought negroes. It was very expensive: a good negro girl cost seven or eight hundred dollars, and that, we must know, was a great deal of money to be laid out in a thing that might lie right down the next day and die. They were not much better either than the hired servants.

Folks up North talked about how badly the negroes were treated; she wished they could see how much work her girls did. She had four of them, and she knew they didn't do half so much work as one good Dutch girl such as she used to have at the North. Oh! the negroes were the laziest things in creation; there was no knowing how much trouble they gave to look after them. Up to the North, if a girl went out into the garden for anything, when she came back she would clean her feet, but these nigger girls will stump right in and track mud all over the house. What do they care? They'd just as lief clean the mud after themselves as anything else—their time isn't any value to themselves. What do they care for the trouble it gives you? Not a bit. And you may scold 'em and whip 'em—you never can break 'em into better habits.

I asked what were servants' wages when they were hired out to do housework? They were paid seven or eight dollars a month; sometimes ten. She didn't use to pay her girl at the North but four dollars, and she knew she would do more work than any six of the niggers, and not give half so much trouble as one. But you couldn't get any other help here but niggers. Northern folks talk about abolishing slavery, but there wouldn't be any use in that; that would be ridiculous, unless you could some way get rid of the niggers. Why, they'd murder us all in our beds—that's what they'd do. Why, over to Fannin, there was a negro woman that killed her mistress with an axe, and her two little ones. The people just flocked together, and hung her right up on the spot; they ought to have piled some wood round her, and burned her to death; that would have been a good lesson to the rest. We afterwards heard her scolding one of her girls; the girl made some exculpatory reply, and getting the best of the argument, the mistress angrily told her if she said another word she would have two hundred lashes given her. She came in and remarked that if she hadn't felt so nervous she would have given that girl a good whipping herself; these niggers are so saucy, it's very trying to one who has to take care of them.

Servants are, it is true, "a trial," in all lands, ages, and nations. But note the fatal reason this woman frankly gives for the inevitable delinquencies of slave-servants, "Their time isn't any value to themselves!"

The women of Eastern Texas seemed to us, in general, far superior to their lords. They have, at least, the tender hearts and some of the gentle delicacy that your "true Texan" lacks, whether mistresses of slaves, or only of their own frying-pan. They are overworked, however, as soon as married, and care gives them thin faces, sallow complexions, and expressions either sad or sour.

Another night we spent at the house of a man who came here, when a boy, from the North. His father was a mechanic, and had emigrated to Texas just before the war of Independence. He joined the army, and his son had been brought up—rather had grown up—Southern fashion, with no training to regular industry. He had learned no trade. What need? His father received some thousand acres of land in payment of his services. The son earned some money by driving a team; bought some cattle, took a wife, and a house, and now had been settled six years, with a young family. He had nothing to do but look after his cattle, go to the nearest town and buy meal and coffee occasionally, and sell a few oxen when the bill was sent in. His house was more comfortless than nine-tenths of the stables of the North. There were several windows, some of which were boarded over, some had wooden shutters, and some were entirely open. There was not a pane of glass. The doors were closed with difficulty. We could see the stars, as we lay in bed, through the openings of the roof; and on all sides, in the walls of the room, one's arm might be thrust out. Notwithstanding, that night the mercury fell below 25° of our Fahrenheit thermometer. There was the standard food and beverage, placed before us night and morning. We asked if there was much game near him? There were a great many deer. He saw them every day. Did he shoot many? He never shot any; 'twas too much trouble. When he wanted "fresh," 'twas easier to go out and stick a hog (the very words he used). He had just corn enough to give our horses one feed —there was none left for the morning. His own horses could get along through the winter on the prairie. He made pets of his children, but was cross and unjust to his wife, who might have been pretty, and was affectionate. He was without care—thoughtless, content, with an unoccupied mind. He took no newspaper—he read nothing. There was, indeed, a pile of old books which his father had brought from the North, but they seemed to be all of the Tract Society sort, and the dust had been undisturbed upon them, it might have been, for many years.

Manchac Spring.—We found a plantation that would have done no discredit to Virginia. The house was large and well constructed, standing in a thick grove, separated from the prairie by a strong worm-fence. Adjacent, within, was the spring, which deserved its prominence of mention upon the maps. It had been tastefully grottoed with heavy limestone rocks, now water-stained and mossy, and the pure stream came gurgling up, in impetuous gallons, to pour itself in a bright current out upon the prairie. The fountains of Italy were what came to mind and "Fontana de Manciocco" would have secured a more natural name.

Everything about the house was orderly and neat. The proprietor came out to receive us, and issued orders about the horses, which we felt, from their quiet tone, would be obeyed without our supervision. When we were ushered into a snug supper-room and found a clean table set with wheat-bread, ham, tea, and preserved fruits, waited on by tidy and ready girls, we could scarce think we had not got beyond the bounds of Texas. We were, in fact, quit, for some time to come, of the lazy poverty of Eastern Texas.

Lower Guadaloupe.—Not finding a suitable camping place, we stumbled, after dark, into a large plantation upon the river bottom.

The irruption of our train within the plantation fences caused a furious commotion among the dogs and little negroes, and it was with no little difficulty we could explain to the planter, who appeared with a candle, which was instantly blown out upon the porch, our peaceable intentions. Finally, after a general striking out of Fanny's heels and the master's boots, aided by the throwing of our loose lariats into the confused crowd, the growling and chattering circle about us was sufficiently enlarged and subdued for us to obtain a hearing, and we were hospitably received.

"Ho, Sam! You Tom, here! Call your missus. Suke! if you don't stop that infernal noise I'll have you drowned! Here, Bill! Josh! some of you! why don't you help the gentleman? Bring a lantern here! Packed, are you, sir. Hold on, you there; leave the gun alone. Now, clear out with you, you little devils, every one of you! Is there no one in the house? St! after 'em, Tiger! Can't any of you find a lantern? Where's Bill, to take these horses? What are you doing there? I tell you to be off, now, every one of you! Tom! take a rail and keep 'em off there!"

In the midst of the noise we go through the familiar motions, and land our saddles and hampers upon the gallery, then follow what appears to be the headmost negro to the stable, and give him a hint to look well out for the horses.

This is our first reintroduction to negro servants after our German experiences, and the contrast is most striking and disagreeable. Here were thirty or forty slaves, but not an order could be executed without more reiteration, and threats, and oaths, and greater trouble to the master and mistress, than would be needed to get a squadron under way. We heard the master threaten his negroes with flogging, at least six times, before we went to bed. In the night a heavy rain came up, and he rose, on hearing it, to arrange the cistern spout, cursing again his infernal niggers, who had turned it off for some convenience of their own. In the morning, we heard the mistress scolding her girls for having left articles outside which had been spoiled by the wet, after repeated orders to bring them in. On visiting the stables we found the door fastened by a board leaned against it.

All the animals were loose, except the mule, which I had fastened myself. The rope attached to my saddle was stolen, and a shorter one substituted for it, when I mentioned the fact, by which I was deceived, until we were too far off to return. The master, seeing the horses had yet had no fodder, called to a boy to get some for them, then, countermanding his order, told the boy to call some one else, and go himself to drive the cows out of the garden. Then, to another boy, he said, "Go and pull two or three bundles of fodder out of the stack and give these horses." The boy soon came with two small bundles. "You infernal rascal, couldn't you tote more fodder than that? Go back and bring four or five bundles, and be quick about it, or I'll lick you." The boy walked slowly back, and returned with four bundles more.

But on entering at night we were struck with the air of comfort that met us. We were seated in rocking-chairs in a well-furnished room, before a blazing fire, offered water to wash, in a little lean-to bed-room, and, though we had two hours to wait for our supper, it was most excellent, and we passed an agreeable evening in intelligent conversation with our host.

After his curiosity about us was satisfied, we learned from him that, though a young man, he was an old settler, and had made a comfortable fortune by his plantation. His wife gave us a picturesque account of their waggon journey here with their people, and described the hardships, dangers, and privations they had at first to endure. Now they were far more comfortable than they could have ever hoped to have been in the State from which they came. They thought their farm the best cotton land in the world. It extended across a mile of timbered bottom land from the river, then over a mile of bottom prairie, and included a large tract of the big prairie "for range." Their field would produce, in a favourable season, three bales to the acre; ordinarily a bale and a half: the "bale" 400 lbs. They had always far more than their hands could pick. It was much more free from weeds than the States, so much so, that three hands would be needed there to cultivate the same area as two here; that is, with the same hands the crop would be one-third greater.

But so anxious is every one in Texas to give all strangers a favourable impression, that all statements as to the extreme profit and healthfulness of lands must be taken with a grain of allowance. We found it very difficult, without impertinent persistence, to obtain any unfavourable facts. Persons not interested informed us, that from one-third to one-half the cotton crop on some of these rich plantations had been cut off by the worm, on several occasions, and that negroes suffered much with dysentery and pneumonia.

It cost them very little to haul their cotton to the coast or to get supplies. They had not been more sickly than they would have been on the Mississippi. They considered that their steady sea-breeze was almost a sure preventive of such diseases as they had higher up the country.

They always employed German mechanics, and spoke well of them. Mexicans were regarded in a somewhat unchristian tone, not as heretics or heathen, to be converted with flannel and tracts, but rather as vermin, to be exterminated. The lady was particularly strong in her prejudices. White folks and Mexicans were never made to live together, anyhow, and the Mexicans had no business here. They were getting so impertinent, and were so well protected by the laws, that the Americans would just have to get together and drive them all out of the country.

On the Chockolate.—"Which way did you come?" asked some one of the old man.

"From ——."

"See anything of a runaway nigger over there, anywhar?"

"No, sir. What kind of a nigger was it?"

"A small, black, screwed-up-faced nigger."

"How long has he been out?"

"Nigh two weeks."

"Whose is he?"

"Judge ——'s, up here. And he cut the judge right bad. Like to have killed the judge. Cut his young master, too."

"Reckon, if they caught him, 'twould go rather hard with him."

"Reckon 'twould. We caught him once, but he got away

from us again. We was just tying his feet together, and he give me a kick in the face, and broke. I had my six-shooter handy, and I tried to shoot him, but every barrel missed fire. Been loaded a week. We shot at him three times with rifles, but he'd got too far off, and we didn't hit, but we must have shaved him close. We chased him, and my dog got close to him once. If he'd grip'd him, we should have got him; but he had a dog himself, and just as my dog got within about a yard of him, his dog turned and fit my dog, and he hurt him so bad we couldn't get him to run him again. We run him close, though, I tell you. Run him out of his coat, and his boots, and a pistol he'd got. But 'twas getting towards dark, and he got into them bayous, and kept swimming from one side to another."

"How long ago was that?"

"Ten days."

"If he's got across the river, he'd get to the Mexicans in two days, and there he'd be safe. The Mexicans'd take care of him."

"What made him run?"

"The judge gave him a week at Christmas, and when the week was up, I s'pose he didn't want to go to work again. He got unruly, and they was a goin' to whip him."

"Now, how much happier that fellow'd 'a' been, if he'd just stayed and done his duty. He might have just worked and done his duty, and his master'd 'a' taken care of him, and given him another week when Christmas come again, and he'd 'a' had nothing to do but enjoy himself again. These niggers, none of 'em, knows how much happier off they are than if they was free. Now, very likely, he'll starve to death, or get shot."

"Oh, the judge treats his niggers too kind. If he was

stricter with them, they'd have more respect for him, and be more contented, too."

"Never do to be too slack with niggers."

We were riding in company, to-day, with a California drover, named Rankin. He was in search of cattle to drive across the plains. He had taken a drove before from Illinois, and told us that people in that State, of equal circumstances, lived ten times better than here, in all matters of comfort and refinement. He had suffered more in travelling in Texas, than ever on the plains or the mountains. Not long before, in driving some mules with his partner, they came to a house which was the last on the road for fourteen miles. They had nothing in the world in the house but a few ears of corn, they were going to grind in their steel mill for their own breakfast, and wouldn't sell on any terms. "We hadn't eaten anything since breakfast, but we actually could get nothing. The only other thing in the cabin, that could be eaten, was a pile of deer-skins, with the hair on. We had to stake our mules, and make a fire, and coil around it. About twelve o'clock there came a norther. We heard it coming, and it made us howl. We didn't sleep a wink for cold."

Houston.—We were sitting on the gallery of the hotel. A tall, jet black negro came up, leading by a rope a downcast mulatto, whose hands were lashed by a cord to his waist, and whose face was horribly cut, and dripping with blood. The wounded man crouched and leaned for support against one of the columns of the gallery—faint and sick.

"What's the matter with that boy?" asked a smoking lounger.

"I run a fork into his face," answered the negro.

"What are his hands tied for?"

"He's a runaway, sir."

"Did you catch him?"

"Yes, sir. He was hiding in the hay-loft, and when I went up to throw some hay to the horses, I pushed the fork down into the mow and it struck something hard. I didn't know what it was, and I pushed hard, and gave it a turn, and then he hollered, and I took it out."

"What do you bring him here, for?"

"Come for the key of the jail, sir, to lock him up."

"What!" said another, "one darkey catch another darkey? Don't believe that story."

"Oh yes, mass'r, I tell for true. He was down in our hay-loft, and so you see when I stab him, I *have to* catch him."

"Why, he's hurt bad, isn't he?"

"Yes, he says I pushed through the bones."

"Whose nigger is he?"

"He says he belong to Mass'r Frost, sir, on the Brazos."

The key was soon brought, and the negro led the mulatto away to jail. He walked away limping, crouching, and writhing, as if he had received other injuries than those on his face. The bystanders remarked that the negro had not probably told the whole story.

We afterwards happened to see a gentleman on horseback, and smoking, leading by a long rope through the deep mud, out into the country, the poor mulatto, still limping and crouching, his hands manacled, and his arms pinioned.

There is a prominent slave-mart in town, which holds a large lot of likely-looking negroes, waiting purchasers. In the windows of shops, and on the doors and columns of the hotel, are many written advertisements, headed "A likely negro girl for sale." "Two negroes for sale." "Twenty negro boys for sale," etc.

South-eastern Texas.—We were unable to procure at Houston any definite information with regard to our proposed route. The known roads thence are those that branch northward and westward from their levee, and so thoroughly within lines of business does local knowledge lie, that the eastern shore is completely terra incognita. The roads east were said to be bad after heavy rains, but the season had been dry, and we determined to follow the direct and the distinct road, laid down upon our map.

Now that I am in a position to give preliminary information, however, there is no reason why the reader should enter this region as ignorant as we did.

Our route took us by Harrisburg and San Jacinto to Liberty, upon the Trinity; thence by Beaumont to the Sabine at Turner's ferry; thence by the Big Woods and Lake Charles to Opelousas, the old capital of St. Landry Parish, at the western head of the intricate navigation from New Orleans.

This large district, extending from the Trinity River to the bayous of the Mississippi, has, throughout, the same general characteristics, the principal of which are, lowness, flatness, and wetness. The soil is variable, but is in greater part a loose, sandy loam, covered with coarse grasses, forming level prairies, which are everywhere broken by belts of pine forests, usually bordering creeks and bayous, but often standing in islands. The surface is but very slightly elevated above the sea; I suppose, upon an average, less than ten feet. It is, consequently, imperfectly drained, and in a wet season a large proportion is literally covered with water, as in crossing it, even in a dry time, we were obliged to wade through many miles of marshy pools. The river-bottoms, still lower than the general level, are subject to constant overflow by tide-water, and what with the fallen timber, the dense undergrowth, the mire-quags, the abrupt gullies, the patches of rotten or floating corduroy, and three or four feet of dirty salt water, the roads through them are not such as one would choose for a morning ride. The country is sparsely settled, containing less than one inhabitant to the square mile, one in four being a slave.

The many pools, through which the usual track took us, were swarming with venemous water-snakes, four or five black moccasins often lifting at once their devilish heads above the dirty surface, and wriggling about our horses' heels. Beyond the Sabine, alligator holes are an additional excitement, the unsuspicious traveller suddenly sinking through the treacherous surface, and sometimes falling a victim, horse and all, to the hideous jaws of the reptile, while overwhelmed by the engulfing mire in which he lurks.

Upon the whole, this is not the spot in which I should prefer to come to light, burn, and expire; in fact, if the nether regions, as was suggested by the dream-gentleman of Nachitoches, be "a boggy country," the avernal entrance might, I should think, with good probabilities, be looked for in this region.

We passed, on both sides the Sabine, many abandoned farms, and the country is but thinly settled. We found it impossible to obtain any information about roads, and frequently went astray upon cattle paths, once losing twenty miles in a day's journey. The people were chiefly herdsmen; cultivating a little cotton upon river-banks, but ordinarily only corn, with a patch of cane to furnish household sugar. We tried in vain to purchase corn for our horses, and were told that "folks didn't make corn enough to bread them, and if anybody had corn to give his horse, he carried it in his hat and went out behind somewhere." The herds were in poor condition, and must in winter be reduced to the verge of starvation. We saw a few hogs, converted, by hardship, to figures so unnatural, that we at first took them for goats. Most of the people we met were old emigrants, from Southern Louisiana and Mississippi, and more disposed to gaiety and cheer than the Texan planters. The houses showed a tendency to Louisiana forms, and the table to a French style of serving the jerked beef, which is the general dish of the country. The meat is dried in strips, over smoky fires, and, if untainted and well prepared, is a tolerably savoury food. I hardly know whether to chronicle it as a border barbarism, or a Creolism, that we were several times, in this neighbourhood, shown to a bed standing next to that occupied by the host and his wife, sometimes with the screen of a shawl, sometimes without.

We met with one specimen of the Virginia habit of "dipping," or snuff-chewing, in the person of a woman who was otherwise neat and agreeable, and observed that a young lady, well-dressed, and apparently engaged, while we were present, in reading, went afterward to light her pipe at the kitchen fire, and had a smoke behind the house.

The condition of the young men appeared to incline decidedly to barbarism. We stopped a night at a house in which a drover, bringing mules from Mexico, was staying; and, with the neighbours who had come to look at the drove, we were thirteen men at table. When speaking with us, all were polite and respectful, the women especially so; but among one another, their coarseness was incredible. The master of the house, a well-known gentleman of the county, who had been absent when we arrived, and at supper-time, came afterwards upon the gallery and commenced cursing furiously, because some one had taken his pipe. Seeing us, he stopped abruptly, and after lighting the pipe, said, in a rather peremptory and formal, but not uncourteous tone: "Where are you from, gentlemen?"

"From Beaumont, sir, last."

"Been out West?"

"Yes, sir."

"Travelling?"

"Yes, sir."

After pausing a moment to make up his mind—

"Where do you live when you are at home, gentlemen, and what's your business in this country?"

"We live in New York, and are travelling to see the country."

"How do you like it?"

"Just here we find it flat and wet."

"What's your name?"

"Olmsted."

"And what's this gentleman's name?"

"Olmsted."

"Is it a Spanish name?"

"No, sir."

He then abruptly left us, and the young men entertained one another with stories of fights and horse-trades, and with vulgar obscenities.

Shortly he returned, saying—

"Show you to bed now, gentlemen, if you wish."

"We are ready, sir, if you will be good enough to get a light."

"A light?"

"Yes, sir."

"*A light?*"

"Yes, sir."

"Get a light?"

"Yes, sir."

"Well" (after a moment's hesitation), "I'll get one."

On reaching the bed-room, which was in a building adjoining, he stood awaiting our pleasure. Thanking him, I turned to take the light, but his fingers were the candlestick. He continued to hold it, and six young men, who had followed us, stood grouped around while we undressed, placing our clothes upon the floor. Judy advanced to lie down by them. One of the young men started forward, and said—

"I've got a right good knife."

"What?"

"I've got a right good knife, if you want it."

"What do you mean?"

"Nothing, only I've got a right good knife, and if you'd like to kill that dog, I'll lend it to you."

"Please to tell me what you mean?"

"Oh, nothing."

"Keep your dog quiet, or I'll kill her," I suppose was the interpretation. When we had covered ourselves in bed, the host said—

"I suppose you don't want the light no more?"

"No, sir;" and all bade us good night; but leaving the door open, commenced feats of prolonged dancing, or stamping upon the gallery, which were uproariously applauded. Then came more obscenities and profanities, apropos to fandango frolics described by the drovers. As we had barely got to sleep, several came to occupy other beds in our room. They had been drinking freely, and continued smoking in bed.

Upon the floor lay two boys of fourteen, who continued shouting and laughing after the others had at length become quiet. Some one soon said to one of them—

"You had better stop your noise; Frank says he'll be damn'd if he don't come in and give you a hiding."

Frank was trying to sleep upon the gallery.

"By ——," the boy cried, raising himself, and drawing a coat from under the pillow, "if he comes in here, I'll be damn'd if I don't kill him. He dare not come in here. I would like to see him come in here," drawing from his coat pocket a revolver, and cocking it. "By ——, you may come in here now. Come in here, come in here! Do you here that?" (revolving the pistol rapidly). "—— damn me, if I don't kill you, if you come near the door."

This continued without remonstrance for some time, when he lay down, asking his companion for a light for his pipe, and continuing the noisy conversation until we fell asleep. The previous talk had been much of knife and pistol fights which had taken place in the county. The same boy was obliging and amiable the next morning, assisting us to bring in and saddle the horses at our departure.

One of the men here was a Yankee, who had lived so long in the Slave States that he had added to his original ruralisms a very complete collection of Southernisms, some of which were of the richest we met with. He had been in the Texas Rangers, and, speaking of the West, said he had been up round the head of the Guadaloupe "heaps and cords of times," at the same time giving us a very picturesque account of the county. Speaking of wolves, he informed us that on the San Jacinto there were "*any dimensions* of them." Obstinacy, in his vocabulary, was represented by "damnation *cussedness*." He was unable to conceive of us in any other light than as two peddlers who had mistaken their ground in coming here.

At another house where we stopped (in which, by the way, we ate our supper by the light of pine knots blazing in the chimney, with an apology for the absence of candles), we heard some conversation upon a negro of the neighbourhood, who had been sold to a free negro, and who refused to live with him, saying he wouldn't be a servant to a nigger. All agreed that he was right, although the man was well known to be kind to his negroes, and would always sell any of them who wished it. The slave had been sold because he wouldn't mind. "If I had a negro that wouldn't mind," said the woman of the house, "I'd break his head, or I'd sell him; I wouldn't have one about me." Her own servant was standing behind her. "I do think it would be better if there wasn't any niggers in the world, they do behave so bad, some of 'em. They steal just like hogs."

South-western Louisiana.—Soon after crossing the Sabine, we entered a "hummock," or tract of more fertile, oak-bearing land, known as the Big Woods. The soil is not rich, but produces cotton, in good seasons nearly a bale to the acre, and the limited area is fully occupied. Upon one plantation we found an intelligent emigrant from Mississippi, who had just bought the place, having stopped on his way into Texas, because the time drew near for the confinement of his wife. Many farms are bought by emigrants, he said, from such temporary considerations; a child is sick, or a horse exhausted; they stop for a few weeks; but summer comes, and they conclude to put in a crop, and often never move again.

It was before reaching the Big Woods, that alligator-holes were first pointed out to us, with a caution to avoid them. They extend from an aperture, obliquely, under ground, to a large cavern, the walls of which are puddled by the motions of the animal; and, being partly filled with water, form a comfortable amphibious residence. A horseman is liable, not only to breaking through near the orifice, but to being precipitated into the den itself, where he will find awaiting him, a disagreeable mixture of mire and angry jaws. In the deep water of the bottoms, we met with no snakes; but the pools were everywhere alive with them. We saw a great variety of long-legged birds, apparently on friendly terms with all the reptiles.

A day's journey took us through the Big Woods, and across Calcasieu to Lake Charles. We were not prepared to find the Calcasieu a superb and solemn river, two hundred and thirty yards across and forty-five feet deep. It is navigable for forty miles, but at its mouth has a bar, on which is sometimes only eighteen inches of water, ordinarily thirty inches. Schooners of light draft ascend it, bringing supplies, and taking out the cotton raised within its reach. Lake Charles is an insignificant village, upon the bank of a pleasant, clear lakelet, several miles in extent.

From the Big Woods to Opelousas, there was no change in the monotonous scenery. Everywhere extended the immense moist plain, being alternate tracts of grass and pine. Nearer Opelousas, oak appears in groups with the pine, and the soil is darker and more fertile. Here the land was mostly taken up, partly by speculators, in view of the Opelousas Railway, then commenced. But in all the western portion of the district, the land is still government property, and many of the people squatters. Sales are seldom made, but the estimated price of the land is fifty cents an acre.

Some of the timbered land, for a few years after clearing, yields good crops of corn and sweet potatoes. Cotton is seldom attempted, and sugar only for family use. Oats are sometimes grown, but the yield is small, and seldom thrashed from the straw. We noted one field of poor rye. So wet a region and so warm a climate suggested rice, and, were the land sufficiently fertile, it would, doubtless, become a staple production. It is now only cultivated for home use, the bayou bottoms being rudely arranged for flowing the crop. But without manure no profitable return can be obtained from breaking the prairie, and the only system of manuring in use is that of ploughing up occasionally the cow-pens of the herdsmen.

The road was now distinctly marked enough, but had frequent and embarrassing forks, which occasioned us almost as much annoyance as the clouds of musquitoes which, east of the Sabine, hovered continually about our horses and our heads. Notions of distance we found incredibly vague. At Lake Charles we were informed that the exact distance to Opelousas was ninety-six miles. After riding eight hours, we were told by a respectable gentleman that the distance from his house was one hundred and twenty miles. The next evening the distance was forty miles; and the following evening a gentleman who met us stated first that it was "a good long way;" next, that it was "thirty or forty miles, and damn'd long ones, too." About four miles beyond him, we reached the twentieth mile-post.

Across the bayous of any size, bridges had been constructed, but so rudely built of logs that the traveller, where possible, left them for a ford.

The people, after passing the frontier, changed in every prominent characteristic. French became the prevailing language, and French the prevailing manners. The gruff Texan bidding, "Sit up, stranger; take some fry!" became a matter of recollection, of which "Monsieur, la soupe est servie," was the smooth substitute. The good-nature of the people was an incessant astonishment. If we inquired the way, a contented old gentleman waddled out and showed us also his wife's house-pet, an immense white crane, his big crop of peaches, his old fig-tree, thirty feet in diameter of shade, and to his wish of "bon voyage" added for each a bouquet of the jessamines we were admiring. The homes were homes, not settlements on speculation; the house, sometimes of logs, it is true, but hereditary logs, and more often of smooth lumber, with deep and spreading galleries on all sides for the coolest comfort. For form, all ran or tended to run to a peaked and many-chimneyed centre, with, here and there, a suggestion of a dormar window. Not all were provided with figs and jessamines, but each had some inclosure betraying good intentions.

The monotonous landscape did not invite to loitering, and we passed but three nights in houses by the road. The first was that of an old Italian-French emigrant, known as "Old Man Corse." He had a name of his own, which he recalled for us, but in forty years it had been lost and superseded by this designation, derived from his birth-place, the island of Corsica. This mixture of nationalities in language must be breeding for future antiquaries a good deal of amusing labour. Next day we were recommended to stop at Jack Bacon's, and, although we would have preferred to avoid an American's, did so rather than go further, and found our Jack Bacon a Creole, named Jacques Béguin. This is equal to Tuckapaw and Nakitosh, the general pronunciation of Attakapas and Nachitoches.

The house of Old Man Corse stood in the shade of oaks, figs, and cypresses, upon the bank of a little bayou, looking out upon the broad prairie. It was large and comfortable, with wide galleries and dormar windows, supported by a negro-hut and a stable. Ornamental axe-work and rude decorative joinery were abundant. The roof was of large split shingles, much warped in the sun. As we entered and took seats by the fire, the room reminded us, with its big fire-place, and old smoke-stained and time-toned cypress beams and ceiling, and its rude but comfortable aspect, of the Acadian fireside:

"In doors, warm by the wide-mouthed fire-place, idly the farmer
Sat in his elbow-chair, and watched how the flames and the smoke-wreaths
Struggled together, like foes in a burning city. Behind him,
Nodding and mocking along the wall, with gestures fantastic,

Darted his own huge shadow, and vanished away into darkness,
Faces, clumsily carved in oak, on the back of his arm-chair,
Laughed in the flickering light, and the pewter plates on the dresser
Caught and reflected the flame, as shields of armies the sunshine."

The tall, elderly, busy housewife bustled about with preparations for supper, while we learned that they had been settled here forty years, and had never had reason to regret their emigration. The old man had learnt French, but no English. The woman could speak some "American," as she properly termed it. Asking her about musquitoes, we received a reply in French, that they were more abundant some years than others; then, as no quantitative adjective of sufficient force occurred to her, she added, "Three years ago, oh! heaps of musquitoes, sir, *heaps!* worse as now."

She laid the table to the last item, and prepared everything nicely, but called a negro girl to wait upon us. The girl stood quiet behind us, the mistress helping us, and practically anticipating all our wants.

The supper was of venison, in ragoût, with a sauce that savoured of the south of France; there was a side dish of hominy, a jug of sweet milk, and wheat-bread in loaf—the first since Houston.

In an evening smoke, upon the settle, we learned that there were many Creoles about here, most of whom learned English, and had their children taught English at the schools. The Americans would not take the trouble to learn French. They often intermarried. A daughter of their own was the wife of an American neighbour. We asked if they knew of a distinct people here called Acadians. Oh yes, they knew many settled in the vicinity, descended from some nation that came here in the last century. They had now no peculiarities. There were but few free negroes just here, but at Opelousas and Niggerville there were many, some of whom were rich and owned slaves, though a part were unmixed black in colour. They kept pretty much by themselves, not attempting to enter white society.

As we went to look at our horses, two negroes followed us to the stable.

"Dat horse a Tennessee horse, mass'r," said one.

"Yes, he was born in Tennessee."

"Born in Tennessee and raised by a Dutchman," said the other, sotto voce, I suppose, quoting a song.

"Why, were you born in Tennessee?" I asked.

"No, sar, I was born in dis State."

"How comes it you speak English so much better than your master?"

"Ho, ho, my old mass'r, he don' speak it at all; my missus she speak it better'n my mass'r do, but you see I war raised on de parara, to der eastward, whar thar's heaps of 'Mericans; so I larned it good."

He spoke it, with a slight accent, while the other, whom he called Uncle Tom, I observed did not. I asked Uncle Tom if he was born in the State.

"*No, sar!* I was born in *Varginny!* in ole Varginny, mass'r. I was raised in —— county [in the West]. I was twenty-two year ole when I came away from thar, and I've been in this country, forty year come next Christmas."

"Then you are sixty years old."

"Yes, sar, amos' sixty. But I'd like to go back to Varginny. Ho, ho! I 'ould like to go back and live in ole Varginny, again."

"Why so? I thought niggers generally liked this country best—I've been told so—because it is so warm here."

"Ho, ho! it's mos' too warm here, sometime, and I can't work at my trade here. Sometimes for three months I don' go in my shop, on'y Sundays to work for mysef."

"What is your trade?"

"I'm a blacksmith, mass'r. I used to work at blacksmithing all the time in ole Virginny, ironin' waggons, and shoein' horses for the folks that work in the mines. But here, can't get nothun' to do. In this here sile, if you sharpen up a plough in the spring o' the year, it'll last all summer, and horses don' want shoeing once a year, here on the parara. I've got a good mass'r here, tho'; the ole man ain't hard on his niggers."

"Was your master hard in Virginia?"

"Well, I wos hired to different mass'rs, sar, thar, afore I wos sole off. I was sole off to a sheriff's sale, mass'r: I wos sole for fifteen hunerd an' fifty dollars; I fetched that on the block, cash, I did, and the man as bought me he brung me down here, and sole me for two thousand two hunerd dollars."

"That was a good price; a very high price in those days."

"Yes, sar, it was that—ho, ho, ho! It was a man by the name of ——, from Tennessee, what bought me. He made a business of goin' roun' and buyin' up people, and bringin' 'em down here, speculatin' on 'em. Ho, ho! he did well that time. But I'd 'a' liked it better, for all that, to have stayed in ole Varginny. 'Tain't the heat, tho' it's too hot here sometimes; but you know, sar, I was born and raised in Varginny, and seems like 'twould be pleasanter to live thar. It's kinder natural to people to hanker arter the place they wos raised in. Ho, ho! I'd like it a heap better, tho' this ole man's a good mass'r; never had no better mass'r."

"I suppose you became a Catholic after you got here?"

"Yes, sar" (hesitatingly).

"I suppose all the people are Catholics here?"

"Here? Oh, no, sar; they was whar I wos first in this here country; they wos all Catholics there."

"Well, they are all Catholics here, too—ain't they?"

"Here, sar? Here, sar? Oh, no, sar!"

"Why, your master is not a Protestant, is he?"

After two deep groans, he replied in a whisper:

"Oh, sar, they don' have no meetin' o' no kind, roun' here!"

"There are a good many free negroes in this country, ain't there?"

"What! here, sar? Oh, no, sar; no such good luck as that in this country."

"At Opelousas, I understood, there were a good many."

"Oh, but them wos born free, sar, under old Spain, sar."

"Yes, those I mean."

"Oh, yes, there's lots o' *them;* some of 'em rich, and some of 'em—a good many of 'em—goes to the penitentiary—you know what that is. White folks goes to the penitenti'ry, too—ho! ho!—sometimes."

"I have understood many of them were quite rich."

"Oh, yes, o' course they is: they started free, and ain't got nobody to work for but theirselves; of course they gets rich. Some of 'em owns slaves—heaps of 'em. That ar ain't right."

"Not right! why not?"

"Why, you don' think it's right for one nigger to own another nigger! One nigger's no business to sarve another. It's bad enough to have to sarve a white man without being paid for it, without having to sarve a black man."

"Don't they treat their slaves well?"

"No, sar, they don't. There ain't no nations so bad masters to niggers as them free niggers, though there's some, I've heard, wos very kind; but—I wouldn't sarve 'em if they wos—no!—Does you live in Tennessee, mass'r?

"No—in New York."

"There's heaps of Quakers in New York, ain't there, mass'r?"

"No—not many."

"I've always heard there was."

"In Philadelphia there are a good many."

"Oh, yes! in Philadelphia, and in Winchester, and in New Jarsey. I know—ho! ho! I've been in those countries, and I've seen 'em. I wos raised nigh by Winchester, and I've been all about there. Used to iron waggons and shoe horses in that country. Dar's a road from Winchester to Philadelphia—right straight. Quakers all along. Right good people, dem Quakers—ho! ho!—I know."*

We slept in well-barred beds, and awoke long after sunrise. As soon as we were stirring, black coffee was sent into us, and at breakfast we had *café au lait* in immense bowls, in the style of the *crêmeries* of Paris. The woman remarked that our dog had slept in their bed-room. They had taken our saddle-bags and blankets with them for security, and Judy had insisted on following them. "Dishonest black people might come here and get into the room," explained the old man. "Yes; and some of our own people in the house might come to them. Such things have happened here, and you never can trust any of them," said the woman, her own black girl behind her chair.

At Mr. Béguin's (Bacon's) we stopped on a Saturday night: and I was obliged to feed my own horse in the morning, the negroes having all gone off before daylight. The proprietor was a Creole farmer, owning a number of labourers, and living in comfort. The house was of the ordinary

* Evidently an allusion to the "underground railroad," or smuggling of runaway slaves, which is generally supposed to be managed mainly by Quakers. This shows how knowledge of the abolition agitation must be carried among the slaves to the most remote districts.

Southern double-cabined style, the people speaking English, intelligent, lively, and polite, giving us good entertainment at the usual price. At a rude corn-mill belonging to Mr. Béguin, we had noticed among the negroes an Indian boy, in negro clothing, and about the house were two other Indians —an old man and a young man; the first poorly clad, the other gaily dressed in a showy printed calico frock, and worked buckskin leggings, with beads and tinsel ornaments, a great turban of Scotch shawl-stuff on his head. It appeared they were Choctaws, of whom a good many lived in the neighbourhood. The two were hired for farm labour at three bits (37½ cents) a day. The old man had a field of his own. in which stood handsome corn. Some of them were industrious, but none were steady at work—often refusing to go on, or absenting themselves from freaks. I asked about the boy at the mill. He lived there and did work, getting no wages, but "living there with the niggers." They seldom consort; our host knew but one case in which a negro had an Indian wife.

At Lake Charles we had seen a troop of Alabamas, riding through the town with baskets and dressed deerskins for sale. They were decked with feathers, and dressed more showily than the Choctaws, but in calico: and over their heads, on horseback—curious progress of manners—all carried open, black cotton *umbrellas*.

Our last night in this region was spent in a house which we reached at sundown of a Sunday afternoon. It proved to be a mere cottage, in a style which has grown to be common along our road. The walls are low, of timber and mud; the roof, high, and sloping from a short ridge in all directions; and the chimney of sticks and mud. The space is divided into one long living-room, having a kitchen at one end and a bed-room at the other. As we rode up, we found only a little boy, who answered us in French. His mother was milking, and his father out in the field.

We rode on to the fence of the field, which enclosed twenty acres, planted in cotton, corn, and sweet potatoes, and waited until the proprietor reached us and the end of his furrow. He stopped before replying, to unhitch his horse, then gave consent to our staying in his house, and we followed his lead to the yard, where we unsaddled our horses. He was a tall, stalwart man in figure, with a large intellectual head, but as uninformed, we afterwards discovered, as any European peasant; though he wore, as it were, an ill-fitting dress of rude independence in manner, such as characterises the Western man.

The field was well cultivated, and showed the best corn we had seen east of the Brazos. Three negro men and two women were at work, and continued hoeing until sunset. They were hired, it appeared, by the proprietor, at four bits (fifty cents) a day. He was in the habit of making use of the Sundays of the slaves of the neighbourhood in this way, paying them sometimes seventy-five cents a day.

On entering the house, we were met by two young boys, gentle and winning in manner, coming up of their own accord to offer us their hands. They were immediately set to work by their father at grinding corn, in the steel-mill, for supper. The task seemed their usual one, yet very much too severe for their strength, as they were slightly built, and not over ten years old. Taking hold at opposite sides of the winch, they ground away, outside the door, for more than an hour, constantly stopping to take breath, and spurred on by the voice of the papa, if the delay were long.

They spoke only French, though understanding questions in English. The man and his wife—an energetic but worn woman—spoke French or English indifferently, even to one another, changing, often, in a single sentence. He could not tell us which was his mother tongue; he had always been as much accustomed to the one as to the other. He said he was not a Frenchman, but a native, American-born; but afterwards called himself a "Dutch-American," a phrase he was unable to explain. He informed us that there were many "Dutch-French" here, that is, people who were Dutch, but who spoke French.

The room into which we were ushered, was actually without an article of furniture. The floor was of boards, while those of the other two rooms were of trodden clay. The mud-walls had no other relief than the mantel, on which stood a Connecticut clock, two small mirrors, three or four cheap cups and saucers, and a paste brooch in the form of a cross, pinned upon paper, as in a jeweller's shop. Chairs were brought in from the kitchen, having deer-hide seats, from which sprang forth an atrocious number of fresh fleas.

We had two or three hours to wait for our late supper, and thus more than ample time to converse with our host, who proceeded to twist and light a shuck cigar. He made, he said, a little cotton, which he hauled ten miles to be ginned and baled. For this service he paid seventy-five cents a hundred weight, in which the cost of bagging was not included. The planter who baled it, also sold it for him, sending it, with his own, to a factor in New Orleans, by steamboat from Niggerville, just beyond Opelousas. Beside cotton, he sold every year some beef cattle. He had a good many cows, but didn't exactly know how many. Corn, too, he sometimes sold, but only to neighbours, who had not raised enough for themselves. It would not pay to haul it to any market. The same applied to sweet potatoes, which were considered worth seventy-five cents a barrel.

The "range" was much poorer than formerly. It was

crowded, and people would have to take their stock somewhere else in four or five years more, or they would starve. He didn't know what was going to become of poor folks, rich people were taking up the public land so fast, induced by the proposed railroad to New Orleans.

More or less stock was always starved in winter. The worst time for them was when a black gnat, called the "eye-breaker," comes out. This insect breeds in the low wood-lands, and when a freshet occurs in winter is driven out in swarms upon the prairies, attacking cattle terribly. They were worse than all manner of musquitoes, flies, or other in-sects. Cattle would herd together then, and wander wildly about, not looking for the best feed, and many would get killed. But this did not often happen.

Horses and cattle had degenerated much within his recol-lection. No pains were taken to improve breeds. People, now-a-days, had got proud, and when they had a fine colt would break him for a carriage or riding-horse, leaving only the common scurvy sort to run with the mares. This was confirmed by our observation, the horses about here being wretched in appearance, and the grass short and coarse.

When we asked to wash before supper, a shallow cake-pan was brought and set upon the window-seat, and a mere rag offered us for towel. Upon the supper-table, we found two wash-bowls, one filled with milk, the other with molasses. We asked for water, which was given us in one battered tin cup. The dishes, besides the bacon and bread, were fried eggs and sweet potatoes. The bowl of molasses stood in the centre of the table, and we were pressed to partake of it, as the family did, by dipping in it bits of bread. But how it was expected to be used at breakfast, when we had bacon and potatoes, with spoons, but no bread, I cannot imagine, the family not breakfasting with us.

The night was warm, and musquitoes swarmed, but we carried with us a portable tent-shaped bar, which we hung over the feather bed, upon the floor, and rested soundly amid their mad singing.

The distance to Opelousas, our Frenchman told us, was fifteen miles by the road, though only ten miles in a direct line. We found it lined with farms, whose division-fences the road always followed, frequently changing its course in so doing at a right angle. The country was very wet and unattractive. About five miles from the town, begin plantations on an extensive scale, upon better soil, and here were large gangs of negroes at work upon cotton, with their hoes.

At the outskirts of the town, we waded the last pool, and entered, with a good deal of satisfaction, the peaceful shaded streets. Reaching the hotel, we were not so instantly struck as perhaps we should have been, with the overwhelming advantages of civilization, which sat in the form of a landlord, slapping with an agate-headed, pliable cane, his patent leather boots, poised, at easy height, upon one of the columns of the gallery. We were suffered to take off our saddle-bags, and to wait until waiting was no longer a pleasure, before civilization, wringing his cane against the floor, but not removing his cigar, brought his patent leathers to our vicinity.

After some conversation, intended as animated upon one side and ineffably indifferent on the other, our horses obtained notice from that exquisitely vague eye, but a further introduction was required before our persons became less than transparent, for the boots walked away, and became again a subject of contemplation upon the column, leaving us, with our saddle-bags, upon the steps. After inquiring of a bystander if this glossy individual were the actual landlord, we attacked him in a tone likely to produce either a revolver-shot or a room, but whose effect was to obtain a removal of the cigar and a gentle survey, ending in a call for a boy to show the gentlemen to number thirteen.

After an hour's delay, we procured water, and were about to enjoy very necessary ablutions, when we observed that the door of our room was partly of uncurtained glass. A shirt was pinned to this, and ceremonies were about beginning, when a step came down the passage, and a gentleman put his hand through a broken pane, and lifted the obstruction, wishing "to see what was going on so damn'd secret in number thirteen." When I walked toward him hurriedly, *in puris naturalibus*, he drew hastily and entered the next room.

On the gallery of the hotel, after dinner, a fine-looking man —who was on the best of terms with every one—familiar with the judge—and who had been particularly polite to me, at the dinner-table, said to another:

"I hear you were very unlucky with that girl you bought of me, last year?"

"Yes, I was; very unlucky. She died with her first child, and the child died, too."

"Well, that was right hard for you. She was a fine girl. I don't reckon you lost less than five thousand dollars, when she died."

"No, sir, not a dollar less."

"Well, it came right hard upon you—just beginning so."

"Yes, I was foolish, I suppose, to risk so much on the life of a single woman; but I've got a good start again now, for all that. I've got two right likely girls; one of them's got a fine boy, four months old, and the other's with child—and old Pine Knot's as hearty as ever."

"Is he? Hasn't been sick at all, eh?"

"Yes; he was sick very soon after I bought him of you; but he got well soon."

"That's right. I'd rather a nigger would be sick early,

after he comes into this country; for he's bound to be acclimated, sooner or later, and the longer it's put off, the harder it goes with him."

The man was a regular negro trader. He told me that he had a partner in Kentucky, and that they owned a farm there, and another one here. His partner bought negroes, as opportunity offered to get them advantageously, and kept them on their Kentucky farm; and he went on occasionally, and brought the surplus to their Louisiana plantation—where he held them for sale.

"So-and-so is very hard upon you," said another man, to him as he still sat, smoking his cigar, on the gallery, after dinner.

"Why so? He's no business to complain; I told him just exactly what the nigger was, before I sold him (laughing, as if there was a concealed joke). It was all right—all right. I heard that he sold him again for a thousand dollars; and the people that bought him, gave him two hundred dollars to let them off from the bargain. I'm sure he can't complain of me. It was a fair transaction. He knew just what he was buying."

An intelligent man whom I met here, and who had been travelling most of the time during the last two years in Louisiana, having business with the planters, described the condition of the new slaveholders and the poorer planters as being very miserable.

He had sometimes found it difficult to get food, even when he was in urgent need of it, at their houses. The lowest class live much from hand to mouth, and are often in extreme destitution. This was more particularly the case with those who lived on the rivers; those who resided on the prairies were seldom so much reduced. The former now live only on those parts of the river to which the back-swamp approaches nearest; that is, where there is but little valuable land, that can be appropriated for plantation-purposes. They almost all reside in communities, very closely housed in poor cabins. If there is any considerable number of them, there is to be always found, among the cluster of their cabins, a church, and a billiard and a gambling-room—and the latter is always occupied, and play going on.

They almost all appear excessively apathetic, sleepy, and stupid, if you see them at home; and they are always longing and waiting for some excitement. They live for excitement, and will not labour, unless it is violently, for a short time, to gratify some passion.

This was as much the case with the women as the men. The women were often handsome, stately, and graceful, and, ordinarily, exceedingly kind; but languid, and incredibly indolent, unless there was a ball, or some other excitement, to engage them. Under excitement, they were splendidly animated, impetuous, and eccentric. One moment they seemed possessed by a devil, and the next by an angel.

The Creoles* are inveterate gamblers—rich and poor alike. The majority of wealthy Creoles, he said, do nothing to improve their estate; and are very apt to live beyond their income. They borrow and play, and keep borrowing to play, as long as they can; but they will not part with their land, and especially with their home, as long as they can help it, by any sacrifice.

The men are generally dissolute. They have large families, and a great deal of family affection. He did not know that they had more than Anglo-Saxons; but they certainly manifested a great deal more, and, he thought, had more domestic

* Creole means simply native of the region, but in Louisiana (a vast region purchased, by the United States, of France, for strategetic reasons, and now proposed to be filibustered away from us), it generally indicates French blood.

happiness. If a Creole farmer's child marries, he will build a house for the new couple, adjoining his own; and when another marries, he builds another house—so, often his whole front on the river is at length occupied. Then he begins to build others, back of the first—and so, there gradually forms a little village, wherever there is a large Creole family, owning any considerable piece of land. The children are poorly educated, and are not brought up to industry, at all.

The planters living near them, as their needs increase, lend them money, and get mortgages on their land, or, in some way or other, if it is of any value, force them them to part with it. Thus they are every year reduced, more and more, to the poorest lands; and the majority now are able to get but a very poor living, and would not be able to live at all in a Northern climate. They are nevertheless—even the poorest of them—habitually gay and careless, as well as kind-hearted, hospitable, and dissolute—working little, and spending much of their time at church, or at balls, or the gaming-table.

There are very many wealthy Creole planters, who are as cultivated and intelligent as the better class of American planters, and usually more refined. The Creoles, he said, did not work their slaves as hard as the Americans; but, on the other hand, they did not feed or clothe them nearly as well, and he had noticed universally, on the Creole plantations, a large number of "used-up hands"—slaves, sore and crippled, or invalided for some cause. On all sugar plantations, he said, they work the negroes excessively, in the grinding season; often cruelly. Under the usual system, to keep the fires burning, and the works constantly supplied, eighteen hours' work was required of every negro, in twenty-four—leaving but six for rest. The work of most of them, too, was very hard. They were generally, during the grinding season, liberally supplied with food and coffee, and were induced, as much as possible, to make a kind of frolic of it; yet, on the Creole plantations, he thought they did not, even in the grinding season, often get meat.

I remarked that the law, in Louisiana, required that meat should be regularly served to the negroes.

"O, those laws are very little regarded."

"Indeed?"

"Certainly. Suppose you are my neighbour; if you maltreat your negroes, and tell me of it, or I see it, am I going to prefer charges against you to the magistrates? I might possibly get you punished according to law; but if I did, or did not, I should have you, and your family and friends, far and near, for my mortal enemies. There is a law of the State that negroes shall not be worked on Sundays; but I have seen negroes at work almost every Sunday, when I have been in the country, since I have lived in Louisiana.* I spent a Sunday once with a gentleman, who did not work his hands at all on Sunday, even in the grinding season; and he had got some of his neighbours to help him build a school-house, which was used as a church on Sunday. He said, there was not a plantation on either side of him, as far as he could see, where the slaves were not generally worked on Sunday; but that, after the church was started, several of them quit the practice, and made their negroes go to the meeting. This made others discontented; and after a year or two, the planters voted new trustees to the school, and these forbid the house to be used for any other than school purposes. This was done, he hadono doubt, for the purpose of breaking up the meetings, and to lessen the discontent of the slaves which were worked on Sunday.

* I also saw slaves at work every Sunday that I was in Louisiana. The law permits slaves to be worked, I believe, on Sunday; but requires that some compensation shall be made to them when they are—such as a subsequent holiday."

It was said that the custom of working the negroes on Sunday was much less common than formerly; if so, he thought that it must have formerly been universal.

He had lived, when a boy, for several years on a farm in Western New York, and afterwards, for some time, at Rochester, and was well acquainted with the people generally, in the valley of the Genesee.

I asked him if he thought, among the intelligent class of farmers and planters, people of equal property lived more happily in New York or Louisiana. He replied immediately, as if he had carefully considered the topic, that, with some rare exceptions, farmers worth forty thousand dollars lived in far greater comfort, and enjoyed more refined and elegant leisure, than planters worth three hundred thousand, and that farmers of the ordinary class, who laboured with their own hands, and were worth some six thousand dollars, in the Genesee valley, lived in far greater comfort, and in all respects more enviably, than planters worth forty thousand dollars in Louisiana. The contrast was especially favourable to the New York farmer, in respect to books and newspapers. He might travel several days, and call on a hundred planters, and hardly see in their houses more than a single newspaper a-piece, in most cases; perhaps none at all: nor any books, except a Bible, and some government publications, that had been franked to them through the post-office, and perhaps a few religious tracts or school-books.

The most striking difference that he observed between the Anglo-Americans of Louisiana and New York, was the impulsive and unreflective habit of the former, in doing business. He mentioned, as illustrative of this, the almost universal passion among the planters for increasing their negro-stock. It appeared evident to him, that the market price of negroes was much higher than the prices of cotton and sugar warranted; but it seemed as if no planter ever made any calculation of that kind. The majority of planters, he thought, would always run in debt to the extent of their credit for negroes, whatever was asked for them, without making any calculation of the reasonable prospects of their being able to pay their debts. When any one made a good crop, he would always expect that his next one would be better, and make purchases in advance upon such expectation. When they were dunned, they would attribute their inability to pay, to accidental short crops, and always were going ahead risking everything, in confidence that another year of luck would favour them, and a big crop make all right.

If they had a full crop, probably there would be good crops everywhere else, and prices would fall, and then they would whine and complain, as if the merchants were to blame for it, and would insinuate that no one could be expected to pay his debts when prices were so low, and that it would be dangerous to press such an unjust claim. And if the crops met with any misfortune, from floods, or rot, or vermin, they would cry about it like children when rain fell upon a holiday, as if they had never thought of the possibility of such a thing, and were very hard used.*

* The following resolutions were proposed (I am not sure that they were adopted) in the Southern Commercial Convention, at New Orleans, in 1855:

"*Resolved*,—That this Convention strongly recommends the Chambers of Commerce and Commission Merchants of our Southern and South-western cities to adopt such a system of laws and regulations as will put a stop to the dangerous practice, heretofore existing, of making advances to planters, in anticipation of their crops—a practice entirely at variance with everything like safety in business transactions, and tending directly to establish the relations of master and slave between the merchant and planter, by bringing the latter into the most abject and servile bondage.

"*Resolved*,—That this Convention recommend, in the most urgent manner, that the planters of the Southern and South-western States patronize exclusively our home merchants, and that our Chambers of Commerce, and merchants gene-

He had talked with many sugar-planters who were strong Cuba war and annexation men, and had rarely found that any of these had given the first thought to the probable effect the annexation of Cuba would have on their home interests. It was mainly a romantic excitement and enthusiasm, inflamed by senseless appeals to their patriotism and their combativeness. They had got the idea, that patriotism was necessarily associated with hatred and contempt of any other country but their own, and the only foreigners to be regarded with favour were those who desired to surrender themselves to us. They did not reflect that the annexation of Cuba would necessarily be attended by the removal of the duty on sugar, and would bring them into competition with the sugar-planters of that island, where the advantages for growing cane were so much greater than in Louisiana.

To some of the very wealthy planters who favoured the movement, and who were understood to have taken some of the Junta* stock, he gave credit for greater sagacity. He thought it was the purpose of these men, if Cuba could be annexed, to get possession of large estates there: then, with the advantages of their greater skill in sugar-making, and better machinery than that which yet was in use in Cuba, and with much cheaper land and labour, and a far better climate for cane growing than that of Louisiana, it would be easy for them to accumulate large fortunes in a few years; but he thought the sugar-planters who remained in Louisiana would be ruined by it.

---

rally, exert all their influence to exclude foreign agents from the purchase and sale of produce in any of our Southern and South-western cities.

"*Resolved, further*,—That this Convention recommend to the legislatures of the Southern and South-western States to pass laws, making it a penitentiary offence for the planters to ask of the merchants to make such pecuniary advances."

* The Junta was a filibustering conspiracy against Cuba.

The principal subscribers to the Junta stock at the South, he thought, were land speculators: persons who expected that, by now favouring the movement, they would be able to obtain from the revolutionary government large grants of land in the island as gratuities in reward of their services or at nominal prices, which after annexation would rise rapidly in value; or persons who now owned wild land in the States, and who thought that if Cuba were annexed the African slave-trade would be re-established, either openly or clandestinely, with the States, and their lands be increased in value, by the greater cheapness with which they could then be stocked with labourers.

I find these views confirmed in a published letter from a Louisiana planter, to one of the members of Congress, from that State; and I insert an extract of that letter, as it is evidently from a sensible and far-thinking man, to show on how insecure a basis rests the prosperity of the slave-holding interest in Louisiana. The fact would seem to be, that, if it were not for the tariff on foreign sugars, sugar could not be produced at all by slave-labour; and that a discontinuance of sugar culture would almost desolate the State.

"The question now naturally comes up to you and to me, Do we Louisianians desire the possession of Cuba? It is not what the provision dealers of the West, or the shipowners of the North may wish for, but what the State of Louisiana, as a State, may deem consistent with her best interests. My own opinion on the subject is not a new one. It was long ago expressed to high officers of our Government, neither of whom ever hesitated to acknowledge that it was, in the main, correct. That opinion was and is, *that the acquisition of Cuba would prove the ruin of our State.* I found this opinion on the following reasons: Cuba has already land enough in cultivation to produce, when directed by American skill, energy, and capital, twenty millions of tons of sugar. In addition to this she has virgin soil, only needing roads to bring it, with a people of the least pretension to enterprise, into active working, sufficient nearly to double this; all of which would be soon brought into productiveness were it our own, with the whole American market free to it. If any man supposes that the culture of sugar in our State can be sustained in the face of this, I have only to say that he can suppose anything. We have very nearly, if not quite, eighty millions invested in the sugar culture. My idea is that *three-fourths of this would, so far as the State is concerned, be annihilated at a blow.* The planter who is in debt, would find his negroes and machinery sold and despatched to Cuba for him, and he who is independent would go there in self-defence. What will become of the other portion of the capital? It consists of land, on which I maintain there can be produced no other crop but sugar, under present auspices, that will bear the contest with cocoa,* and the expense and risk of levees, as it regards the larger part of it, and the difficulty of transportation for the remainder. But supposing that it will be taken up by some other cultivation, that in any case must be a work of time, and in this case a very long time for unacclimated men. It is not unreasonable, then, to suppose that this whole capital will, for purposes of taxation, be withdrawn from Louisiana. From whence, then, is to come the revenue for the support of our State government, for the payment of the interest on our debt, and the eventual redemption of the principal? Perhaps repudiation may be recommended; but you and I, my dear sir, are too old-fashioned to rob in that manner, or in any other. The only resort, then, is double taxation on the cotton planter, which will drive him, without much difficulty, to Texas, to Arkansas, and Mississippi."

Washington.—The inn, here, when we arrived, was well filled with guests, and my friend and I were told that we must sleep together. In the room containing our bed there were three other beds; and although the outside of the house was pierced with windows, nowhere more than four feet apart, not one of them opened out of our room. A door opened into the hall, another into the dining-room, and at the side of our bed was a window into the dining-room, through which, betimes in the morning, we could, with our heads on our pillows, see the girls setting the breakfast-tables. Both the doors were provided with glass windows, without curtains. Hither, about eleven o'clock, we "retired." Soon afterwards,

* Cocoa is a grass much more pernicious, and more difficult of extirpation when it once gets a footing upon a sugar plantation, than the Canada thistle, or any other weed known at the North. Several plantations have been ruined by it, and given up as worthless by their owners.

hearing something moving under the bed, I asked, "Who's there?" and was answered by a girl, who was burrowing for eggs; part of the stores of the establishment being kept in boxes, in this convenient locality. Later, I was awakened by a stranger attempting to enter my bed. I expostulated, and he replied that it was his bed, and nobody else had a right to his place in it. Who was I, he asked, angrily, and where was his partner? "Here I am," answered a voice from another bed; and without another word, he left us. I slept but little, and woke feverish, and with a headache, caused by the want of ventilation.

While at the dinner-table, a man asked, as one might at the North, if the steamer had arrived, if there had been "any fights to-day?" After dinner, while we were sitting on the gallery, loud cursing, and threatening voices were heard in the direction of the bar-room, which, as at Nachitoches, was detached, and at a little distance from the hotel. The company, except myself and the other New-Yorker, immediately ran towards it. After ten minutes, one returned, and said—

"I don't believe there'll be any fight; they are both cowards."

"Are they preparing for a fight?"

"O, yes; they are loading pistols in the coffee-room, and there's a man outside, in the street, who has a revolver and a knife, and who is challenging another to come out. He swears he'll wait there till he does come out; but in my opinion he'll think better of it, when he finds that the other feller's got pistols, too."

"What's the occasion of the quarrel?"

"Why, the man in the street says the other one insulted him this morning, and that he had his hand on his knife, at the very moment he did so, so he couldn't reply. And now he says he's ready to talk with him, and he wants to have him come out, and as many of his friends as are a mind to, may come with him; he's got enough for all of 'em, he says. He's got two revolvers, I believe."

We did not hear how it ended; but, about an hour afterwards, I saw three men, with pistols in their hands, coming from the bar-room.

The next day, I saw, in the streets of the same town, two boys running from another, who was pursuing them with a large, open dirk-knife in his hand, and every appearance of ungovernable rage in his face.

The boat, for which I was waiting, not arriving, I asked the landlady—who appeared to be a German Jewess—if I could not have a better sleeping-room. She showed me one, which she said I might use for a single night; but, if I remained another, I must not refuse to give it up. It had been occupied by another gentleman, and she thought he might return the next day, and would want it again; and, if I remained in it, he would be very angry that they had not reserved it for him, although they were under no obligation to him. "He is a dangerous man," she observed, "and my husband, he's a quick-tempered man, and, if they get to quarrelling about it, ther'll be knives about, sure. It always frightens me to see knives drawn."

A Texas drover, who stayed over night at the hotel, being asked, as he was about to leave in the morning, if he was not going to have his horse shod, replied:

"No sir! it'll be a damn'd long spell 'fore I pay for having a horse shod. I reckon, if God Almighty had thought it right hosses should have iron on thar feet, he'd a put it thar himself. I don't pretend to be a pious man myself; but I a'nt a-goin' to run agin the will of God Almighty, though thar's some, that calls themselves ministers of Christ, that does it."

CHAPTER II.

A TRIP INTO NORTHERN MISSISSIPPI.

Vicksburg, March 18th.—I arrived at this place last night, about sunset, and was told that there was no hotel in the town except on the wharf-boat, the only house used for that purpose having been closed a few days ago on account of a difference of opinion between its owner and his tenant.

There are no wharves on the Mississippi, or any of the southern rivers. The wharf-boat is an old steamboat, with her paddle boxes and machinery removed and otherwise dismantled, on which steamboats discharge passengers and freight. The main deck is used as a warehouse, and in place of the furnace, has in this case a dram shop, a chandler's shop, a forwarding agency, and a telegraph office. Overhead, the saloon and state-rooms remain, and with the bar-room and clerk's office, kitchen and barber's shop, constitute a stationary, though floating hostelry.

Though there were fifty or more rooms, and not a dozen guests, I was obliged, about twelve o'clock, to admit a stranger who had been gambling all the evening in the saloon, to occupy the spare shelf of my closet. If a disposition to enjoy occasional privacy, or to exercise a choice in one's room-mates were a sure symptom of a monomania for incendiarism, it could not be more carefully thwarted than it is at all public-houses in this part of the world.

Memphis, March 20th.—I reached this place to-day in forty-eight hours by steamboat from Vicksburg.

Here, at the "Commercial Hotel," I am favoured with an unusually good-natured room-mate. He is smoking on the bed—our bed—now, and wants to know what my business is here, and whether I carry a pistol about me; also whether I believe that it isn't lucky to play cards on Sundays; which I do most strenuously, especially as this is a rainy Sunday, and his second cigar is nearly smoked out.

This is a first-class hotel, and has, of course, printed bills of fare, which, in a dearth of other literature, are not to be dropped at the first glance. A copy of to-day's is presented on the opposite page.

Being in a distant quarter of the establishment when a crash of the gong announced dinner, I did not get to the table as early as some others. The meal was served in a large, dreary room exactly like a hospital ward; and it is a striking illustration of the celerity with which everything is accomplished in our young country, that beginning with the soup, and going on by the fish to the roasts, the first five dishes I inquired for—when at last I succeeded in arresting one of the negro boys—were "all gone;" and as the waiter had to go to the head of the dining-room, or to the kitchen, to ascertain this fact upon each demand, the majority of the company had left the table before I was served at all. At length I said I would take anything that was still to be had, and thereupon was provided immediately with some grimy bacon, and greasy cabbage. This I commenced eating, but I no sooner paused for a moment, than it was suddenly and surreptitiously removed, and its place supplied, without the expression of any desire on my part, with some other Memphitic chef d'œuvre, a close investigation of which left me in doubt whether it was that denominated "sliced potatoe pie," or "Irish pudding."

I congratulate myself that I have lived to see the day in which an agitation for reform in our GREAT HOTEL SYSTEM has been commenced, and I trust that a Society for the Revival of Village Inns will ere long form one of the features of the May anniversaries.

COMMERCIAL HOTEL.

BY D. COCKRELL.

BILL OF FARE.

MARCH 20.

SOUP.
Oyster.

FISH.
Red.

BOILED.
Jole and Green.
Ham.
Corned beef.
Bacon and turnips.
Codfish egg sauce.
Beef heart egg sauce.
Leg of mutton caper sauce.
Barbecued rabits.
Boiled tongue.

ROAST.
Veal.
Roast pig.
Muscovie ducks.
Kentucky beef.
Mutton.
Barbecued shoat.
Roast bear meat.
Roast pork.

ENTREES.
Fricasee pork.
Calf feet mushroom sauce.
Bear sausages.
Harricane tripe.
Stewed mutton.
Browned rice.
Calf feet madeira sauce.
Stewed turkey wine sauce.
Giblets volivon.
Mutton omelett.
Beef's heart fricaseed.
Cheese macaroni.
Chicken chops robert sauce.
Breast chicken madeira sauce.
Beef kidney pickle sauce.
Cod fish baked.
Calf head wine sauce.

FRUIT.
Almonds.
Rasins.
Pecans.

VEGETABLES.
Boiled cabbage.
Turnips.
Cold slaugh.
Hot slaugh.
Pickled beets.
Creole hominy.
Crout cabbage.
Oyster plant fried.
Parsneps gravied.
Stewed parsneps.
Fried cabbage.
Sweet potatoes spiced.
Carrot.
Sweet potatoes baked.
Cabbage stuffed.
Onions, boiled.
Irish potatoes creamed and mashed.
Irish potatoes browned.
Boiled shellots.
Scolloped carrots.
Boiled turnips drawn butter.
White beans.

PASTRY.
Currant pies.
Lemon custard.
Rice pudding.
Cocoanut pie.
Cranberry pies.
Sliced potato pie.
Chess cake.
Irish pudding.
Orange custard.
Cranberry shapes.
Green peach tarts.
Green peach puff paste.
Grape tarts.
Huckle berry pies.
Pound cake.
Rheubarb tarts.
Plum tarts.
Calves feet jelly.
Blamonge.
Orange jelly

A stage-coach conveyed the railroad passengers from the hotel to the station, which was a mile or two out of town. As we were entering the coach the driver observed with a

Mephistophelean smile that we "needn't calk'late we were gwine to ride very fur," and, as soon as we had got into the country he stopped and asked all the men to get out and walk, for, he condescended to explain, "it was as much as his hosses could do to draw the ladies and the baggage." It was quite true; the horses were often obliged to stop, even with the diminished load, and as there was a contract between myself and the proprietors by which, for a stipulated sum of money by me to them in hand duly paid, they had undertaken to convey me over this ground, I thought it would have been no more than honest if they had looked out beforehand to have either a stronger team, or a better road, provided. As is the custom of our country, however, we allowed ourselves to be thus robbed with great good-nature, and waded along ankle-deep in the mud, joking with the driver and ready to put our shoulders to the wheels if it should be necessary. Two portmanteaus were jerked off in heavy lurches of the coach; the owners picked them up and carried them on their shoulders till the horses stopped to breathe again. The train of course had waited for us, and it continued to wait until another coach arrived, when it started twenty minutes behind time.

After some forty miles of rail, nine of us were stowed away in another stage coach. The road was bad, the weather foul. We proceeded slowly, were often in imminent danger of being upset, and once were all obliged to get out and help the horses drag the coach out of a slough; but with smoking, and the occasional circulation of a small black bottle, and a general disposition to be as comfortable as circumstances would allow, four hours of coaching proved less fatiguing than one of the ill-ventilated rail-cars.

Among the passengers was a "Judge," resident in the vicinity, portly, dignified, and well-informed; and a young man, who was a personal friend of the member of Congress from the district, and who, as he informed me, had, through the influence of this friend, a promise from the President of honourable and lucrative employment under Government. He was known to all the other passengers, and hailed by every one on the road-side, by the title of Colonel. The Judge was ready to converse about the country through which we were passing, and while perfectly aware, as no one else seemed to be, that it bore anything but an appearance of prosperity or attractiveness to a stranger, he assured me that it was really improving in all respects quite rapidly. There were few large plantations, but many small planters or rather farmers, for cotton, though the principal source of cash income, was much less exclusively an object of attention than in the more southern parts of the State. A larger space was occupied by the maize and grain crops. There were not a few small fields of wheat. In the afternoon, when only the Colonel and myself were with him, the Judge talked about slavery in a candid and liberal spirit. At present prices, he said, nobody could afford to own slaves, unless he could engage them almost exclusively in cotton-growing. It was undoubtedly a great injury to a region like this, which was not altogether well adapted to cotton, to be in the midst of a slaveholding country, for it prevented efficient free labour. A good deal of cotton was nevertheless grown hereabouts by white labour—by poor men who planted an acre or two, and worked it themselves, getting the planters to gin and press it for them. It was not at all uncommon for men to begin in this way and soon purchase negroes on credit, and eventually become rich men. Most of the plantations in this vicinity, indeed, belonged to men who had come into the country with nothing within twenty years. Once a man got a good start with negroes, unless the luck was much against him, nothing but his own folly could prevent his becoming rich. The increase of his negro property by births, if he took good care of it, must, in a few years, make him independent. The worst thing, and the most difficult to remedy, was the deplorable ignorance which prevailed. Latterly, however, people were taking more pride in the education of their children. Some excellent schools had been established, the teachers generally from the North, and a great many children were sent to board in the villages—county-seats—to attend them. This was especially true of girls, who liked to live in the villages rather than on the plantations. There was more difficulty in making boys attend school, until, at least, they were too old to get much good from it.

The "Colonel" was a rough, merry, good-hearted, simple-minded man, and kept all the would-be sober-sides of our coach body in irrepressible laughter with queer observations on passing occurrences, anecdotes and comic songs. It must be confessed that there is no charge which the enemies of the theatre bring against the stage, that was not duly illustrated, and that with a broadness which the taste of a metropolitan audience would scarcely permit. Had Doctor —— and Doctor —— been with me they would thereafter for ever have denied themselves, and discountenanced in others, the use of such a means of travel. The Colonel, notwithstanding, was of a most obliging disposition, and having ascertained in what direction I was going, enumerated at least a dozen families on the road, within some hundred miles, whom he invited me to visit, assuring me that I should find pretty girls in all of them, and a warm welcome, if I mentioned his name.

He told the Judge that his bar-bill on the boat, coming up from New Orleans, was forty dollars—seventeen dollars the first night. But he had made money—had won forty dollars of one gentleman. He confessed, however, that he had lost fifteen by another, "but he saw how he did it. He did not want to accuse him publicly, but he saw it and he meant to write to him and tell him of it. He did not want to insult the gentleman, only he did not want to have him think that he was so green as not to know how he did it."

While stopping for dinner at a village inn, a young man came into the room where we all were, and asked the coachman what was to be paid for a trunk which had been brought for him. The coachman said the charge would be a dollar, which the young man thought excessive. The coachman denied that it was so, said that it was what he had often been paid; he should not take less. The young man finally agreed to wait for the decision of the proprietor of the line. There was a woman in the room; I noticed no loud words or angry tones, and had not supposed that there was the slightest excitement. I observed, however, that there was a profound silence for a minute afterwards, which was interrupted by a jocose remark of the coachman about the delay of our dinner. Soon after we re-entered the coach, the Colonel referred to the trunk owner in a contemptuous manner. The Judge replied in a similar tone. "If I had been in the driver's place, I should have killed him sure," said the Colonel. With great surprise, I ventured to ask for what reason. "Did not you see the fellow put his hand to his breast when the driver denied that he had ever taken less than a dollar for bringing a trunk from Memphis?"

"No, I did not; but what of it?"

"Why, he meant to frighten the driver, of course."

"You think he had a knife in his breast?"

"Of course he had, sir."

"But you wouldn't kill him for that, I suppose?"

"When a man threatens to kill me, you wouldn't have me wait for him to do it, would you, sir?"

The roads continued very heavy; some one remarked, "There's been a heap of rain lately," and rain still kept falling. We passed a number of cotton waggons which had stopped in the road; the cattle had been turned out and had strayed off into the woods, and the drivers lay under the tilts asleep on straw.

The Colonel said this sight reminded him of his old camp-meeting days. "I used to be very fond of going to camp-meetings. I used to go first for fun, and, oh Lord! haint I had some fun at camp meetings? But after a while I got a conviction—needn't laugh, gentlemen. I tell you it was sober business for me. I'll never make fun of that. The truth just is, I am a melancholy case; I thought I was a pious man once, I did—I'm damn'd if I didn't. Don't laugh at what I say, now; I don't want fun made of that; I give you my word I experienced religion, and I used to go to the meetings with as much sincerity and soberness as anybody could. That was the time I learned to sing—learned to pray too, I did; could pray right smart. I did think I was a converted man, but of course I ain't, and I 'spose 'twarnt the right sort, and I don't reckon I shall have another chance. A gentleman has a right to make the most of this life, when he can't calculate on anything better than roasting in the next. Aint that so, Judge? I reckon so. You mustn't think hard of me, if I do talk wicked some. Can't help it."

I was forced by the stage arrangements to travel night and day. The Colonel told me that I should be able to get a good supper at a house where the coach was to stop about midnight —"good honest fried bacon, and hot Christian corn-bread—nothing like it, to fill a man up and make him feel righteous. You get a heap better living up in this country than you can at the St. Charles, for all the fuss they make about it. It's lucky you'll have something better to travel on to-night than them French friterzeed Dutch flabbergasted hell-fixins: for you'll have the——" (another most extraordinary series of imprecations on the road over which I was to travel).

Before dark all my companions left me, and in their place I had but one, a young gentleman with whom I soon became very intimately acquainted. He was seventeen years old, so he said; he looked older; and the son of a planter in the "Yazoo bottoms." The last year he had "follered overseein'" on his father's plantation, but he was bound for Tennessee, now, to go to an academy, where he could learn geography. There was a school near home at which he had studied reading and writing and ciphering, but he thought a gentleman ought to have some knowledge of geography. At ten o'clock the next morning the stage-coach having progressed at the rate of exactly two miles and a half an hour, for the previous sixteen hours, during which time we had been fasting, the supper-house, which we should have reached before midnight, was still ten miles ahead, the driver sulky and refusing to stop until we reached it. We had been pounded till we ached in every muscle. I had had no sleep since I left Memphis. We were passing over a hill country which sometimes appeared to be quite thickly inhabited, yet mainly still covered with a pine forest, through which the wind moaned lugubriously.

I had been induced to turn this way in my journey in no slight degree by reading the following description in a statistical article of De Bow's Review:

"The settling of this region is one among the many remarkable events in the history of the rise of the Western States. Fifteen years ago it was an Indian wilderness, and now it has reached and passed in its population, other portions of the State of ten times its age, and this population, too, one of the finest in all the West. Great attention has been given to schools and education, and here, [at Memphis,] has been located the

University of Mississippi; so amply endowed by the State, and now just going into operation under the auspices of some of the ablest professors from the eastern colleges. There is no overgrown wealth among them, and yet no squalid poverty; the people being generally comfortable, substantial, and independent farmers. Considering its climate, soil, wealth, and general character of its inhabitants, I should think no more desirable or delightful residence could be found than among the hills and sunny valleys of the Chickasaw Cession."*

And here among the hills of this Paradise of the South-west, we were, Yazoo and I—he, savagely hungry, as may be guessed from his observations upon "the finest people of the West," among whose cabins in the pine-wood toiled our stage-coach.

The whole art of driving was directed to the discovery of a passage for the coach among the trees and through the fields, where there were fields, adjoining the road—the road itself being impassable. Occasionally, when the coachman, during the night, found it necessary, owing to the thickness of the forest on each side, to take to the road, he would first leave the coach and make a survey with his lantern, sounding the ruts of the cotton-waggons, and finally making out a channel by guiding-stakes which he cut from the underwood with a hatchet, usually carried in the holster. If, after diligent sounding, he found no passage sufficiently shallow, he would sometimes spend half an hour in preparing one, bringing rails from the nearest fence, or cutting brushwood for the purpose. We were but once or twice during the night called upon to leave the coach, or to assist in road-making, and my companion frequently expressed his gratitude for this—gratitude not to the driver but to Providence, who had made a country, as he thought, so unusually well adapted for stage-coaching. The night before, he had been on a much worse road, and was half the time, with numerous other passengers, engaged in bringing rails, and prying the coach out of sloughs.

* See "Resources;" article, "Mississippi," etc.

They had been obliged to keep on the track, because the water was up over the adjoining country. Where the wooden causeway had floated off, they had passed through water so deep that it entered the coach body. With our road of to-day, then, he could only express satisfaction; not so with the residents upon it. "Look at 'em!" he would say. "Just look at 'em! What's the use of such people's living? 'Pears to me I'd die if I couldn't live better 'n that. When I get to be representative, I'm going to have a law made that all such kind of men shall be took up by the State and sent to the penitentiary, to make 'em work and earn something to support their families. I pity the women; I haint nuthin agin them; they work hard enough, I know; but the men—I know how 'tis. They just hang around groceries and spend all the money they can get—just go round and live on other people, and play keerds, and only go home to nights; and the poor women, they hev to live how they ken."

"Do you think it's so? It is strange we see no men—only women and children."

"Tell you they're off, gettin' a dinner out o' somebody. Tell you I know it's so. It's the way all these people do. Why there's one poor man I know, that lives in a neighbourhood of poor men, down our way, and he's right industrious, but he can't get rich and he never ken, cause all these other poor men live on him."

"What do you mean? Do they all drop in about dinner time?"

"No, not all on 'em, but some on 'em every day. And they keep borrowin' things of him. He haint spunk enough to insult 'em. If he'd just move into a rich neighbourhood and jest be a little sassy, and not keer so much about what folks said of him, he'd get rich; never knew a man that was industrious and sassy in this country that didn't get rich, quick, and get niggers to do his work for him. Anybody ken that's smart. Thar's whar they tried to raise some corn. Warn't no corn grew thar; that's sartin. Wonder what they live on? See the stalks. They never made no corn. Plowed right down the hill! Did you ever see anything like it? As if this sile warn't poor enough already. There now. Just the same. Only look at 'em! 'Pears like they never see a stage afore. This ain't the right road, the way they look at us. No, sartin, they never see a stage. Lord God! see the babies. They never see a stage afore. No, the stage never went by here afore, I know. This damn'd driver's just taken us round this way to show off what he can do and pass away the time before breakfast. Couldn't get no breakfast here if he would stop—less we ate a baby. That's right! step out where you ken see her good; prehaps you'll never see a stage again; better look now, right sharp. Yes, oh yes, sartin; fetch out all the babies. Haint you got no more? Well, I should hope not. Now, what is the use of so many babies? That's the worst on't. I'd get married to-morrow if I wasn't sure I'd hev babies. I hate babies, can't bear 'em round me, and won't have 'em. I would like to be married. I know several gals I'd marry if 'twarn't for that. Well, it's a fact. Just so. I hate the squallin' things. I know I was born a baby, but I couldn't help it, could I? I wish I hadn't been. I hate the squallin' things. If I had to hev a baby round me I should kill it."

"If you had a baby of your own, you'd feel differently about it."

"That's what they tell me. I s'pose I should, but I don't want to feel differently. I hate 'em. I hate 'em."

The coach stopped at length. We got out and found ourselves on the bank of an overflowed brook. A part of the bridge was broken up, the driver declared it impossible to ford the stream, and said he should return to the shanty, four miles back, at which we had last changed horses. We persuaded him to take one of his horses from the team and let us see if we could not get across. I succeeded in doing this without difficulty, and turning the horse loose he returned. The driver, however, was still afraid to try to ford the stream with the coach and mails, and after trying our best to persuade him, I told him if he returned he should do it without me, hoping he would be shamed out of his pusillanimity. Yazoo joined me, but the driver having again recovered the horse upon which he had forded the stream, turned about and drove back. We pushed on, and after walking a few miles, came to a neat new house, with a cluster of old cabins about it. It was much the most comfortable establishment we had seen during the day. Truly a "sunny valley" home of northern Mississippi. We entered quietly, and were received by two women who were spinning in a room with three outside doors all open, though a fine fire was burning, merely to warm the room, in a large fire-place, within. Upon our asking if we could have breakfast prepared for us, one of the women went to the door and gave orders to a negro, and in a moment after, we saw six or seven black boys and girls chasing and clubbing a hen round the yard for our benefit. I regret to add that they did not succeed in making her tender. At twelve o'clock we breakfasted, and were then accommodated with a bed, upon which we slept together for several hours. When I awoke I walked out to look at the premises.

The house was half a dozen rods from the high road, with a square yard all about it, in one corner of which was a small enclosure for stock, and a log stable and corn-crib. There were also three negro cabins; one before the house, and two behind it. The house was a neat building of logs, boarded over and painted on the outside. On the inside, the logs were neatly hewn to a plane face, and exposed. One of the lower rooms contained a bed, and but little other furniture; the other was the common family apartment, but also was furnished with a bed. A door opened into another smaller log house in the rear, in which were two rooms—one of them the family dining-room; the other the kitchen. Behind this was still another log erection, fifteen feet square, which was the smoke-house, and in which a great store of bacon was kept. The negro cabins were small, dilapidated, and dingy; the walls were not chinked, and there were no windows—which, indeed, would have been a superfluous luxury, for there were spaces of several inches between the logs, through which there was unobstructed vision. The furniture in the cabins was of the simplest and rudest imaginable kind, two or three beds with dirty clothing upon them, a chest, a wooden stool or two made with an axe, and some earthenware and cooking apparatus. Everything within the cabins was coloured black by smoke. The chimneys of both the house and the cabins were built of splinters and clay, and on the outer side of the walls. At the door of each cabin were literally "heaps" of babies and puppies, and behind or beside it a pig-stye and poultry coop, a ley-tub, and quantities of home-carded cotton placed upon boards to bleach. Within each of them was a woman or two, spinning with the old-fashioned great wheel, and in the kitchen another woman was weaving coarse cotton shirting with the ancient rude hand-loom. The mistress herself was spinning in the living-room, and asked, when we had grown acquainted, what women at the North could find to do, and how they could ever pass the time, when they gave up spinning and weaving. She made the common every-day clothing for all her family and her servants. They only bought a few "store-goods" for their "dress-up" clothes. She kept the negro girls spinning all through the winter, and at all times when they were not needed in the field. She supposed they would begin to plant corn now in a few days, and then the girls would go to work out of doors. I noticed that all the bed-clothing, the towels, curtains, etc., in the house, were of homespun.

The proprietor, who had been absent on a fishing excursion, during the day, returned at dusk. He was a man of the fat, slow-and-easy style, and proved to be good-natured, talkative, and communicative. He had bought the tract of land he now occupied, and moved upon it about ten years before. He had made a large clearing, and could now sell it for a good deal more than he gave for it. He intended to sell whenever he could get a good offer, and move on West. It was the best land in this part of the country, and he had got it well fenced, and put up a nice house: there were a great many people that like to have these things done for them in advance—and he thought he should not have to wait long for a purchaser. He liked himself to be clearing land, and it was getting too close settled about here to suit him. He did not have much to do but to hunt and fish, and the game was getting so scarce it was too much trouble to go after it. He did not think there were so many cat in the creek as there used to be either, but there were more gar-fish. When he first bought this land he was not worth much—had to run in debt—hadn't but three negroes. Now he was pretty much out of debt and owned twenty negroes, seven of them prime field-hands, and he reckoned I had not seen a better lot anywhere.

During the evening, all the cabins were illuminated by great fires, and, looking into one of them, I saw a very picturesque family group; a man sat on the ground making a basket, a woman lounged on a chest in the chimney corner smoking a pipe, and a boy and two girls sat in a bed which had been drawn up opposite to her, completing the fireside circle. They were talking and laughing cheerfully.

The next morning when I turned out I found Yazoo looking with the eye of a connoisseur at the seven prime field-hands, who at half-past seven were just starting off with hoes and axes for their day's work. As I approached him, he exclaimed with enthusiasm :—

"Aren't them a right keen lookin' lot of niggers?"

And our host soon after coming out, he immediately walked up to him, saying :—

"Why, friend, them yer niggers o' yourn would be good for seventy bales of cotton, if you'd move down into our country."

Their owner was perfectly aware of their value, and said everything good of them.

"There's something ruther singlar, too, about my niggers; I don't know as I ever see anything like it anywhere else."

"How so, sir?"

"Well, I reckon it's my way o' treatin' 'em, much as anything. I never hev no difficulty with 'em. Hen't licked a nigger in five year, 'cept maybe sprouting some of the young ones sometimes. Fact, my niggers never want no lookin' arter; they jus tek ker o' themselves. Fact, they do tek a greater interest in the crops than I do myself. There's another thing—I 'spose 'twill surprise you—there ent one of my niggers but what can read; read good, too—better 'n I can, at any rate."

"How did they learn?"

"Taught themselves. I b'lieve there was one on 'em that I bought, that could read, and he taught all the rest. But niggers is mighty apt at larnin', a heap more 'n white folks is."

I said that this was contrary to the generally received opinion.

"Well, now, let me tell you," he continued; "I had a boy to work, when I was buildin', and my boys jus teachin' him night times and such, he warn't here more'n three months, and he larned to read as well as any man I ever heerd, and I know he didn't know his letters when he come here. It didn't seem to me any white man could have done that; does it to you, now?

"How old was he?"

"Warn't more'n seventeen, I reckon."

"How do they get books—do you get them for them?"

"Oh, no; get 'em for themselves."

"How?"

"Buy 'em."

"How do they get the money?"

"Earn it."

"How?"

"By their own work. I tell you my niggers have got more money 'n I hev."

"What kind of books do they get?"

"Religious kind a books ginerally—these stories; and some of them will buy novels, I believe. They won't let on to that, but I expect they do it."

They bought them of peddlers. I inquired about the law to prevent negroes reading, and asked if it allowed books to be sold to negroes. He had never heard of any such law—didn't believe there was any. The Yazoo man said there was such a law in his country. Negroes never had anything to read there. I asked our host if his negroes were religious, as their choice of works would have indicated.

"Yes; all on 'em, I reckon. Don't s'pose you'll believe it, but I tell you it's a fact; I haint heerd a swear on this place for a twelvemonth. They keep the Lord's day, too, right tight, in gineral."

"Our niggers is mighty wicked down in Yallerbush county," said my companion; "they dance."

"Dance on Sunday?" I asked.

"Oh, no, we don't allow that."

"What do they do, then—go to meeting?"

"Why, Sundays they sleep mostly; they've been at work hard all the week, you know, and Sundays they stay in their cabins, and sleep and talk to each other. There's so many of 'em together, they don't want to go visiting off the place."

"Are your negroes Baptists or Methodists?" I inquired of our host.

"All Baptists; niggers allers want to be ducked, you know. They ain't content to be just titch'd with water; they must be ducked in all over. There was two niggers jined the Methodists up here last summer, and they made the minister put 'em into the branch; they wouldn't jine 'less he'd duck 'em."

"The Bible says baptize, too," observed Yazoo.

"Well, they think they must be ducked all under, or 'tain't no good."

"Do they go to meeting?"

"Yes, they hev a meeting among themselves."

"And a preacher?"

"Yes; a nigger preacher."

"Our niggers is mighty wicked; they dance!" repeated Yazoo.

"Do you consider dancing so very wicked, then?" I asked.

"Well, I don't account so myself, as I know on, but they do, you know—the pious people, all kinds, except the 'Piscopers; some o' them, they do dance themselves, I believe. Do you dance in your country?"

"Yes."

"What sort of dances—cotillions and reels?"

"Yes; what do you?"

"Well, we dance cotillions and reels too, and we dance on a plank; that's the kind of dancin' I like best."

"How is it done?"

"Why, don't you know that? You stand face to face with your partner on a plank and keep a dancin'. Put the plank up on two barrel heads, so it'll kind o' spring. At some of our parties—that's among common kind o' people, you know—it's great fun. They dance as fast as they can, and the folks all stand round and holler, '*Keep it up, John!*' '*Go it, Nance!*' '*Don't give it up so!*' '*Old Virginny never tire!*' '*Heel and toe, ketch a fire!*' and such kind of observations, and clap and stamp 'em."

"Do your negroes dance much?"

"Yes, they are mighty fond on't. Saturday night they dance all night, and Sunday nights too. Daytime they sleep and rest themselves, and Sunday nights we let 'em dance and sing if they want. It does 'em good, you know, to enjoy theirselves."

"They dance to the banjo, I suppose?"

"Banjos and violins; some of 'em has got violins."

"I like to hear negroes sing," said I.

"Niggers is allers good singers nat'rally," said our host. "I reckon they got better lungs than white folks, they hev such powerful voices."

We were sitting at this time on the rail fence at the corner of a hog-pen and a large half-cleared field. In that part of this field nearest the house, among the old stumps, twenty or thirty small fruit trees had been planted. I asked what sorts they were.

"I don't know—good kinds tho', I expect; I bought 'em for that at any rate."

"Where did you buy them?"

"I bought 'em of a feller that came a peddlin' round here last fall; he said I'd find 'em good."

"What did you pay for them?"

"A bit apiece."

"That's very cheap, if they're good for anything; you are sure they're grafted, arn't you?"

"Only by what he said—he said they was grafted kinds. I've got a paper in the housen he gin me, tells about 'em; leastways, he said it did. They's the curosest kinds of trees printed into it you ever heerd on. But I did not buy none, only the fruit kinds."

Getting off the fence I began to pick about the roots of one of them with my pocket-knife. After exposing the trunk for five or six inches below the surface, I said, "You've planted these too deep, if they're all like this. You should have the ground dished about it or it won't grow." I tried another, and after picking some minutes without finding any signs of the "collar," I asked if they had all been planted so deeply.

"I don't know—I told the boys to put 'em in about two feet, and I expect they did, for they fancied to have apple-trees growin'."

The catalogue of the tree-peddler, which afterwards came into my possession, quite justified the opinion my host expressed of the kinds of trees described in it. The reader shall judge for himself, and I assure him that the following is a literal transcript of it, omitting the sections headed "Ancebus new," "Camelias," "Rhododendrums," "Bubbs Pæony," "Rosiers," "Wind's flowers of the greatest scarcity," "Bulbous Roots, and of various kinds of graines."

SPECIAL CATALOGUE

OF THE PLANTS, FLOWERS, SHRUBS IMPORTED BY

ROUSSET

MEMBER OF SEVERAL SOCIETIES.

At Paris (France), boulevard of Hopital, and at Chambery, faubourg de Mache.

Mr Rousset beg to inform they are arrived in this town, with a large assortment of the most rare vegetable plants, either flowerd on fruit bearer, onion bulbous, seeds, &c., &c. Price very moderate.

Their store is situated

CHOIX D'ARBRES A FRUIT.

Choice of Fruit Trees.

Pear Trees.

1 Good Louisa from Avranche.
2 Winter's Perfume.
3 Saint-John-in-Iron.
4 Leon-the-Clerc.
5 Bergamot from England.
6 Duchess of Angoulème.
7 Goulu-Morceau.
8 Tarquin Pear.
9 Summer's Good (large) Christian.
10 Good Turkisk Christian.
11 Grey (large) Beurré.
12 Royal Beurré from England.

1 Bon-Chrétien d'été,
2 — d'hiver.
3 — de Pâque.
4 Doyenné blanc.
5 Duchesse d'Angora-New.
6 Belle Angevine, fondante.
7 Crassane d'hiver.
8 Louise d'Orleans, sucré.
9 Double fleur hâtif.
10 Angélique de Tour.

1 Borgamotte de Milan, Gros.
2 — d'Aiençon, très-gros.
3 Beurrê gris d'hiver.
4 — Amanlis.
5 — d'Hardenpont, précoce.
6 Fortunè, fondant.
7 Josephine, chair fine.
8 Martin-sec, sucrè.
9 Messire, gris.
10 Muscat d'etè.
11 Doyenné d'automne.
12 — d'hiver, sucré.
13 Virgouleuse fondonte.
14 Bezy-Lamotte.
15 Gros-Blanquet.

Apples.

1 Renetto of Spain.
2 — Green.
3 Apple Coin.
4 — Friette.
5 Calville, white, winter's fruit.
6 — red, autumn's fruit.
7 — red, winter's fruit.
8 Violet or of the Four-Taste.
9 Renette from England, or Gold-Apple.
10 Golded Renette, a yellow backward plant.
11 White — of a great perfume.
12 Renette, red, winter's fruit.

1 Renette, yellow, heavy fruit.
2 — grey, very delicate.
3 — Princess noble.
4 Apple d'Api.
5 — d'Eve.
6 Winter's Postophe.
7 Plein gney fenouillet.
8 Renette franc.
9 — of St. Laurent.
10 Sammers Numbourg.
11 Belle du Havre.
12 Belle Hollandaise.

1 Violet Apple or of the 4 taste; the fruit may be preserved 2 years.
2 Princess Renette, of a gold yellow, spotted with red of a delicious taste.
3 White Renette from Canada, of 'which the skin is lite scales strange by its size.
4 The Cythère Apple.
5 The Caynoite Apple.
6 Apple Trees with double flowers. Blooms twice a year, Camélia's flowers like.
106 others kinds of Apples of the newest choice.

Apricots.

1 The Ladie's Apricots.
2 The Peack Apricots.
3 The Royal Apricots.

4 The Gros Muscg Apricots.
5 The Pourret Apricots.
6 Portugal Apricots.
7 Apricats monstruous from America, of a gold yellow, of an enormous size, and of the pine's apple taste.

Peach Trees.

1 Peach Grosse Mignonne.
2 — Bello Beauty.
3 — Godess.
4 — Beauty of Paris.
4 — From Naples ! said without stone,
6 Brugnon, musc taste.
7 Admirable; Belle of Vitry.
8 The Large Royal.
9 Monstruous Pavie.
10 The Cardinal, very forward.
11 Good Workman.
12 Lêtitia Bonaparte.
13 The Prince's Peach, melting in the mouth.
14 The Prince's Peach from Africa, with large white fruit, weighing pound and half each; hearly, new kind.
50 others new kinds of Peach Trees.

Plum Trees.

1 Plum Lamorte.
2 Surpasse Monsieur.
3 Damas with musc taste.
4 Royale of Tonrs.
5 Green Gage, of a violet colour.
6 Large Mirabelle.
7 Green gage, golded.
8 Imperial, of a violet colour.
9 Empress, of a white colour.
10 Ste-Catherine, zellow, suger taste like.

Cherry Trees.

1 Cherry from the North.
2 — Royal, gives from 18 to 20 cherries weihing one pound, 4 differentes kinds.
3 Cherry Reina Hortense.
4 — Montmorency.
5 — with thort stalk (Gros-Gobet),
6 — Le Mercier.
7 — Four for a pound.
8 Cherry Beauty of Choicy.
9 — The English.
10 Cherry-Duck.
11 — Créole with bunches.
12 — Bigarrot or monster of new Mézel.

Currant Trees.

1 Currant Three with red bunches (grapes).
2 — — with white bunches.
3 Gooseberries of 1st choice (Raspherries) six kinds of alégery.
4 New kind of currants, of which the grapes are as big as the wine grapes.

Grapes Wines.

1 Chasselas of Fontainebleau, with large gold grains.
2 Chasselas, black very good.
3 — red, of musc teste.
4 Verdal, the sweetest and finest fruit for desert.
5 White Muscadine grape, or of Frontignan.
6 Muscat of Alexandrie, musc taste.
7 Cornichon, white, sweet sugar like, very good.
8 Tokay, red and white.
9 Verjus from Bordeaux, large yellow fruit.
10 St. Peter large and fine fruit.
11 Red Muscadine Graper.
12 Raisin of Malaga.
13 The Celestial Wine Mree, or the amphibious grain, weighing two ounces, the grain of a red and violet colour.

New Strawberry Plants.

1 The Strawberry Cremont.
2 — — the Queen.
3 — — monster, new kind.
4 — — from Clili.
5 Caperon of a raspberry taste.
6 Scarlat from Venose, very forward plant.
7 Prince Albert, fruit of very greatz beauty.
8 Grinston colalant, very large.
9 Rose-Berry, big fruit and of a long form.
10 Bath chery, very good.
11 The Big Chinese Strawberry, weihing 16 to a pound, produce fruit all year round, of the pine apple's taste.
12 Vilmoth full.

New Fig Trees of a Monstruous Size.

1 Diodena white, of a large size.
2 Duchess of Maroc, green fruit.
3 Donne-à-Dieu, blue fruit.
4 La Sanspareille, yellow fruit.

The Perpetual Rapsberry Tree, imported from Indies producing a fruit large as an egg, taste delicious 3 kinds, red, violet and white.

The Rapsberry Tree from Fastolff, red fruit, very good of an extraordinary size, very hearly forward plant.

Cherry Currant Tree, with large bunches, it has a great production. Its numerous and long bunches cover entirely the old wood and looks like grapes; the fruit of a cherry pink colour is very large and of the best quality.

Asparagus from Africa, new kinds, good to eat the same year of their planting (seeds of two years). 1000 varieties of annual and perpetual flower's grains also of kitchen garden grains.

PAULNOVIA INPERIALIS. Magnificent hardy plant from 12 to 15 yards of higth: its leave come to the size of 75 to 80 centimeter and its fine and larg flowers of a fine blue, gives when the spring comes, a soft and agréable perfume.

Besides these plants the amateur will fine at M. ROUSSET, *stores, a great number of other Plants and Fruit Trees of which would be to long to describe.*

NOTICE.

The admirable and strange plant called *Trompette du Jugement* (The Judgment Trompette) of that name having not yet found its classification.

This marvellous plant was send to us from China by the cleuer and courageous botanist collector M. Fortune, from l'Himalaya, near summet of the Chamalari Macon.

This splendid plant deserves the first rank among all kinds of plant wich the botanical science has produce till now in spite of all the new discoveries.

This bulbous plant gives several stems on the same subject. It grows to the height of 6 feet. It is furnished with flowers from bottom to top. The bud looks by his from like a big cannon ball of a heavenly blue. The center is of an aurora yellewish colour. The vegetation of that plant is to fouitfull that when it is near to blossom it gives a great heat when tassing it in hand and when the bud opens it produces a naite Similar to a pistole shot. Immediately the vegetation takes fire and burns like alcohol about an hour and a half. The flowers succeeding one to the other gives the satisfaction of having flowers during 7 or 8 months.

The most intense cold can not hurt this plant and can be culvivated in pots, in appartments or gpeen houses.

Wa call the public attention to this plant as a great curiosity.

Havre—Printed by F. HUE, rue de Paris, 89.

"But come," said the farmer, "go in; take a drink. Breakfast'll be ready right smart."

"I don't want to drink before breakfast, thank you."

"Why not?"

"I'm not accustomed to it, and I don't find it's wholesome."

Not wholesome to drink before breakfast! That was "a new kink" to our jolly host, and troubled him as much as a new "ism" would an old fogy. Not wholesome? He had always reckoned it warn't very wholesome not to drink before breakfast. He did not expect I had seen a great many healthier men than he was, had I? and he always took a drink before breakfast. If a man just kept himself well strung up, without ever stretching himself right tight, he didn't reckon damps or heat would ever do him much harm. He had never had a sick day since he came to this place, and he reckoned that this was owin' considerable to the good rye whisky he took. It was a healthy trac' of land, though, he believed, a mighty healthy trac'; everything seemed to thrive here. We must see a nigger-gal that he was raisin'; she was just coming five, and would pull up nigh upon a hundred weight.

"Two year ago," he continued, after taking his dram, as we sat by the fire in the north room, "when I had a carpenter here to finish off this house, I told one of my boys he must come in and help him. I reckoned he would larn quick, if he was a mind to. So he come in, and a week arterwards he fitted the plank and laid this floor, and now you just look at it; I don't believe any man could do it better. That was two year ago, and now he's as good a carpenter as you ever see. I bought him some tools after the carpenter left, and he can do anything with 'em—make a table or a chest of drawers or anything. I think niggers is somehow nat'rally ingenious; more so 'n white folks. They is wonderful apt to any kind of slight."

I took out my pocket-map, and while studying it, asked Yazoo some questions about the route East. Not having yet studied geography, as he observed, he could not answer. Our host inquired where I was going, that way. I said I should go on to Carolina.

"Expect you're going to buy a rice-farm, in the Carolinies, aint you? and I reckon you're up here speckylating arter nigger stock, aint you now?"

"Well," said I, "I would n't mind getting that fat girl of yours, if we can made a trade. How much a pound will you sell her at?"

"We don't sell niggers by the pound in this country."

"Well, how much by the lump?"

"Well, I don't know; reckon I don't keer about sellin' her just yet."

After breakfast, I inquired about the management of the farm. He said that he purchased negroes, as he was able, from time to time. He grew rich by the improved saleable value of his land, arising in part from their labour, and from their natural increase and improvement, for he bought only such as would be likely to increase in value on his hands. He had been obliged to spend but little money, being able to live and provide most of the food and clothing for his family and his people, by the production of his farm. He made a little cotton, which he had to send some distance to be ginned and baled, and then waggoned it seventy miles to a market; also raised some wheat, which he turned into flour at a neighbouring mill, and sent to the same market. This transfer engaged much of the winter labour of his man-slaves.

I said that I supposed the Memphis and Charleston railroad, as it progressed east, would shorten the distance to which it would be necessary to draw his cotton, and so be of much service to him. He did not know that. He did not know as he should ever use it. He expected they would charge pretty high for carrying cotton, and his niggers hadn't any thing else to do. It did not really cost him anything now to send it to Memphis, because he had to board the niggers and the cattle anyhow, and they did not want much more on the road than they did at home.

He made a large crop of corn, which, however, was mainly consumed by his own force, and he killed annually about one hundred and fifty hogs, the bacon of which was all consumed in his own family and by his people, or sold to passing travellers. In the fall, a great many drovers and slave-dealers passed over the road with their stock, and they frequently camped against this house, so as to buy corn and bacon of him. This they cooked themselves.

There were sometimes two hundred negroes brought along together, going South. He didn't always have bacon to spare for them, though he killed one hundred and fifty swine. They were generally bad characters, and had been sold for fault by their owners. Some of the slave-dealers were high-minded, honourable men, he thought; "high-toned gentlemen, as ever he saw, some of 'em, was."

Niggers were great eaters, and wanted more meat than white folks; and he always gave his as much as they wanted, and more too. The negro cook always got dinner for them, and took what she liked for it; his wife didn't know much about it. She got as much as she liked, and he guessed she didn't spare it. When the field-hands were anywhere within a reasonable distance, they always came up to the house to get their dinner. If they were going to work a great way off, they would carry their dinner with them. They did as they liked about it. When they hadn't taken their dinner, the cook called them at twelve o'clock with a conch. They ate in the kitchen, and he had the same dinner that they did, right out of the same frying-pan; it was all the same, only they ate in the kitchen, and he ate in the room we were in, with the door open between them.

I brought up the subject of the cost of labour, North and South. He had no apprehension that there would ever be any want of labourers at the South, and could not understand that the ruling price indicated the state of the demand for them. He thought negroes would increase more rapidly than the need for their labour. "Niggers," said he, "breed faster than white folks, a 'mazin' sight, you know; they begin younger."

"How young do they begin?"

"Sometimes at fourteen, sometimes at sixteen, and sometimes at eighteen."

"Do you let them marry so young as that?" I inquired. He laughed, and said, "They don't very often wait to be married."

"When they marry, do they have a minister to marry them?"

"Yes, generally one of their own preachers."

"Do they with you?" I inquired of Yazoo.

"Yes, sometimes they hev a white minister, and sometimes a black one, and if there arn't neither handy, they get some of the pious ones to marry 'em. But then very often they only just come and ask our consent, and then go ahead, without any more ceremony. They just call themselves married. But most niggers likes a ceremony, you know, and they generally make out to hev one somehow. They don't very often get married for good, though, without trying each other, as they say, for two or three weeks, to see how they are going to like each other."

I afterwards asked how far it was to the post-office. It was six miles. "One of my boys," said our host, "always gets the paper every week. He goes to visit his wife, and passes by the post-office every Sunday. Our paper hain't come, though, now, for three weeks. The mail don't come very regular." All of his negroes, who had wives off the place, left an hour before sunset on Saturday evening. One of them, who had a wife twenty miles away, left at twelve o'clock Saturday, and got back at twelve o'clock Monday.

"We had a nigger once," said Yazoo, "that had a wife fifteen miles away, and he used to do so; but he did some rascality once, and he was afraid to go again. He told us his wife was so far off, 't was too much trouble to go there, and he believed he'd give her up. We was glad of it. He was a darned rascally nigger—allers getting into scrapes. One time we sent him to mill, and he went round into town and sold some of the meal. The storekeeper wouldn't pay him for't, 'cause he hadn't got an order. The next time we were in town, the storekeeper just showed us the bag of meal; said he reckoned 't was stole; so when we got home we just tied him up to the tree and licked him. He's a right smart nigger; rascally niggers allers is smart. I'd rather have a rascally nigger than any other—they's so smart allers. He is about the best nigger we've got."

"I have heard," said I, "that religious negroes were generally the most valuable. I have been told that a third more would be given for a man if he were religious." "Well, I never heerd of it before," said he. Our host thought there was no difference in the market value of sinners and saints.

"Only," observed Yazoo, "the rascalier a nigger is, the better he'll work. Now that yer nigger I was tellin' you on, he's worth more'n any other nigger we've got. He's a yaller nigger."

I asked their opinion as to the comparative value of black and yellow negroes. Our host had two bright mulatto boys among his—didn't think there was much difference, "but allers reckoned yellow fellows was the best a little; they worked smarter. He would rather have them." Yazoo would not; he "didn't think but what they'd work as well; but he didn't fancy yellow negroes 'round him; would rather have real black ones."

I asked our host if he had no foreman or driver for his negroes, or if he gave his directions to one of them in particular for all the rest. He did not. They all did just as they pleased, and arranged the work among themselves. They never needed driving.

"If I ever notice one of 'em getting a little slack, I just talk to him; tell him we must get out of the grass, and I want to hev him stir himself a little more, and then, maybe, I slip a dollar into his hand, and when he gits into the field he'll go ahead, and the rest seeing him, won't let themselves be distanced by him. My niggers never want no lookin' arter. They tek more interest in the crop than I do myself, every one of 'em."

Religious, instructed, and seeking further enlightenment; industrious, energetic, and self directing; well fed, respected, and trusted by their master, and this master an illiterate, indolent, and careless man! A very different state of things, this, from what I saw on a certain great cotton planter's estate, where a profit of $100,000 was made in a single year, but where five hundred negroes were constantly kept under the whip, where religion was only a pow-wow or cloak for immorality, and where the negro was considered to be of an inferior race, especially designed by Providence to be kept in the position he there occupied! A very different thing; and strongly suggesting what a very different thing this negro servitude might be made in general, were the ruling disposition of the South more just and sensible.

About half-past eleven, a stage coach, which had come earlier in the morning from the East, and had gone on as far as the brook, returned, having had our luggage transferred to it from the one we had left on the other side. In the transfer a portion of mine was omitted and never recovered. Up to this time our host had not paid the smallest attention to any work his men were doing, or even looked to see if they had fed the cattle, but had lounged about, sitting upon a fence, chewing tobacco, and talking with us, evidently very glad to have somebody to converse with. He went in once again, after a drink; showed us the bacon he had in his smoke-house, and told a good many stories of his experience in life, about a white man's "dying hard" in the neighbourhood, and of a tree falling on a team with which one of his negroes was ploughing cotton, "which was lucky"—that is, that it did not kill the negro—and a good deal about "hunting" when he was younger and lighter.

Still absurdly influenced by an old idea which I had brought to the South with me, I waited, after the coach came in sight, for Yazoo to put the question, which he presently did, boldly enough.

"Well; reckon we're goin' now. What's the damage?"

"Well; reckon seventy-five cents 'll be right."

CHAPTER III.

THE INTERIOR COTTON DISTRICTS—CENTRAL MISSISSIPPI, ALABAMA, ETC.

Central Mississippi, May 31st.—Yesterday was a raw, cold day, wind north-east, like a dry north-east storm at home. Fortunately I came to the pleasantest house and household I had seen for some time. The proprietor was a native of Maryland, and had travelled in the North; a devout Methodist, and somewhat educated. He first came South, as I understood, for the benefit of his health, his lungs being weak.

His first dwelling, a rude log cabin, was still standing, and was occupied by some of his slaves. The new house, a cottage, consisting of four rooms and a hall, stood in a small grove of oaks; the family were quiet, kind, and sensible.

When I arrived, the oldest boy was at work, holding a plough in the cotton-field, but he left it and came at once, with confident and affable courtesy, to entertain me.

My host had been in Texas, and after exploring it quite thoroughly, concluded that he much preferred to remain where he was. He found no part of that country where good land, timber, and a healthy climate were combined: in the West he did not like the vicinage of the Germans and Mexicans; moreover, he didn't "fancy" a prairie county. Here, in favourable years, he got a bale of cotton to the acre. Not so much now as formerly. Still, he said, the soil would be good enough for him here, for many years to come.

I went five times to the stable without being able to find a servant there. I was always told that "the boy" would feed my horse, and take good care of him, when he came;

and so at length I had to go to bed, trusting to this assurance. I went out just before breakfast next morning, and found the horse with only ten *dry* cobs in the manger. I searched for the boy; could not find him, but was told that my horse had been fed. I said, "I wish to have him fed more—as much as he will eat." Very well, the boy should give him more. When I went out after breakfast the boy was leading out the horse. I asked if he had given him corn this morning.

"Oh yes, sir."

"How many ears did you give him?"

"Ten or fifteen—or sixteen, sir; he eats very hearty."

I went into the stable and saw that he had not been fed; there were the same ten cobs (dry) in the manger. I doubted, indeed, from their appearance, if the boy had fed him at all the night before. I fed him with leaves myself, but could not get into the corn crib. The proprietor was, I do not doubt, perfectly honest, but the negro had probably stolen the corn for his own hogs and fowls.

The next day I rode more than thirty miles, having secured a good feed of corn for the horse at midday. At nightfall I was much fatigued, but had as yet failed to get lodging. It began to rain, and grew dark, and I kept the road with difficulty. About nine o'clock I came to a large, comfortable house.

An old lady sat in the verandah, of whom I asked if I could be accommodated for the night: "Reckon so," she replied: then after a few moments' reflection, without rising from her chair she shouted, "Gal!—gal!" Presently a girl came.

"Missis?"

"Call Tom!"

The girl went off, while I remained, waiting for a more definite answer. At length she returned: "Tom ain't there, missis."

"Who is there?"

"Old Pete."

"Well, tell him to come and take this gentleman's horse."

Pete came, and I went with him to the gate where I had fastened my horse. Here he called for some younger slave to come and take him down to "the pen," while he took off the saddle.

All this time it was raining, but any rapidity of movement was out of the question. Pete continued shouting. "Why not lead the horse to the pen yourself?" I asked. "I must take care of de saddle and tings, massa; tote 'em to de house whar dey'll be safe. Dese niggers is so treacherous, can't leave nothin' roun' but dey'll hook suthing off of it."

Next morning, at dawn of day, I saw honest Pete come into the room where I was in bed and go stealthily to his young master's clothes, probably mistaking them for mine. I moved and he dropped them, and slunk out to the next room, where he went loudly to making a fire. I managed to see the horse well fed night and morning.

There were three pretty young women in this house, of good manners and well dressed, except for the abundance of rings and jewelry which they displayed at breakfast. One of them surprised me not a little at the table. I had been offered, in succession, fried ham and eggs, sweet potatoes, apple-pie, corn-bread, and molasses; this last article I declined, and passed it to the young lady opposite, looking to see how it was to be used. She had, on a breakfast plate, fried ham and eggs and apple-pie, and poured molasses between them.

June 1st.—I stopped last evening at the house of a man who was called "Doctor" by his family, but who was, to judge from his language, very illiterate. His son, by whom I was first received, followed me to the stable. He had ordered a negro child to lead my horse, but as I saw the little fellow could n't hold him I went myself. He had no fodder (corn-leaves), and proposed to give the horse some shucks (corn-husks) dipped in salt water, and, as it was now too late to go further, I assented. Belshazzar licked them greedily, but would not eat them, and they seemed to destroy his appetite for corn, for late in the evening, having groped my way into the stable, I found seven small ears of corn, almost untasted, in the manger. I got the young man to come out and give him more.

The "Doctor" returned from "a hunt," as he said, with no game but a turtle, which he had taken from a "trot line"—a line, with hooks at intervals, stretched across the river.

The house was large, and in a good-sized parlour or common room stood a handsome centre table, on which were a few books and papers, mostly Baptist publications. I sat here alone in the evening, straining my eyes to read a wretchedly printed newspaper, till I was offered a bed. I was very tired and sleepy, having been ill two nights before. The bed was apparently clean, and I gladly embraced it.

My host, holding a candle for me to undress by (there was no candlestick in the house), called to a boy on the outside to fasten the doors, which he did by setting articles of furniture against them. When I had got into bed he went himself into an inner room, the door of which he closed and fastened in the same manner. No sooner was the light withdrawn than I was attacked by bugs. I was determined, if possible, not to be kept awake by them, but they soon conquered me. I never suffered such incessant and merciless persecution from them before. In half an hour I was nearly frantic, and leaped from bed. But what to do? There was no use in making a disturbance about it; doubtless every other bed and resting place in the house was full of them. I shook out my day clothes carefully and put them on, and then pushing away the barricade, opened the door and went into the parlour. At first I thought that I would arrange the chairs in a row and sleep on them; but this I found impracticable, for the seats of the chairs were too narrow, and moreover of deerskin, which was sure to be full of fleas if not of bugs. Stiff and sore and weak, I groaningly lay down where the light of the moon came through a broken window, for bugs feed but little except in darkness, and with my saddle-bags for a pillow, again essayed to sleep. Fleas! instantly. There was nothing else to be done; I was too tired to sit up, even if that would have effectually removed the annoyance. Finally I dozed—not long, I think, for I was suddenly awakened by a large insect dropping upon my eye. I struck it off, and at the moment it stung me. My eyelid swelled immediately, and grew painful, but at length I slept in spite of it. I was once more awakened by a large beetle which fell on me from the window; once more I got asleep, till finally at four o'clock I awoke with that feverish dryness of the eyes which indicates a determination to sleep no more. It was daylight, and I was stiff and shivering; the inflammation and pain of the sting in my eyelid had in a great degree subsided. I pushed back the bolt of the outside door-lock, and went to the stable. The negroes were already at work in the field. Belshazzar had had a bad night too: that was evident. The floor of the stall, being of earth, had been trodden into two hollows at each end, leaving a small rough hillock in the centre. Bad as it was, however, it was the best in the stable; only one in four of the stalls having a manger that was not broken down. A wee little black girl and boy were cleaning their master's horses—mine they were afraid of. They had managed to put some fresh corn in his manger, however, and as he refused to eat, I took a curry-comb and brush, and in the next two hours gave him the first thorough grooming he had enjoyed since I owned him. I could not detect the reason of his loss of appetite. I had been advised by an old southern traveller to examine the corn when my horse refused to eat—if corn were high I might find that it had been greased. From the actions of the horse, then and subsequently, I suspect some trick of this kind was here practised upon me. When I returned to the house and asked to wash, water was given me in a vessel which, though I doubted the right of my host to a medical diploma, certainly smelt strongly of the shop—it was such as is used by apothecaries in mixing drugs. The title of Doctor is often popularly given at the South to druggists and venders of popular medicines; very probably he had been one, and had now retired to enjoy the respectability of a planter.

June 2nd.—I met a ragged old negro, of whom I asked the way, and at what house within twelve miles I had better stop. He advised me to go to one more than twelve miles distant.

"I suppose," said I, "I can stop at any house along the road here, can't I? They'll all take in travellers?"

"Yes, sir, if you'll take rough fare, such as travellers has to, sometimes. They're all damn'd rascals along dis road, for ten or twelve miles, and you'll get nothin' but rough fare. But I say, massa, rough fare 's good enough for dis world; ain't it, massa? Dis world ain't nothin; dis is hell, dis is, I calls it; hell to what 's a comin' arter, ha! ha! Ef you 's prepared? you says. I don't look much 's if I was prepared, does I? nor talk like it, nuther. De Lord he cum to me in my cabin in de night time, in de year '45."

"What?"

"De Lord! massa, de bressed Lord! He cum to me in

de night time, in de year '45, and he says to me, says he, 'I'll spare you yet five year longer, old boy!' So when '50 cum round I thought my time had cum, sure; but as I didn't die, I reckon de Lord has 'cepted of me, and I 'specs I shall be saved, dough I don't look much like it, ha! ha! ho! ho! de Lord am my rock, and he shall not perwail over me. I will lie down in green pastures and take up my bed in hell, yet will not His mercy circumwent me. Got some baccy, master?"

A little after sunset I came to an unusually promising plantation, the dwelling being within a large enclosure, in which there was a well-kept southern sward shaded by fine trees. The house, of the usual form, was painted white, and the large number of neat out-buildings seemed to indicate opulence, and, I thought, unusual good taste in its owner. A lad of sixteen received me, and said I could stay; I might fasten my horse, and when the negroes came up he would have him taken care of. When I had done so, and had brought the saddle to the verandah, he offered me a chair, and at once commenced a conversation in the character of entertainer. Nothing in his tone or manner would have indicated that he was not the father of the family, and proprietor of the establishment. No prince royal could have had more assured and nonchalant dignity. Yet a northern stable-boy, or apprentice, of his age, would seldom be found as ignorant.

"Where do you live, sir, when you are at home?" he asked.

"At New York."

"New York is a big place, sir, I expect?"

"Yes, very big."

"Big as New Orleans, is it, sir?"

"Yes, much bigger."

"Bigger 'n New Orleans? It must be a bully city."

"Yes; the largest in America."

"Sickly there now, sir?"

"No, not now; it is sometimes."

"Like New Orleans, I suppose?"

"No, never so bad as New Orleans sometimes is."

"Right healthy place, I expect, sir?"

"Yes, I believe so, for a place of its size."

"What diseases do you have there, sir?"

"All sorts of diseases—not so much fever, however, as you have hereabouts."

"Measles and hooping-cough, sometimes, I reckon?"

"Yes, 'most all the time, I dare say."

"All the time! People must die there right smart. Some is dyin' 'most every day, I expect, sir?"

"More than a hundred every day, I suppose."

"Gosh! a hundred every day! Almighty sickly place 't must be?"

"It is such a large place, you see—seven hundred thousand people."

"Seven hundred thousand—expect that's a heap of people, ain't it?"

His father, a portly, well-dressed man, soon came in, and learning that I had been in Mexico, said, "I suppose there's a heap of Americans flocking in and settling up that country along on the line, ain't there, sir?"

"No, sir, very few. I saw none, in fact—only a few Irishmen and Frenchmen, who called themselves Americans. Those were the only foreigners I saw, except negroes."

"Niggers! Where were they from?"

"They were runaways from Texas."

"But their masters go there and get them again, don't they?"

"No, sir, they can't."

"Why not?"

"The Mexicans are friendly to the niggers, and protect them."

"But why not go to the Government?"

"The Government considers them as free, and will not let them be taken back."

"But that's stealing, sir. Why don't our Government make them deliver them up? What good is the Government to us if it don't preserve the rights of property, sir? Niggers are property, ain't they? and if a man steals my property, ain't the Government bound to get it for me? Niggers are property, sir, the same as horses and cattle, and nobody's any more right to help a nigger that's run away than he has to steal a horse."

He spoke very angrily, and was excited. Perhaps he was indirectly addressing me, as a Northern man, on the general subject of fugitive slaves. I said that it was necessary to have special treaty stipulations about such matters. The Mexicans lost their *peons*—bounden servants; they ran away to our side, but the United States Government never took any measures to restore them, nor did the Mexicans ask it. "But," he answered, in a tone of indignation, "those are not niggers, are they? They are white people, sir, just as white as the Mexicans themselves, and just as much right to be free."

My horse stood in the yard till quite dark, the negroes not coming in from the cotton-field. I twice proposed to take him to the stable, but he said, "No: the niggers would come up soon and attend to him." Just as we were called to supper, the negroes began to make their appearance, getting over a fence with their hoes, and the master called to one to put the horse in the stable, and to "take good care of him." "I want him to have all the corn he'll eat," said I. "Yes, sir; feed him well; do you hear there?"

The house was meagrely furnished within, not nearly as well as the most common New England farm-house. I saw no books and no decorations. The interior wood-work was unpainted.

At supper there were three negro girls in attendance—two children of twelve or fourteen years of age, and an older one, but in a few moments they all disappeared. The mistress called aloud several times, and at length the oldest came, bringing in hot biscuit.

"Where's Suke and Bet?"

"In the kitchen, missus."

"Tell them both to come to me, right off."

A few minutes afterwards, one of the girls slunk in and stood behind me, as far as possible from her mistress. Presently, however, she was discovered.

"You Bet, you there? Come here! come here to me! close to me! *(Slap, slap, slap.)* Now, why don't you stay in here? *(Slap, slap, slap,* on the side of the head.) I know! you want to be out in the kitchen with them Indians! *(Slap, slap, slap.)* Now see if you can stay here." *(Slap!)* The other girl didn't come at all, and was forgotten.

As soon as supper was over my hostess exclaimed, "Now, you Bet, stop crying there, and do you go right straight home; mind you run every step of the way, and if you stop one minute in the kitchen you'd better look out. Begone!" During the time I was in the house she was incessantly scolding the servants, in a manner very disagreeable for me to hear, though they seemed to regard it very little.

The Indians, I learned, lived some miles away, and were hired to hoe cotton. I inquired their wages. "Well, it costs me about four bits (fifty cents) a day," (including food, probably). They worked well for a few days at a time; were better at picking than at hoeing. "They don't pick so much in a day as niggers, but do it better." The women said they were good for nothing, and her husband had no business to plant so much cotton that he couldn't 'tend it with his own slave hands.

While at table a young man, very dirty and sweaty, with a ragged shirt and no coat on, came in to supper. He was surly and rude in his actions, and did not speak a word; he left the table before I had finished, and lighting a pipe, laid himself at full length on the floor of the room to smoke. This was the overseer.

Immediately after supper the master told me that he was in the habit of going to bed early, and he would show me where I was to sleep. He did so, and left me without a candle. It was dark, and I did not know the way to the stables, so I soon went to bed. On a feather bed I did not enjoy much rest, and when I at last awoke and dressed, breakfast was just ready. I said I would go first to look after my horse, and did so, the planter following me. I found him standing in a miserable stall, in a sorry state; he had not been cleaned, and there were no cobs or other indications of his having been fed at all since he had been there. I said to my host—

"He has not been fed, sir!"

"I wonder! hain't he? "Well, I'll have him fed. I s'pose the overseer forgot him."

But, instead of going to the crib and feeding him at once himself, he returned to the house and blew a horn for a negro; when after a long time one came in sight from the cotton-fields, he called to him to go to the overseer for the key of the corn-crib and feed the gentleman's horse, and asked me now to come to breakfast. The overseer joined us as a supper; nothing was said to him about my horse, and he was perfectly silent, and conducted himself like an angry or sulky man in all his actions. As before, when he had finished his meal, without waiting for others to leave the table, he lighted a pipe and lay down to rest on the floor. I went to the stable and found my horse had been supplied with seven poor ears of corn only. I came back to ask for more, but could find neither master nor overseer. While I was packing my saddle-bags preparatory to leaving, I heard my host call a negro to "clean that gentleman's horse and bring him here." As it was late, I did not interpose. While I was putting on the bridle, he took off the musquito tent attached to the saddle and examined it. I explained why I carried it.

"You won't want it any more," said he; "no musquitoes of any account where you are going now; you'd better give it to me, sir; I should like to use it when I go a-fishing; musquitoes are powerful bad in the swamp." After some further solicitation, as I seldom used it, I gave it to him. Almost immediately afterwards he charged me a dollar for my entertainment, which I paid, notwithstanding the value of the tent was several times that amount. Hospitality to travellers is so entirely a matter of business with the common planters.

I passed the hoe-gang at work in the cotton-field, the overseer lounging among them carrying a whip; there were ten or twelve of them; not one looked up at me. Within ten minutes I passed five who were ploughing, with no overseer or driver in sight, and each stopped his plough to gaze at me.

June 3rd.—Yesterday I met a well-dressed man upon the road, and inquired of him if he could recommend me to a comfortable place to pass the night.

"Yes, I can," said he; "you stop at John Watson's. He is a real good fellow, and his wife is a nice, tidy woman; he's got a good house, and you'll be as well taken care of there as in any place I know."

"What I am most concerned about is a clean bed," said I.

"Well, you are safe for that, there."

So distinct a recommendation was unusual, and when I reached the house he had described to me, though it was not yet dark, I stopped to solicit entertainment.

In the gallery sat a fine, stalwart man, and a woman, who in size and figure matched him well. Some ruddy, fat children were playing on the steps. The man wore a full beard, which is very uncommon in these parts. I rode to a horse-block near the gallery, and asked if I could be accommodated for the night. "Oh, yes, you can stay here if you can get along without anything to eat; we don't have anything to eat but once a week." "You look as if it agreed with you, I reckon I'll try it for one night." "Alight, sir, alight. Why, you came from Texas, didn't you? Your rig looks like it," he said, as I dismounted. "Yes, I've just crossed Texas, all the way from the Rio Grande." "Have you though? Well, I'll be right glad to hear something of that country." He threw my saddle and bags across the rail of the gallery, and we walked together to the stable.

"I hear that there are a great many Germans in the western part of Texas," he said presently.

"There are a great many; west of the Guadaloupe, more Germans than Americans born."

"Have they got many slaves?"

"No."

"Well, won't they break off and make a free State down there, by and by?"

"I should think it not impossible that they might."

"I wish to God they would; I would like right well to go and settle there if it was free from slavery. You see Kansas and all the Free States are too far north for me; I was raised in Alabama, and I don't want to move into a colder climate; but I would like to go into a country where they had not got this curse of slavery."

He said this not knowing that I was a Northern man. Greatly surprised, I asked, "What are your objections to slavery, sir?"

"Objections! The first's here" (striking his breast); "I never could bring myself to like it. Well, sir, I know slavery is wrong, and God 'll put an end to it. It 's bound to come to an end, and when the end does come, there'll be woe in the land. And, instead of preparing for it, and trying to make it as light as possible, we are doing nothing but make it worse and worse. That's the way it appears to me, and I'd rather get out of these parts before it comes. Then I've another objection to it. I don't like to have slaves about me. Now, I tell a nigger to go and feed your horse; I never know if he's done it unless I go and see; and if he didn't know I would go and see, and would whip him if I found he hadn't fed him, would he feed him? He'd let him starve. I've got as good niggers as anybody, but I never can depend on them; they will lie, and they will steal, and take advantage of me in every way they dare. Of course they will, if they are slaves. But lying and stealing are not the worst of it. I've got a family of children, and I don't like to have such degraded beings round my house while they are growing up. I know what the consequences are to children, of growing up among slaves."

I here told him that I was a Northern man, and asked if he could safely utter such sentiments among the people of this district, who bore the reputation of being among the most extreme and fanatical devotees of slavery. "I've been told a hundred times I should be killed if I were not more prudent in expressing my opinions, but, when it comes to killing, I'm as good as the next man, and they know it. I never came the worst out of a fight yet since I was a boy. I never am afraid to speak what I think to anybody. I don't think I ever shall be."

"Are there many persons here who have as bad an opinion of slavery as you have?"

"I reckon you never saw a conscientious man who had been brought up among slaves who did not think of it pretty much as I do—did you?"

"Yes, I think I have, a good many."

"Ah, self-interest warps men's minds wonderfully, but I don't believe there are many who don't think so, sometimes—it's impossible, I know, that they don't."

Were there any others in this neighbourhood, I asked, who avowedly hated slavery? He replied that there were a good many mechanics, all the mechanics he knew, who felt slavery to be a great curse to them, and who wanted to see it brought to an end in some way. The competition in which they were constantly made to feel themselves engaged with slave-labour was degrading to them, and they felt it to be so. He knew a poor, hard-working man who was lately offered the services of three negroes for six years each if he would let them learn his trade, but he refused the proposal with indignation, saying he would starve before he helped a slave to become a mechanic.* There was a good deal of talk now among them

* At Wilmington, North Carolina, on the night of the 27th of July (1857), the frame-work of a new building was destroyed by a number of persons, and a placard attached to the disjointed lumber, stating that a similar course would be pursued in all cases, against edifices that should be erected by negro contractors or carpenters, by one of which class of men the house had been constructed. There was a public meeting called a few days afterwards, to take this outrage into con-

about getting laws passed to prevent the owners of slaves from having them taught trades, and to prohibit slave-mechanics from being hired out. He could go out to-morrow, he supposed, and in the course of a day get two hundred signatures to a paper alleging that slavery was a curse to the people of Mississippi, and praying the Legislature to take measures to relieve them of it as soon as practicable. (The county contains three times as many slaves as whites.)

He considered a coercive government of the negroes by the whites, forcing them to labour systematically, and restraining them from a reckless destruction of life and property, at present to be necessary. Of course, he did not think it wrong to hold slaves, and the profits of their labour were not more than enough to pay a man for looking after them—not if he did his duty to them. What was wrong, was making slavery so much worse than was necessary. Negroes would improve very rapidly, if they were allowed, in any considerable measure, the ordinary incitements to improvement. He knew hosts of negroes who showed extraordinary talents, considering their opportunities: there were a great many in this part of the country who could read and write, and calculate mentally as well as the general run of white men who had been to schools. There were Colonel ——'s negroes, some fifty of them; he did not suppose there were any

sideration, which was numerously attended. Resolutions were adopted, denouncing the act, and the authorities were instructed to offer a suitable reward for the detection and conviction of the rioters. "The impression was conveyed at the meeting," says the *Wilmington Herald*, "that the act had been committed by members of an organized association, said to exist here, and to number some two hundred and fifty persons, and possibly more, who, as was alleged, to right what they considered a grievance in the matter of negro competition with white labour, had adopted the illegal course of which the act in question was an illustration." Proceedings of a similar significance had occurred at various points, especially in Virginia.

fifty more contented people in the world; they were not driven hard, and work was stopped three times a day for meals; they had plenty to eat, and good clothes; and through the whole year they had from Friday night to Monday morning to do what they liked with themselves. Saturdays, the men generally worked in their patches (private gardens), and the women washed and mended clothes. Sundays, they nearly all went to a Sabbath School which the mistress taught, and to meeting, but they were not obliged to go; they could come and go as they pleased all Saturday and Sunday; they were not looked after at all. Only on Monday morning, if there should any one be missing, or any one should come to the field with ragged or dirty clothes, he would be whipped. He had often noticed how much more intelligent and sprightly these negroes all were than the common run; a great many of them had books and could read and write; and on Sundays they were smartly dressed, some of them better than he or his wife ever thought of dressing. These things were purchased with the money they made out of their patches, working Saturdays.

There were two other large plantations near him, in both of which the negroes were turned out to work at half-past three every week-day morning—I might hear the bell ring for them—and frequently they were not stopped till nine o'clock at night, Saturday nights the same as any other. One of them belonged to a very religious lady, and on Sunday mornings at half-past nine she had her bell rung for Sunday School, and after Sunday School they had a meeting, and after dinner another religious service. Every negro on the plantation was obliged to attend all these exercises, and if they were not dressed clean they were whipped. They were never allowed to go off the plantation, and if they were caught speaking to a negro from any other place, they were whipped.

They could all of them repeat the catechism, he believed, but they were the dullest, and laziest, and most sorrowful looking negroes he ever saw.

As a general rule, the condition of the slaves, as regards their material comfort, had greatly improved within twenty years. He did not know that it had in other respects. It would not be a bit safer to turn them free to shift for themselves, than it would have been twenty years ago. Of this he was quite confident. Perhaps they were a little more intelligent, knew more, but they were not as capable of self-guidance, not as much accustomed to work and contrive for themselves, as they used to be, when they were not fed and clothed nearly as well as now.

Beyond the excessive labour required of them on some plantations, he did not think slaves were often treated with unnecessary cruelty. It was necessary to use the lash occasionally. Slaves never really felt under any moral obligation to obey their masters. Faithful service was preached to them as a Christian duty, and they pretended to acknowledge it, but the fact was that they were obedient just so far as they saw that they must be to avoid punishment; and punishment was necessary, now and then, to maintain their faith in their master's power. He had seventeen slaves, and he did not suppose that there had been a hundred strokes of the whip on his place for a year past.

He asked if there were many Americans in Texas who were opposed to slavery, and if they were free to express themselves. I said that the wealthy Americans there were all slaveholders themselves; that their influence all went to encourage the use of slave-labour, and render labour by whites disreputable. "But are there not a good many northern men there?" he asked. The northern men, I replied, were chiefly merchants or speculators, who had but one idea, which was to make money as fast as they could; and nearly all the little money there was in that country was in the hands of the largest slaveholders.

If that was the way of things there, he said, there could not be much chance of its becoming a Free State. I thought the chances were against it, but if the Germans continued to flock into the country, it would rapidly acquire all the characteristic features of a free-labour community, including an abundance and variety of skilled labour, a home market for a variety of crops, denser settlements, and more numerous social, educational, and commercial conveniences. There would soon be a large body of small proprietors, not so wealthy that the stimulus to personal and active industry would have been lost, but yet able to indulge in a good many luxuries, to found churches, schools, and railroads, and to attract thither tradesmen, mechanics, professional men, and artists. Moreover, the labourers who were not landholders would be intimately blended with them in all their interests; the two classes not living dissociated from each other, as was the case generally at the South, but engaged in a constant fulfilment of reciprocal obligations. I told him that if such a character of society could once be firmly and extensively established before the country was partitioned out into these little independent negro kingdoms, which had existed from the beginning in every other part of the South, I did not think any laws would be necessary to prevent slavery. It might be a slave State, but it would be a free people.

On coming from my room in the morning, my host met me with a hearty grasp of the hand. "I have slept very little with thinking of what you told me about western Texas. I think I shall have to go there. If we could get rid of slavery in this region, I believe we would soon be the most prosperous people in the world. What a disadvantage it must be to have your ground all frozen up, and to be obliged to fodder your cattle five months in the year, as you do at the North. I don't see how you live. I think I should like to buy a small farm near some town where I could send my children to school—a farm that I could take care of with one or two hired men. One thing I wanted to ask you, are the Germans learning English at all?" "Oh, yes; they teach the children English in their schools." "And have they good schools?" "Wherever they have settled at all closely they have. At New Braunfels they employ American as well as German teachers, and instruction can be had in the classics, natural history, and the higher mathematics." "Upon my word, I think I must go there," he replied. (Since then, as I hear, an educational institution of a high character, has been established by German influence in San Antonio, teachers in which are from Harvard.)

When I left he mounted a horse and rode on with me some miles, saying he did not often find an intelligent man who liked to converse with him on the question of slavery. It seemed to him there was an epidemic insanity on the subject. It is unnecessary to state his views at length. They were precisely those which used to be common among all respectable men at the South.

As we rode an old negro met and greeted us warmly. My companion hereupon observed that he had never uttered his sentiments in the presence of a slave, but in some way all the slaves in the country had, he thought, been informed what they were, for they all looked to him as their special friend. When they got into trouble, they would often come to him for advice or assistance. This morning before I was up, a negro came to him from some miles distant, who had been working for a white man on Sundays till he owed him three dollars, which, now that the negro wanted it, he said he could not pay. He had given the negro the three dollars, for he thought he could manage to get it from the white man.

He confirmed an impression I had begun to get of the purely dramatic character of what passed for religion with most of the slaves. One of his slaves was a preacher, and a favourite among them. He sometimes went to plantations twenty miles away—even further—on a Sunday, to preach a funeral sermon, making journeys of fifty miles a day on foot. After the sermon, a hat would be passed round, and he sometimes brought home as much as ten dollars. He was a notable pedestrian; and once when he had committed some abominable crime for which he knew he would have to be punished, and had run away, he (Mr. Watson) rode after him almost immediately, often got in sight of him, but did not overtake him until the second day, when starting early in the morning he overhauled him crossing a broad, smooth field. When the runaway parson saw that he could not escape, he jumped up into a tree and called out to him, with a cheerful voice, "I gin ye a good run dis time, didn't I, massa?" He was the most rascally negro, the worst liar, thief, and adulterer on his place. Indeed, when he was preaching, he always made a strong point of his own sinfulness, and would weep and bellow about it like a bull of Bashan, till he got a whole camp meeting into convulsions.

The night after leaving Mr. Watson's I was kindly received by a tradesman, who took me, after closing his shop, to his mother's house, a log cabin, but more comfortable than many more pretentious residences at which I passed a night on this journey. For the first time in many months tea was offered me. It was coarse Bohea, sweetened with honey, which was stirred into the tea as it boiled in a kettle over the fire, by the old lady herself, whose especial luxury it seemed to be. She asked me if folks ever drank tea at the North, and when I spoke of green tea said she had never heard of that kind of tea before. They owned a number of slaves, but the young man looked after my horse himself. There was a good assortment of books and newspapers at this house, and the people were quite intelligent and very amiable.

The next day, I passed a number of small Indian farms, very badly cultivated—the corn nearly concealed by weeds. The soil became poorer than before, and the cabins of poor people more frequent. I counted about ten plantations, or negro-cultivated farms, in twenty miles. A planter, at whose house I called after sunset, said it was not convenient for him to accommodate me, and I was obliged to ride until it was quite dark. The next house at which I arrived was one of the commonest sort of cabins. I had passed twenty like it during the day, and I thought I would take the opportunity to get an interior knowledge of them. The fact that a horse and waggon were kept, and that a considerable area of land in the rear of the cabin was planted with cotton, showed that the family were by no means of the lowest class, yet, as they were not able even to hire a slave, they may be considered to represent very favourably, I believe, the condition of the poor whites of the plantation districts. The whites of the county, I observe, by the census, are three to one of the slaves; in the nearest adjoining county, the proportion is reversed; and within a few miles the soil was richer, and large plantations occurred.

It was raining, and nearly nine o'clock. The door of the cabin was open, and I rode up and conversed with the occupant as he stood within. He said that he was not in the habit of taking in travellers, and his wife was about sick, but if I was a mind to put up with common fare, he didn't care.

Grateful, I dismounted and took the seat he had vacated by the fire, while he led away my horse to an open shed in the rear—his own horse ranging at large, when not in use, during the summer.

The house was all comprised in a single room, twenty-eight by twenty-five feet in area, and open to the roof above. There was a large fireplace at one end and a door on each side—no windows at all. Two bedsteads, a spinning-wheel, a packing-case, which served as a bureau, a cupboard, made of rough hewn slabs, two or three deer-skin seated chairs, a Connecticut clock, and a large poster of Jayne's patent medicines, constituted all the visible furniture, either useful or ornamental in purpose. A little girl, immediately, without having had any directions to do so, got a frying-pan and a chunk of bacon from the cupboard, and cutting slices from the latter, set it frying for my supper. The woman of the house sat sulkily in a chair tilted back and leaning against the logs, spitting occasionally at the fire, but took no notice of me, barely nodding when I saluted her. A baby lay crying on the floor. I quieted it and amused it with my watch till the little girl, having made "coffee" and put a piece of corn-bread on the table with the bacon, took charge of it.

I hoped the woman was not very ill.

"Got the headache right bad," she answered. "Have the headache a heap, I do. Knew I should have it to-night. Been cuttin' brush in the cotton this arternoon. Knew't would bring on my headache. Told him so when I begun."

As soon as I had finished my supper and fed Jude, the little girl put the fragments and the dishes in the cupboard, shoved the table into a corner, and dragged a quantity of quilts from one of the bedsteads, which she spread upon the floor, and presently crawled among them out of sight for the night. The woman picked up the child—which, though still a suckling, she said was twenty-two months old—and nursed it, retaking her old position. The man sat with me by the fire, his back towards her. The baby having fallen asleep was laid away somewhere, and the woman dragged off another lot of quilts from the beds, spreading them upon the floor. Then taking a deep tin pan, she filled it with alternate layers of corn-cobs and hot embers from the fire. This she placed upon a large block, which was evidently used habitually for the purpose, in the centre of the cabin. A furious smoke arose from it, and we soon began to cough. "Most *too* much smoke," observed the man. "Hope 'twill drive out all the gnats, then," replied the woman. (There is a very minute flying insect here, the bite of which is excessively sharp.)

The woman suddenly dropped off her outer garment and stepped from the midst of its folds, in her petticoat; then, taking the baby from the place where she had deposited it, lay down and covered herself with the quilts upon the floor. The man told me that I could take the bed which remained on one of the bedsteads, and kicking off his shoes only, rolled himself into a blanket by the side of his wife. I ventured to take off my cravat and stockings, as well as my boots, but almost immediately put my stockings on again, drawing their tops over my pantaloons. The advantage of this arrangement was that, although my face, eyes, ears, neck, and hands, were immediately attacked, the vermin did not reach my legs for two or three hours. Just after the clock struck two, I distinctly heard the man and the woman, and the girl and the dog scratching, and the horse out in the shed stamping and gnawing himself. Soon afterward the man exclaimed, "Good God Almighty—mighty! mighty! mighty!" and jumping up pulled off one of his stockings, shook it, scratched his foot vehemently, put on the stocking, and lay down again with a groan. The two doors were open, and through the logs and the openings in the roof, I saw the clouds divide and the moon and stars reveal themselves. The woman, after having been nearly smothered by the smoke from the pan which she had originally placed close to her own pillow, rose and placed it on the sill of the windward door, where it burned feebly and smoked lustily, like an altar to the Lares, all night. Fortunately the cabin was so open that it gave us little annoyance, while it seemed to answer the purpose of keeping all flying insects at a distance.

When, on rising in the morning, I said that I would like to wash my face, water was given me for the purpose in an earthen pie-dish. Just as breakfast, which was of exactly the same materials as my supper, was ready, rain began to fall, presently in such a smart shower as to put the fire out and compel us to move the table under the least leaky part of the roof.

At breakfast occurred the following conversation :—

"Are there many niggers in New York?"

"Very few."

"How do you get your work done?"

"There are many Irish and German people constantly coming there who are glad to get work to do."

"Oh, and you have them for slaves?"

"They want money and are willing to work for it. A great many American-born work for wages, too."

"What do you have to pay?"

"Ten or twelve dollars a month."

"There was a heap of Irishmen to work on the railroad; they was paid a dollar a day; there was a good many Americans, too, but mostly they had little carts and mules, and hauled dirt and sich like. They was paid twenty-five or thirty dollars a month and found."

"What did they find them?"

"Oh, blanket and shoes, I expect; they put up kind o' tents like for 'em to sleep in altogether."

"What food did they find them?"

"Oh, common food; bacon and meal."

"What do they generally give the niggers on the plantations here?"

"A peck of meal and three pound of bacon is what they call 'lowance, in general, I believe. It takes a heap o' meat on a big plantation. I was on one of William R. King's plantations over in Alabamy, where there was about fifty niggers, one Sunday last summer, and I see 'em weighin' outen the meat. Tell you, it took a powerful heap on it. They had an old nigger to weigh it out, and he warn't no ways partickler about the weight. He just took and chopped it off, middlins, in chunks, and he'd throw them into the scales, and if a piece weighed a pound or two over he wouldn't mind it; he never took none back. Ain't niggers all-fired sassy at the North?"

"No, not particularly."

"Ain't they all free, there? I hearn so."

"Yes."

"Well, how do they get along when they 's free?"

"I never have seen a great many, to know their circumstances very well. Right about where I live they seem to me to live quite comfortably; more so than the niggers on these big plantations do, I should think."

"Oh, they have a mighty hard time on the big plantations. I 'd ruther be dead than to be a nigger on one of these big plantations."

"Why, I thought they were pretty well taken care of on them."

The man and his wife both looked at me as if surprised, and smiled.

"Why, they are well fed, are they not?"

"Oh, but they work 'em so hard. My God, sir, in pickin' time on these plantations they start 'em to work 'fore light, and they don't give 'em time to eat."

"I supposed they generally gave them an hour or two at noon."

"No, sir; they just carry a piece of bread and meat in their pockets and they eat it when they can, standin' up. They have a hard life on 't, that 's a fact. I reckon you can get along about as well withouten slaves as with 'em, can't you, in New York?"

"In New York there is not nearly so large a proportion of very rich men as here. There are very few people who farm over three hundred acres, and the greater number—nineteen out of twenty, I suppose—work themselves with the hands they employ. Yes, I think it's better than it is here, for all concerned, a great deal. Folks that can't afford to buy niggers get along a great deal better in the Free States, I think; and I guess that those who could afford to have niggers get along better without them."

"I no doubt that's so. I wish there warn't no niggers here. They are a great cuss to this country, I expect. But 'twouldn't do to free 'em; that wouldn't do nohow!"

"Are there many people here who think slavery a curse to the country?"

"Oh, yes, a great many. I reckon the majority would be right glad if we could get rid of the niggers. But it wouldn't never do to free 'em and leave 'em here. I don't know anybody, hardly, in favour of that. Make 'em free and leave 'em here and they'd steal everything we made. Nobody couldn't live here then."

These views of slavery seem to be universal among people of this class. They were repeated to me at least a dozen times.

"Where I used to live [Alabama], I remember when I was a boy—must ha' been about twenty years ago—folks was dreadful frightened about the niggers. I remember they built pens in the woods where they could hide, and Christmas time they went and got into the pens, 'fraid the niggers was risin'."

"I remember the same time where we was in South Carolina," said his wife; "we had all our things put up in bags, so we could tote 'em, if we heerd they was comin' our way."

They did not suppose the niggers ever thought of rising now, but could give no better reason for not supposing so than that "everybody said there warn't no danger on 't now."

Hereabouts the plantations were generally small, ten to twenty negroes on each; sometimes thirty or forty. Where he used to live they were big ones—forty or fifty, sometimes a hundred on each. He had lived here ten years. I could not make out why he had not accumulated wealth, so small a family and such an inexpensive style of living as he had. He generally planted twenty to thirty acres, he said; this year he had sixteen in cotton and about ten, he thought, in corn. Decently cultivated, this planting should have produced him five hundred dollars' worth of cotton, besides supplying him with bread and bacon—his chief expense, apparently. I suggested that this was a very large planting for his little family; he would need some help in picking time. He ought to have some now, he said; grass and bushes were all overgrowing him; he had to work just like a nigger; this durnation rain would just make the weeds jump, and he didn't expect he should have any cotton at all. There warn't much use in a man's trying to get along by himself; every thing seemed to set in agin him. He'd been trying to hire somebody, but he couldn't, and his wife was a sickly kind of a woman.

His wife reckoned he might hire some help if he'd look round sharp.

My horse and dog were as well cared for as possible, and a "snack" of bacon and corn-bread was offered me for noon, which has been unusual in Mississippi. When I asked what I should pay, the man hesitated and said he reckoned what I had had, wasn't worth much of anything; he was sorry he could not have accommodated me better. I offered him a dollar, for which he thanked me warmly. It is the first instance of hesitation in charging for a lodging which I have met with from a stranger at the South.

Northern Alabama, June 15th.—I have to-day reached a more distinctly hilly country—somewhat rocky and rugged, but with inviting dells. The soil is sandy and less frequently fertile; cotton-fields are seen only at long intervals, the crops on the small proportion of cultivated land being chiefly corn and oats. I notice also that white men are more commonly at work in the fields than negroes, and this as well in the cultivation of cotton as of corn.

The larger number of the dwellings are rude log huts, of only one room, and that unwholesomely crowded. I saw in and about one of them, not more than fifteen feet square, five grown persons, and as many children. Occasionally, however, the monotony of these huts is agreeably varied by neat, white, frame houses. At one such, I dined to-day, and was comfortably entertained. The owner held a number of slaves, but made no cotton. He owned a saw mill, was the postmaster of the neighbourhood, and had been in the Legislature.

I asked him why the capital had been changed from Tuscaloosa to Montgomery. He did not know. "Because Montgomery is more central and easy of access, probably," I suggested. "No, I don't think that had anything to do with it." "Is Tuscaloosa an unhealthy place?" "No, sir; healthier than Montgomery, I reckon." "Was it then simply because the people of the southern districts were stronger, and used their power to make the capital more convenient of access to themselves?" "Well, no, I don't think that was it, exactly. The fact is, sir, the people here are not like you northern people; they don't reason out everything so. They are fond of change, and they got tired of Tuscaloosa; the Montgomery folks wanted it there and offered to pay for moving it, so they let 'em have it; 't was just for a change." "If there really was no better reason, was it not rather wasteful to give up all the public buildings at Tuscaloosa?" "Oh, the Montgomery people wanted it so bad they promised to pay for building a new State House; so it did not cost anything."

Quite on a par with the economics of southern commercial conventions.

I passed the night at the second framed house that I saw during the day, stopping early in order to avail myself of its promise of comfort. It was attractively situated on a hill-top, with a peach orchard near it. The proprietor owned a dozen slaves, and "made cotton," he said, "with other crops." He had some of his neighbours at tea and at breakfast; sociable, kindly people, satisfied with themselves and their circumstances, which I judged from their conversation had been recently improving. One coming in, remarked that he had discharged a white labourer whom he had employed for some time past; the others congratulated him on being "shet" of him; all seemed to have noticed him as a bad, lazy man; he had often been seen lounging in the field, rapping the negroes with his hoe if they didn't work to suit him. "He was about the meanest white man I ever see," said a woman; "he was a heap meaner 'n niggers. I reckon niggers would come somewhere between white folks and such as he." "The first thing I tell a man," said another, "when I hire him, is, 'if there's any whippin' to be done on this place I want to do it myself.' If I saw a man rappin' my niggers with a hoe-handle, as I see him, durned if I wouldn't rap him—the lazy whelp."

One of the negroes complimented my horse. "Dar's a heap of genus in dat yar hoss's head!" The proprietor looked after the feeding himself.

These people were extremely kind; inquiring with the simplest good feeling about my domestic relations and the purpose of my journey. When I left, one of them walked a quarter of a mile to make sure that I went upon the right road. The charge for entertainment, though it was unusually good, was a quarter of a dollar less than I have paid before, which I mention, not as Mr. De Bow would suppose,* out of gratitude for the moderation, but as an indication of the habits of the people, showing, as it may, either closer calculation, or that the district grows its own supplies, and can furnish food cheaper than those in which attention is more exclusively given to cotton.

June 17*th*.—The country continues hilly, and is well populated by farmers, living in log huts, while every mile or two, on the more level and fertile land, there is a larger farm, with ten or twenty negroes at work. A few whites are usually working near them, in the same field, generally ploughing while the negroes hoe.

About noon, my attention was attracted towards a person upon a ledge, a little above the road, who was throwing up earth and stone with a shovel. I stopped to see what the purpose of this work might be, and perceived that the shoveller

* See De Bow's Review, for August, 1857, p. 117.

was a woman, who, presently discovering me, stopped and called to others behind her, and immediately a stout girl and two younger children, with a man, came to the edge and looked at me. The woman was bareheaded, and otherwise half-naked, as perhaps needed to be, for her work would have been thought hard by our stoutest labourers, and it was the hottest weather of the summer, in the latitude of Charleston, and on a hill-side in the full face of the noon sun. I pushed my horse up the hill until I reached them, when another man appeared, and in answer to my inquiries told me that they were getting out iron ore. One was picking in a vein, having excavated a short adit; the other man picked looser ore exterior to the vein. The women and children shovelled out the ore and piled it on kilns of timber, where they roasted it to make it crumble. It was then carted to a forge, and they were paid for it by the load. They were all clothed very meanly and scantily. The women worked, so far as I could see, as hard as the men. The children, too, even to the youngest—a boy of eight or ten—were carrying large lumps of ore, and heaving them into the kiln, and shovelling the finer into a screen to separate the earth from it.

Immediately after leaving them I found a good spot for nooning. I roped my horse out to graze, and spread my blanket in a deep shade. I noticed that the noise of their work had ceased, and about fifteen minutes afterwards, Jude suddenly barking, I saw one of the men peering at me through the trees, several rods distant. I called to him to come up. He approached rather slowly and timidly, examined the rope with which my horse was fastened, eyed me vigilantly, and at length asked if I was resting myself. I replied that I was; and he said that he did not know but I might be sick, and had come to see me. I thanked him, and offered him a seat upon my blanket, which he declined.

Presently he took up a newspaper that I had been reading, looked at it for a moment, then he told me he couldn't read. "Folks don't care much for edication round here; it would be better for 'em, I expect, if they did." He began then to question me closely about my circumstances—where I came from, whither I was going, etc.

When his curiosity was partially appeased he suddenly laughed in a silly manner, and said that the people he had been working with had watched me after I left them; they saw me ride up the hill and stop, ride on again, and finally take off my saddle, turn my horse loose and tote my saddle away, and they were much frightened, thinking I must be crazy at least. When he started to come toward me they told him he wouldn't dare to go to me, but he saw how it was, well enough—I was just resting myself.

"If I should run down hill now," said he, "they'd start right off and wouldn't stop for ten mile, reckoning you was arter me. That would be fun; oh, we have some good fun here sometimes with these green folks. There's an amazin' ignorant set round here."

I asked if they were foreigners.

"Oh, no; they are common, no account people; they used to live over the hill, here; they come right nigh starvin' thar, I expect."

They had not been able to get any work to do, and had been "powerful poor," until he got them to come here. They had taken an old cabin, worked with him, and were doing right well now. He didn't let them work in the vein—he kept that for himself—but they worked all around, and some days they made a dollar and a half—the man, woman, and children together. They had one other girl, but she had to stay at home to take care of the baby and keep cattle and hogs out of their "gardien." He had known the woman when she was a girl; "she was always a good one to work. She'd got a voice like a bull, and she was as smart as a wild cat; but the man warn't no account."

He had himself followed this business (mining) since he was a young man, and could earn three dollars a day by it if he tried; he had a large family and owned a small farm: never laid up anything, always kept himself a little in debt at the store.

He asked if I had not found the people "more friendly like" up in this country to what they were down below, and assured me that I would find them grow more friendly as I went further North, so at least he had heard, and he knew where he first came from (Tennessee) the people were more friendly than they were here. "The richer a man is," he continued, pursuing a natural association of ideas, "and the more niggers he's got, the poorer he seems to live. If you want to fare well in this country you stop to poor folks' housen; they try to enjoy what they've got, while they ken, but these yer big planters they don' care for nothing but to save. Now, I never calculate to save anything; I tell my wife I work hard, and I mean to enjoy what I earn as fast as it comes."

Sometimes he "took up bee-huntin' for a spell," and made money by collecting wild honey. He described his manner of finding the hives and securing the honey, and, with a hushed voice, told me a "secret," which was, that if you carried three leaves, each of a different tree (?) in your hand, there was never a bee would dare to sting you.

I asked about his children. He had one grown-up son, who was doing very well; he was hired by the gentleman who owned the forge, to cart ore. He had nothing to do but to drive a team; he didn't have to load, and he had a nigger to take care of the horses when his day's teaming was done.

His wages were seven dollars a month, and board for himself and wife. They ate at the same table with the gentleman, and had good living, beside having something out of the store, "tobacco and so on—tobacco for both on 'em, and two people uses a good deal of tobacco you know; so that's pretty good wages—seven dollars a month besides their keep and tobacco." Irishmen, he informed me, had been employed occasionally at the forge. "They do well at first, only they is apt to get into fights all the time; but after they've been here a year or two, they get to feel so independent and keer-less-like, you can't get along with 'em." He remained about half an hour, and not till he returned did I hear again the noise of picking and shovelling, and cutting timber.

At the forges, I was told, slave labour is mainly employed—the slaves being owned by the proprietors of the forges.

I spent that night at a large inn in a village. In the morning as I sat waiting in my room, a boy opened the door. Without looking up I asked, "Well?"

"I didn't say nuthin', sar," with a great grin.

"What are you waiting there for?" "Please, massa, I b'leve you's owin' me suthin', sar." "Owing you something? What do you mean?" "For drying yer clothes for yer, sar, last night." I had ordered him immediately after tea to go up stairs and get my clothes, which had been drenched in a shower, and hang them by the kitchen fire, that they might be dry if I should wish to leave early in the morning. When I went to my bedroom at nine o'clock I found the clothes where I had left them. I went down and reported it to the landlord, who directly sent the boy for them. In the morning, when I got them again I found they were not dry except where they were burned. I told him to be gone; but with the door half open, he stood putting in his head, bowing and grinning. "Please, sar, massa sent me out of an errand, and I was afeard you would be gone before I got back; dat's the reason why I mention it, sar; dat's all, sar; I hope you'll skuse me, sar."

During the afternoon I rode on through a valley, narrow and apparently fertile, but the crops indifferent. The general social characteristics were the same that I met with yesterday.

At night I stopped at a large house having an unusual number of negro cabins and stables about it. The proprietor, a hearty old farmer, boasted much of his pack of hounds, saying they had pulled down five deer before he had had a shot at them. He was much interested to hear about Texas, the Indians and the game. He reckoned there was "a heap of big varmint out thar."

His crop of cotton did not average two bales to the hand, and corn not twenty bushels to the acre.

He amused me much with a humorous account of an oyster supper to which he had been invited in town, and his attempts to eat the "nasty things" without appearing disconcerted before the ladies.

An old negro took my horse when I arrived, and half an hour afterward, came to me and asked if I wanted to see him fed. As we walked toward the stables, he told me that he always took care not to forget gentlemen's hosses, and to treat them well; "then," he said, bowing and with emphasis, "they looks out and don't forget to treat me well."

The same negro was called to serve me as a candlestick at bedtime. He held the candle till I got into bed. As he retired I closed my eyes, but directly afterward, perceiving the light return, I opened them. Uncle Abram was bending over me, holding the candle, grinning with his toothless gums, winking and shaking his head in a most mysterious manner.

"Hush! massa," he whispered. "You hain't got something to drink, in dem saddle-bags, has you, sar?"

The farmer told me something about "nigger dogs;" they didn't use foxhounds, but bloodhounds—not pure, he thought, but a cross of the Spanish bloodhound with the common hounds, or curs. There were many men, he said, in the country below here, who made a business of nigger-hunting, and they had their horses trained, as well as the dogs, to go over any common fence, or if they couldn't leap it, to break it down. Dogs were trained, when pups, to follow a nigger—not allowed to catch one, however, unless they were quite young, so that they couldn't hurt him much, and they were always taught to hate a negro, never being permitted to see one except to be put in chase of him. He believed that only two of a pack were kept kenneled all the time—these were old, keen ones, who led the rest when they were out; they were always kept coupled together with a chain, except when trailing. He had seen a pack of thirteen who would follow a trail two days and a half old, if rain had not fallen in the mean time. When it rained immediately after a negro got off, they had to scour the country where they supposed he might be, till they scented him.

When hard pushed, a negro always took to a tree; sometimes, however, they would catch him in an open field. When this was the case the hunter called off the dogs as soon as he could, unless the negro fought—"that generally makes 'em mad (the hunters), and they'll let 'em tear him a spell. The owners don't mind having them kind o' niggers tore a good deal; runaways ain't much account nohow, and it makes the rest more afraid to run away, when they see how they are sarved." If they caught the runaway within two or three days, they got from $10 to $20; if it took a longer time, they were paid more than that; sometimes $200. They asked their own price; if an owner should think it exorbitant, he supposed, he said in reply to an inquiry, they'd turn the nigger loose, order him to make off, and tell his master to catch his own niggers.

Sunday.—I rode on, during the cool of the morning, about eight miles, and stopped for the day, at a house pleasantly situated by a small stream, among wooded hills. During the forenoon, seven men and three women, with their children, gathered at the house. All of them, I concluded, were non-slaveholders, as was our host himself; though, as one told me, "with his five boys he makes a heap more crop than Mrs. ——, who's got forty niggers." "How is that?" "Well, she's a woman, and she can't make the niggers work; she won't have a overseer, and niggers won't work, you know, unless there's somebody to drive 'em."

Our host, when I arrived, had just been pulling weeds out of his potato patch, which he mentioned as an apology for not being a little clean, like the rest.

Beside the company I have mentioned, and the large family of the house, there was another traveller and myself to dinner, and three bountiful tables were spread, one after another.

The traveller was said to be a Methodist preacher, but gave no indication of it, except that he said grace before meat, and used the Hebrew word for Sunday. He was, however, a man of superior intelligence to the others, who were ignorant and stupid, though friendly and communicative. He asked me "what a good nigger man could be bought for in New York;" he didn't seem surprised, or make any further inquiry, when I told him we had no slaves there. Some asked me much about crops, and when I told them that my crops of wheat for six years had averaged twenty-eight bushels, and that I had once reaped forty from a single acre, they were amazed beyond expression, and anxious to know how I "put it in." I described the process minutely, which astonished them still more; and one man said he had often thought they might get more wheat if they put it in differently; he had thought that perhaps more wheat would grow if more seed were sown, but he never tried it. The general practice, they told me, was to sow wheat on ground from which they had taken maize, without removing the maize stumps, or ploughing it at all; they sowed three pecks of wheat to the acre, and then ploughed it in—that was all. They used the cradle, but had never heard of reaping machines; the crop was from five to ten bushels an acre; ten bushels was extraordinary, six was not thought bad. Of cotton, the ordinary crop was five hundred pounds to the acre, or from one to two bales to a hand. Of maize, usually from ten to twenty bushels to the acre; last year not over ten; this year they thought it would be twenty-five on the best land.

The general admiration of Jude brought up the topic of negro dogs again, and the clergyman told a story of a man who hunted niggers near where he lived. He was out once with another man, when after a long search, they found the dogs barking up a big cottonwood tree. They examined the tree closely without finding any negro, and concluded that the dogs must have been foiled, and they were about to go away, when Mr.——, from some distance off, thought he saw a negro's leg very high up in the tree, where the leaves and moss were thick enough to hide a man lying on the top of a limb with his feet against the trunk. He called out, as if he really saw a man, telling him to come down, but nothing stirred. He sent for an axe, and called out again, saying he would cut the tree to the ground if he didn't come down. There was no reply. He then cut half through the tree on one side, and was beginning on the other, when the negro halloed out that if he would stop he would come down. He stopped cutting, and the negro descended to the lowest limb, which was still far from the ground, and asked the hunter to take away his dogs, and promise they shouldn't tear him. But the hunter swore he'd make no conditions with him after having been made to cut the tree almost down.

The negro said no more, but retained his position until the tree was nearly cut in two. When it began to totter, he slid down the trunk, the dogs springing upon him as soon as he was within their reach. He fought them hard, and got hold of one by the ear; that made them fiercer, and they tore him till the hunter was afraid they'd kill him, and stopped them.

"Are dogs allowed to tear the negroes when they catch them?

"When the hunters come up they always call them off, unless the nigger fights. If the nigger fights 'em that makes 'em mad, and they let 'em tear him good," said the clergyman.

There were two or three young women present, and the young men were sparking with them in the house, sitting on the beds for want of sofas, the chairs being all in use outside; the rest of the company sat on the gallery most of the time, but there was little conversation. It was twice remarked to me, "Sunday's a dull day—nothing to do."

As the Methodist and I were reading after dinner, I noticed that two or three were persuading the others to go with them somewhere, and I asked where they purposed to go. They said they wanted to go over the mountain to hunt a bull.

"To shoot him?"

"Oh, no, it's a working bull; they got his mate yesterday. There ain't but one pair of cattle in this neighbourhood, and they do all the hauling for nine families." They belonged, together with their waggon, to one man, and the rest borrowed of him. They wanted them this week to cart in their oats. The stray bull was driven in toward night, yoked with another to a waggon, and one of the women, with her family, got into the waggon and was carried home. The bulls were fractious and had to be led by one man, while another urged them forward with a cudgel.

Last night by the way a neighbour came into the house of Uncle Abram's master, and in the course of conversation about crops, said that on Sunday he went over to John Brown's to get him to come out and help him at his harvesting. He found four others there for the same purpose, but John said he didn't feel well, and he reckoned he couldn't work. He offered him a dollar and a half a day to cradle for him; but when he tried to persuade him, John spoke out plainly and said, "he'd be d—d if he was going to work anyhow;" so he said to the others, "Come, boys, we may as well go; you can't make a lazy man work when he's determined he won't." He supposed that remark made him mad, for on Thursday John came running across his cotton patch, where he was ploughing. He didn't speak a word to him, but cut along over to his neighbour's house, and told him that he had shot two deer, and wanted his hounds to catch 'em, promising to give him half the venison if he succeeded. He did catch one of them, and kept his promise.

This man Brown, they told me, had a large family, and lived in a little cabin on the mountain. He pretended to plant a corn patch, but he never worked it, and didn't make any corn. They reckoned he lived pretty much on what corn and hogs he could steal, and on game. The children were described as pitiably, "scrawny," half-starved little wretches. Last summer his wife had come to one of them, saying they had no corn, and she wanted to pick cotton to earn some. He had let her go in with the niggers and pick. She kept at it for two days, and took her pay in corn. Afterward he saw her little boy "toting" it to the mill to be ground—much too heavy a load for him.

I asked if there were many such vagabonds.

"Yes, a great many on the mountain, and they make a heap of trouble. There is a law by which they might be taken up [if it could be proved that they have no 'visible means of support'] and made to work to support their families; but the law is never used."

Speaking of another man, one said: "He'll be here to breakfast, at your house to dinner, and at Dr. ——'s to supper, leaving his family to live as best they can." They "reckoned" he got most of his living in that way, while his family had to get theirs by stealing. He never did any work except hunting, and they "reckoned" he killed about as many shoats and yearlings as deer and turkeys.

They said that this sort of people were not often intemperate; they had no money to buy liquor with; now and then, when they'd sold some game or done a little work to raise money, they'd have a spree; but they were more apt to gamble it off or spend it for fine clothes and things to trick out their wives.

June —. To-day, I am passing through a valley of thin, sandy soil, thickly populated by poor farmers. Negroes are rare, but occasionally neat, new houses, with other improvements, show the increasing prosperity of the district. The majority of dwellings are small log cabins of one room, with another separate cabin for a kitchen; each house has a well, and a garden inclosed with palings. Cows, goats, mules and swine, fowls and doves are abundant. The people are more social than those of the lower country, falling readily into friendly conversation with a traveller. They are very ignorant; the agriculture is wretched and the work hard. I have seen three white women hoeing field crops to-day. A spinning-wheel is heard in every house, and frequently a loom is clanging in the gallery, always worked by women; every one wears homespun. The negroes have much more individual freedom than in the rich cotton country, and are not unfrequently heard singing or whistling at their work.

Tennessee, June 29th.—At nightfall I entered a broader and more populous valley than I had seen before during the day, but for some time there were only small single room log cabins, at which I was loath to apply for lodging. At length I reached a large and substantial log house with negro cabins. The master sat in the stoop. I asked if he could accommodate me.

"What do you want?"

"Something to eat for myself and horse, and room to sleep under your roof."

"The wust on't is," he said, getting up and coming toward me, "we haven't got much for your horse."

"You've got corn, I suppose."

"No, hain't got no corn but a little that we want for ourselves, only just enough to bread us till corn comes again."

"Well, you have oats?"

"Hain't got an oat."

"Haven't you hay?"

"No."

"Then I must go further, for my horse can't travel on fodder."

"Hain't got nary fodder nuther."

Fortunately I did not have to go much further before I came to the best house I had seen during the day, a large, neat, white house, with negro shanties, and an open log cabin in the front yard. A stout, elderly, fine-looking woman, in a cool white muslin dress sat upon the gallery, fanning herself. Two little negroes had just brought a pail of fresh water, and she was drinking of it with a gourd, as I came to the gate. I asked if it would be convenient for her to accommodate me for the night, doubtingly, for I had learned to distrust the accommodations of the wealthy slaveholders.

"Oh yes, get down; fasten your horse there, and the niggers will take care of him when they come from their work. Come up here and take a seat."

I brought in my saddle-bags.

"Bring them in here, into the parlour," she said, "where they'll be safe."

The interior of the house was furnished with unusual comfort. "The parlour," however, had a bed in it. As we came out, she locked the door.

We had not sat long, talking about the weather (she was suffering much from the heat), when her husband came. He was very hot also, though dressed coolly enough in merely a pair of short-legged, unbleached cotton trousers, and a shirt with the bosom spread open—no shoes nor stockings. He took his seat before speaking to me, and after telling his wife it was the hottest day he ever saw, squared his chair toward me, threw it back so as to recline against a post, and said gruffly, "Good evening, sir; you going to stay here to-night?"

I replied, and he looked at me a few moments without speaking. He was, in fact, so hot that he spoke with difficulty. At length he got breath and asked abruptly: "You a mechanic, sir, or a dentist, eh—or what?"

Supper was cooked by two young women, daughters of the master of the house, assisted by the two little negro boys. The cabin in front of the house was the kitchen, and when the bacon was dished up, one of the boys struck an iron triangle at the door. "Come to supper," said the host, and led the way to the kitchen, which was also the supper-room. One of the young ladies took the foot of the table, the other seated herself apart by the fire, and actually waited on the table, though the two negro boys stood at the head and foot, nominally waiters, but always anticipated by the Cinderella, when anything was wanted.

A big lout of a youth who came from the field with the negroes, looked in, but seeing me, retired. His father called, but his mother said, " 't wouldn't do no good—he was so bashful."

Speaking of the climate of the country, I was informed that a majority of the folks went barefoot all winter, though they had snow much of the time four or five inches deep, and the man said he didn't think most of the men about here had more than one coat, and they never wore any in winter except on holidays. "That was the healthiest way," he reckoned, "just to toughen yourself and not wear no coat; no matter how cold it was, he didn't wear no coat."

The master held a candle for me while I undressed, in a large room above stairs; and gave me my choice of the four beds in it. I found one straw bed (with, as usual, but one sheet), on which I slept comfortably. At midnight I was awakened by some one coming in. I rustled my straw, and a voice said, "Who is there in this room?"

"A stranger passing the night; who are you?"

"All right; I belong here. I've been away and have just come home."

He did not take his clothes off to sleep. He turned out to be an older son who had been fifty miles away, looking after a stray horse. When I went down stairs in the morning, having been wakened early by flies, and the dawn of day through an open window, I saw the master lying on his bed in the "parlour," still asleep in the clothes he wore at supper. His wife was washing her face on the gallery, being already dressed for the day; after using the family towel, she went into the kitchen, but soon returned, smoking a pipe, to her chair in the doorway.

Yet everything betokened an opulent and prosperous man —rich land, extensive field crops, a number of negroes, and considerable herds of cattle and horses. He also had capital invested in mines and railroads, he told me. His elder son spoke of him as "the squire."

A negro woman assisted in preparing breakfast (she had probably been employed in the field labour the night before), and both the young ladies were at the table. The squire observed to me that he supposed we could buy hands very cheap in New York. I said we could hire them there at moderate wages. He asked if we couldn't buy as many as we wanted, by sending to Ireland for them and paying their passage. He had supposed we could buy them and hold them as slaves for a term of years, by paying the freight on them. When I had corrected him, he said, a little hesitatingly, "You don't have no black slaves in New York?" "No, sir." "There's niggers there, ain't there, only they're all free?" "Yes, sir." "Well, how do they get along so?" "So far as I know, the most of them live pretty comfortably." (I have changed my standard of comfort lately, and am inclined to believe that the majority of the negroes at the North live more comfortably than the majority of whites at the South.) "I wouldn't like that," said the old lady. "I wouldn't like to live where niggers was free, they are bad enough when they are slaves: it's hard enough to get along with them here, they're so bad. I reckon that niggers are the meanest critters on earth; they are so mean and nasty" (she expressed disgust and indignation very strongly in her face). "If they was to think themselves equal to we, I don't think white folks could abide it—they're such vile saucy things." A negro woman and two boys were in the room as she said this.

North Carolina, July 13th.—I rode late last night, there

being no cabins for several miles in which I was willing to spend the night, until I came to one of larger size than usual, with a gallery on the side toward the road and a good stable opposite it. A man on the gallery was about to answer (as I judged from his countenance), "I reckon you can," to my inquiry if I could stay, when the cracked voice of a worryful woman screeched out from within, "We don't foller takin' in people."

"No, sir," said the man, "we don't foller it."

"How far shall I have to go?"

"There's another house a little better than three quarters of a mile further on."

To this house I proceeded—a cabin of one room and a loft, with a kitchen in a separate cabin. The owner said he never turned anybody away, and I was welcome. He did not say that he had no corn, until after supper, when I asked for it to feed my horse. The family were good-natured, intelligent people, but very ignorant. The man and his wife and the daughters slept below, the boy and I in the cock-loft. Supper and breakfast were eaten in the detached kitchen. Yet they were by no means poor people. The man told me that he had over a thousand acres of rich tillable land, besides a large extent of mountain range, the most of which latter he had bought from time to time as he was able, to prevent the settlement of squatters near his valley-land. "There were people who would be bad neighbours, I knew," he said, "that would settle on most any kind of place, and everybody wants to keep such as far away from them as they can." (When I took my bridle off, I hung it up by the stable-door; he took it down and said he'd hang it in a safer place. "He'd never had anything stolen from here, and he didn't mean to have—it was just as well not to put temptation before people," and he took it into the house and put it under his bed.)

Besides this large tract of land here, he owned another tract of two hundred acres with a house upon it, rented for one-third the produce, and another smaller farm, similarly rented; he also owned a grist mill, which he rented to a miller for half the tolls. He told me that he had thought a good deal formerly of moving to new countries, but he had been doing pretty well and had stayed here now so long, he didn't much think he should ever budge. He reckoned he'd got enough to make him a living for the rest of his life, and he didn't know any use a man had for more'n that.

I did not see a single book in the house, nor do I think that any of the family could read. He said that many people here were talking about Iowa and Indiana; "was Iowa (Hiaway) beyond the Texies?" I opened my map to show him where it was, but he said he "wasn't scollar'd enough" to understand it, and I could not induce him to look at it. I asked him if the people here preferred Iowa and Indiana to Missouri at all because they were Free States. "I reckon," he replied, "they don't have no allusion to that. Slavery is a great cuss, though, I think, the greatest there is in these United States. There ain't no account of slaves up here in the west, but down in the east part of this State about Fayetteville there's as many as there is in South Carolina. That's the reason the West and the East don't agree in this State; people out here hates the Eastern people."

"Why is that?"

"Why you see they vote on the slave basis, and there's some of them nigger counties where there ain't more'n four or five hundred white folks, that has just as much power in the Legislature as any of our mountain counties where there'll be some thousand voters."

He made further remarks against slavery and against slave-holders. When I told him that I entirely agreed with him, and said further, that poor white people were usually far better off in the Free than in the Slave States, he seemed a little surprised and said, "New York ain't a Free State, is it?"

Labourers' wages here, he stated, were from fifty cents to one dollar a day, or eight dollars a month. "How much by the year?" "They's never hired by the year."

"Would it be $75 a year?"

"'Twouldn't be over that, anyhow, but 'tain't general for people to hire here only for harvest time; fact is, a man couldn't earn his board, let alone his wages, for six months in the year."

"But what do these men who hire out during harvest time do during the rest of the year; do they have to earn enough in those two or three months to live on for the other eight or nine?"

"Well, they gets jobs sometimes, and they goes from one place to another."

"But in winter time, when you say there's not work enough to pay their board?"

"Well, they keeps a goin' round from one place to another, and gets their living somehow."

"The fact on't is," he said at length, as I pressed the inquiry, "there ain't anybody that ever means to work any in this country, except just along in harvest—folks don't keep working here as they do in your country, I expect."

"But they must put in their crops?"

"Yes, folks that have farms of their own, they do put in their craps and tend 'em, but these fellows that don't have farms, they won't work except in harvest, when they can get high wages [$8 a month]. I hired a fellow last spring for six months; I wanted him to help me plant and tend my corn. You see I had a short crap last year, and this spring I had to pay fifty cents a bushel for corn for bread, and I didn't want to get caught so again, not this year, so I gin this fellow $6 a month for six months— $36 I gin him in hard silver."

"Paid it to him in advance?"

"Yes, he wouldn't come 'less I'd pay him right then. Well, he worked one month, and maybe eight days—no, I don't think it was more than six days over a month, and then he went away, and I hain't seen a sight on him since. I expect I shall lose my money—reckon he don't ever intend to come back; he knows I'm right in harvest, and want him now, if ever I do."

"What did he go away for?"

"Why, he said he was sick, but if he was, he got well mighty easy after he stopped working."

"Do you know where he is now?"

"Oh, yes, he's going round here."

"What is he doing?"

"Well, he's just goin' round."

"Is he at work for any one else?"

"Reckon not—no, he's just goin' round from one place to another."

At supper and breakfast surprise was expressed that I declined coffee, and more still that I drank water instead of milk. The woman observed, "'twas cheap boarding me." The man said he must get home a couple more cows; they ought to drink milk more, coffee was so high now, and he believed milk would be just as healthy. The woman asked the price of coffee in New York; I could not tell her, but said I believed it was uncommonly high; the crops had been short. She asked how coffee grew. I told her as well as I was able, but concluded by saying I had never seen it growing. "Don't you raise coffee in New York?" she asked; "I thought that was where it came from."

The butter was excellent. I said so, and asked if they

never made any for sale. The woman said she could make "as good butter as any ever was made in the yarth, but she couldn't get anything for it; there warn't many of the merchants would buy it, and those that did, would only take it at eight cents a pound for goods." The man said the only thing he could ever sell for ready money was cattle. Drovers bought them for the New York market, and lately they were very high—four cents a pound. He had driven cattle all the way to Charleston himself, to sell them, and only got four cents a pound there. He had sold corn here for twelve and a half cents a bushel.

Although the man could not read, he had honoured letters by calling one of his children "Washington Irving;" another was known as Matterson (Madison?). He had never tried manuring land for crops, but said, "I do believe it is a good plan, and if I live I mean to try it sometime."

July 16th.—I stopped last night at the pleasantest house I have yet seen in the highlands; a framed house, painted white, with a log kitchen attached. The owner was a man of superior standing. I judged from the public documents and law books on his table, that he had either been in the Legislature of the State, or that he was a justice of the peace. There were also a good many other books and newspapers, chiefly of a religious character. He used, however, some singularly uncouth phrases common here. He had a store, and carried on farming and stock raising. After a conversation about his agriculture, I remarked that there were but few slaves in this part of the country. He wished that there were fewer. They were not profitable property here, I presumed. They were not, he said, except to raise for sale; but there were a good many people here who would not have them if they were profitable, and yet who were abundantly able to buy them. They were horrid things, he thought; he would not take one to keep it if it should be given to him. 'Twould be a great deal better for the country, he believed, if there was not a slave in it. He supposed it would not be right to take them away from those who had acquired property in them, without any remuneration, but he wished they could all be sent out of the country—sent to Liberia. That was what ought to be done with them. I said it was evident that where there were no slaves, other things being equal, there was greater prosperity than where slavery supplied the labour. He didn't care so much for that, he said; there was a greater objection to slavery than that, in his mind. He was afraid that there was many a man who had gone to the bad world, who wouldn't have gone there if he hadn't had any slaves. He had been down in the nigger counties a good deal, and he had seen how it worked on the white people. It made the rich people, who owned the niggers, passionate and proud, and ugly, and it made the poor people mean. "People that own niggers are always mad with them about something; half their time is spent in swearing and yelling at them."

"I see you have 'Uncle Tom's Cabin' here," said I; "have you read it?"

"Oh, yes."

"And what do you think of it?"

"Think of it? I think well of it."

"Do most of the people here in the mountains think as you do about slavery?"

"Well, there's some thinks one way and some another, but there's hardly any one here that don't think slavery's a curse to our country, or who wouldn't be glad to get rid of it."

I asked what the people about here thought of the Nebraska Bill. He couldn't say what the majority thought.

Would people moving from here to Nebraska now, be likely to vote for the admission of slavery there? He thought not; "most people would much rather live in a Free State." He told me that he knew personally several persons who had gone to California, and taken slaves with them, who had not been able to bring them back. There were one or two cases where the negroes had been induced to return, and these instances had been made much of in the papers, as evidence that the slaves were contented.

"That's a great lie," he said; "they are not content, and nine-tenths of 'em would do 'most anything to be free. It's only now and then that slaves, who are treated unusual kind, and made a great deal of, will choose to remain in slavery if freedom is put in their way." He knew one man (giving his name) who tried to bring two slaves back from California, and had got started with them, when some white people suspecting it, went on board the ship and told him it was against the law to hold negroes as slaves in California, and his negroes shouldn't go back with him unless they were willing to. Then they went to the slaves and told them they need not return if they preferred to stay, and the slaves said they had wanted very much to go back to North Carolina, yet they would rather remain in California, if they could be free, and so they took them ashore. He had heard the slave owner himself relating this, and cursing the men who interfered. He had told him that they did no more than Christians were obliged to do.

I overtook upon the road, to-day, three young men of the poorest class. Speaking of the price of land and the profit of farming, one of them said, believing me to be a southerner—

"We are all poor folks here; don't hardly make enough to keep us in liquor. Anybody can raise as much corn and hogs on the mountains as he'll want to live on, but there ain't no rich people here. Nobody's got any black ones—only three or four; no one's got fifty or a hundred, like as they have down in the East." "It would be better," interrupted another, somewhat fiercely, "there warn't any at all; that's my mind about it; they're no business here; they ought to be in their own country and take care of themselves, that's what I believe, and I don't care who hears it." But let the reader not be deceived by these expressions; they indicate simply the weakness and cowardice of the class represented by these men. It is not slavery they detest; it is simply the negro competition, and the monopoly of the opportunities to make money by negro owners, which they feel and but dimly comprehend.

If you meet a man without stopping, the salutation here always is, "How d'ye do, sir?" never "Good morning;" and on parting it is, "I wish you well, sir," more frequently than "Good-bye." You are always commanded to appear at the table, as elsewhere throughout the South, in a rough, peremptory tone, as if your host feared you would try to excuse yourself.

"Come in to supper." "Take a seat." "Some of the fry?" "Help yourself to anything you see that you can eat."

They ask your name, but do not often call you by it, but hail you "Stranger," or "Friend."

Texas is always spoken of in the plural—"the Texies." "Bean't the Texies powerful sickly?"

"Ill" is used for "vicious." "Is your horse ill?" "Not that I am aware of. Does he appear so?" "No; but some horses will bite a stranger if he goes to handling on 'em."

"Is your horse ill?" "No, I believe not." "I see he kind o' drapt his ears when I came up, 'zif he was playful."

Everybody I've met in the last three counties—after ascertaining what parts I came from, and which parts I'm going to, where I got my horse, what he cost, and of what breed he is, what breed the dog is, and whether she's followed me all the way from the Texies, if her feet ain't worn out, and if I don't think I'll have to tote her if I go much further, and if I don't want to give her away, how I like the Texies, etc.—has asked me whether I didn't see a man by the name of Baker in the Texies, who was sheriff of ——— county, and didn't behave exactly the gentleman, or another fellow by the name of ———, who ran away from the same county, and cut to the Texies. I've been asked if they had done fighting yet in the Texies, referring to the war with Mexico, which was ended ten years ago. Indeed the ignorance with regard to everything transpiring in the world outside, and the absurd ideas and reports I hear, are quite incredible. It cannot be supposed that having been at home in New York, there should be any one there whom I do not personally know, or that, having passed through Texas, I should be unable to speak from personal knowledge of the welfare of every one in that State.

North-eastern Tennessee, ——.—Night before last I spent at the residence of a man who had six slaves; last night, at the home of a farmer without slaves. Both houses were of the best class common in this region; two-story framed buildings, large, and with many beds, to accommodate drovers and waggoners, who, at some seasons, fill the houses which are known to be prepared with stabling, corn, and beds for them. The slaveholder was much the wealthier of the two, and his house originally was the finer, but he lived in much less comfort than the other. His house was in great need of repair, and was much disordered; it was dirty, and the bed given me to sleep in was disgusting. He and his wife made the signs of pious people, but were very morose or sadly silent, when not scolding and re-ordering their servants. Their son, a boy of twelve, was alternately crying and bullying his mother all the evening till bed-time, because his father had refused to give him something that he wanted. He slept in the same room with me, but did not come to bed until after I had once been asleep, and then he brought another boy to sleep with him. He left the candle burning on the floor, and when, in five minutes after he had got into bed, a girl came after it, he cursed her with a shocking volubility of filthy blackguardism, demanding why she had not come sooner. She replied gently and entreatingly, "I didn't think you 'd have more 'n got into bed yet, master John." The boys were talking and whispering obscenity till I fell asleep again. The white women of the house were very negligent and sluttish in their attire; the food at the table badly cooked, and badly served by negroes.

The house of the farmer without slaves, though not in good repair, was much neater, and everything within was well-ordered and unusually comfortable. The women and girls were clean and neatly dressed; every one was cheerful and kind. There was no servant. The table was abundantly supplied with the most wholesome food—I might almost say the first wholesome food—I have had set before me since I was at the hotel at Natchez; loaf bread for the first time; chickens, stewed instead of fried; potatoes without fat; two sorts of simple preserved fruit, and whortleberry and blackberry tarts. (The first time I have had any of these articles at a private house since I was in Western Texas.) All the work, both within and without the house, was carried on regularly and easily, and it was well done, because done by parties interested in the result, not by servants interested only to escape reproof or punishment.

Doubtless two extreme cases were thus brought together,

but similar, if less striking, contrasts are found the general rule, according to my experience. It is a common saying with the drovers and waggoners of this country, that if you wish to be well taken care of, you must not stop at houses where they have slaves.

The man of the last described house was intelligent and an ardent Methodist. The room in which I slept was papered with the "Christian Advocate and Journal," the Methodist paper of New York.* At the slaveholder's house, my bedroom was partially papered with "Lottery Schemes."

The free labouring farmer remarked, that, although there were few slaves in this part of the country, he had often said to his wife that he would rather be living where there were none. He thought slavery wrong in itself, and deplorable in its effects upon the white people. Of all the Methodists whom he knew in North-eastern Tennessee and South-western Virginia, he believed that fully three fourths would be glad to join the Methodist Church North, if it were "convenient." They generally thought slavery wrong, and believed it the duty of the church to favour measures to bring it to an end. He was not an Abolitionist, he said; he didn't think slaves could be set free at once, but they ought to be sent back to their own country, and while they were here they ought to be educated. He had perceived that great injustice was done by the people both of the North and South, towards each other. At the South, people were very apt to believe that

* Religion in Virginia.—A mass meeting of citizens of Taylor county, Virginia, was held at Boothesville recently, at which the following, among other resolutions, was passed unanimously:

"That the five *Christian Advocates*, published in the cities of New York, Pittsburg, Cincinnati, St. Louis, and Chicago, having become Abolition sheets of the rankest character, we ask our commonwealth's attorneys and post-masters to examine them, and, if found to be of an unlawful character, to deal with them and their agents as the laws of our State direct."—*Washington Republic.*

the Northerners were wanting not only to deprive them of their property, but also to incite the slaves to barbarity and murder. At the North, people thought that the negroes were all very inhumanely treated. That was not the case, at least hereabouts, it wasn't. If I would go with him to a camp meeting here, or to one of the common Sunday meetings, I would see that the negroes were generally better dressed than the whites. He believed that they were always well fed, and they were not punished severely. They did not work hard, not nearly as hard as many of the white folks; they were fat and cheerful. I said that I had perceived this, and it was so generally, to a great degree, throughout the country; yet I was sure that on the large plantations it was necessary to treat the slaves with great severity. He "expected" it was so, for he had heard people say, who had been on the great rice and cotton plantations in South Carolina, that the negroes were treated very hard, and he knew there was a man down here on the railroad, a contractor, who had some sixty hands which he had hired in Old Virginny ("that's what we call Eastern Virginia here"), and everybody who saw them at work, said he drove them till they could hardly stand, and did not give them half what they ought to have to eat. He was opposed to the Nebraska Bill, he said, and to any further extension of slavery, on any pretext; the North would not do its Christian duty if it allowed slavery to be extended; he wished that it could be abolished in Tennessee. He thought that many of the people who went hence to Kansas would vote to exclude slavery, but he wasn't sure that they would do it generally, because they would consider themselves Southerners, and would not like to go against other Southerners. A large part of the emigration from this part of the country went to Indiana, Illinois, and Iowa; those States being preferred to Missouri, because they were Free States. There were fewer slaves hereabouts now, than there were when he was a boy. The people all thought slavery wrong, except, he supposed, some slaveholders who, because they had property in slaves, would try to make out to themselves that it was right. He knew one rich man who had owned a great many slaves. He thought slavery was wrong, and he had a family of boys growing up, and he knew they wouldn't be good for anything as long as he brought them up with slaves; so he had told his slaves that if they wanetd to be free, he would free them, send them to Liberia, and give them a hundred dollars to start with, and they had all accepted the offer. He himself never owned a slave, and never would own one for his own benefit, if it were given to him, "first, because it was wrong; and secondly, because he didn't think they ever did a man much good."

I noticed that the neighbours of this man on each side owned slaves; and that their houses and establishments were much poorer than his.

CHAPTER IV.

THE EXCEPTIONAL LARGE PLANTERS.

*Feliciana.**—A deep notch of sadness marks in my memory the morning of the May day on which I rode out of the chattering little town of Bayou Sara, and I recollect little of its immediate suburbs but the sympathetic cloud-shadows slowly going before me over the hill of St. Francis. At the top is an old French hamlet.

One from among the gloomy, staring loungers at the door of the tavern, as I pass, throws himself upon a horse, and overtaking me, checks his pace to keep by my side. I turn towards him, and being full of aversion for the companionship of a stranger, nod, in such a manner as to say, "Your equaility is acknowledged; go on." Not a nod; not the slightest deflection of a single line in the austere countenance; not a ripple of radiance in the sullen eyes, which wander slowly over, and, at distinct intervals, examine my horse, my saddle-bags, my spurs, lariat, gloves, finally my face, with such stern deliberation that, at last, I should not be sorry if he would speak. But he does not; does not make the smallest response to the further turning of my head, which acknow-

* "This latter received its beautiful and expressive name from its beautifully variegated surface of hills and valleys, and its rare combination of all the qualities that are most desired in a planting country. It is a region of almost fairy beauty and wealth. Here are some of the wealthiest and most intelligent planters and the finest plantations in the State, the region of princely taste and more than patriarchal hospitality," etc.—*Norman's New Orleans.*

ledges the reflex interest in my own mind; his eyes rest as fixedly upon me as if they were a dead man's. I can, at length, no longer endure this in silence, so I ask, in a voice attuned to his apparent humour—

"How far to Woodville?"

The only reply is a slight grunt, with an elevation of the chin.

"You don't know?"

"No."

"Never been there."

"No."

"I can ride there before night, I suppose?"

No reply.

"Good walker, your horse?"

Not a nod.

"I thought mine pretty good."

Not a sneer, or a gleam of vanity, and Belshazzar and I warmed up together. Scott's man of leather occurred to my mind, and I felt sure that I could guess my man's chord. Cotton! I touched it, and in a moment he became animated, civil; hospitable even. I was immediately informed that this was a famous cotton region: "when it was first settled up by 'Mericans, used to be reckoned the gardying of the world. The almightiest rich sile God Almighty ever shuck down. All on't owned by big-bugs." Finally he confided to me that he was an overseer for one of them, "one of the biggest sort." This greatest of the local hemipteras was not now on his plantation, but had "gone North to Paris or Saratogy, or some of them places."

Wearing no waistcoat, the overseer carried a pistol, without a thought of concealment, in the fob of his trousers. The distance to Woodville, which, after he had exhausted his subject of cotton, I tried again to ascertain, he did not know, and would not attempt to guess. The ignorance of the more brutalized slaves is often described by saying of them that they cannot count above twenty. I find many of the whites but little more intelligent. At all events, it is rarely that you meet, in the plantation districts, a man, whether white or black, who can give you any clear information about the roads, or the distances between places in his own vicinity. While in or near Bayou Sara and St. Francisville, I asked, at different times, ten men, black and white, the distance to Woodville (the next town to the northward on the map). None answered with any appearance of certainty, and those who ventured to give an opinion, differed in their estimates as much as ten miles. I found the actual distance to be, I think, about twenty-four miles. After riding by my side for a mile or two the overseer suddenly turned off at a fork in the road, with hardly more ceremony than he had used in joining me.

For some miles about St. Francisville the landscape has an open, suburban character, with residences indicative of rapidly accumulating wealth, and advancement in luxury, or careless expenditure, among the proprietors. For twenty miles to the north of the town, there is on both sides a succession of large sugar and cotton plantations. Much land still remains uncultivated, however. The roadside fences are generally hedges of roses—Cherokee and sweet brier. These are planted first by the side of a common rail fence, which, while they are young, supports them in the manner of a trellis; as they grow older they fall each way, and mat together, finally forming a confused, sprawling, slovenly thicket, often ten feet in breadth and four to six feet high. Trumpet creepers, grapevines, green-briers, and in very rich soil, cane, grow up through the mat of roses, and add to its strength. It is not as pretty as a more upright hedge, yet very agreeable, and, at one or two points, where the road was narrow, deep, and lane like, delightful memories of England were brought to mind.

There were frequent groves of magnolia grandiflora, large trees, and every one in the glory of full blossom. The magnolia does not, however, mass well, and the road-side woods were much finer, where the beech, elm, and liquid amber formed the body, and the magnolias stood out against them, magnificent chandeliers of fragrance. The large-leaved magnolia, very beautiful at this season, was more rarely seen.

The soil seems generally rich, though much washed off the higher ground. The ploughing is directed with some care not to favour this process. Young pine trees, however, and other indications of rapid impoverishment, are seen on many plantations.

The soil is a sandy loam, so friable that the negroes always working in large gangs, superintended by a driver with a whip, continued their hoeing in the midst of quite smart showers, and when the road had become a poaching mud.

Only once did I see a gang which had been allowed to discontinue its work on account of the rain. This was after a heavy thunder shower, and the appearance of the negroes whom I met crossing the road in returning to the field, from the gin-house to which they had retreated, was remarkable. First came, led by an old driver carrying a whip, forty of the largest and strongest women I ever saw together; they were all in a simple uniform dress of a bluish check stuff, the skirts reaching little below the knee; their legs and feet were bare; they carried themselves loftily, each having a hoe over the shoulder, and walking with a free, powerful swing. Behind them came the cavalry, thirty strong, mostly men, but a few of them women, two of whom rode astride on the plough mules. A lean and vigilant white overseer, on a brisk pony, brought up the rear. The men wore small blue Scotch bonnets; many of the women, handkerchiefs, turban fashion, and a few nothing at all on their heads. They were evidently a picked lot. I thought that every one would pass for a "prime" cotton hand.

The slaves generally of this district appear uncommonly well—doubtless, chiefly, because the large incomes of their owners enables them to select the best from the yearly exportations of Virginia and Kentucky, but also because they are systematically well fed.

The plantation residences were of a cottage class, sometimes, but not usually, with extensive and tasteful grounds about them.

An old gentleman, sensible, polite, and communicative, who rode a short distance with me, said that many of the proprietors were absentees—some of the plantations had dwellings only for the negroes and the overseer. He called my attention to a field of cotton which, he said, had been ruined by his overseer's neglect. The negroes had been allowed at a critical time to be careless in their hoeing, and it would now be impossible to recover the ground then lost. Grass grew so rampantly in this black soil, that if it once got a good start ahead, you could never overtake it. That was the devil of a rainy season. Cotton could stand drouth better than it could grass.*

* "FINE PROSPECT FOR HAY.—While riding by a field the other day, which looked as rich and green as a New England meadow, we observed to a man sitting on the fence, 'You have a fine prospect for hay, neighbour.' 'Hay! that's *cotton, sir*,' said he, with an emotion that betrayed an excitement which we cared to provoke no further; for we had as soon sport with a rattlesnake in the blind days of August as a farmer at this season of the year, badly in the grass. * * *

"All jesting aside, we have never known so poor a prospect for cotton in this region. In some instances the fields are clean and well worked, but the cotton is diminutive in size and sickly in appearance. We have seen some fields so foul that it was almost impossible to tell what had been planted.

"All this backwardness is attributable to the cold, wet weather that we have had almost constantly since the planting season commenced. When there was a warm spell, it was raining so that ploughs could not run to any advantage; so, between the cold and the rain, the cotton crop is very unpromising. * * *

The inclosures are not often of less area than a hundred acres. Fewer than fifty negroes are seldom found on a plantation; many muster by the hundred. In general the fields are remarkably free from weeds and well tilled.

I arrived shortly after dusk at Woodville, a well-built and pleasant court-town, with a small but pretentious hotel. Court was in session, I fancy, for the house was filled with guests of somewhat remarkable character. The landlord was inattentive, and, when followed up, inclined to be uncivil. At the ordinary—supper and breakfast alike—there were twelve men beside myself, all of them wearing black cloth coats black cravats, and satin or embroidered waistcoats; all, too, sleek as if just from a hairdresser's, and redolent of perfumes, which really had the best of it with the exhalations of the kitchen. Perhaps it was because I was not in the regulation dress that I found no one ready to converse with me, and could obtain not the slightest information about my road, even from the landlord.

I might have left Woodville with more respect for this decorum if I had not, when shown by a servant to my room, found two beds in it, each of which proved to be furnished with soiled sheets and greasy pillows, nor was it without reiterated demands and liberal cash in hand to the servant, that I succeeded in getting them changed on the one I selected. A gentleman of embroidered waistcoat took the other bed as it was, with no apparent reluctance, soon after I had effected my own arrangements. One wash-bowl, and

"The low, flat lands this year have suffered particularly. Thoroughly saturated all the time, and often overflowed, the crops on them are small and sickly, while the weeds and grass are luxurious and rank.

"A week or two of dry hot weather will make a wonderful change in our agricultural prospects, but we have no idea that any sort of seasons could bring the cotton to more than an average crop."—*Hernando (Miss.) Advance, June* 22, 1854.

a towel which had already been used, was expected to answer for both of us, and would have done so but that I carried a private towel in my saddle-bags. Another requirement of a civilized household was wanting, and its only substitute unavailable with decency.

The bill was excessive, and the black ostler, who had left the mud of yesterday hanging all along the inside of Belshazzar's legs, and who had put the saddle on so awkwardly that I resaddled him myself after he had brought him to the door, grumbled, in presence of the landlord, at the smallness of the gratuity which I saw fit to give him.

The country, for some distance north of Woodville, is the most uneven, for a non-mountainous region, I ever saw. The road seems well engineered, yet you are nearly all the time mounting or descending the sides of protuberances or basins, ribs or dykes. In one place it follows along the top of a crooked ridge, as steep-sided and regular for nearly a quarter of a mile, as a high railroad embankment. A man might jump off anywhere and land thirty feet below. The ground being too rough here for cultivation, the dense native forest remains intact.

This ridge, a man told me, had been a famous place for robberies. It is not far from the Mississippi bottoms.

"Thar couldn't be," said he, "a better location for a feller that wanted to foller that business. There was one chap there a spell ago, who built himself a cabin t'other side the river. He used to come over in a dug-out. He could paddle his dug-out up the swamp, you see, to within two mile of the ridge; then, when he stopped a man, he'd run through the woods to his dug-out, and before the man could get help, he'd be t'other side the Mississippi, a sittin' in his housen as honest as you be."

The same man had another story of the ridge:—

"Mr. Allen up here caught a runaway once, and started to take him down to Woodville to the jail. He put him in irons and carried him along in his waggin. The nigger was peaceable and submissive till they got along onto that yer ridge place. When they got thar, all of a sudden he gin a whop like, and over he went twenty foot plum down the side of the ridge. 'Fore Allen could stop his hoss he'd tumbled and rolled himself 'way out of sight. He started right away arter him, but he never cotched a sight on him again."

Not far north of the ridge, plantations are found again, though the character of the surface changes but little. The hill-sides are carefully ploughed so that each furrow forms a contour line. After the first ploughing the same lines are followed in subsequent cultivation, year in and year out, as long as enough soil remains to grow cotton upon with profit. On the hills recently brought into cultivation, broad, serpentine ditches, having a fall of from two to four inches in a rod, have been frequently constructed: these are intended to prevent the formation of gullies leading more directly down the hill during heavy rains. But all these precautions are not fully successful, the cultivated hills, in spite of them, losing soil every year in a melancholy manner.

I passed during the day four or five large plantations, the hill-sides worn, cleft, and channelled like icebergs; stables and negro quarters all abandoned, and everything given up to nature and decay.

In its natural state the virgin soil appears the richest I have ever seen, the growth upon it from weeds to trees being invariably rank and rich in colour. At first it is expected to bear a bale and a half of cotton to the acre, making eight or ten bales for each able field-hand. But from the cause described its productiveness rapidly decreases.

Originally, much of this country was covered by a natural growth of cane, and by various nutritious grasses. A good northern farmer would deem it a crying shame and sin to attempt to grow any crops upon such steep slopes, except grasses or shrubs which do not require tillage. The waste of soil which attends the practice is much greater than it would be at the North, and, notwithstanding the unappeasable demand of the world for cotton, its bad economy, considering the subject nationally, cannot be doubted.

If these slopes were thrown into permanent terraces, with turfed or stone-faced escarpments, the fertility of the soil might be preserved, even with constant tillage. In this way the hills would continue for ages to produce annual crops of greater value than those which are at present obtained from them at such destructive expense—from ten to twenty crops of cotton rendering them absolute deserts. But with negroes at fourteen hundred dollars a head, and fresh land in Texas at half a dollar an acre, nothing of this sort can be thought of. The time will probably come when the soil now washing into the adjoining swamps will be brought back by our descendants, perhaps on their heads, in pots and baskets, in the manner Huc describes in China,—and which may be seen also in the Rhenish vineyards,—to be relaid on these sunny slopes, to grow the luxurious cotton in.

The plantations are all large, but, except in their size and rather unusually good tillage, display few signs of wealthy proprietorship. The greater number have but small and mean residences upon them. No poor white people live upon the road, nor in all this country of rich soils are they seen, except *en voyage*. In a distance of seventy-five miles I saw no houses without negro-cabins attached, and I calculated that there were fifty slaves, on an average, to every white family resident in the country under my view. (There is a small sandy region about Woodville, which I passed through after nightfall, and which, of course, my note does not include.)

I called in the afternoon, at a house, almost the only one I had seen during the day which did not appear to be the residence of a planter or overseer, to obtain lodging. No one was at home but a negro woman and children. The woman said that her master never took in strangers; there was a man a few miles further on who did; it was the only place she knew at which I was likely to "get in."

I found the place: probably the proprietor was the poorest white man whose house I had passed during the day, but he had several slaves; one of them, at least, a very superior man, worth fully $2,000.

Just before me, another traveller, a Mr. S., from beyond Natchez, had arrived. Learning that I was from Texas, he immediately addressed me with volubility.

"Ah! then you can tell us something about it, and I would be obliged to you if you would. Been out west about Antonio? Ranchering's a good business, eh, out west there? Isn't it? Make thirty per cent. by it, eh? I hear so. Should think that would be a good business. How much capital ought a man to have to go into ranchering, good, eh? So as to make it a good business?"

He was a middle-aged, well-dressed man, devouring tobacco prodigiously; nervous and wavering in his manner; asking questions, a dozen at a breath, and paying no heed to the answers. He owned a plantation in the bottoms, and another on the upland; the latter was getting worn out, it was too unhealthy for him to live in the bottoms, and so, as he said, he had had "a good notion to go into ranchering. Just for ease and pleasure."

"Fact is, though, I've got a family, and this is no country

for children to be raised in. All the children get such foolish notions. I don't want my children to be brought up here. Ruins everybody. Does sir, sure. Spoils 'em. Too bad. 'Tis so. Too bad. Can't make anything of children here, sir. Can't sir. Fact."

He had been nearly persuaded to purchase a large tract of land at a point upon a certain creek where, he had been told, was a large court-house, an excellent school, etc. The waters of the creek he named are brackish, the neighbouring country is a desert, and the only inhabitants, savages. Some knavish speculator had nearly got a customer, but could not quite prevail on him to purchase until he examined the country personally, which it was his intention soon to do. He gave me no time to tell him how false was the account he had had, but went on, after describing its beauties and advantages—

"But negro property isn't very secure there, I'm told. How is't? Know?"

"Not at all secure, sir; if it is disposed to go, it will go: the only way you could keep it would be to make it always contented to remain. The road would always be open to Mexico; it would go when it liked."

"So I hear. Only way is, to have young ones there and keep their mothers here, eh? Negroes have such attachments, you know. Don't you think that would fix 'em, eh? No? No, I suppose not. If they got mad at anything, they'd forget their mothers, eh? Yes, I suppose they would. Can't depend on niggers. But I reckon they'd come back. Only to be worse off in Mexico—eh?"

"Nothing but——"

"Being free, eh? Get tired of that, I should think. Nobody to take care of them. No, I suppose not. Learn to take care of themselves."

Then he turned to our host and began to ask him about his neighbours, many of whom he had known when he was a boy, and been at school with. A sorry account he got of most. Generally they had run through their property; their lands had passed into new hands; their negroes had been disposed of; two were now, he thought, "strikers" for gamblers in Natchez.

"What is a striker?" I asked the landlord at the first opportunity.

"Oh! to rope in fat fellows for the gamblers; they don't do that themselves, but get somebody else. I don't know as it is so; all I know is, they don't have no business, not till late at night; they never stir out till late at night, and nobody knows how they live, and that's what I expect they do. Fellows that come into town flush, you know—sold out their cotton and are flush—they always think they must see everything, and try their hands at everything—they get hold of 'em and bring 'em in to the gamblers, and get 'em tight for 'em, you know."

"How's —— got along since his father died?" asked Mr. S.

"Well, ——'s been unfortunate. Got mad with his overseer; thought he was lazy and packed him off; then he undertook to oversee for himself, and he was unfortunate. Had two bad crops. Finally the sheriff took about half his niggers. He tried to work the plantation with the rest, but they was old, used-up hands, and he got mad that they would not work more, and tired o' seein' 'em, and 'fore the end of the year he sold 'em all."

Another young man, whom he inquired about, had had his property managed for him by a relative till he came of age, and had been sent North to college. When he returned and got into his own hands, the first year he ran it in debt

$16,000. The income from it being greatly reduced under his management, he had put it back in the care of his relative, but continued to live upon it. "I see," continued our host, "every time any of their teams pass from town they fetch a barrel or a demijohn. There is a parcel of fellows, who, when they can't liquor anywhere else, always go to him."

"But how did he manage to spend so much," I inquired, "the first year after his return, as you said,—in gambling?"

"Well, he gambled some, and run horses. He don't know anything about a horse, and, of course, he thinks he knows everything. Those fellows up at Natchez would sell him any kind of a tacky for four or five hundred dollars, and then after he'd had him a month, they'd ride out another and make a bet of five or six hundred dollars they'd beat him. Then he'd run with 'em, and of course he'd lose it."

"But sixteen thousand dollars is a large sum of money to be worked off even in that way in a year," I observed.

"Oh, he had plenty of other ways. He'd go into a bar-room, and get tight and commence to break things. They'd let him go on, and the next morning hand him a bill for a hundred dollars. He thinks that's a smart thing, and just laughs and pays it, and then treats all around again."

By one and the other, many stories were then told of similar follies of young men. Among the rest, this:—

A certain man had, as was said to be the custom when running for office, given an order at a grocery for all to be "treated" who applied in his name. The grocer, after the election, which resulted in the defeat of the treater, presented what was thought an exorbitant bill. He refused to pay it, and a lawsuit ensued. A gentleman in the witness box being asked if he thought it possible for the whole number of people taking part in the election to have consumed the quantity of liquor alleged, answered—

"Moy Goad! Judge!" (reproachfully): "Yes, sir! Why, I've been charged for a hundred and fifty drinks *'fore breakfast*, when I've stood treat, and I never thought 'o disputin' it."

At supper, Mr. S., looking at the daughter of our host, said—

"What a pretty girl that is. My dear, do you find any schools to go to, out here—eh? I reckon not. This isn't the country for schools. There'll not be a school in Mississippi 'fore long, I reckon. Nothing but Institutes, eh? Ha! ha! ha! Institutes, humph! Don't believe there's a school between this and Natchez, is there?"

"No, sir."

"Of course there isn't."*

"What sort of a country is it, then, between here and Natchez?" I asked. "I should suppose it would be well settled."

"Big plantations, sir. Nothing else. Aristocrats. Swell-heads, I call them, sir. Nothing but swell-heads, and you can't get a night's lodging, sir. Beyond the ferry, I'll be bound, a man might die on the road 'fore he'd get a lodging with one of them. Eh, Mr. N.? So, isn't it? 'Take a stranger in, and I'll clear you out!' That's the rule. That's

* "Sectional excitement" had given a great impetus to educational projects in the South, and the Mississippi newspapers about this time contained numerous advertisements of a similar character to the following:

"CALHOUN INSTITUTE—FOR YOUNG LADIES; MAÇON, NOXUBEE COUNTY, MISSISSIPPI.—W. R. POINDEXTER, A.M., Principal and Proprietor.—The above School, formerly known as the 'Maçon Female Institute,' will be reopened on the first of October, 1855, with an entirely new corps of teachers from Principal down. Having purchased the property at public sale, and thus become *sole proprietor*, the Principal has determined to use all means he can now command, as well as he may realize for several years yet to come, in building, refitting and procuring such appurtenances as shall enable him to contribute his full quota, as a professional man, to the progress of the great cause of 'SOUTHERN EDUCATION.'"

what they tell their overseers, eh? Yes, sir; just so inhospitable as that. Swell-heads! Swell-heads, sir. Every plantation. Can't get a meal of victuals or a night's lodging from one of them, I don't suppose, not if your life depended on it. Can you, Mr. N.?"

"Well, I believe Mr. ——, his place is right on the road, and it's half way to the ferry, and I believe he tells his overseer if a man comes and wants something to eat, he must give it to him, but he must not take any pay for it, because strangers must have something to eat. They start out of Natchez, thinking it's as 'tis in other countries; that there's houses along, where they can get a meal, and so they don't provide for themselves, and when they get along about there, they are sometimes desperate hungry. Had to be something done."

"Do the planters not live themselves on their plantations?"

"Why, a good many of them has two or three plantations, but they don't often live on any of them."

"Must have ice for their wine, you see," said Mr. S., "or they'd die. So they have to live in Natchez or New Orleans. A heap of them live in New Orleans."

"And in summer they go up into Kentucky, do they not? I've seen country houses there which were said to belong to cotton-planters from Mississippi."

"No, sir. They go North. To New York, and Newport, and Saratoga, and Cape May, and Seneca Lake. Somewhere that they can display themselves more than they do here. Kentucky is no place for that. That's the sort of people, sir, all the way from here to Natchez. And all round Natchez, too. And in all this section of country where there's good land. Good God! I wouldn't have my children educated, sir, among them, not to have them as rich as Dr. ——, every one of them. You can know their children as far off as you can see them. Young swell-heads! You'll take note of 'em in Natchez. You can tell them by their walk. I noticed it yesterday at the Mansion House. They sort o' throw out their legs as if they hadn't got strength enough to lift 'em and put them down in any particular place. They do want so bad to look as if they weren't made of the same clay as the rest of God's creation."

Some allowance is of course to be made for the splenetic temperament of this gentleman, but facts evidently afford some justification of his sarcasms. This is easily accounted for. The farce of the vulgar-rich has its foundation in Mississippi, as in New York and in Manchester, in the rapidity with which certain values have advanced, especially that of cotton, and, simultaneously, that of cotton lands and negroes.* Of course, there are men of refinement and cultivation among the rich planters of Mississippi, and many highly estimable and intelligent persons outside of the wealthy class, but the number of such is smaller in proportion to that of the immoral, vulgar, and ignorant newly-rich, than in any other part of the United States. And herein is a radical difference between the social condition of this region and that of the sea-board slave States, where there are fewer wealthy families, but where among the few people of wealth, refinement and education are more general.

I asked how rich the sort of men were of whom he spoke.

* As "A SOUTHERN LAWYER," writing for *Harper's Weekly* (February, 1859), observes: "The sudden acquisition of wealth in the cotton-growing region of the United States, in many instances by planters commencing with very limited means, is almost miraculous. Patient, industrious, frugal, and self-denying, nearly the entire amount of their cotton-crops is devoted to the increase of their capital. The result is, in a few years large estates, as if by magic, are accumulated. The fortunate proprietors then build fine houses, and surround themselves with comforts and luxuries to which they were strangers in their earlier years of care and toil."

"Why, sir, from a hundred thousand to ten million."

"Do you mean that between here and Natchez there are none worth less than a hundred thousand dollars?"

"No, sir, not beyond the ferry. Why, any sort of a plantation is worth a hundred thousand dollars. The niggers would sell for that."

"How many negroes are there on these plantations?"

"From fifty to a hundred."

"Never over one hundred?"

"No; when they've increased to a hundred they always divide them; stock another plantation. There are sometimes three or four plantations adjoining one another, with an overseer for each, belonging to the same man. But that isn't general. In general, they have to strike off for new land."

"How many acres will a hand tend here?"

"About fifteen—ten of cotton, and five of corn; some pretend to make them tend twenty."

"And what is the usual crop?"

"A bale and a half to the acre on fresh land and in the bottom. From four to eight bales to a hand they generally get: sometimes ten and better, when they are lucky."

"A bale and a half on fresh land? How much on old?"

"Well, you can't tell. Depends on how much it's worn and what the season is so much. Old land, after a while, isn't worth bothering with."

"Do most of these large planters who live so freely, anticipate their crops as the sugar planters are said to—spend the money, I mean, before the crop is sold?"

"Yes, sir, and three and four crops ahead generally."

"Are most of them the sons of rich men? are they old estates?"

"No, sir; lots of them were overseers once."

"Have you noticed whether it is a fact that these large properties seldom continue long in the same family? Do the grandsons of wealthy planters often become poor men?"

"Generally the sons do. Almost always their sons are fools, and soon go through with it."

"If they don't kill themselves before their fathers die," said the other.

"Yes. They drink hard and gamble, and of course that brings them into fights."

This was while they were smoking on the gallery after supper. I walked to the stable to see how my horse was provided for, and took my notes of the conversation. When I returned they were talking of negroes who had died of yellow fever while confined in the jail at Natchez. Two of them were spoken of as having been thus "happily released," being under sentence of death, and unjustly so, in their opinion.

A man living in this vicinity having taken a runaway while the fever was raging in the jail at Natchez, a physician advised him not to send him there. He did not, and the negro escaped; was some time afterward recaptured, and the owner having learned from him that he had been once before taken and not detained according to law, he made a journey to inquire into the matter, and was very angry. He said, "Whenever you catch a nigger again, you send him to jail, no matter what's to be feared. If he dies in the jail, you are not responsible. You've done your duty, and you can leave the rest to Providence."

"That was right, too," said Mr. P. "Yes, he ought to a' minded the law. Then if he'd died in jail, he'd know 'twasn't his fault."

Next morning, near the ferry house, I noticed a set of

stocks, having holes for the head as well as the ankles; they stood unsheltered and unshaded in the open road.

I asked an old negro what it was.

"Dat ting, massa?" grinning; "well, sah, we calls dat a ting to put black people, niggers, in, when dey misbehaves bad, and to put runaways in, sah. Heaps o' runaways, dis country, sah. Yes, sah, heaps on 'em round here."*

Mr. S. and I slept in the same room. I went to bed some time before him; he sat up late, to smoke, he said. He woke me when he came in, by his efforts to barricade the door with our rather limited furniture. The room being small, and without a window, I expostulated. He acknowledged it would probably make us rather too warm, but he shouldn't feel safe if the door were left open. "You don't know," said he; "there may be runaways around."

* The following is a characteristic newspaper item of this vicinity:—

From the *West Feliciana Whig*.—"On Saturday last, a runaway negro was killed in the parish of East Baton Rouge, just below the line of this parish, under the following circumstances: Two citizens of Port Hudson, learning that a negro was at work on a flat boat, loading with sand, just below that place, who was suspected of being a runaway, went down in a skiff for the purpose of arresting him.

"Having seized him and put him into the skiff they started back, but had not proceeded far when the negro, who had been at the oars, seized a hatchet and assaulted one of them, wounding him very seriously. A scuffle ensued, in which both parties fell overboard. They were both rescued by the citizen pulling to them with the skiff. Finding him so unmanageable, the negro was put ashore, and the parties returned to Port Hudson for arms and a pack of negro dogs, and started again with the intention to capture him. They soon got on his trail, and when found again he was standing at bay upon the outer edge of a large raft of drift wood, armed with a club and pistol.

"In this position he bade defiance to men and dogs—knocking the latter into the water with his club, and resolutely threatening death to any man who approached him. Finding him obstinately determined not to surrender, one of his pursuers shot him. He fell at the third fire, and so determined was he not to be captured, that when an effort was made to rescue him from drowning he made battle with his club, and sunk waving his weapon in angry defiance at his pursuers. He refused to give the name of his owner."

He then drew two small revolvers, hitherto concealed under his clothing, and began to examine the caps. He was certainly a nervous man, perhaps a madman. I suppose he saw some expression of this thought in my face, for he said, placing them so they could be easily taken up as he lay in bed, "Sometimes a man has a use for them when he least expects it. There was a gentleman on this road a few days ago. He was going to Natchez. He overtook a runaway, and he says to him, 'Bad company's better'n none, boy, and I reckon I'll keep you along with me into Natchez.' The nigger appeared to be pleased to have company, and went along, talking with him, very well, till they came to a thicket place, about six miles from Natchez. Then he told him he reckoned he would not go any further with him. 'What! you black rascal,' says he; 'you mean you won't go in with me? You step out and go straight ahead, and if you turn your face till you get into Natchez, I'll shoot you.' 'Aha! massa,' says the nigger, mighty good-natured, 'I reckon you 'aint got no shootin' irons;' and he bolted off into the thicket, and got away from him."

At breakfast, Mr. S. came late. He bowed his head as he took his seat, and closed his eyes for a second or two; then, withdrawing his quid of tobacco and throwing it in the fireplace, he looked round with a smile, and said:—

"I always think it a good plan to thank the Lord for His mercies. I'm afraid some people'll think I'm a member of the church. I aint, and never was. Wish I was. I am a Son, though [of Temperance?] Give me some water, girl. Coffee first. Never too soon for coffee. And never too late, I say. Wait for anything but coffee. These swell-heads drink their coffee after they've eaten all their dinner. I want it with dinner, eh? Don't nothing taste good without coffee, I reckon."

Before he left, he invited me to visit his plantations, giving me careful directions to find them, and saying that if he should not have returned before I reached them, his wife and his overseer would give me every attention if I would tell them he told me to visit them. He said again, and in this connection, that he believed this was the most inhospitable country in the world, and asked, "as I had been a good deal of a traveller, didn't I think so myself?" I answered that my experience was much too small to permit me to form an opinion so contrary to that generally held.

If they had a reputation for hospitality, he said, it could only be among their own sort. They made great swell-head parties; and when they were on their plantation places, they made it a point to have a great deal of company; they would not have anything to do if they didn't. But they were all swell-heads, I might be sure; they'd never ask anybody but a regular swell-head to see them.

His own family, however, seemed not to be excluded from the swell-head society.

Among numerous anecdotes illustrative of the folly of his neighbours, or his own prejudices and jealousy, I remember none which it would be proper to publish but the following:—

"Do you remember a place you passed?" [describing the locality].

"Yes," said I; "a pretty cottage with a large garden, with some statues or vases in it."

"I think it likely. Got a foreign gardener, I expect. That's all the fashion with them. A nigger isn't good enough for them. Well, that belongs to Mr. A. J. Clayborn.[?] He's got to be a very rich man. I suppose he's got as many as five hundred people on all his places. He went out to Europe a few years ago, and sometime after he came back, he came up to Natchez. I was there with my wife at the same time, and as she and Mrs. Clayborn came from the same section of country, and used to know each other when they were girls, she thought she must go and see her. Mrs. Clayborn could not talk about anything but the great people they had seen in Europe. She was telling of some great nobleman's castle they went to, and the splendid park there was to it, and how grandly they lived. For her part, she admired it so much, and they made so many friends among the people of quality, she said, she didn't care if they always stayed there. In fact, she really wanted Mr. Clayborn to buy one of the castles, and be a nobleman himself. 'But he wouldn't,' says she; 'he's such a strong Democrat, you know.' Ha! ha! ha! I wonder what old Tom Jeff. would have said to these swell-head Democrats."

I asked him if there were no poor people in this country. I could see no houses which seemed to belong to poor people.

"Of course not, sir. Every inch of the land bought up by the swell-heads on purpose to keep them away. But you go back on to the pine ridge. Good Lord! I've heard a heap about the poor folks at the North; but if you ever saw any poorer people than them, I should like to know what they live on. Must be a miracle if they live at all. I don't see how these people live, and I've wondered how they do a great many times. Don't raise corn enough, great many of them, to keep a shoat alive through the winter. There's no way they can live, 'less they steal."

At the ferry of the Homochitto I fell in with a German, originally from Dusseldorf, whence he came seventeen years ago, first to New York; afterward he had resided successively in Baltimore, Cincinnati, New Orleans, Pensacola, Mobile, and Natchez. By the time he reached the last place he had lost all his money. Going to work as a labourer in the town, he soon earned enough again to set him up as a trinket peddler;

and a few months afterward he was able to buy "a leetle coach-dray." Then, he said, he made money fast; for he would go back into the country, among the poor people, and sell them trinkets, and calico, and handkerchiefs, and patent medicines. They never had any money. "All poor folks," he said; "dam poor; got no money; oh no; but I say, 'dat too bad, I don't like to balk you, my frind; may be so, you got some egg, some fedder, some cheeken, some rag, some sass, or some skin vot you kill.' I takes dem dings vot they's got, and ven I gets my load I cums to Natchez back and sells dem, alvays dwo or dree times so much as dey coss me; and den I buys some more goots. Not bad beesnes—no. Oh, dese poor people dey deenk me is von fool ven I buy some dime deir rag vat dey bin vear; dey calls me de ole Dutch cuss. But dey don't know nottin' vot it is vorth. I deenk dey neever see no money; may be so dey geev all de cheeken vot they been got for a leetle breaspin vot cost me not so much as von beet. Sometime dey be dam crazy fool; dey know not how do make de count at all. Yees, I makes some money, a heap."

From the Homochitto to the suburbs of Natchez, a good half-day's ride, I found the country beautiful; fewer hills than before, the soil very rich, and the land almost all inclosed in plantations, the roadside boundaries of which are old rose-hedges. The road is well constructed, and often, in passing through the hills, with high banks on each side, coped with thick and dark, but free and sportive hedges, out of which grow bending trees, brooding angle-like over the traveller, the sentiment of the most charming Herefordshire lanes is reproduced. There are also frequent oak-woods, the trees often of great height. Sometimes these have been inclosed with neat palings, and slightly and tastefully thinned out, so as to form noble grounds around the residences of the planters, which are always very simple and unostentatious wooden houses. Near two of these are unusually good ranges of negro-houses. On many of the plantations, perhaps most, no residence is visible from the road, and the negro quarters, when seen, are the usual comfortless log-huts.

Within three miles of the town the country is entirely occupied by houses and grounds of a villa character; the grounds usually paltry with miniature terraces, and trees and shrubs planted and trimmed with no regard to architectural or landscape considerations. There is, however, an abundance of good trees, much beautiful shrubbery, and the best hedges and screens of evergreen shrubs that I have seen in America. The houses are cheap and shabby.

I was amused to recognize specimens of the "swell-head" fraternity, described by my nervous friend, as soon as I got into the villa district. First came two boys in a skeleton waggon, pitching along with a racking pony, which ran over Jude; she yelped, I wheeled round, and they pulled up and looked apologetic. She was only slightly hurt, but thereafter gave a quicker and broader sheer to approaching vehicles than her Texas experience had taught her to do.

Then came four youthful riders, and two old, roué-looking men, all upon a match-trot; the young fellows screaming, breaking up, and swearing. After them cantered a mulatto groom, white-gloved and neatly dressed, who, I noticed, bowed politely, lifting his hat and smiling to a very aged and ragged negro with a wheelbarrow and shovel, on the foot path.

Next came—and it was a swelteringly hot afternoon—an open carriage with two ladies taking an airing. Mr. S. had said that the swell-heads had "got to think that their old maumy niggers were not good enough for their young ones;" and here, on the front seat of the carriage, was a white and veritable French bonne, holding a richly-belaced baby. The ladies sat back, good-looking women enough, prettily dressed, and excessively demure. But the dignity of the turn-out chiefly reposed in the coachman, an obese old black man, who had, by some means, been set high up in the sun's face, on the bed-like cushion of the box, to display a great livery top-coat, with the wonted capes and velvet, buttoned brightly and tightly to the chin, and crowned by the proper emblazoned narrow-brimmed hat; his elbows squared, the reins and whip in his hands, the sweat in globules all over his ruefully-decorous face, and his eyes fast closed in sleep.

The houses and shops within the town itself are generally small, and always inelegant. A majority of the names on the signs are German; the hotel is unusually clean, and the servants attentive; and the stable at which I left Belshazzar is excellent, and contains several fine horses. Indeed, I never saw such a large number of fine horses as there is here, in any other town of the size. At the stable and the hotel there is a remarkable number of young men, extraordinarily dressed, like shop-boys on a Sunday excursion, all lounging or sauntering, and often calling at the bar; all smoking, all twisting lithe walking-sticks, all "talking horse."

But the grand feature of Natchez is the bluff, terminating in an abrupt precipitous bank over the river, with the public garden upon it. Of this I never had heard; and when, after seeing my horse dried off and eating his oats with great satisfaction—the first time he has ever tasted oats, I suppose, and I had not seen them before for many months—I strolled off to see the town, I came upon it by surprise. I entered a gate and walked up a slope, supposing that I was approaching the ridge or summit of a hill, and expecting to see beyond it a corresponding slope and the town again, continuing in terraced streets to the river. I suddenly found myself on the very edge of a great cliff, and before me an indescribably vast expanse of forest, extending on every hand to a hazy horizon, in which, directly in front of me, swung the round, red, setting sun. Through the otherwise unbroken forest, the Father of Waters had opened a passage for himself, forming a perfect arc, the hither shore of the middle of the curve being hidden under the crest of the cliff, and the two ends lost in the vast obscurity of the Great West. Overlooked from such an eminence, the size of the Mississippi can be realized—which is difficult under ordinary circumstances; but though the fret of a swelling torrent is not wanting, it is perceptible only as the most delicate chasing upon the broad, gleaming expanse of polished steel, which at once shamed all my previous conceptions of the appearance of the greatest of rivers.

Coming closer to the edge and looking downward, you see the lower town, of Natchez, its roofs with water flowing all around them, and its pigmy people wading, and labouring to carry upward their goods and furniture, in danger from a rising movement of the great water. Poor people, "emigrants and niggers" only.

I laid down, and would have reposed my mind in the infinite vision westward, but was presently disturbed by a hog which came grunting near me, rooting in the poor turf of this wonderful garden. I rose and walked its length. Little more has been done than to inclose a space along the edge, which it would have been dangerous to build upon, to cut out some curving alleys now recaptured by the grass and weeds, and to plant a few succulent trees. A road to the lower town, cutting through it, is crossed by slight wooden foot-bridges, and there are some rough plank benches, adorned with stencilled "medical" advertisements. Some shrubs are planted on the crumbling face of the cliff, so near the top that the swine can obtain access to them. A man, bearded and smoking, and a woman with him, sitting at the extreme end, were the only visitors except myself and the swine.

As I am writing there is a bustle in the street. A young man is being lifted up and carried into the bar-room. He is insensible. A beautiful mare, from which he has evidently been thrown, is led back from around the corner, quivering with excitement.

I could find no reading-room; no recent newspapers except *The Natchez Free Trader*, which has nothing but cotton and river news and steamboat puffs; no magazines but aged Harpers; and no recent publications of any sort are for sale or to be seen at the booksellers'; so, after supper, I went to the bluff again, and found it most solemnly beautiful; the young moon shining through rents in the clouds: the great gleaming crescent of water; the dim, ungapped horizon; the earth sensibly a mere swinging globe.

Of all the town, only five Germans, sitting together, but smoking in silence, had gathered for this evening worship.

As I returned up the main street, I stopped opposite a house from which there came the sound of excellent music—a violin and piano. I had heard no music since I was in Western Texas, and I leaned upon a lamp-post for an hour, listening. Many stopped near me for a few minutes, and went on. At length, a man who had remained some time, addressed me, speaking in a foreign tongue. "Can't you speak English?" said I.

"You are not an American?"

"Yes."

"I should tzink it not."

"I am; I am a New Yorker."

"So ?—O yes, perhaps, but not zis country."

"What are you ?"

"Italian."

"Do you live here ?"

"Yes."

"Are there many Italians in Natchez ?"

"Yes—some many—seven. All big dam rascaal. Yes. Ha ! ha ! ha ! True. Dam rascaal all of us."

"What do you do for a living here ?"

"For me it is a cigar-store ; fruit ; confectionary."

"And the rest ?"

"Oh, everytzing. I don't expect dem be here so much long now."

"Why—what will they do ?"

"Dey all go to Cuba. Be vawr zair soon now. All go. All dam rascaal go, can go, ven ze vawr is. Good ting dat for Natchez, eh ? Yes, I tzink."

He told me the names of the players ; the violinist, an Italian, he asserted to be the best in America. He resided in Natchez, I understood, as a teacher ; and, I presume, the town has metropolitan advantages for instruction in all fashionable accomplishments. Yet, with a population of 18,601, the number of children registered for the public schools and academies, or "Institutes," of the county seat, is but 1,015 ; and among these must be included many sent from other parts of the State, and from Arkansas and Louisiana ; the public libraries contain but 2,000 volumes, and the churches seat but 7,700.*

Franklin, the next county in the rear of the county in

* This may be compared with the town of Springfield, county of Sangammon, Illinois, in which, with a population of 19,228 (nearer to that of Natchez than any other town I observe in the Free States), the number of registered school children is 3,300, the public libraries contain 20,000 volumes, and the churches can accommodate 28,000 sitters.

which Natchez is situated (Adams), has a population of 6,000, and but 132 children attending school.

Mr. Russell (*North America: its Agriculture and Climate*, page 258) states that he had been led to believe that "as refined society was to be found at Natchez as in any other part of the United States;" but *his personal observation* is, that "the chief frequenters of the best hotel are low, drunken fellows." I find a crowd of big, silly boys, not drunk, but drinking, smoking, chewing, and betting, and a few men who look like dissolute fourth-rate comedians, who have succeeded in swindling a swell-mob tailor.

The first night after leaving Natchez I found lodging with a German, who, when I inquired if he could accommodate me, at once said, "Yes, sir, I make it *a business* to lodge travellers."

He had a little farm, and owned four strong negro men and a woman with several children. All his men, however, he hired out as porters or servants in Natchez, employing a white man, a native of the country, to work with him on his farm.

To explain the economy of this arrangement, he said that one of his men earned in Natchez $30 a month clear of all expenses, and the others much more than he could ever make their labour worth to him. A negro of moderate intelligence would hire, as a house-servant, for $200 a year and his board, which was worth $8 a month; whereas he hired this white fellow, who was strong and able, for $10 a month; and he believed he got as much work out of him as he could out of a negro. If labour were worth so much as he got for that of his negroes, why did the white man not demand more? Well—he kept him in whisky and tobacco beside his wages, and he was content. Most folks here did not like white labourers. They had only been used to have niggers do their work, and they did not know how to manage with white labourers; but he had no difficulty.

I asked if eight dollars would cover the cost of a man's board? He supposed it might cost him rather more than that to keep the white man; eight dollars was what it was generally reckoned in town to cost to keep a negro; niggers living in town or near it were expected to have "extras;" out on the plantations, where they did not get anything but bacon and meal, of course it did not cost so much. Did he know what it cost to keep a negro generally upon the plantations? It was generally reckoned, he said, that a nigger ought to have a peck of meal and three pounds of bacon a week; some didn't give so much meat, but he thought it would be better to give them more.

"You are getting rich," I said. "Are the Germans generally, hereabouts, doing well? I see there are a good many in Natchez."

"Oh yes; anybody who is not too proud to work can get rich here."

The next day, having ridden thirty tedious miles through a sombre country, with a few large plantations, about six o'clock I called at the first house standing upon or near the road which I have seen for some time, and solicited a lodging. It was refused, by a woman. How far was it to the next house? I asked her. Two miles and a half. So I found it to be, but it was a deserted house, falling to decay, on an abandoned plantation. I rode several miles further, and it was growing dark, and threatening rain, before I came in sight of another. It was a short distance off the road, and approached by a private lane, from which it was separated by a grass plat. A well dressed man stood between the gate and the house. I stopped and bowed to him, but he turned his back upon me and walked to the house. I opened a gate and rode in. Two men were upon the gallery, but as they paid no attention to my presence when I stopped near them, I doubted if either were the master of the house. I asked, "Could I obtain a lodging here to-night, gentlemen?" One of them answered, surlily, "No." I paused a moment that they might observe me—evidently a stranger benighted, with a fatigued horse, and then asked, "Can you tell me, sir, how far it is to a public-house?" "I don't know," replied the same man. I again remained silent a moment. "No public-houses in this section of the country, I reckon, sir," said the other. "Do you know how far it is to the next house on the road, north of this?" "No," answered one. "You'll find one about two miles, or two miles and a half from here," said the other. "Is it a house in which I shall be likely to get a lodging, do you know?" "I don't know, I'm sure."

"Good night, gentlemen; you'll excuse me for troubling you. I am entirely a stranger in this region."

A grunt, or inarticulate monosyllable, from one of them, was the only reply, and I rode away, glad that I had not been fated to spend an evening in such company.

Soon afterward I came to a house and stables close upon the road. There was a man on the gallery playing the fiddle. I asked, "Could you accommodate me here to-night, sir?" He stopped fiddling, and turned his head toward an open door, asking, "Wants to know if you can accommodate him?" "Accommodate him with what?" demanded a harsh-toned woman's voice. "With a bed of course—what do you s'pose—ho! ho! ho!" and he went on fiddling again. I had, during this conversation, observed ranges of negro huts behind the stables, and perceived that it must be the overseer's house of the plantation at which I had previously called. "Like master, like man," I thought, and rode on, my inquiry not having been even answered.

I met a negro boy on the road, who told me it was about two miles to the next house, but he did not reckon that I would get in there. "How far to the next house beyond that?" "About four miles, sir, and I reckon you can get in there, master; I've heerd they did take in travellers to that place."

Soon after this it began to rain and grow dark; so dark that I could not keep the road, for soon finding Belshazzar in difficulty, I got off and discovered that we were following up the dry bed of a small stream. In trying to get back I probably crossed the road, as I did not find it again, and wandered cautiously among trees for nearly an hour, at length coming to open country and a fence. Keeping this in sight, I rode on until I found a gate, entering at which, I followed a nearly straight and tolerable good road full an hour, as it seemed to me, at last coming to a large negro "settlement."

I passed through it to the end of the rows, where was a cabin larger than the rest, facing on the space between the two lines of huts. A shout brought out the overseer. I begged for a night's lodging; he was silent; I said that I had travelled far, was much fatigued and hungry; my horse was nearly knocked up, and I was a stranger in the country; I had lost my road, and only by good fortune had found my way here. At length, as I continued urging my need, he said—

"Well, I suppose you must stop. Ho, Byron! Here, Byron, take this man's horse, and put him in *my* stable. 'Light, sir, and come in."

Within I found his wife, a young woman, showily dressed —a caricature of the fashions of the day. Apparently, they had both been making a visit to neighbours, and but just come home. I was not received kindly, but at therequest of her husband she brought out and set before me some cold corn-bread and fat bacon.

Before I had finished eating my supper, however, they both quite changed their manner, and the woman apologized for not having made coffee. The cook had gone to bed and the fire was out, she said. She presently ordered Byron, as he brought my saddle in, to get some "light-wood" and make a fire; said she was afraid I had made a poor supper, and set a chair by the fire-place for me as I drew away from the table.

I plied the man with inquiries about his business, got him interested in points of difference between Northern and Southern agriculture, and soon had him in quite a sociable and communicative humour. He gave me much overseer's lore about cotton culture, nigger and cattle maladies, the right way to keep sweet potatoes, etc.; and when I proposed to ride over the plantation with him in the morning, he said he "would be very thankful for my company."

I think they gave up their own bed to me, for it was double, and had been slept in since the sheets were last changed; the room was garnished with pistols and other arms and ammunition, rolls of negro-cloth, shoes and hats, handcuffs, a large medicine chest, and several books on medical and surgical subjects and farriery; while articles of both men's and women's wearing apparel hung against the walls, which were also decorated with some large patent-medicine posters. One of them is characteristic of the place and the times.*

* "THE WASHINGTON REMEDIES—TO PLANTERS AND OTHERS.—These Remedies, now offered to the public under the title of the Washington Remedies, are composed of ingredients, many of which are not even known to Botany. No apothecary has them for sale; they are supplied to the subscriber by the native red-men of Louisiana. The recipes by which they are compounded have descended

We had a good breakfast in the morning, and immediately afterward mounted and rode to a very large cotton-field, where the whole field-force of the plantation was engaged.

It was a first-rate plantation. On the highest ground stood a large and handsome mansion, but it had not been occupied for several years, and it was more than two years since the overseer had seen the owner. He lived several hundred miles away, and the overseer would not believe that I did not know him, for he was a rich man and an honourable, and had several times been where I came from—New York.

The whole plantation, including the swamp land around it, and owned with it, covered several square miles. It was four miles from the settlement to the nearest neighbour's house. There were between thirteen and fourteen hundred acres under cultivation with cotton, corn, and other hoed crops, and two hundred hogs running at large in the swamp. It was the intention that corn and pork enough should be raised to keep the slaves and cattle. This year, however, it has been found necessary to purchase largely, and such was probably usually the case,* though the overseer intimated the

---

to the present possessor, M. A. MICKLEJOHN, from ancestors who obtained them from the friendly Indian tribes, prior to and during the Revolution, and they are now offered to the public with that confidence which has been gained from a knowledge of the fact that during so long a series of years there has never been known an instance in which they have failed to perform a speedy and permanent cure. The subscribers do not profess these remedies will cure *every* disarrangement of the human system, but in such as are enumerated below they feel they cannot fail. The directions for use have only to be strictly followed, and however despairing the patient may have been he will find cause for blissful *hope* and renewed *life*.

"*These preparations are no Northern patent humbug*, but are manufactured in New Orleans by a Creole, who has long used them in private practice, rescuing many unfortunate victims of disease from the grave, after they have been given up by their physicians as incurable, or have been tortured beyond endurance by laceration and painful operations."

* "The bacon is almost entirely imported from the Northern States, as well as

owner had been displeased, and he "did not mean to be caught so bad again."

There were 135 slaves, big and little, of which 67 went to field regularly—equal, the overseer thought, to fully 60 prime hands. Besides these, there were 3 mechanics (blacksmith, carpenter, and wheelwright), 2 seamstresses, 1 cook, 1 stable servant, 1 cattle-tender, 1 hog-tender, 1 teamster, 1 house servant (overseer's cook), and one midwife and nurse. These were all first-class hands; most of them would be worth more, if they were for sale, the overseer said, than the best field-hands. There was also a driver of the hoe-gang who did not labour personally, and a foreman of the plough-gang. These two acted as petty officers in the field, and alternately in the quarters.

There was a nursery for sucklings at the quarters, and twenty women at this time who left their work four times each day, for half an hour, to nurse their young ones. These women, the overseer counted as half-hands—that is, expected to do half the day's work of a prime field-hand in ordinary condition.

He had just sold a bad runaway to go to Texas, he happened to remark. He was whipping the fellow, when he turned and tried to stab him—then broke from him and ran away. He had him caught almost immediately with the dogs. After catching him, he kept him in irons till he had a chance to sell him. His niggers did not very often run

---

a considerable quantity of Indian corn. This is reckoned bad management by intelligent planters. * * * On this plantation as much Indian corn was raised as was needed, but little bacon, which was mostly imported from Ohio. The sum annually paid for this article was upwards of eight hundred pounds. Large plantations are not suited to the rearing of hogs; for it is found almost impossible to prevent the negroes from stealing and roasting the pigs." Mr. Russell, visiting the plantation of a friend near Natchez.—*North America: its Agriculture*, etc., p. 265.

away, he said, because they had found that he was almost sure to catch them. As soon as he saw that one was gone he put the dogs on, and if rain had not just fallen, they would soon find him. Sometimes they did manage to outwit the dogs, but then they almost always kept in the neighbourhood, because they did not like to go where they could not sometimes get back and see their families, and he would soon get wind of where they had been; they would come round their quarters to see their families and to get food, and as soon as he knew it, he would find their tracks and put the dogs on again. Two months was the longest time any of them ever kept out. He had dogs trained on purpose to run after niggers, and never let out for anything else.

We found in the field thirty ploughs; moving together, turning the earth from the cotton plants, and from thirty to forty hoers, the latter mainly women, with a black driver walking about among them with a whip, which he often cracked at them, sometimes allowing the lash to fall lightly upon their shoulders. He was constantly urging them also with his voice. All worked very steadily, and though the presence of a stranger on the plantation must have been a most unusual occurrence, I saw none raise or turn their heads to look at me. Each gang was attended by a "water-toter," that of the hoe-gang being a straight, sprightly, plump little black girl, whose picture, as she stood balancing the bucket upon her head, shading her bright eyes with one hand, and holding out a calabash with the other to maintain her poise, would have been a worthy study for Murillo.

I asked at what time they began to work in the morning. "Well," said the overseer, "I do better by my niggers than most. I keep 'em right smart at their work while they do work, but I generally knock 'em off at 8 o'clock in the morning, Saturdays, and give 'em all the rest of the day to themselves, and I always gives 'em Sundays, the whole day. Pickin' time, and when the crap's bad in grass, I sometimes keep 'em to it till about sunset, Saturdays, but I never work 'em Sundays."

"How early do you start them out in the morning, usually?"

"Well, I don't never start my niggers 'fore daylight, 'less 'tis in pickin' time, then maybe I get 'em out a quarter of an hour before. But I keep 'em right smart to work through the day." He showed an evident pride in the vigilance of his driver, and called my attention to the large area of ground already hoed over that morning; well hoed, too, as he said.

"At what time do they eat?" I asked. They ate "their snacks" in their cabins, he said, before they came out in the morning (that is before daylight—the sun rising at this time at a little before five, and the day dawning, probably, an hour earlier); then at 12 o'clock their dinner was brought to them in a cart—one cart for the plough-gang and one for the hoe-gang. The hoe-gang ate its dinner in the field, and only stopped work long enough to eat it. The plough-gang drove its teams to the "weather houses"—open sheds erected for the purpose in different parts of the plantation, under which were cisterns filled with rain water, from which the water-toters carried drink to those at work. The mules were fed with as much oats (in straw), corn and fodder as they would eat in two hours; this forage having been brought to the weather houses by another cart. The ploughmen had nothing to do but eat their dinner in all this time. All worked as late as they could see to work well, and had no more food nor rest until they returned to their cabins.* At half-past nine o'clock the

* This would give at this season hardly less than sixteen hours of plodding labour, relieved by but one short interval of rest, during the daylight, for the hoe-gang. It is not improbable. I was accustomed to rise early and ride late, resting

drivers, each on an alternate night, blew a horn, and at ten visited every cabin to see that its occupants were at rest, and not lurking about and spending their strength in fooleries, and that the fires were safe—a very unusual precaution; the negroes are generally at liberty after their day's work is done till they are called in the morning. When washing and patching were done, wood hauled and cut for the fires, corn ground, etc., I did not learn: probably all chores not of daily necessity were reserved for Saturday. Custom varies in this respect. In general, with regard to fuel for the cabins, the negroes are left to look out for themselves, and they often have to go to "the swamp" for it, or at least, if it has been hauled, to cut it to a convenient size, after their day's work is done. The allowance of food was a peck of corn and four pounds of pork per week, each. When they could not get "greens" (any vegetables) he generally gave them five pounds of pork. They had gardens, and raised a good deal for themselves; they also had fowls, and usually plenty of eggs. He added, "the man who owns this plantation does more for his niggers than any other man I know. Every Christmas he sends me up a thousand or fifteen hundred dollars' [equal to eight or ten dollars each] worth of molasses and coffee, and tobacco, and calico, and Sunday tricks for 'em. Every family on this plantation gets a barrel of molasses at Christmas." *

---

during the heat of the day, while in the cotton district, but I always found the negroes in the field when I first looked out, and generally had to wait for the negroes to come from the field to have my horse fed when I stopped for the night. I am told, however, and I believe, that it is usual in the hottest weather, to give a rest of an hour or two to all hands at noon. I never happened to see it done. The legal limit of a slave's day's work in South Carolina is fifteen hours.

* I was told by a gentleman in North Carolina, that the custom of supplying molasses to negroes in Mississippi, was usually mentioned to those sold away from his part of the country, to reconcile them to going thither.

Beside which, the overseer added, they are able, if they choose, to buy certain comforts for themselves—tobacco for instance—with money earned by Saturday and Sunday work. Some of them went into the swamps on Sunday, and made boards (which means slabs worked out with no other instrument than an axe). One man sold last year as much as fifty dollars' worth.

Finding myself nearer the outer gate than the "quarters," when at length my curiosity was satisfied, I did not return to the house. After getting a clear direction how to find my way back to the road I had been upon the previous day, I said to the overseer, with some hesitation, "You will allow me to pay you for the trouble I have given you?" He looked a little disconcerted by my putting the question in this way, but answered in a matter-of-course tone, "It will be a dollar and a quarter, sir."

This was the only large plantation I had an opportunity of seeing at all closely, over which I was not chiefly conducted by an educated gentleman and slave owner, by whose habitual impressions and sentiments my own were probably somewhat influenced. From what I saw in passing, and from what I heard by chance of others, I suppose it to have been a very favourable specimen of those plantations on which the owners do not reside. A merchant of the vicinity recently in New York tells me that he supposes it to be a fair enough example of plantations of its class. There is nothing remarkable in its management, so far as he had heard. When I asked about the molasses and Christmas presents, he said he reckoned the overseer must have rather stretched that part of his story, but the owner was a very good man. A magistrate of the district, who had often been on the plantation, said in answer to an inquiry from me, that the negroes were very well treated upon it, though he did not think they were extraordinarily so. His comparison was with plantations in general.* He also spoke well of the overseer. He had been a long time on this plantation—I think he said ever since it had begun to be cultivated. This is very rare; it was the only case I met with in which an overseer had kept the same place ten years, and it was a strong evidence of his comparative excellence, that his employer had been so long satisfied with him. Perhaps it was a stronger evidence that the owner of the negroes was a man of good temper, systematic and thorough in the management of his property.†

The condition of the fences, of the mules and tools, and tillage, which would have been considered admirable in the best farming district of New York—the dress of the negroes and the neatness and spaciousness of their "quarters," which were superior to those of most of the better class of plantations on which the owners reside, all bore testimony to a very unusually prudent and provident policy.

* In De Bow's 'Resources of the South,' vol. i., p. 150, a table is furnished by a cotton-planter to show that the expenses of raising cotton are "generally greatly underrated." It is to be inferred that they certainly are not underrated in the table. On "a well improved and properly organized plantation," the expense of feeding one hundred negroes, "as deduced from fifteen years' experience" of the writer, is asserted in this table to be $750 per annum, or seven dollars and a half each; in this sum is included, however, the expenses of the "hospital and the overseer's table." This is much less than the expense for the same purposes, if the overseer's account was true, of the plantation above described. Clothing, shoes, bedding, *sacks for gathering cotton, and so forth*, are estimated by the same authority to cost an equal sum—$7.50 for each slave. I have just paid on account of a day labourer on a farm in New York, his board bill, he being a bachelor living at the house of another Irish labourer with a family. The charge is twenty-one times as large as that set down for the slave.

† "I was informed that some successful planters, who held several estates in this neighbourhood [Natchez] made it a rule to *change their overseers every year*, on the principle that the *two* years' service system is sure to spoil them."—*Russell's North America: its Agriculture*, etc., p. 258.

"Overseers are changed every year; a few remain four or five years, but the average time they remain on the same plantation does not exceed two years."—*Southern Agriculturist*, vol. iv., p. 351.

I made no special inquiries about the advantages for education or means of religious instruction provided for the slaves. As there seems to be much public desire for definite information upon that point, I regret that I did not. I did not need to put questions to the overseer to satisfy my own mind, however. It was obvious that all natural incitements to self-advancement had been studiously removed or obstructed, in subordination to the general purpose of making the plantation profitable. Regarding only the balance-sheet of the owner's ledger, it was admirable management. I am sorry to have to confess to an impression that it is rare, where this is the uppermost object of the cotton-planter, that an equally frugal economy is maintained; and as the general character of the district along the Mississippi, which is especially noticeable for the number of large and very productive plantations which it contains, has now been sufficiently illustrated, I will here present certain observations which I wish to make upon the peculiar aspect of slavery in that and other districts where its profits to the owners of slaves are most apparent.

CHAPTER V.

SLAVERY IN ITS PROPERTY ASPECT—MORAL AND RELIGIOUS INSTRUCTION OF THE SLAVES, ETC.

In a hilly part of Alabama, fifty miles north of the principal cotton-growing districts of that State, I happened to have a tradesman of the vicinity for a travelling companion, when, in passing an unusually large cluster of negro cabins, he called my attention to a rugged range of hills behind them which, he said, was a favourite lurking-ground for runaway negroes. It afforded them numerous coverts for concealment during the day, and at night the slaves of the plantation we were passing would help them to find the necessaries of existence. He had seen folks who had come here to look after niggers from plantations two hundred miles to the south, ward. "I suppose," said he, "'t would seem kind o' barbarous to you to see a pack of hounds after a human being?"

"Yes, it would."

"Some fellows take as much delight in it as in runnin' a fox. Always seemed to me a kind o' barbarous sport." [A pause.] "It's necessary, though."

"I suppose it is. Slavery is a custom of society which has come to us from a barbarous people, and, naturally, barbarous practices have to be employed to maintain it."

"Yes, I s'pose that's so. But niggers is generally pretty well treated, considering. Some people work their niggers too hard, that's a fact. I know a man at ——; he's a merchant there, and I have had dealings with him; he's got three plantations, and he puts the hardest overseers he can get on them. He's all the time a' buying niggers, and they say around there he works 'em to death. On these small plantations, niggers ain't very often whipped bad; but on them big plantations, they've got to use 'em hard to keep any sort of control over 'em. The overseers have to always go about armed; their life wouldn't be safe, if they didn't. As 't is, they very often get cut pretty bad." (Cutting is knifing; it may be stabbing, in south-western parlance).

He went on to describe what he had seen on some large plantations which he had visited for business purposes—indications, as he thought, in the appearance of "the people," that they were being "worked to death." "These rich men," he said, "are always bidding for the overseer who will make the most cotton; and a great many of the overseers didn't care for anything but to be able to say they've made so many bales in a year. If they make plenty of cotton, the owners never ask how many niggers they kill."

I suggested that this did not seem quite credible; a negro was a valuable piece of property. It would be foolish to use him in such a way.

"Seems they don't think so," he answered. "They are always bragging—you must have heard them—how many bales their overseer has made, or how many their plantation has made to a hand. They never think of anything else. You see, if a man did like to have his niggers taken care of, he couldn't bear to be always hearing that all the plantations round had beat his. He'd think the fault was in his overseer. The fellow who can make the most cotton always gets paid the best."

Overseers' wages were ordinarily from $200 to $600, but a real driving overseer would very often get $1,000. Sometimes they'd get $1,200 or $1,500. He heard of $2,000 being paid one fellow. A determined and perfectly relentless man —I can't recall his exact words, which were very expressive —a real devil of an overseer, would get almost any wages he'd ask; because, when it was told round that such a man had made so many bales to the hand, everybody would be trying to get him.

The man who talked in this way was a native Alabamian, ignorant, but apparently of more than ordinarily reflective habits, and he had been so situated as to have unusually good opportunities for observation. In character, if not in detail, I must say that his information was entirely in accordance with the opinions I should have been led to form from the conversations I heard by chance, from time to time, in the richest cotton districts. That his statements as to the bad management of large plantations, in respect to the waste of negro property, were not much exaggerated, I find frequent evidence in southern agricultural journals. The following is an extract from one of a series of essays published in *The Cotton Planter*, the chief object of which is to persuade planters that they are under no necessity to employ slaves exclusively in the production of cotton. The writer, Mr. M. W. Phillips, is a well-known, intelligent, and benevolent planter, who resides constantly on his estate, near Jackson, Mississippi :—

"I have known many in the rich planting portion of Mississippi especially, and others elsewhere, who, acting on the policy of the boy in the fable, who 'killed the goose for the golden egg,' accumulated property, yet among those who have relied solely on their product in land and negroes, I doubt if this be the true policy of plantation economy. With the former everything has to bend, give way to large crops of cotton, land has to be cultivated wet or dry, negroes to work, cold or hot. Large crops planted, and they must be cultivated, or done so after a manner. When disease comes about, as, for instance, cholera, pneumonia, flux, and other violent diseases, these are more subject, it seemeth to me, than others, or even if not, there is less vitality to work on, and, therefore, in like situations and similar in severity, they must sink with more certainty ; or even should the animal economy rally under all these trials, the neglect consequent upon this 'cut and cover' policy must result in greater mortality. Another objection, not one-fourth of the children born are raised, and perhaps not over two-thirds are born on the place, which, under a different policy, might be expected. And this is not all : hands, and teams, and land must wear out sooner ; admitting this to be only one year sooner in twenty years, or that lands and negroes are less productive at forty than at forty-two, we see a heavy loss. Is this not so ? I am told of negroes not over thirty-five to forty-five, who look older than others at forty-five to fifty-five. I know a man now, not short of sixty, who might readily be taken for forty-five; another on the same place full fifty (for I have known both for twenty-eight years, and the last one for thirty-two years), who could be sold for thirty-five, and these negroes are very leniently dealt with. Others, many others, I know and have known twenty-five to thirty years, of whom I can speak of as above. As to rearing children, I can point to equally as strong cases ; ay, men who are, 'as it were,' of one family, differing as much as four and eight bales in cropping, and equally as much in raising young negroes. The one scarcely paying expenses by his crop, yet in the past twenty-five years raising over seventy-five to a hundred negroes, the other buying more than raised, and yet not as many as the first.

"I regard the 'just medium' to be the correct point. Labour is conducive to health ; a healthy woman will rear most children. I favour good and fair work, yet not overworked so as to tax the animal economy, that the woman cannot rear healthy children, nor should the father be over-wrought, that his vital powers be at all infringed upon.

"If the policy be adopted, to make an improvement in land visible, to raise the greatest number of healthy children, to make an abundance of provision, to rear a portion at least of work horses, rely on it we will soon find by our tax list that our country is improving. * * *

"Brethren of the South, we must change our policy. *Overseers are not interested in raising children, or meat, in improving land, or improving productive qualities of seed, or animals. Many of them do not care whether property has depreciated or improved, so they have made a crop [of cotton] to boast of.*

"As to myself, I care not who has the credit of making crops at Log Hall ; and I would prefer that an overseer, who has been one of my family for a year or two, or more, should be benefited ; but this thing is to be known and well understood. I plant such fields in such crops as I see fit ; I plant acres in corn, cotton, oats, potatoes, etc., as I select, and the general policy of rest, cultivation, etc., must be preserved which I lay down. A self-willed overseer may fraudulently change somewhat in the latter, by not carrying out orders—that I cannot help. What I have written, I have written, and think I can substantiate."

From the *Southern Agriculturist*, vol. iv., page 317 :—

"OVERSEERS.

* * * "When they seek a place, they rest their claims entirely on the number of bags they have heretofore made to the hand, and generally the employer unfortunately recognizes the justice of such claims.

"No wonder, then, that the overseer desires to have entire control of the plantation. No wonder he opposes all experiments, or, if they are persisted in, neglects them; *presses everything at the end of the lash; pays no attention to the sick, except to keep them in the field as long as possible; and drives them out again at the first moment, and forces sucklers and breeders to the utmost. He has no other interest than to make a big cotton crop.* And if this does not please you, and induce you to increase his wages, he knows men it will please, and secure him a situation with."

From the Columbia *South Carolinian* :—

* * * "Planters may be divided into two great classes, viz., those who attend to their business, and those who do not. And this creates corresponding classes of overseers. The planter who does not manage his own business must, of course, surrender everything into the hands of his overseer. Such a planter usually rates the merits of the overseer exactly in proportion to the number of bags of cotton he makes, and of course the overseer cares for nothing but to make a large crop. To him it is of no consequence that the old hands are worked down, or the young ones overstrained; that the breeding women miscarry, and the sucklers lose their children; that the mules are broken down, the plantation tools destroyed, the stock neglected, and the lands ruined: *so that he has the requisite number of cotton bags, all is overlooked;* he is re-employed at an advanced salary, and his reputation increased. Everybody knows that by such a course, a crop may be increased by the most inferior overseer, in any given year, unless his predecessors have so entirely exhausted the resources of the plantation, that there is no part of the capital left which can be wrought up into current income. * * * Having once had the sole management of a plantation, and imbibed the idea that the only test of good planting is to make a large crop of cotton, an overseer becomes worthless. He will no longer obey orders; he will not stoop to details; he scorns all improvements, and *will not* adopt any other plan of planting than simply to work lands, negroes, and mules to the top of their bent, which necessarily proves fatal to every employer who will allow it.

"It seems scarcely credible, that any man owning a plantation will so abandon it and his people on it entirely to a hireling, no matter what his confidence in him is. Yet there are numbers who do it habitually; and I have even known overseers to stipulate that their employers should not give any order, nor interfere in any way with their management of the plantation. There are also some proprietors of considerable property and pretension to being planters, who give their overseer a proportion of the crop for his wages; thus bribing him by the strongest inducements of self-interest, to overstrain and work down everything committed to his charge.

"No planter, who attends to his own business, can dispense with agents and sub-agents. It is *impossible*, on a plantation of any size, for the proprietor to attend to all the details, many of which are irksome and laborious, and he requires more intelligence to assist him than slaves usually possess. To him, therefore, a good overseer is a blessing. But an overseer who would answer the views of such a planter is most difficult to find. The men engaged in that occupation who combine the most intelligence, industry, and character, are allured into the service of those who place all power in their hands, and are ultimately spoiled."

An English traveller writes to the London *Daily News* from Mississippi (1857):—

"On crossing the Big Block river, I left the sandhills and began to find myself in the rich loam of the valley of the Mississippi. The plantations became larger, the clearings more numerous and extensive, and the roads less hilly, but worse. Along the Yazoo river one meets with some of the richest soil in the world, and some of the largest crops of cotton in the Union. My first night in that region was passed at the house of a planter who worked but few hands, was a fast friend of slavery, and yet drew for my benefit one of the most mournful pictures of a slave's life I have ever met with. He said, and I believe truly, that the negroes of small planters are, on the whole, well treated, or at least as well as the owners can afford to treat them. Their master not unfrequently works side by side with them in the fields. * * * But on the large plantations, where the business is carried on by an overseer, and everything is conducted with military strictness and discipline, he described matters as being widely different. *The future of the overseer depends altogether on the quantity of cotton he is able to make up for the market.* Whether the owner be resident or non-resident, if the plantation be large, and a great number of hands be employed upon it, the overseer gets credit for a large crop, and blame for a small one. His professional reputation depends in a great measure upon the number of bales or hogsheads he is able to produce, and neither his education nor his habits are such as to render it likely that he would allow any consideration for the negroes to stand in the way of his advancing it. His 'interest is to get as much work out of them as they can possibly perform. His 'skill consists in knowing exactly how hard they may be driven without incapacitating them for future exertion. The larger the plantation the less chance there is, of course, of the owner's softening the rigour of the overseer, or the sternness of discipline by personal interference. So, as Mr. H—— said, a vast mass of the slaves pass their lives, from the moment they are able to go afield in the picking season till they drop worn out into the grave, in incessant labour, in all sorts of weather, at all seasons of the year, without any other change or relaxation than is furnished by sickness, without the smallest hope of any improvement either in their condition, in their food, or in their clothing, which are of the plainest and coarsest kind, and indebted solely to the forbearance or good temper of the overseer for exemption from terrible physical suffering. They are rung to bed at nine o'clock, almost immediately after bolting the food which they often have to cook after coming home from their day's labour, and are rung out of bed at four or five in the morning. The interval is one long round of toil. Life has no sunny spots for them. Their only refuge or consolation in this world is in their own stupidity and grossness. The nearer they are to the beast, the happier they are likely to be. Any mental or moral rise is nearly sure to bring unhappiness with it."

The same gentleman writes from Columbus :—

"One gets better glimpses of the real condition of the negroes from conversations one happens to overhear than from what is told to one's-self—above all, when one is known to be a stranger, and particularly an Englishman. The cool way in which you hear the hanging of niggers, the shooting of niggers, and the necessity for severe discipline among niggers talked of in bar-rooms, speaks volumes as to the exact state of the case. A negro was shot when running away, near Greensboro', a small town on my road, the day before I passed through, by a man who had received instructions from the owner to take him alive, and shoot him if he resisted. I heard the subject discussed by some 'loafers' in the bar, while getting my horse fed, and I found, to my no small—I do not know whether to say horror or amusement—that the point in dispute was not the degree of moral guilt incurred by the murderer, but the degree of loss and damage for which he had rendered himself liable to the owner of the slave in departing from the letter of his commission. One of the group summed up the arguments on both sides, by exclaiming, 'Well, this shootin' of niggers should be put a stop to, that's a fact.' The obvious inference to be deduced from this observation was, that 'nigger shootin'' was a slight contravention of police regulations—a little of which might be winked at, but which, in this locality, had been carried to such an extent as to call for the interference of the law."

I do not think that I have ever seen the sudden death of a negro noticed in a Southern newspaper, or heard it referred to in conversation, that the loss of property, rather than the extinction of life, was not the evident occasion of interest. Turning over several Southern papers at this moment, I fall at once upon these examples :—

"We are informed that a negro man, the property of Mr. William Mays, of this city, was killed last Thursday by a youth, the son of Mr. William Payne, of Campbell county. The following are the circumstances, as we have received them. Two sons of Mr. Payne were shooting pigeons on the plantation of Mr. Mays, about twenty miles from this place, and went to the tobacco-house, where the overseer and hands were housing tobacco; one of the boys had a string of pigeons and the other had none. On reaching the house, the negro who was killed asked the boy who had no pigeons, 'where his were.' He replied that he killed none, but could kill him (the negro), and raised his gun and fired. The load took effect in the head, and caused death in a few hours. *The negro was a valuable one. Mr. Mays had refused* $1,200 *for him.*"—*Lynchburg Virginian.*

"*A valuable negro boy, the property of* W. A. Phipps, living in the upper end of this county, was accidentally drowned in the Holston river a few days ago."—*Rogersville Times.*

"Mr. Tilghman Cobb's barn at Bedford, Va., was set fire to by lightning on Friday, the 11th, and consumed. Two negroes and three horses perished in the flames."—*New Orleans Daily Crescent.*

I have repeated these accounts, not to convey to the reader's mind the impression that slaves are frequently shot by their masters, which would be, no doubt, a mistaken inference, but to show in what manner I was made to feel, as I was very strongly in my journey, that what we call the sacredness of human life, together with a great range of kindred instincts, scarcely attaches at all, with most white men, to the slaves, and also in order to justify the following observation:—that I found the lives and the comfort of negroes, in the rich cotton-planting districts especially, habitually regarded, by all classes, much more from a purely pecuniary point of view than I had ever before supposed they could be; and yet that, as property, negro life and negro vigour were generally much less carefully economized than I had always before imagined them to be.

As I became familiar with the circumstances, I saw reasons for this, which, in looking from a distance, or through the eyes of travellers, I had not been able adequately to appreciate. I will endeavour to state them:—

It is difficult to handle simply as property, a creature possessing human passions and human feelings, however debased and torpid the condition of that creature may be; while, on the other hand, the absolute necessity of dealing with property as a thing, greatly embarrassed a man in any attempt to treat it as a person. And it is the natural result of this complicated state of things, that the system of slave-management is irregular, ambiguous, and contradictory; that it is never either consistently humane or consistently economical.

As a general rule, the larger the body of negroes on a plantation or estate, the more completely are they treated as mere property, and in accordance with a policy calculated to insure the largest pecuniary returns. Hence, in part, the greater proportionate profit of such plantations, and the tendency which everywhere prevails in the planting districts to the absorption of small, and the augmentation of large estates. It may be true, that among the wealthier slave-owners there is oftener a humane disposition, a better judgment, and a greater ability to deal with their dependents indulgently and bountifully, but the effects of this disposition are chiefly felt, even on those plantations where the proprietor resides permanently, among the slaves employed about the house and stables, and perhaps a few old favourites in the quarters. It is more than balanced by the difficulty of acquiring a personal interest in the units of a large body of slaves, and an acquaintance with the individual characteristics of each. The treatment of the mass must be reduced to a system, the ruling idea of which will be, to enable one man to force into the same channel of labour the muscles of a large number of men of various and often conflicting wills.

The chief difficulty is to overcome their great aversion to labour. They have no objection to eating, drinking, and resting, when necessary, and no general disinclination to receive instruction. If a man own many slaves, therefore, the faculty which he values highest, and pays most for, in an overseer, is that of making them work. Any fool could see that they were properly supplied with food, clothing, rest, and religious instruction.

The labourers we see in towns, at work on railroads and steamboats, about stations and landings; the menials of our houses and hotels, are less respectable, moral, and intelligent than the great majority of the whole labouring class of the North. The traveller at the South has to learn that there the reverse is the case to a degree which can hardly be sufficiently estimated. I have been obliged to think that many amiable travellers who have received impressions with regard to the condition of the slaves very different from mine, have failed to make a sufficient allowance for this. The rank-and-file plantation negroes are not to be readily made acquaintance with by chance or through letters of introduction.

I have described in detail, in former chapters, two large plantations, which were much the best in respect to the happiness of the negroes, of all that I saw in the South. I am now about to describe what I judged to be the most profitable estate that I visited. In saying this I do not compare it with others noticed in this chapter, my observations of which were too superficial to warrant a comparison. It was situated upon a tributary of the Mississippi, and accessible only by occasional steamboats; even this mode of communication being frequently interrupted at low stages of the rivers. The slaves upon it formed about one twentieth of the whole population of the county, in which the blacks considerably outnumber the whites. At the time of my visit, the owner was sojourning upon it, with his family and several invited guests, but his usual residence was upon a small plantation, of little productive value, situated in a neighbourhood somewhat noted for the luxury and hospitality of its citizens, and having a daily mail, and direct railroad and telegraphic communication with New York. This was, if I am not mistaken, his second visit in five years.

The property consisted of four adjoining plantations, each with its own negro-cabins, stables, and overseer, and each worked to a great extent independently of the others, but all contributing their crop to one gin-house and warehouse, and all under the general superintendence of a bailiff or manager, who constantly resided upon the estate, and in the absence of the owner, had vice-regal power over the overseers, controlling, so far as he thought fit, the economy of all the plantations.

The manager was himself a gentleman of good education, generous and poetic in temperament, and possessing a capacity for the enjoyment of nature and a happiness in the bucolic life, unfortunately rare with Americans. I found him a delightful companion, and I have known no man with whose natural tastes and feelings I have felt, on so short acquaintance, a more hearty sympathy. The gang of toiling negroes to him, however, was as essential an element of the poetry of nature as flocks of peaceful sheep and herds of lowing kine, and he would no more appreciate the aspect in which an Abolitionist would see them, than would Virgil have honoured the feelings of a vegetarian, sighing at the sight of flocks and herds destined to feed the depraved appetite of the carnivorous savage of modern civilization. The overseers were superior to most of their class, and, with one exception, frank, honest, temperate, and industrious, but their feelings toward negroes were such as naturally result from their occupation. They were all married, and lived with their families, each in a cabin or cottage, in the hamlet of the slaves of which he had especial charge. Their wages varied from $500 to $1,000 a year each.

These five men, each living more than a mile distant from either of the others, were the only white men on the estate, and the only others within several miles of them were a few skulking vagabonds. Of course, to secure their own personal safety and to efficiently direct the labour of such a large number of ignorant, indolent, and vicious negroes, rules, or rather habits and customs, of discipline, were necessary, which would in particular cases be liable to operate unjustly and cruelly. It is apparent, also, that, as the testimony of negroes against them would not be received as evidence in court, that there was very little probability that any excessive severity would be restrained by fear of the law. A provision of the law intended to secure a certain privilege to slaves, was indeed disregarded under my own observation, and such infraction of the law was confessedly customary with one of the overseers, and was permitted by the manager, for the reason that it seemed to him to be, in a certain degree, justifiable and expedient under the circumstances, and because he did not like to interfere unnecessarily in such matters.

In the main, the negroes appeared to be well taken care of and abundantly supplied with the necessaries of vigorous physical existence. A large part of them lived in commodious and well-built cottages, with broad galleries in front, so that each family of five had two rooms on the lower floor, and a loft. The remainder lived in log huts, small and mean in appearance, but those of their overseers were little better, and preparations were being made to replace all of these by neat boarded cottages. Each family had a fowl-house and hog-sty (constructed by the negroes themselves), and kept fowls and swine, feeding the latter during the summer on weeds and fattening them in the autumn on corn, *stolen* (this was mentioned to me by the overseers as if it were a matter of course) from their master's corn-fields. I several times saw gangs of them eating the dinner which they had brought, each man for himself, to the field, and observed that they generally had plenty, often more than they could eat, of bacon, corn-bread, and molasses. The allowance of food is weighed and measured under the eye of the manager by the drivers, and distributed to the head of each family weekly: consisting of—for each person, 3 pounds of pork, 1 peck of meal; and from January to July, 1 quart of molasses. Monthly, in addition, 1 pound tobacco, and 4 pints salt. No drink is ever served but water, except after unusual exposure, or to ditchers working in water, who get a glass of whisky at night. All hands cook for themselves after work at night, or whenever they please between nightfall and daybreak, each family in its own cabin. Each family has a garden, the products of which, together with eggs, fowls, and bacon, they frequently sell, or use in addition to their regular allowance of food. Most of the families buy a barrel of flour every year. The manager endeavours to encourage this practice; and that they may spend their money for flour instead of liquor, he furnishes it to them at rather less than what it costs him at wholesale. There are many poor whites within a few miles who will always sell liquor to the negroes, and encourage them to steal, to obtain the means to buy it of them. These poor whites are always spoken of with anger by the overseers, and they each have a standing offer of much more than the intrinsic value of their land, from the manager, to induce them to move away.

The negroes also obtain a good deal of game. They set traps for raccoons, rabbits, and turkeys; and I once heard the stock-tender complaining that he had detected one of the vagabond whites stealing a turkey which had been caught in his pen. I several times partook of game, while on the plantation, that had been purchased of the negroes. The stock-tender, an old negro, whose business it was to ride about in the woods and keep an eye on the stock cattle that were pastured in them, and who was thus likely to know where the deer ran, had an ingenious way of supplying himself with venison. He lashed a scythe blade or butcher's knife to the end of a pole so that it formed a lance; this he set near a fence or fallen tree which obstructed a path in which the deer habitually ran, and the deer in leaping over the obstacle would leap directly on the knife. In this manner he had killed two deer the week before my visit.

The manager sent to him for some of this venison for his own use, and justified himself to me for not paying for it on the ground that the stock-tender had undoubtedly taken time which really belonged to his owner to set his spear. Game taken by the field-hands was not looked upon in the same light, because it must have been got at night when they were excused from labour for their owner.

The first morning I was on the estate, while at breakfast with the manager, an old negro woman came into the room and said to him, "Dat gal's bin bleedin' agin' dis mornin'."

"How much did she bleed?"

"About a pint, sir."

"Very well; I'll call and see her after breakfast."

"I come up for some sugar of lead, masser; I gin her some powdered alum 'fore I come away."

"Very well; you can have some."

After breakfast the manager invited me to ride with him on his usual daily round of inspection through the plantations.

On reaching the nearest "quarters," we stopped at a house, a little larger than the ordinary cabins, which was called the loom-house, in which a dozen negroes were at work making shoes, and manufacturing coarse cotton stuff for negro clothing. One of the hands so employed was insane, and most of the others were cripples, invalids with chronic complaints, or unfitted by age, or some infirmity, for field-work.

From this we went to one of the cabins, where we found the sick woman who had been bleeding at the lungs, with the old nurse in attendance upon her. The manager examined and prescribed for her in a kind manner. When we came out he asked the nurse if any one else was sick.

"Oney dat woman Carline."

"What do you think is the matter with her?"

"Well, I don't tink dere's anyting de matter wid her, masser; I mus' answer you for true, I don't tink anyting de matter wid her, oney she's a little sore from dat whippin' she got."

We went to another cabin and entered a room where a woman lay on a bed, groaning. It was a dingy, comfortless room, but a musquito bar, much patched and very dirty, covered the bed. The manager asked the woman several times what was the matter, but could get no distinct reply. She appeared to be suffering great pain. The manager felt her pulse and looked at her tongue, and after making a few more inquiries, to which no intelligible reply was given, told her he did not believe she was ill at all. At this the woman's groans redoubled. "I have heard of your tricks," continued the manager; "you had a chill when I came to see you yesterday morning; you had a chill when the mistress came here, and you had a chill when the master came. I never knew a chill to last the whole day. So you'll just get up now and go to the field, and if you don't work smart, you'll get a dressing; do you hear?"

We then left. The manager said that he rarely—almost never—had occasion to employ a physician for the people.

Never for accouchements; the women, from their labour in the field, were not subject to the difficulty, danger, and pain which attended women of the better classes in giving birth to their offspring. (I do not suppose that there was a physician within a day's journey of the plantations.)

Near the first quarters we visited there was a large blacksmith's and wheelwright's shop, in which a number of mechanics were at work. Most of them, as we rode up, were eating their breakfast, which they warmed at their fires. Within and around the shop there were some fifty ploughs which they were putting in order. The manager inspected the work, found some of it faulty, sharply reprimanded the workmen for not getting on faster, and threatened one of them with a whipping for not paying closer attention to the directions which had been given him.

The overseer of this plantation rode up while we were at the shop, and in a free and easy style, reported to the manager how all his hands were employed. There were so many at this and so many at that, and they had done so much since yesterday. "There's that girl, Caroline," said the manager; "she's not sick, and I told her she must go to work; put her to the hoeing; there's nothing the matter with her, except she's sore with the whipping she got. You must go and get her out." A woman passing at the time, the manager told her to go and tell Caroline she must get up and go to work, or the overseer would come and start her. She returned in a few minutes, and reported that Caroline said she could not get up. The overseer and manager rode toward the cabin, but before they reached it, the girl, who had probably been watching us from the window, came out and went to the field with her hoe. They then returned to me and continued their conversation. Just before we left the overseer, he said, "I think that girl who ran away last week was in her cabin last night." The manager told me, as we rode on, that the people often ran away after they have been whipped, or something else had happened to make them angry. They hide in the swamp, and come in to the cabins at night to get food. They seldom remain away more than a fortnight, and when they come in they are whipped. The woman, Caroline, he said, had been delivered of a dead child about six weeks before, and had been complaining and getting rid of work ever since. She was the laziest woman on the estate. This shamming illness gave him the most disagreeable duty he had to perform. Negroes were famous for it. "If it was not for her bad character," he continued, "I should fear to make her go to work to-day; but her pulse is steady, and her tongue perfectly smooth. We have to be sharp with them; if we were not, every negro on the estate would be a-bed."

We rode on to where the different gangs of labourers were at work, and inspected them one after another. I observed, as we were looking at one of the gangs, that they were very dirty. "Negroes are the filthiest people in the world," said the manager; "there are some of them who would not keep clean twenty-four hours at a time if you gave them thirty suits a year." I asked him if there were any rules to maintain cleanliness. There were not, but sometimes the negroes were told at night that any one who came into the field the next morning without being clean would be whipped. This gave no trouble to those who were habitually clean, while it was in itself a punishment to those who were not, as they were obliged to spend the night in washing.

They were furnished with two suits of summer, and one of winter clothing each year. Besides which, most of them got presents of holiday finery (calico dresses, handkerchiefs, etc.), and purchased more for themselves, at Christmas. One of the drivers now in the field had on a uniform coat of an officer of artillery. After the Mexican war, a great deal of military clothing was sold at auction in New Orleans, and much of it was bought by the planters at a low price, and given to their negroes, who were greatly pleased with it.

Each overseer regulated the hours of work on his own plantation. I saw the negroes at work before sunrise and after sunset. At about eight o'clock they were allowed to stop for breakfast, and again about noon, to dine. The length of these rests was at the discretion of the overseer or drivers, usually, I should say, from half an hour to an hour. There was no rule.

The number of hands directed by each overseer was considerably over one hundred. The manager thought it would be better economy to have a white man over every fifty hands, but the difficulty of obtaining trustworthy overseers prevented it. Three of those he then had were the best he had ever known. He described the great majority as being passionate, careless, inefficient men, generally intemperate, and totally unfitted for the duties of the position. The best overseers, ordinarily, are young men, the sons of small planters, who take up the business temporarily, as a means of acquiring a little capital with which to purchase negroes for themselves.

The ploughs at work, both with single and double mule teams, were generally held by women, and very well held, too. I watched with some interest for any indication that their sex unfitted them for the occupation. Twenty of them were ploughing together, with double teams and heavy ploughs. They were superintended by a negro man who carried a whip, which he frequently cracked at them, permitting no dawdling or delay at the turning; and they twitched their ploughs around on the head-land, jerking their reins, and yelling to their mules, with apparent ease, energy, and rapidity. Throughout the South-west the negroes, as a rule, appear to be worked much harder than in the Eastern and Northern Slave States. I do not think they accomplish as much in the same time as agricultural labourers at the North usually do, but they certainly labour much harder, and more unremittingly. They are constantly and steadily driven up to their work, and the stupid, plodding, machine-like manner in which they labour, is painful to witness. This was especially the case with the hoe-gangs. One of them numbered nearly two hundred hands (for the force of two plantations was working together), moving across the field in parallel lines, with a considerable degree of precision. I repeatedly rode through the lines at a canter, with other horsemen, often coming upon them suddenly, without producing the smallest change or interruption in the dogged action of the labourers, or causing one of them, so far as I could see, to lift an eye from the ground. I had noticed the same thing with smaller numbers before, but here, considering that I was a stranger, and that strangers could but very rarely visit the plantation, it amazed me very much. I think it told a more painful story than any I had ever heard, of the cruelty of slavery. It was emphasized by a tall and powerful negro who walked to and fro in the rear of the line, frequently cracking his whip, and calling out in the surliest manner, to one and another, "Shove your hoe, there! shove your hoe!" But I never saw him strike any one with the whip.

The whip was evidently in constant use, however. There were no rules on the subject, that I learned; the overseers and drivers punished the negroes whenever they deemed it necessary, and in such manner, and with such severity, as they thought fit. "If you don't work faster," or "If you don't work better," or "If you don't recollect what I tell you, I will have you flogged," I often heard. I said to one of the overseers, "It must be disagreeable to have to punish them as much as you do?" "Yes, it would be to those who are not used to it—but it's my business, and I think nothing of it. Why, sir, I wouldn't mind killing a nigger more than I would a dog." I asked if he had ever killed a negro? "Not quite that," he said, but overseers were often obliged to. Some negroes are determined never to let a white man whip them, and will resist you, when you attempt it; of course you must kill them in that case.* Once a negro, whom he was about to whip in the field, struck at his head with a hoe. He parried the blow with his whip, and, drawing a pistol, tried to shoot him; but the pistol missing fire, he rushed in and knocked him down with the butt of it. At another time, a negro whom he was punishing insulted and threatened him. He went to the house for his gun, and as he was returning, the negro, thinking he would be afraid of spoiling so valuable a piece of property by firing, broke for the woods. He fired at once, and put six buck-shot into his hips. He always carried a bowie-knife, but not a pistol unless he anticipated some unusual act of insubordination. He always kept a pair of pistols ready loaded over the mantel-piece, however, in case they should be needed. It was only when he first came upon a plantation that he ever had much trouble. A great many overseers were unfit for their business, and too easy and slack with the negroes. When he succeeded such a man, he had

* "On Monday last, as James Allen (overseer on Prothro's plantation at St. Maurice) was punishing a negro boy named Jack, for stealing hogs, the boy ran off before the overseer had chastised him sufficiently for the offence. He was immediately pursued by the overseer, who succeeded in catching him, when the negro drew a knife and inflicted a terrible gash in his abdomen. The wounds of the overseer were dressed by Dr. Stephens, who pronounces it a very critical case, but still entertains hope of his recovery."—*Nachitoches Chronicle.*

hard work for a time to break the negroes in; but it did not take long to teach them their place. His conversation on the subject was exactly like what I have heard said, again and again, by northern shipmasters and officers, with regard to seamen.

I happened to see the severest corporeal punishment of a negro that I witnessed at the South while visiting this estate. I suppose, however, that punishment equally severe is common; in fact, it must be necessary to the maintenance of adequate discipline on every large plantation. It is much more necessary than on shipboard, because the opportunities of hiding away and shirking labour, and of wasting and injuring the owner's property without danger to themselves, are far greater in the case of the slaves than in that of the sailors, but, above all, because there is no real moral obligation on the part of the negro to do what is demanded of him. The sailor performs his duty in obedience to a voluntary contract; the slave is in an involuntary servitude. The manner of the overseer who inflicted the punishment, and his subsequent conversation with me about it, indicated that it was by no means unusual in severity. I had accidentally encountered him, and he was showing me his plantation. In going from one side of it to the other, we had twice crossed a deep gully, at the bottom of which was a thick covert of brushwood. We were crossing it a third time, and had nearly passed through the brush, when the overseer suddenly stopped his horse exclaiming, "What's that? Hallo! who are you, there?"

It was a girl lying at full length on the ground at the bottom of the gully, evidently intending to hide herself from us in the bushes.

"Who are you, there?"

"Sam's Sall, sir."

"What are you skulking there for?"

The girl half rose, but gave no answer.

"Have you been here all day?"

"No, sir."

"How did you get here?"

The girl made no reply.

"Where have you been all day?"

The answer was unintelligible.

After some further questioning, she said her father accidentally locked her in, when he went out in the morning.

"How did you manage to get out?"

"Pushed a plank off, sir, and crawled out."

The overseer was silent for a moment, looking at the girl, and then said, "That won't do; come out here." The girl arose at once, and walked towards him. She was about eighteen years of age. A bunch of keys hung at her waist, which the overseer espied, and he said, "Your father locked you in; but you have got the keys." After a little hesitation, she replied that these were the keys of some other locks; her father had the door-key.

Whether her story were true or false, could have been ascertained in two minutes by riding on to the gang with which her father was at work, but the overseer had made up his mind.

"That won't do;" said he, "get down." The girl knelt on the ground; he got off his horse, and holding him with his left hand, struck her thirty or forty blows across the shoulders with his tough, flexible, "raw-hide" whip (a terrible instrument for the purpose). They were well laid on, at arm's length, but with no appearance of angry excitement on the part of the overseer. At every stroke the girl winced and exclaimed, "Yes, sir!" or "Ah, sir!" or "Please, sir!" not groaning or screaming. At length he stopped and said, "Now tell me the truth." The girl repeated the same story. "You have not got enough yet," said he; "pull up your clothes—lie down." The girl without any hesitation, without a word or look of remonstrance or entreaty, drew closely all her garments under her shoulders, and lay down upon the ground with her face toward the overseer, who continued to flog her with the raw hide, across her naked loins and thighs, with as much strength as before. She now shrunk away from him, not rising, but writhing, grovelling, and screaming, "Oh, don't sir! oh, please stop, master! please, sir! please, sir! oh, that's enough, master! oh, Lord! oh, master, master! oh, God master, do stop! oh, God, master! oh, God, master!"

A young gentleman of fifteen was with us; he had ridden in front, and now, turning on his horse, looked back with an expression only of impatience at the delay. It was the first time I had ever seen a woman flogged. I had seen a man cudgelled and beaten, in the heat of passion, before, but never flogged with a hundredth part of the severity used in this case. I glanced again at the perfectly passionless but rather grim business-like face of the overseer, and again at the young gentleman, who had turned away; if not indifferent he had evidently not the faintest sympathy with my emotion. Only my horse chafed. I gave him rein and spur and we plunged into the bushes and scrambled fiercely up the steep acclivity. The screaming yells and the whip strokes had ceased when I reached the top of the bank. Choking, sobbing, spasmodic groans only were heard. I rode on to where the road, coming diagonally up the ravine, ran out upon the cotton-field. My young companion met me there, and immediately afterward the overseer. He laughed as he joined us, and said:

"She meant to cheat me out of a day's work, and she has done it, too."

"Did you succeed in getting another story from her?" I asked, as soon as I could trust myself to speak.

"No; she stuck to it."

"Was it not perhaps true?"

"Oh no, sir; she slipped out of the gang when they were going to work, and she's been dodging about all day, going from one place to another as she saw me coming. She saw us crossing there a little while ago, and thought we had gone to the quarters, but we turned back so quick, we came into the gully before she knew it, and she could do nothing but lie down in the bushes."

"I suppose they often slip off so."

"No, sir; I never had one do so before—not like this; they often run away to the woods, and are gone some time, but I never had a dodge-off like this before."

"Was it necessary to punish her so severely?"

"Oh yes, sir," (laughing again.) "If I hadn't, she would have done the same thing again to-morrow, and half the people on the plantation would have followed her example. Oh, you've no idea how lazy these niggers are; you Northern people don't know anything about it. They'd never do any work at all if they were not afraid of being whipped."

We soon afterward met an old man, who, on being closely questioned, said that he had seen the girl leave the gang as they went to work after dinner. It appeared that she had been at work during the forenoon, but at dinner-time the gang was moved, and as it passed through the gully she slipped out. The driver had not missed her. The overseer said that when he first took charge of this plantation, the negroes ran away a great deal—they disliked him so much. They used to say, 'twas hell to be on his place; but after a few months they got used to his ways, and liked him better than any of the rest. He had not had any run away now for some time. When they ran away they would generally return within a fortnight. If many of them went off, or if they stayed out long, he would make the rest of the force work Sundays, or deprive them of some of their usual privileges until the runaways returned. The negroes on the plantation could always bring them in if they chose to do so. They depended on them for their food, and they had only to stop the supplies to oblige them to surrender.

Accepting the position of the overseer, I knew that his method was right, but it was a red-hot experience to me, and has ever since been a fearful thing in my memory. Strangely so, I sometimes think, but I suppose the fact that the delicate and ingenuous lad who was with me, betrayed not even the slightest flush of shame, and that I constrained myself from the least expression of feeling of any kind, made the impression in my brain the more intense and lasting.

Sitting near a gang with an overseer and the manager, the former would occasionally call out to one and another by name, in directing or urging their labour. I asked if he knew them all by name. He did, but I found that the manager did not know one in five of them. The overseer said he generally could call most of the negroes on a plantation by their names in two weeks after he came to it, but it was rather difficult to learn them on account of there being so many of the same name, distinguished from each other by a prefix. "There's a Big Jim here, and a Little Jim, and Eliza's Jim, and there's Jim Bob, and Jim Clarisy."

"What's Jim Clarisy?—how does he get that name?"

"He's Clarisy's child, and Bob is Jim Bob's father. That fellow ahead there, with the blue rag on his head, his name is Swamp; he always goes by that name, but his real name is Abraham, I believe; is it not, Mr. [Manager]?"

"His name is Swamp on the plantation register—that's all I know of him."

"I believe his name is Abraham," said the overseer; "he told me so. He was bought of Judge ——, he says, and he told me his master called him Swamp because he ran away so much. He is the worst runaway on the place."

I inquired about the increase of the negroes on the estate, and the manager having told me the number of deaths and births the previous year, which gave a net increase of four per cent.—on Virginia estates it is often twenty per cent.—I asked if the negroes began to have children at a very early age. "Sometimes at sixteen," said the manager. "Yes, and at fourteen," said the overseer; "that girl's had a child"—pointing to a girl that did not appear older than fourteen. "Is she married?" "No." "You see," said the manager, "negro girls are not remarkable for chastity; their habits indeed rather hinder them from having children. They'd have them younger than they do, if they would marry or live with but one man, sooner than they do.* They often do not have children till they are twenty-five years old." "Are those who are married true to each other?" I asked. The overseer laughed heartily at the idea, and described a disgusting state of things. Women were almost common property, though sometimes the men were not all inclined to acknowledge it; for when I asked: "Do you not try to discourage this?" the overseer answered: "No, not unless they quarrel." "They get jealous and quarrel among themselves sometimes about it," the manager explained, "or come to the overseer and complain, and he has them punished." "Give all hands a damned good hiding," said the overseer. "You punish for adultery, then, but not for

* Mr. Russell makes an observation to the same effect with regard to the Cuba plantations, p. 230. On these large cotton plantations there are frequently more men than women, men being bought in preference to women for cotton picking.

The contrary is usually the case on the small plantations, where the profits of breeding negroes are constantly in view.

fornication?" "Yes," answered the manager, but "No," insisted the overseer, "we punish them for quarrelling; if they don't quarrel I don't mind anything about it, but if it makes a muss, I give all four of 'em a warning."

Riding through a large gang of hoers, with two of the overseers, I observed that a large proportion of them appeared to be thorough-bred Africans. Both of them thought that the "real black niggers" were about three-fourths of the whole number, and that this would hold as an average on Mississippi and Louisiana plantations. One of them pointed out a girl—"That one is pure white; you see her hair?" (It was straight and sandy.) "She is the only one we have got." It was not uncommon, he said, to see slaves so white that they could not be easily distinguished from pure-blooded whites. He had never been on a plantation before, that had not more than one on it.* "Now," said I, "if that girl should dress herself well, and run away, would she be suspected of being a slave?" (I could see nothing myself by which to distinguish her, as she passed, from an ordinary poor white girl.)

"Oh, yes; you might not know her if she got to the North, but any of us would know her."

"How?"

"By her language and manners."

"But if she had been brought up as house-servant?"

"Perhaps not in that case."

* "A woman, calling herself Violet Ludlow, was arrested a few days ago, and committed to jail, on the supposition that she was a runaway slave belonging to A. M. Mobley, of Upshur county, Texas, who had offered through our columns a reward of fifty dollars for her apprehension. On being brought before a justice of the peace, she stated that she was a white woman, and claimed her liberty. She states that she is a daughter of Jeremiah Ludlow, of Pike county, Alabama, and was brought from that country in 1853, by George Cope, who emigrated to Texas. After arriving in Texas, she was sold by George Cope to a Doctor Terry, in Upshur county, Texas, and was soon after sold by him to a Mrs. Hagen, or Hagens, of the

The other thought there would be no difficulty; you could always see a slave girl quail when you looked in her eyes.

I asked if they thought the mulattoes or white slaves were weaker or less valuable than the pure negroes.

"Oh, no; I'd rather have them a great deal," said one. "Well, I had not," said the other; "the blacker the better for me." "The white ones," added the first, "are more active, and know more, and I think they do the most work." "Are they more subject to illness, or do they appear to be of weaker constitutions?" One said they were not, the other that they did not seem to bear the heat as well. The first thought that this might be so, but that, nevertheless, they would do more work. I afterwards asked the manager's opinion. He thought they did not stand excessive heat as well as the pure negroes, but that, from their greater activity and willingness, they would do more work. He believed they were equally strong and no more liable to illness; had never had reason to think them of weaker constitution. They often had large families, and he had not noticed that their

---

same county. Violet says that she protested against each sale made of her, declaring herself a free woman. She names George Gilmer, Thomas Rogers, John Garret, and others, residents of Pike county, Alabama, as persons who have known her from infancy as the daughter of one Jeremiah Ludlow and Rene Martin, a widow at the time of her birth, and as being a free white woman, and her father a free white man. Violet is about instituting legal proceedings for her freedom."—*Shreveport Southwestern.*

"Some days since, a woman named Pelasgie was arrested as a fugitive slave, who has lived for more than twelve years in this city as a free woman. She was so nearly white that few could detect any traces of her African descent. She was arrested at the instance of a man named Raby, who claimed her as belonging to an estate of which he is heir-at-law. She was conveyed to the First District guard-house for safe keeping, and while there she stated to Acting Recorder Filleul that she was free, had never belonged to Raby, and had been in the full and unquestioned enjoyment of her freedom in this city for the above-mentioned period. She also stated that she had a house, well furnished, which she was in the habit of letting out in rooms."—*New Orleans Picayune.*

children were weaker or more subject to disease than others. He thought that perhaps they did not have so many children as the pure negroes, but he had supposed the reason to be that they did not begin bearing so young as the others, and this was because they were more attractive to the men, and perhaps more amorous themselves. He knew a great many mulattoes living together, and they generally had large and healthy families.

Afterwards, at one of the plantation nurseries, where there were some twenty or thirty infants and young children, a number of whom were evidently the offspring of white fathers, I asked the nurse to point out the healthiest children to me, and of those she indicated more were of the pure than of the mixed breed. I then asked her to show me which were the sickliest, and she did not point to any of the latter. I then asked if she noticed any difference in this respect between the black and the yellow children. "Well, dey do say, master, dat de yellow ones is de sickliest, but I can't tell for true dat I ever see as dey was."

Being with the proprietor and the manager together, I asked about the religious condition of the slaves. There were "preachers" on the plantations, and they had some religious observances on a Sunday; but the preachers were the worst characters among them, and, they thought, only made their religion a cloak for habits of especial depravity. They, were, at all events, the most deceitful and dishonest slaves on the plantation, and oftenest required punishment. The negroes of all denominations, and even those who ordinarily made no religious pretensions, would join together in exciting religious observances. They did not like to have white men preach on the estate; and in future they did not intend to permit them to do so. It excited the negroes so much as to greatly interfere with the subordination and order which were necessary to obtain the profitable use of their labour. They would be singing and dancing every night in their cabins, till dawn of day, and utterly unfit themselves for work.

With regard to the religious instruction of slaves, widely different practices of course prevail. There are some slave-holders, like Bishop Polk of Louisiana,* who oblige, and many others who encourage, their slaves to engage in religious exercises, furnishing them certain conveniences for the purpose. Among the wealthier slaveowners, however, and in all those parts of the country where the enslaved portion of the population outnumbers the whites, there is generally a visible, and often an avowed distrust of the effect of religious exercises upon slaves, and even the preaching of white clergymen to them is permitted by many with reluctance. The prevailing impression among us, with regard to the important influence of slavery in promoting the spread of religion among the blacks, is an erroneous one in my opinion. I have heard northern clergymen speak as if they supposed

* "Bishop Polk, of Louisiana, was one of the guests. He assured me that he had been all over the country on Red River, the scene of the fictitious sufferings of 'Uncle Tom,' and that he had found the temporal and spiritual welfare of the negroes well cared for. He had confirmed thirty black persons near the situation assigned to Legree's estate. He is himself the owner of four hundred slaves, whom he endeavours to bring up in a religious manner. He tolerates no religion on his estate but that of the Church. He baptizes all the children, and teaches them the Catechism. All, without exception, attend the Church service, and the chanting is creditably performed by them, in the opinion of their owner. Ninety of them are communicants, marriages are celebrated according to the Church ritual, and the state of morals is satisfactory. Twenty infants had been baptized by the bishop just before his departure from home, and he had left his whole estate, his keys, &c., in the sole charge of one of his slaves, without the slightest apprehension of loss or damage. In judging of the position of this Christian prelate as a slave-owner, the English reader must bear in mind that, by the laws of Louisiana, emancipation has been rendered all but impracticable, and, that, if practicable, it would not necessarily be, in all cases, an act of mercy or of justice." —*The Western World Revisited.* By the Rev. Henry Caswall, M.A., author of "America and the American Church," etc. Oxford, John Henry Parker, 1854.

a regular daily instruction of slaves in the truths of Christianity to be general. So far is this from being the case, that although family prayers were held in several of the fifty planters' houses in Mississippi and Alabama, in which I passed a night, I never in a single instance saw a field-hand attend or join in the devotion of the family.

In South Carolina, a formal remonstrance, signed by over three hundred and fifty of the leading planters and citizens, was presented to a Methodist clergyman who had been chosen by the Conference of that State, as being a cautious and discreet person, to preach especially to slaves. It was his purpose, expressly declared beforehand, to confine himself to verbal instruction in religious truth. "Verbal instruction," replied the remonstrants, "will increase the desire of the black population to learn. * * * Open the missionary sluice, and the current will swell in its gradual onward advance. We thus expect *a progressive system of improvement* will be introduced, or will follow from the nature and force of circumstances, which, if not checked (though it may be shrouded in sophistry and disguise), *will ultimately revolutionize our civil institutions.*"

The missionary, the Rev. T. Tupper, accordingly retired from the field. The local newspaper, the *Grenville Mountaineer*, in announcing his withdrawal, stated that the great body of the people were manifestly opposed to the religious instruction of their slaves, even if it were only given orally.

Though I do not suppose this view is often avowed, or consciously held by intelligent citizens, such a formal, distinct, and effective manifestation of sentiment made by so important an integral portion of the slaveholding body, cannot be supposed to represent a merely local or occasional state of mind; and I have not been able to resist the impression, that even where the economy, safety, and duty of some sort of religious education of the slaves is conceded, so much caution, reservation, and restriction is felt to be necessary in their instruction, that the result in the majority of cases has been merely to furnish a delusive clothing of Christian forms and phrases to the original vague superstition of the African savage.

In the county of Liberty, in Georgia, a Presbyterian minister has been for many years employed exclusively in labouring for the moral enlightenment of the slaves, being engaged and paid for this especial duty by their owners. From this circumstance, almost unparalleled as it is, it may be inferred that the planters of that county are, as a body, remarkably intelligent, liberal, and thoughtful for the moral welfare of the childlike wards Providence has placed under their care and tutorship. According to my private information, there is no body of slaveowners more, if any as much so, in the United States. I heard them referred to with admiration of their reputation in this particular, even as far away as Virginia and Kentucky. I believe, that in no other district has there been displayed as general and long-continued an interest in the spiritual well-being of the negroes. It must be supposed that nowhere else are their circumstances more happy and favourable to Christian nurture.*

* In White's 'Statistics of Georgia' (page 377), the citizens of Liberty county are characterized as "unsurpassed for the great attention paid to the duties of religion."—Dr. Stevens, in his 'History of Georgia,' describes them as "worthy of their sires," who were, "the moral and intellectual nobility of the province," "whose accession was an honour to Georgia, and has ever proved one of its richest blessings."—In the biography of General Scrivens the county of Liberty is designated "proud spot of Georgia's soil!"—Dr. J. M. B. Harden, in a medical report of the county, says: "The use of intoxicating drinks has been almost entirely given up" by its people.—White says ('Statistics,' p. 373), "The people of Liberty, from their earliest settlement, have paid much attention to the subject of education. Excellent schools are found in different portions of the county, and it is believed a greater number of young men from Liberty graduate at our colleges than from any [other] section of Georgia. Indeed, it has been proverbial for furnishing able ministers and instructors."

After labouring thirteen years with a zeal and judgment which had made him famous, this apostle to the slaves of Liberty was called to the professorship of theology in the University of South Carolina. On retiring from his field of labour as a missionary, he addressed a valedictory sermon to his patrons, which has been published. While there is no unbecoming despondency or absence of proper gratitude for such results as have rewarded his protracted labour, visible in this document, the summing up is not such as would draw unusual cheers if given in the report of an African missionary at the Tabernacle or Exeter Hall. Without a word on which the most vigilant suspicion could rest a doubt of his entire loyalty to the uttermost rights of property which might be claimed by those whom he addressed, he could not avoid indicating, in the following passages, what he had been obliged to see to be the insurmountable difficulty in the way of any vital elevation of character among those to whom he had been especially charged to preach the Gospel wherewith Christ blessed mankind :—

"They [his pastoral charge] are, in the language of Scripture, '*your money.*' They are the source, the means of your wealth; by their labour do you obtain the necessaries, the conveniences, and comforts of life. The increase of them is the general standard of your worldly prosperity: without them you would be comparatively poor. *They are consequently sought after and desired as property, and when possessed, must be so taken care of and managed as to be made profitable.*

"Now, it is exceedingly difficult to use them as money; to treat them as property, and at the same time render to them that which is just and equal as immortal and accountable beings, and as heirs of the grace of life, equally with ourselves. They are associated in our business, and thoughts, and feelings, with labour, and interest, and gain, and wealth. Under the influence of the powerful feeling of self-interest, there is a tendency to view and to treat them as instruments of labour, as a means of wealth, and to forget or pass over lightly, the fact that they are what they are, under the eye and government of God. There is a tendency to rest satisfied with very small and miserable efforts for their moral improvement, and to give one's self but little trouble to correct immoralities and reform wicked practices and habits, should they do their work quietly and profitably, and enjoy health, and go on to multiply and increase upon the earth."

This is addressed to a body of "professing evangelical Christians," in a district in which more is done for the elevation of the slaves than in any other of the South. What they are called to witness from their own experience, as the tendency of a system which recognizes slaves as absolute property, mere instruments of labour and means of wealth, "exceedingly difficult" for them to resist, is, I am well convinced, the *entirely irresistible effect* upon the mass of slaveholders. Fearing that moral and intellectual culture may injure their value as property, they oftener interfere to prevent than they endeavour to assist their slaves from using the poor opportunities that chance may throw in their way.

Moreover, the missionary adds:—

"The current of the conversation and of business in society, in respect to negroes, runs in the channel of interest, and thus increases the blindness and insensibility of owners. * * * And this custom of society acts also on the negroes, who, seeing, and more than seeing, *feeling and knowing, that their owners regard and treat them as their money—as property only*—are inclined to lose sight of their better character and higher interests, and, in their ignorance and depravity, to estimate themselves, and religion, and virtue, no higher than their owners do."

Again, from the paramount interest of owners in the property quality of these beings, they provide them only such accommodations for spending the time in which they are not actively employed, as shall be favourable to their bodily health, and enable them to comply with the commandment, to "increase and multiply upon the earth," without regard to their moral health, without caring much for their obedience to the more pure and spiritual commands of the Scriptures.

"The consequent mingling up of husbands and wives, children and youths, banishes the privacy and modesty essential to domestic peace and purity, and opens wide the door to dishonesty, oppression, violence, and profligacy. The owner may see, or hear, or know little of it. His servants may appear cheerful, and go on in the usual way, and enjoy health, and do his will, yet their actual moral state may be miserable. * * * *If family relations are not preserved and protected, we cannot look for any considerable degree of moral and religious improvement.*"

It must be acknowledged of slavery, as a system, not only in Liberty county, but as that system finds the expression of the theory on which it is based in the laws of every Southern State, that family relations are not preserved and protected under it. As we should therefore expect, the missionary finds that

"One of the chief causes of the immorality of negroes arises from the indifference both of themselves and of their owners to family relations."

Large planters generally do not allow their negroes to marry off the plantation to which they belong, conceiving "that their own convenience and interest, and," says the missionary, "the comfort and *real* happiness of their people" are thereby promoted. Upon this point, however, it is but just to quote the views of the editor of the *Southern Agriculturist*, who, in urging planters to adopt and strictly maintain such a regulation, says: "If a master has a servant, and no suitable one of the other sex for a companion, he had better give an extra price for such an one as his would be willing to marry, than to have one man owning the husband, and the other the wife."

But this mode of arranging the difficulty seems not to have occurred to the Liberty county missionary; and while arguing against the course usually pursued, he puts the following, as a pertinent suggestion:—

"Admitting that they are people having their preferences as well as others, *and there be a supply*, can that love which is the foundation and essence of the marriage state be forced?"

Touching honesty and thrift among the negroes, he says:

"While some discipline their people for every act of theft committed against their interests, they have no care whatever what amount of pilfering and stealing the people carry on *among themselves*. Hence, in some places, thieves thrive and honest men suffer, until it becomes a practice 'to keep if you can what is your own, and get all you can besides that is your neighbour's. Things come to such a pass, that the saying of the negroes is literally true, 'The people live upon one another.'"

Referring to the evil of intemperance, it is observed:

"Whatever toleration masters use towards ardent spirits in others, they are generally inclined to use none in respect to their servants; and in effecting this reformation, masters and mistresses should set the example; for without example, precepts and persuasions are powerless. Nor can force effect this reformation as surely and perfectly as persuasion —appealing to the character and happiness of the servant himself, the appeal recognizes him in such a manner as to produce self-respect, and it tends to give elevation of conduct and character. I will not dwell upon this point."

He will not dwell on this point; yet, is it not evident that until this point can be dwelt upon, all effort for the genuine Christianization of the negro race in the South must be ineffectual?

The benefit to the African which is supposed to be incidental to American slavery, is confessedly proportionate to the degree in which he is forced into intercourse with a superior race and made subject to its example. Before I visited the South, I had believed that the advantages accruing from slavery, in this way, far outweighed the occasional cruelties, and other evils incidental to the system. I found, however, the mental and moral condition of the negroes, even in Virginia, and in those towns and districts containing the largest proportion of whites, much lower than I had anticipated; and as soon as I had an opportunity to examine one of the extensive plantations of the interior, although one inherited by its owner, and the home of a large and virtuous white family, I was satisfied that the advantages arising to the blacks from association with their white masters were very inconsiderable, scarcely appreciable, for the great majority of the field-hands. Even the overseer had barely acquaintance enough with the slaves, individually, to call them by name; the owner could not determine if he were addressing one of his own chattels, or whether it was another man's property, he said, when by chance he came upon a negro off the work. Much less did the slaves have an opportunity to cultivate their minds by intercourse with other white people. Whatever of civilization, and of the forms, customs, and shibboleths of Christianity, they were acquiring by example, and through police restraints, might, it occurred to me, after all, but poorly compensate the effect of the systematic withdrawal from them of all the usual influences which tend to nourish the moral nature and develope the intellectual faculties, in savages as well as in civilized free men.

This doubt, as my Northern friends well know, for I had habitually assumed the opposite, in all previous discussions of the slavery question, was unexpected and painful to me. I resisted it long, and it was not till I had been more than twelve months in the South, with my attention constantly fixed upon the point, that I ceased to suspect that the circumstances which brought me to it were exceptional and deceptive. It grew constantly stronger with every opportunity I had of observing the condition, habits, and character of slaves whom I could believe to present fair examples of the working of the system with the majority of those subject to it upon the large plantations.

The frequency with which the slaves use religious phrases of all kinds, the readiness with which they engage in what are deemed religious exercises, and fall into religious ecstacies. with the crazy, jocular manner in which they often talk of them, are striking and general characteristics. It is not at all uncommon to hear them refer to conversations which they allege, and apparently believe themselves to have had with Christ, the apostles, or the prophets of old, or to account for some of their actions by attributing them to the direct influence of the Holy Spirit, or of the devil. It seems to me that this state of mind is fraught with more danger to their masters than any to which they could possibly have been brought by general and systematic education, and by the unrestricted study of the Bible, even though this involved what is so much dreaded, but which is, I suspect, an inevitable accompaniment of moral elevation, the birth of an ambition to look out for themselves. Grossly ignorant and degraded in mind, with a crude, undefined, and incomplete system of theology and ethics, credulous and excitable, intensely superstitious and fanatical, what better field could a cunning monomaniac or a sagacious zealot desire in which to set on foot an appalling crusade?

The African races, compared with the white, at least with the Teutonic, have greater vanity or love of approbation, a stronger dramatic and demonstrative character, more excitability, less exact or analytic minds, and a nature more sensuous, though (perhaps from want of cultivation) less refined. They take a real pleasure, for instance, such as it is a rare thing for a white man to be able to feel, in bright and strongly contrasting colours, and in music, in which nearly all are proficient to some extent. They are far less adapted for steady, uninterrupted labour than we are, but excel us in feats demanding agility and tempestuous energy. A Mississippi steamboat manned by negro deck-hands will wood up a third quicker than one manned by the same number of whites; but white labourers of equal intelligence and under equal stimulus will cut twice as much wood, split twice as many rails, and hoe a third more corn in a day than negroes. On many plantations, religious exercises are almost the only habitual recreation not purely sensual, from steady dull labour, in which the negroes are permitted to indulge, and generally all other forms of mental enjoyment are discouraged. Religious exercises are rarely forbidden, and a greater freedom to individual impulse and talent is allowed while engaged in them than is ever tolerated in conducting mere amusements or educational exercises.

Naturally and necessarily all that part of the negro's nature which is otherwise suppressed, bursts out with an intensity and vehemence almost terrible to witness, in forms of religious worship and communion; and a "profession" of piety which it is necessary to make before one can take a very noticeable part in the customary social exercises, is almost universal, except on plantations where the ordinary tumultuous religious meetings are discouraged, or in towns where other recreations are open to the slaves.*

Upon the value of the statistics of "coloured church membership," which are often used as evidence that the evils of

* The following newspaper paragraph indicates the wholesale way in which slaves may be nominally Christianized :—

"REVIVAL AMONG THE SLAVES.—Rev. J. M. C. Breaker, of Beaufort, S.C., writes to the *Southern Baptist*, that within the last three months he has baptized by immersion three hundred and fifty persons, *all of them, with a few exceptions, negroes.* These conversions were the result of a revival which has been in progress during the last six months. On the 12th inst., he baptized two hundred and twenty-three converts—all blacks but three—and the ceremony, although performed with due deliberation, occupied only one hour and five minutes. This is nearly four a minute, and Mr. Breaker considers it a demonstration that the three thousand converted on the day of Pentecost could easily have been baptized by the twelve apostles—each taking two hundred and fifty—in an hour and thirteen minutes."

slavery are fully compensated by its influence in Christianizing the slaves, some light is thrown by the following letter from the white pastor of a town church in that part of the South in which the whites are most numerous, and in which the negroes enjoy the most privileges.

"*To the Editor of the Richmond (Virginia) Religious Herald.*

* * * "The truth is, the teachings of the pulpit (at least among Baptists) have nothing to do with the matter. Let me furnish a case in proof. Of two churches which the writer serves, his immediate predecessor was pastor for about twenty-five years. It would be only necessary to give his name, to furnish the strongest and most satisfactory assurance that nothing which ever fell from his lips could be construed into the support of ignorance, superstition, or fanaticism. During the five or six years I have served these churches, whatever may have been my errors and failings (and I am ready to admit that they have been numerous and grievous enough, in all conscience), I know I have never uttered a sentiment which could be tortured into the support of the superstitions prevailing among the coloured people. And yet in both these churches, the coloured members are as superstitious and fanatical as they are elsewhere. Indeed, this was to be expected, for I certainly claim no superiority over my brethren in the ministry, and I am satisfied that many of them are far better qualified than I am to expose error and to root out superstition. This state of things, then, is not due to the teachings of the pulpit. Nor is it the result of private instructions by masters. Indeed, these last have been afforded so sparingly, till within a few years since, that they could produce but little effect of any sort. And, besides, those who own servants, and are willing to teach them, are far too intelligent to countenance superstition in any way. I repeat the inquiry, then, Why is it that so many of our coloured members are ignorant, superstitious, and fanatical? It is the effect of instructions received from leading men among themselves, and the churches are responsible for this effect, in so far as they receive into fellowship those who have listened to these instructions, ground their hopes upon them, and guide their lives by them. Whatever we may say against superstition, so long as we receive into our churches those who are its slaves, they will believe that we think them Christians; and naturally relying on our judgment as expressed by their reception, they will live deluded, and die but to be lost.

"But some one will say, 'We never receive coloured persons when they manifest these superstitions—when they talk of visions, dreams, sounds,' etc. This is right as far as it goes. In every such case they should be rejected. But superstition of a fatal character often exists where nothing is said about dreams and visions. It is just as fatally superstitious to trust in prayers and feelings, as in dreams and visions. And this is the sort of superstition which now prevails among the coloured people. They have found that sights and sounds will not answer before the whites, and now (reserving these, perhaps, for some chosen auditory of their own colour), they substitute prayers and feelings. In illustration permit me to record, in no spirit of levity, the stereotyped experience which generally passes current, and, in ninety-nine cases out of a hundred, introduces the coloured candidate into the church. The pastor is informed, by one of the 'coloured deacons,' that a man wishes to offer to the church with a view to baptism. The fact is announced, a meeting of the church called, and the candidate comes forward.

"*Pastor.*—'Well, John, tell me in a few words, in your own way, your religious experience. What have been your feelings, and what are your present hopes and purposes?'

"*John.*—'I see other people trying, and so I thought I would try too, as I had a soul to save. So I went to pray, and the more I pray the wus I felt; so I kept on praying, and the more I pray the wus I felt. I felt heavy—I felt a weight—and I kept on praying till at last I felt light—I felt easy—I felt like I loved all Christian people—I felt like I loved everybody.'

"Now this is positively the whole of the experience which is generally related by coloured candidates for baptism. There may be a slight variation of expression now and then, but the sense is almost invariably the same. On this experience, hundreds have been received into the churches—I have received many upon it myself. I am somewhat curious to know how many of the seventy, baptized by my good brother Bagby, told this tale. I'll warrant not less than fifty. Have any of us been right in receiving persons on such a relation as this? In the whole of it, there is not one word of gospel, not one word about sorrow for sin, not one word about faith, not one word about Christ. I know that all these things are subsequently brought out by questions; and were this not the case, I have no idea that the candidate would be in any instance received. *But that these questions may be understood, they are made necessarily 'leading questions,'* such as suggest their answers; and consequently these answers are of comparatively little value. * * * I am aware that, as brother Bagby suggests, private instructions by masters have been too much neglected. *But these can accomplish but little good, so long as they are counteracted by the teachings of leading coloured members, in whose views, after all our efforts, the coloured people will have most confidence.*"

Not the smallest suggestion, I observe, in all the long article from which the above is derived, is ventured, that the negroes are capable of education, or that their religious condition would improve if their general enlightenment of mind were not studiously prevented.

"I have often heard the remark made," says the Rev. C. C. Jones, in a treatise on the "Religious Instruction of Slaves," printed at Savannah, Georgia, 1842, "by men whose standing and office in the churches afforded them abundant opportunity for observation, that the more they have had to do with coloured members, the less confidence they have been compelled to place in their Christian professions."

A portion of a letter written for publication by the wife of the pastor of a church in the capital of Alabama, given below, naïvely reveals the degree of enlightenment prevailing among the Christianized Africans at a point where their means of instruction are a thousand times better than they are on an average throughout the country.

"Having talked to him seriously, and in the strongest light held up to him the enormity of the crime of forsaking his lawful wife and taking another, Colly replied, most earnestly, and not taking in at all the idea of guilt, but deeply distressed at having offended his master:

"'Lor, Massa Harry, what was I to do, sir? She tuk all I could git, and more too, sir, to put on her back; and tellin' de truf, sir, dress herself as no poor man's wife hav' any right to. I 'monstrated wid her, massa, but to no purpose; and den, sir, w'y I jis did all a decent man could do—lef' her, sir, for some oder nigger better off 'an I is.'

"'Twas no use. Colly could not be aroused to conscientiousness on the subject.

"Not one in a thousand, I suppose, of these poor creatures have any conception whatever of the sanctity of marriage; nor can they be made to have; yet, strange to say, they are perfect models of conjugal fidelity and devotion while the temporary bondage lasts. I have known them to walk miles after a hard day's work, not only occasionally, but every night, to see the old woman, and cut her wood for her, etc. But to see the coolness with which they throw off the yoke is diverting in the extreme.

"I was accosted one morning in my husband's study by a respectable-looking negro woman, who meekly inquired if Mr. B. was at home.

"'No, he is not. Is it anything particular you want?—perhaps I can help you.'

"'Yes, ma'am; it's partickler business wid himself.'

"Having good reason to believe it was the old story of a 'mountain in labour and brought forth a mouse,' I pressed the question, partly to save my better half some of the petty annoyances to which he was almost daily subjected by his sable flock, and partly, I own, to gratify a becoming and laudable curiosity, after all this show of mystery. Behold the answer in plain English, or rather nigger English.

"'I came to ask, please ma'am, if I might have another husband.'

"Just at this crisis the oracle entered, who, having authority by a few spoken words, to join together those whom no man may put asunder, these poor people simply imagine him gifted with equal power to annul the contract with a breath of his mouth.

"I was heartily amused to find that this woman was really no widow, as I had supposed, but merely from caprice, or some reason satisfactory to herself, no doubt, took it into her head to drop her present spouse and look out for another. The matter was referred to the 'Quarterly Conference,' where an amusing scene occurred, which resulted in the discomfiture of the disconsolate petitioner, who returned to her home rather crest-fallen.

"These Quarterly Conference debates, for flights of oratory, and superlativeness of diction, beggar all description. Be it understood, that negroes, as a class, have more 'business' to attend to than any other people—that is, provided they can thereby get a chance to 'speak 'fore white folks.' To make a speech is glory enough for Sambo, if he happen to have the 'gift of gab;' and to speak before the preacher is an honour unparalleled. And, by the way, if the preacher have will and wit enough to manage and control the discordant elements of a negro Quarterly Conference, he will be abundantly rewarded with such respect and gratitude as a man seldom may lay claim to. They account him but a very little 'lower than the angels;' and their lives, their fortunes, and their sacred honour, are equally his at command. But wo be to the unfortunate pastor who treats them with undue indulgence; they will besiege him daily and hourly with their petty affairs, and their business meetings will be such a monopoly of his time and patience, that but for the farcical character of the same, making them more like dramatic entertainments than sober realities, he would be in despair. Far into the short hours of morning will they speechify and magnify, until nothing but the voice of stern authority, in a tone of command not to be mistaken, can stop the current."

An Alabama gentleman whom I questioned with regard to the chastity of the so-called pious slaves, confessed, that four negro women had borne children in his own house, all of them at the time members in good standing of the Baptist church, and none of them calling any man husband. The only negro man in the house was also a church member, and he believed that he was the father of the four children. He said that he did not know of more than one negro woman whom he could suppose to be chaste, yet he knew hosts who were members of churches.*

A Northern clergyman who had been some years in another town in Alabama, where also the means of instruction offered the slaves were unusually good, answered my inquiry, What proportion of the coloured members of the churches in the town had any clear comprehension of the meaning of the articles of faith which they professed? "Certainly not more than one in seven."

The acknowledgment that "the coloured people will, in spite of all our efforts, have more confidence in the views of leading coloured members," made by the writer of the letter taken from the "Religious Herald," has been generally made by all clergymen at the South with whom I have conversed. A clergyman of the Episcopal Church, of very frank and engaging manners, said in my presence that he had been striving for seven years to gain the confidence of the small number of Africans belonging to his congregation, and with extreme humility he had been lately forced to acknowledge that all his apparent success hitherto had been most delusive.

* "A small farmer," who "has had control of negroes for thirty years and has been pursuing his present system with them for twenty years," and who "owning but a few slaves is able," as he observes, "to do better by them" than large planters, writing to Mr. De Bow, says: "I have tried faithfully to break up immorality. I have not known an oath to be sworn for a long time. I know of no quarrelling, no calling harsh names, and but little stealing. *Habits of amalgamation, I cannot stop.* I can only check it in name. I am willing to be taught, for I have tried everything I know." He has his field-negroes attend his own family prayers on Sunday, prayer meetings at four o'clock Sunday mornings, etc.—*De Bow's Resources*, vol. ii., p. 337.

When asked how he accounted for it, he at once ascribed it to the negro's habitual distrust of the white race, and in discussing the causes of this distrust he asked how, if he pretended to believe that the Bible was the Word of God, addressed equally to all the human race, he could explain to a negro's satisfaction why he should fear to put it directly into his hands and instruct him to read it and judge for himself of his duty? A planter present, a member of his church, immediately observed that these were dangerous views, and advised him to be cautious in the expression of them. The laws of the country forbade the education of negroes, and the church was, and he trusted always would remain, the bulwark of the laws. The clergyman replied that he had no design to break the laws, but he must say that he considered that the law which withheld the Bible from the negro was unnecessary and papistical in character.*

The "Methodist Protestant," a religious newspaper edited by a clergyman, in Maryland, where the slave population is to the free only in the ratio of one to twenty-five, lately printed an account of a slave auction in Java (translated from a Dutch paper), at which the father of a slave family was permitted to purchase his wife and children at a nominal price, owing to the humanity of the spectators. The account concluded as follows:—

"It would be difficult to describe the joy experienced by these slaves on hearing the fall of the hammer which thus gave them their liberty;

* The "Southern Presbyterian," in reviewing some observations made before a South Carolina Bible Society, in which it had been urged that if slaves were permitted to read the Bible, they would learn from it to be more submissive to the authority which the State gives the master over them, says that the speaker "seems to be uninformed of the fact that the Scriptures are read in our churches every Sabbath day, and those very passages which inculcate the relative duties of masters and servants in consequence of their textual, *i. e.* legally prescribed connections, are *more frequently read* than any other portions of the Bible."

and this joy was further augmented by the presents given them by numbers of the spectators, in order that they might be able to obtain a subsistence till such time as they could procure employment.

"These are the acts of a noble generosity that deserves to be remembered, and which, at the same time, testify that the inhabitants of Java begin to abhor the crying injustice of slavery, and are willing to entertain measures for its abolition."

To give currency to such ideas, even in Maryland, would be fatal to what ministers call their "influence," and which they everywhere value at a rather dangerous estimate; accordingly, in the editorial columns prominence is given to the following salve to the outraged sensibilities of the subscribers:

"SLAVE AUCTION IN JAVA.

"A brief article, with this head, appears on the fourth page of our paper this week. It is of a class of articles we *never select*, because they are very often manufactured by paragraphists for a purpose, and are not reliable. It was put in by our printer in place of something we had *marked out*. We did not see this objectionable substitute until the outside form was worked off, and are therefore not responsible for it."*

The habitual caution imposed on clergymen and public teachers must, and obviously does have an important secondary effect, similar to that usually attributed by Protestants to papacy, upon the minds of all the people, discountenancing and retarding the free and fearless exercise of the mind upon subjects of a religious or ethical nature, and the necessity of accepting and apologizing for the exceedingly low morality of the nominally religious slaves, together with the familiarity with this immorality which all classes acquire, renders the existence of a very elevated standard of morals among the whites almost an impossibility.†

In spite of the constant denunciations by the Southern

* Organized action for the abolition of slavery in the island of Java, has since been authentically reported.

† Twice it happened to come to my knowledge that sons of a planter, by whom I was lodged while on this journey—lads of fourteen or sixteen—who were supposed to have slept in the same room with me, really spent the night, till after daybreak, in the negro cabins. A southern merchant, visiting New York, to whom I ex-

newspapers, of those who continued to patronize Northern educational institutions, I never conversed with a cultivated Southerner on the effects of slavery, that he did not express a wish or intention to have his own children educated where they should be free from demoralizing association with slaves. That this association is almost inevitably corrupting and dangerous, is very generally (I may say, excepting by the extremest fanatics of South Carolina, universally) admitted. Now, although the children of a few wealthy men may, for a limited period, be preserved from this danger, the children of the million cannot be. Indeed it requires a man of some culture, and knowledge of the rest of the world, to appreciate the danger sufficiently to guard at all diligently against it. If habitual intercourse with a hopelessly low and immoral class is at all bad in its effects on young minds, the people of the South are, as a people, educated subject to this bad influence, and must bear the consequences. In other words, if the slaves must not be elevated, it would seem to be a necessity that the citizens should steadily degenerate,

Change and grow more marked in their peculiarities with every generation, they certainly do, very obviously. "The South" has a traditional reputation for qualities and habits in

---

pressed the view I had been led to form of the evil of slavery in this way, replied that he thought I over-estimated the evil to boys on the plantations, but that it was impossible to over-estimate it in towns. "I have personal knowledge," he continued, "that there are but two lads, sixteen years old, in our town, [a small market town of Alabama,] who have not already had occasion to resort to remedies for the penalty of licentiousness." "When on my brother's plantation, just before I came North," said another Southern merchant, on his annual visit to New York, "I was informed that each of his family-servants were suffering from ——, and I ascertained that each of my brother's children, girls and boys, had been informed of it, and knew how and from whom it had been acquired. The negroes being their familiar companions, I tried to get my brother to send them North with me to school. I told him he might as well have them educated in a brothel at once, as in the way they were growing up."

which I think the Southern people, as a whole, are to-day more deficient than any other nation in the world. The Southern gentleman, as we ordinarily conceive him to be, is as rare a phenomenon in the South at the present day as is the old squire of Geoffry Crayon in modern England. But it is unnecessary to argue how great must be the influence, upon people of a higher origin, of habitual association with a race systematically kept at the lowest ebb of intellect and morals. It has been elaborately and convincingly described by Mr. Jefferson, from his personal experience and observation of his neighbours. What he testified to be the effect upon the Virginians, in his day, of owning and associating with slaves, is now to be witnessed to a far greater and more deplorable extent throughout the whole South, but most deplorably in districts where the slave population predominates, and where, consequently, the action of slavery has been most unimpeded.*

* Jefferson fails to enumerate, among the evils of slavery, one of its influences which I am inclined to think as distinct and as baneful to us nationally as any other. How can men retain the most essential quality of true manhood who daily, without remonstrance or interference, see men beaten, whose position renders effective resistance totally impracticable—and not only men, but women, too! Is it not partially the result of this, that self-respect seldom seems to suggest to an angry man at the South that he should use anything like magnanimity? that he should be careful to secure fair play for his opponent in a quarrel? A gentleman of veracity, now living in the South, told me that among his friends he had once numbered two young men, who were themselves intimate friends, till one of them, taking offence at some foolish words uttered by the other, challenged him. A large crowd assembled to see the duel, which took place on a piece of prairie ground. The combatants came armed with rifles, and at the first interchange of shots the challenged man fell disabled by a ball in the thigh. The other, throwing down his rifle, walked toward him, and kneeling by his side, drew a bowie knife, and deliberately butchered him. The crowd of bystanders not only permitted this, but the execrable assassin still lives in the community, has since married, and, as far as my informant could judge, his social position has been rather advanced than otherwise, from thus dealing with his enemy. In what other English—in what other civilized or half-civilized community would such cowardly atrocity have been endured?

What proportion of the larger cotton plantations are resided upon by their owners, I am unable to estimate with confidence. Of those having cabin accommodations for fifty slaves each, which came under my observation from the road, while I was travelling through the rich cotton district bordering the Mississippi river, I think more than half were unprovided with a habitation which I could suppose to be the ordinary residence of a man of moderate wealth. I should judge that a large majority of all the slaves in this district, were left by their owners to the nearly unlimited government of hireling overseers the greater part of the time. Some of these plantations are owned by capitalists, who reside permanently and constantly in the North or in Europe. Many are owned by wealthy Virginians and Carolinians, who reside on the "show plantations" of those States—country seats, the exhausted soil of which will scarcely produce sufficient to feed and clothe the resident slaves, whose increase is constantly removed to colonize these richer fields of the West.

A still larger number are merely occasional sojourning places of their owners, who naturally enough prefer to live, as soon as they can afford to do so, where the conveniences and luxuries belonging to a highly civilized state of society are more easily obtained than they can ever be in a country of large plantations. It is rare that a plantation of this class can have a dozen intelligent families residing within a day's ride of it. Any society that a planter enjoys on his estate must, therefore, consist in a great degree of permanent guests. Hence the name for hospitality of wealthy planters. A large plantation is necessarily a retreat from general society, and is used by its owner, I am inclined to think, in the majority of cases, in winter, as Berkshire villas and farms are in summer by rich people of New York and Boston. I have never been on a plantation numbering fifty field-hands, the owner of which was accustomed to reside steadily through the year upon it. Still I am aware that there are many such, and possibly it is a minority of them who are regularly absent with their families from their plantations during any considerable part of the year.

The summer visitors to our Northern watering places, and the European tourists, from the South, are, I judge, chiefly of the migratory, wealthy class. Such persons, it is evident, are much less influenced in their character and habits, by association with slaves, than any other at the South.

The number of the very wealthy is, of course, small, yet as the chief part of the wealth of these consists in slaves, no inconsiderable proportion of all the slaves belong to men who deputize their government in a great measure to overseers. It may be computed, from the census of 1850, that about one half the slaves of Louisiana and one third that of Mississippi, belong to estates of not less than fifty slaves each, and of these, I believe, nine-tenths live on plantations which their owners reside upon, if at all, but transiently.

The number of plantations of this class, and the proportion of those employed upon them to the whole body of negroes in the country, is, as I have said, rapidly increasing At the present prices of cotton the large grower has such advantages over the small, that the owner of a plantation of fifty slaves, favourably situated, unless he lives very recklessly, will increase in wealth so rapidly and possess such a credit that he may very soon establish or purchase other plantations, so that at his death his children may be provided for without reducing the effective force of negroes on any division of his landed estate. The excessive credit given to such planters by negro dealers and tradesmen renders this the more practicable. The higher the price of cotton the higher is that of negroes, and the higher the price of negroes the less is it in the power of men of small capital to buy them. Large plantations of course pay a much larger per centage on the capital invested in them than smaller ones; indeed the only plausible economical defence of slavery is simply an explanation of the advantages of associated labour, advantages which are possessed equally by large manufacturing establishments in which free labourers are brought together and employed in the most effective manner, and which I can see no sufficient reason for supposing could not be made available for agriculture did not the good results flowing from small holdings, on the whole, counterbalance them. If the present high price of cotton and the present scarcity of labour at the South continues, the cultivation of cotton on small plantations will by-and-by become unusual, for the same reason that hand-loom weaving has become unusual in the farm houses of Massachusetts.

But whatever advantages large plantations have, they accrue only to their owners and to the buyers of cotton; the mass of the white inhabitants are dispersed over a greater surface, discouraged and driven toward barbarism by them, and the blacks upon them, while rapidly degenerating from all that is redeeming in savage-life, are, it is to be feared, gaining little that is valuable of civilization.

In the report of the Grand Jury of Richland District, South Carolina, in eighteen hundred and fifty-four, calling for a re-establishment of the African slave trade,* it is observed: "As to the moralty of this question, it is scarcely necessary for us to allude to it; when the fact is remarked

* Richland District contains seven thousand white, and thirteen thousand slave population. The Report is published in the *Charleston Standard*, October 12th, 1854.

that the plantations of Alabama, Mississippi, Louisiana, and Texas have been and are daily settled by the removal of slaves from the more northern of the Slave States, and that in consequence of their having been raised in a more healthy climate and in most cases trained to pursuits totally different, the mortality even on the best-ordered farms is so great that in many instances the entire income is expended in the purchase of more slaves from the same source in order to replenish and keep up those plantations, while in *every case* the condition of the slave, if his life is spared, is made worse both physically and morally. * * * And if you look at the subject in a religious point of view, the contrast is equally striking, for when you remove a slave from the more northern to the more southern parts of the slaveholding States, you thereby diminish his religious opportunities."

I believe that this statement gives an exaggerated and calumnious report of the general condition of the slaves upon the plantations of the States referred to—containing, as they do, nearly one half of the whole slave population of the South—but I have not been able to resist the conviction that in the districts where cotton is now grown most profitable to the planters, the oppression and deterioration of the negro race is much more lamentable than is generally supposed by those who like myself have been constrained, by other considerations, to accept it as a duty to oppose temperately but determinately the modern policy of the South, of which this is an immediate result. Its effect on the white race, I still consider to be infinitely more deplorable.

CHAPTER VI.

SLAVERY AS A POOR-LAW SYSTEM.

In the year 1846 the Secretary of the Treasury of the United States addressed a circular of inquiries to persons engaged in various businesses throughout the country, to obtain information of the national resources. In reply to this circular, forty-eight sugar-planters, of St. Mary's Parish, Louisiana, having compared notes, made the following statement of the usual expenses of a plantation, which might be expected to produce, one year with another, one hundred hogsheads of sugar:—

Household and family expenses		$1,000
Overseer's salary		400
Food and clothing for 15 working hands, at $30 ..		450
Food and clothing for 15 old negroes and children, at $15		225
1½ per cent. on capital invested (which is about $40,000), to keep it in repair		600
		2,675
50 hogsheads sugar, at 4 cents per pound (net proceeds)	$2,000	
25 hogsheads sugar, at 3 cents per pound (net proceeds)	750	
25 hogsheads sugar, at 2 cents per pound (net proceeds)	500	
4,000 gallons of molasses, at 10 cents	400	3,650
Leaving a profit of		$975

Another gentleman furnished the following estimate of the expenses of one of the larger class of plantations, working one hundred slaves, and producing, per annum, four to five hundred hogsheads of sugar:—

Overseer	$1,500
Physician's attendance (by contract, $3 a head, of all ages)	300
Yearly repairs to engine, copper work, resetting of sugar kettles, etc., at least	900
Engineer, during grinding season	200
Pork, 50 pounds per day—say, per annum, 90 hogsheads, at $12	1,080
Hoops	80
Clothing, two full suits per annum, shoes, caps, hats, and 100 blankets, at least $15 per slave	1,500
Mules or horses, and cattle to replace, at least	500
Implements of husbandry, iron, nails, lime, etc., at least	1,000
Factor's commission, 2½ per cent.	500
	$7,560

(It should be noticed that in this estimate the working force is considered as being equal, in first-class hands, to but one-third of the whole number of slaves.)

In the report of an Agricultural Society, the work of one hand, on a well-regulated sugar-estate, is put down at the cultivation of five acres—producing 5,000 pounds of sugar, and 125 gallons of molasses; the former valued on the spot at 5½ cents per pound, and the latter at 18 cents per gallon —together, $297.50. The annual expenses, per hand, including wages paid, horses, mules, and oxen, physician's bills, etc., $105. An estate of eighty negroes annually costs $8,330. The items are as follows—Salt meat and spirits, $830; clothing, $1,200; medical attendance and medicines, $400; Indian corn, $1,090 (total for food and drink of negroes, and other live stock, $24 per head of the negroes, per annum. For clothing $15); overseer and sugar-maker's salary, $1,000; taxes $300. The capital invested in 1,200 acres of land, with its stock of slaves, horses, mules, and working oxen, is estimated at $147,200. One-third, or 400 acres, being cultivated annually in cane, it is estimated, will yield 400,000 pounds, at 5½ cents, and 10,000 gallons molasses at 18 cents—together $23,800. Deduct annual expense, as before, $8,330, an apparent profit remains of $15,470 or 10 3-7 per cent. interest on the investment. The crop upon which these estimates were based, has been considered an uncommonly fine one.

These estimates are all made by persons anxious to maintain the necessity of protection to the continued production of sugar in the United States, and who are, therefore, under strong temptation to over-estimate expenditures.

In the first statement, the cost of clothing and boarding a first-rate, hard-working man is stated to be $30 a year. A suit of winter clothing and a pair of trousers for summer, a blanket for bedding, a pair of shoes and a hat, must all at least be included under the head of clothing; and these, however poor, could not certainly cost, altogether, less than $10. For food, then, $20 a year is a large estimate, which is 5½ cents. a day. This is for the best hands; light hands are estimated at half this cost. Does the food of a first-rate labourer, anywhere in the free world, cost less? The lowest price paid by agricultural labourers in the Free States of America for board is 21 cents a day, that is, $1.50 a week; the larger part probably pay at least twice as much as this.

On most plantations, I suppose, but by no means on all, the slaves cultivate "patches," and raise poultry for themselves. The produce is nearly always sold to get money to buy tobacco and Sunday finery. But these additions to the usual allowance cannot be said to be provided for them by their masters. The labour expended in this way for themselves does not average half a day a week per slave; and many planters will not allow their slaves to cultivate patches, because it tempts them to reserve for and to expend in the night-work the strength they want employed in their service during the day, and also because the produce thus obtained is made to cover much plundering of their master's crops, and of his live stock.* The free labourer also, in addition to his board, nearly always spends something for luxuries—tobacco, fruit, and confections, to say nothing of dress and luxuries and recreations.

The fact is, that ninety-nine in a hundred of our free labourers, from choice and not from necessity—for the same provisions cost more in Louisiana than they do anywhere in the Northern States—live, in respect to food, at least four times as well as the average of the hardest-worked slaves on the Louisiana sugar-plantations. And for two or three months in the year I have elsewhere shown that these are worked with much greater severity than free labourers at the North ever are. For on no farm, and in no factory, or mine, even when double wages are paid for night-work, did I ever hear of men or women working regularly eighteen hours a day. If ever done, it is only when some accident makes it especially desirable for a few days.

I have not compared the comfort of the light hands, in which, besides the aged and children, are evidently included

* "Most persons allow their negroes to cultivate a small crop of their own. For a number of reasons the practice is a bad one. It is next to impossible to keep them from working the crop on the Sabbath. They labour at night when they should be at rest. There is no saving more than to give them the same amount; for, like all other animals, the negro is only capable of doing a certain amount of work without injury. To this point he may be worked at his regular task, and any labour beyond this is an injury to both master and slave. They will pilfer to add to what cotton or corn they have made. If they sell the crop and trade for themselves, they are apt to be cheated out of a good portion of their labour. They will have many things in their possession, under colour of purchases, which we know not whether they have oained honestly."—*Southern Cultivator.*

most of the females of the plantation, with that of factory girls and apprentices; but who of those at the North was ever expected to find board at four cents a day, and obliged to save money enough out of such an allowance to provide him or herself with clothing? But that, manifestly and beyond the smallest doubt of error (except in favour of free labour), expresses the condition of the Louisiana slave. Forty-eight of the most worthy planters of the State attest it in an official document, published by order of Congress.

There is no reason for supposing that the slaves are much, if any, better fed elsewhere than in Louisiana. I was expressly told in Virginia that I should find them better fed in Louisiana than anywhere else. In the same Report of Mr. Secretary Walker, a gentleman in South Carolina testifies that he considers that the "furnishing" (food and clothing) of "full-tasked hands" costs $15 a year.*

The United States army is generally recruited from our labouring class, and a well-conditioned and respectable labourer is not very often induced to join it. The following, taken from an advertisement, for recruits, in the *Richmond Enquirer*, shows the food provided:

"*Daily Rations.*—One and a quarter pounds of beef, one and three-sixteenths pounds of bread; and at the rate of eight quarts of beans, eight pounds of sugar, four pounds of coffee, two quarts of salt, four pounds of candles, and four pounds of soap, to every hundred rations."

From an advertisement for slaves to be hired by the year, to work on a canal, in the *Daily Georgian:*

"*Weekly Allowance.*—They will be provided with three and a half pounds of pork or bacon, and ten quarts of gourd seed corn per week, lodged in comfortable shanties, and attended by a skilful physician."

* P. W. Fraser, p. 574, Pub. Doc. VI., 1846.

The expense of boarding, clothes, taxes, and so forth, of a male slave, is estimated by Robert C. Hall, a Maryland planter, at $45 per annum; this in a climate but little milder than that of New York, and in a breeding state. By J. D. Messenger, Jerusalem, Virginia: "The usual estimate for an able-bodied labourer—three barrels of corn, and 250 pounds of well-cured bacon, seldom using beef or pork; peas and potatoes substitute about one-third the allowance of bread" (maize). By R. G. Morris, Amherst County, Va.: "Not much beef is used on our estates; bacon, however, is used much more freely, three pounds a week being the usual allowance. The quantity of milk used by slaves is frequently considerable."—*Pat. Office Report*, 1848."

On the most valuable plantation, with one exception, which I visited in the South, no meat was regularly provided for the slaves, but a meal of bacon was given them "occasionally."

Louisiana is the only State in which meat is required, by law, to be furnished the slaves. I believe the required ration is four pounds a week, with a barrel of corn (flour barrel of ears of maize) per month, and salt. (This law is a dead letter, many planters in the State making no regular provision of meat for their force.) In North Carolina the law fixes "a quart of corn per day" as the proper allowance of food for a slave. In no other States does the law define the quantity, but it is required, in general terms, to be sufficient for the health of the slave; and I have no doubt that suffering from want of food is rare. The food is everywhere, however, coarse, crude, and wanting in variety; much more so than that of our prison convicts.

Does argument, that the condition of free-labourers is, on the whole, better than that of slaves, or that simply they are generally better fed, and more comfortably provided, seem to any one to be unnecessary? Many of our newspapers, of the largest circulation, and certainly of great influence among people—probably not very reflective, but certainly not fools—take the contrary for granted, whenever it suits their purpose. The Southern newspapers, so far as I know, do so, without exception. And very few Southern writers, on any subject whatever, can get through a book, or even a business or friendly letter, to be sent North, without, in some form or other, asserting that Northern labourers might well envy the condition of the slaves. A great many Southern gentlemen—gentlemen whom I respect much for their moral character, if not for their faculties of observation—have asserted it so strongly and confidently, as to shut my mouth, and by assuring me that they had personally observed the condition of Northern labourers themselves, and really knew that I was wrong, have for a time half convinced me against my long experience. I have, since my return, received letters to the same effect: I have heard the assertion repeated by several travellers, and even by Northerners, who had resided long in the South: I have heard it publicly repeated in Tammany Hall, and elsewhere, by Northern Democrats: I have seen it in European books and journals: I have, in times past, taken its truth for granted, and repeated it myself. Such is the effect of the continued iteration of falsehood.

Since my return I have made it a subject of careful and extended inquiry. I have received reliable and unprejudiced information in the matter, or have examined personally the food, the wages, and the habits of the labourers in more than one hundred different farmers' families, in every Free State (except California), and in Canada. I have made personal observations and inquiries of the same sort in Great Britain, Germany, France, and Belgium. In Europe, where there are large landed estates, which are rented by lordly proprietors to the peasant farmers, or where land is divided into such small portions that its owners are unable to make use of the best modern labour-saving implements, the condition of the labourer, as respects food, often is as bad as that of the slave often is—never worse than that sometimes is. But in general, even in France, I do not believe it is generally or frequently worse; I believe it is, in the large majority of cases, much better than that of the majority of slaves. And as respects higher things than the necessities of life—in their intellectual, moral, and social condition, with some exceptions on large farms and large estates in England, bad as is that of the mass of European labourers, the man is a brute or a devil who, with my information, would prefer that of the American slave. As to our own labourers, in the Free States, I have already said enough for my present purpose.

But it is time to speak of the extreme cases, of which so much use has been made, in the process of destroying the confidence of the people of the United States in the freedom of trade, as applied to labour.

In the year 1855, the severest winter ever known occurred at New York, in conjunction with unprecedentedly high prices of food and fuel, extraordinary business depression, unparalleled marine disasters, and the failure of establishments employing large numbers of men and women. At the same time, there continued to arrive, daily, from five hundred to one thousand of the poorer class of European peasantry. Many of these came, expecting to find the usual demand and the usual reward for labour, and were quite unprepared to support themselves for any length of time unless they could obtain work and wages. There was consequently great distress.

We all did what we thought we could, or ought, to relieve it; and with such success, that not one single case of actual starvation is known to have occurred in a close compacted population of over a million, of which it was generally reported fifty thousand were out of employment. Those who needed charitable assistance were, in nearly every case, recent foreign immigrants, sickly people, cripples, drunkards, or knaves taking advantage of the public benevolence, to neglect to provide for themselves. Most of those who received assistance would have thrown a slave's ordinary allowance in the face of the giver, as an insult; and this often occurred with more palatable and suitable provisions. Hundreds and hundreds, to my personal knowledge, during the worst of this dreadful season, refused to work for money-wages that would have purchased them ten times the slave's ordinary allowance of the slave's ordinary food. In repeated instances, men who represented themselves to be suffering for food refused to work for a dollar a day. A labourer, employed by a neighbour of mine, on wages and board, refused to work unless he was better fed. "What's the matter," said my neighbour; "don't you have enough?" "Enough; yes, such as it is." "You have good meat, good bread, and a variety of vegetables; what do you want else?" "Why, I want pies and puddings, too, to be sure." Another labourer left another neighbour of mine, because, as he alleged, he never had any meat offered him except beef and pork; he "didn't see why he shouldn't have chickens."

And these men went to New York, and joined themselves to that army on which our Southern friends exercise their pity—of labourers out of work—of men who are supposed to envy the condition of the slave, because the "slave never dies for want of food."*

* Among the thousands of applicants for soup, and bread, and fuel, as charity, I never saw, during "the famine" in New York, one negro. Five Points Pease said to me, "The negro seems to be more provident than the Celt. The poor

In the depth of winter, a trustworthy man wrote us from Indiana :—

"Here, at Rensselaer, a good mechanic, a joiner or shoemaker, for instance—and numbers are needed here—may obtain for his labour in one week :

2 bushels of corn.	25 pounds of pork.
1 bushel of wheat.	1 good turkey.
5 pounds of sugar.	3 pounds of butter.
½ pound of tea.	1 pound of coffee.
10 pounds of beef.	1 bushel of potatoes.

and have a couple of dollars left in his pocket, to start with the next Monday morning."

The moment the ice thawed in the spring, the demand for mechanics exceeded the supply, and the workmen had the master-hand of the capitalists. In June, the following rates were willingly paid to the different classes of workmen—some of the trades being on strike for higher :—

	Dollars per Week.		Dollars per Week.
Boiler-maker	12 to 20	Harness-maker	10
Blacksmith	12 to 20	Mason	10 to 15
Baker	9 to 14	Omnibus-driver	10
Barber	7 to 10	Printer	10 to 25
Bricklayer	14 to 15	Plumber	15
Boat-builder	15	Painter (house)	15
Cooper	8 to 12	Pianoforte maker	10 to 14
Carpenter (house)	15	Shipwright	18
Confectioner	8 to 12	Ship-caulker	18
Cigar-maker	9 to 25	Ship-fastener	18
Car-driver (city cars)	10	Shoemaker	16
Car-conductor "	10½	Sign painter	25 to 30
Engineer, common	12 to 15	Sail-maker	15
Engineer, locomotive	15	Tailor	8 to 17

---

blacks always manage to keep themselves more decent and comfortable than the poor whites. They very rarely complain, or ask for charity; and I have often found them sharing their food with white people, who were too poor to provide for themselves." A great deal of falsehood is circulated and accredited about the sufferings of the free negroes at the North. Their condition is bad enough, but no worse than that of any men educated and treated as they are, must be; and it is, on an average, far better than that of the slave.

At this time I engaged a gardener, who had been boarding for a month or two in New York, and paying for his board and lodging $3 a week. I saw him at the dinner-table of his boarding house, and I knew that the table was better supplied with a variety of wholesome food, and was more attractive, than that of the majority of slaveowners with whom I have dined.

Amasa Walker, formerly Secretary of State in Massachusetts, is the authority for the following table, showing the average wages of a common (field-hand) labourer in Boston (where immigrants are constantly arriving, and where, consequently, there is often a necessity, from their ignorance and accidents, of charity, to provide for able-bodied persons), and the prices of ten different articles of sustenance, at three different periods:—

WAGES OF LABOUR AND FOOD AT BOSTON.

	1836. Wages. $1·25 per day.	1840. Wages. $1 per day.	1843. Wages. $1 per day.
	Dollars.	Dollars.	Dollars.
1 barrel flour	9·50	5·50	4·75
25 lbs. sugar, at 9c.	2·25	2·00	1·62
10 gals. molasses, 42½c. ..	4·25	2·70	1·80
100 lbs. pork	4·50	8·50	5·00
14 lbs. coffee, 12½c.	1·75	1·50	5·00
28 lbs. rice	1·25	1·00	75
1 bushel corn meal	96	65	62
1 do. rye meal	1·08	83	73
30 lbs. butter, 22c.	6·60	4·80	4·20
20 lbs. cheese, 10c.	2·00	1·60	1·40
	44·00	28·98	22·00

This shows that in 1836 it required the labour of thirty-four and a half days to pay for the commodities mentioned; while in 1840 it required only the labour of twenty-nine days, and in 1843 that of only twenty-three and a half days to pay for the same. If we compare the ordinary allowance of food given to slaves per month—as, for instance, sixteen pounds pork, one bushel corn meal, and, say one quart of molasses on an average, and a half pint of salt—with that which it is shown by this table the free labourer is usually able to obtain by a month's labour, we can estimate the comparative general comfort of each.

I am not all disposed to neglect the allegation that there is sometimes great suffering among our free labourers. Our system is by no means perfect; no one thinks it so: no one objects to its imperfections being pointed out. There was no subject so much discussed in New York that winter as the causes, political and social, which rendered us liable to have labourers, under the worst possible combination of circumstances, liable to difficulty in procuring satisfactory food.

But this difficulty, as a serious thing, is a very rare and exceptional one (I speak of the whole of the Free States): that it is so, and that our labourers are ordinarily better fed and clothed than the slaves, is evident from their demands and expectations, when they are deemed to be suffering. When any real suffering does occur, it is mainly a consequence and a punishment of their own carelessness and improvidence, and is in the nature of a remedy.

And in every respect, for the labourer, the competitive system, in its present lawless and uncertain state, is far preferable to the slave system; and any labourer, even if he were a mere sensualist and materialist, would be a fool to wish himself a slave.

One New York newspaper, having a very large circulation at the South, but a still larger at the North, in discussing this matter, last winter, fearlessly and distinctly declared—as if its readers were expected to accept the truth of the assertion at once, and without argument—that the only sufficient prevention of destitution among a labouring class was to be found in slavery; that there was always an abundance of food in the Slave States, and hinted that it might yet be necessary, as a security against famine, to extend slavery over the present Free States. This article is still being copied by the Southern papers, as testimony of an unwilling witness to the benevolence and necessity of the eternal slavery of working people.

The extracts following, from Southern papers, will show what has occurred in the slave country in the meanwhile:

"For several weeks past, we have noticed accounts of distress among the poor in some sections of the South, for the want of bread, particularly in Western Georgia, East and Middle Alabama. Over in Coosa, corn-cribs are lifted nightly; and one poor fellow (corn thief) lately got caught between the logs, and killed! It is said there are many grain-hoarders in the destitute regions, awaiting higher prices! The L—d pity the poor, for his brother man will not have any mercy upon his brother."—*Pickens Republican, Carrolton, Ala., June* 5, 1855.

"We regret that we are unable to publish the letter of Governor Winston, accompanied by a memorial to him from the citizens of a portion of Randolph county, showing a great destitution of breadstuffs in that section, and calling loudly for relief.

"The Claiborne *Southerner* says, also, that great destitution in regard to provisions of all kinds, especially corn, prevails in some portions of Perry county."—*Sunny South, Jacksonville, Ala., May* 26, 1855.

"As for wheat, the yield in Tallad̀ega, Tallapoosa, Chambers, and Macon, is better even than was anticipated. Flour is still high, but a fortnight will lower the price very materially. We think that wheat is bound to go down to $1·25 to $1·50 per bushel, though a fine article commands now $2·25.

"Having escaped famine—as we hope we have—we trust the planting community of Alabama will never again suffer themselves to be brought so closely in view of it. Their want of thrift and foresight has come remarkably near placing the whole country in an awful condition. It is only to a kind Providence that we owe a deliverance from a great calamity, which would have been clearly the result of man's short-sightedness."—*Montgomery Mail, copied in Savannah Georgian, June* 25, 1855.

"Wheat crops, however, are coming in good, above an average; but oats are entirely cut off. I am issuing commissary, this week, for the county, to distribute some corn bought by the Commissioner's Court, for the destitute of our county; and could you have witnessed the applicants, and heard their stories, for the last few days, I am satisfied you could draw a picture that would excite the sympathy of the most selfish heart. I am free to confess that I had no idea of the destitution that prevails in this county. Why, sir, what do you think of a widow and her children living, for three days and nights, on boiled weeds, called pepper grass?—yet such, I am credibly informed, has been the case in Chambers County." —*From a letter to the editor of the Montgomery (Ala.) Journal, from Hon. Samuel Pearson, Judge of Probate, for Chambers County, Alabama.*

"FAMINE IN UPPER GEORGIA.—We have sad news from the north part of Georgia. The *Dalton Times* says that many people are without corn, or means to procure any. And, besides, there is none for sale. In some neighbourhoods, a bushel could not be obtained for love or money. Poor men are offering to work for a peck of corn a day. If they plead, 'Our children will starve,' they are answered, 'So will mine, if I part with the little I have.' Horses and mules are turned out into the woods, to wait for grass, or starve. The consequence is, that those who have land can only plant what they can with the hoe—they cannot plough. It is seriously argued that, unless assisted soon, many of the poor class of that section will perish."—*California Paper.**

No approach to anything like such a state of things as those extracts portray (which extended over parts of three agricultural States) ever occurred, I am sure, in any rural district of the Free States. Even in our most thickly-peopled manufacturing districts, to which the staple articles of food are brought from far-distant regions, assistance from abroad, to sustain the poor, has never been asked; nor do I believe the poor have ever been reduced, for weeks together, to a diet of corn. But this famine at the South occurred in a region where most productive land can be purchased for from three to seven dollars an acre; where maize and wheat

* In the obscure country papers of Northern Alabama and Georgia, and Western South Carolina, I have seen many more descriptions, similar to these, of this famine; but I cannot now lay my hand on them. These I have by accident, not having taken pains to collect them for this purpose. In a district of the Slave States, where it is boasted that more than a hundred bushels of maize to the acre has been raised, and where not one out of five hundred of the people is engaged in any other than agricultural industry, I have myself bought maize, which had been raised by free labour, in Ohio, at two dollars a bushel.

grow kindly; where cattle, sheep, and hogs, may be pastured over thousands of acres, at no rent; where fuel has no value, and at a season of the year when clothing or shelter is hardly necessary to comfort.

It is a remarkable fact that this frightful famine, unprecedented in North America, was scarcely noticed, in the smallest way, by any of those Southern papers which, in the ordinary course of things, ever reach the North. In the Charleston, Savannah, and Mobile papers, received at our commercial reading-rooms, I have not been able to find any mention of it at all—a single, short, second-hand paragraph in a market report excepted. But these journals had columns of reports from our papers, and from their private correspondents, as well as pages of comment, on the distress of the labourers in New York City the preceding winter.

In 1837, the year of repudiation in Mississippi, a New Orleans editor describes the effect of the money-pressure upon the planters, as follows:—

"They are now left without provisions, and the means of living and using their industry for the present year. In this dilemma, planters, whose crops have been from 100 to 700 bales, find themselves forced to sacrifice many of their slaves, in order to get the common necessaries of life, for the support of themselves and the rest of their negroes. In many places, heavy planters compel their slaves to fish for the means of subsistence, rather than sell them at such ruinous rates. There are, at this moment, thousands of slaves in Mississippi, that know not where the next morsel is to come from. The master must be ruined, to save the wretches from being starved."

Absolute starvation is as rare, probably, in slavery, as in freedom; but I do not believe it is more so. An instance is just recorded in the *New Orleans Delta*. Other papers omit to notice it—as they usually do facts which it may be feared will do discredit to slavery—and even the *Delta*, as will be seen, is anxious that the responsibility of the publication should be fixed upon the coroner:

"INQUEST.—DEATH FROM NEGLECT AND STARVATION.—The body of an old negro, named Bob, belonging to Mr. S. B. Davis, was found lying dead in the woods, near Marigny Canal, on the Gentilly Road, yesterday. The coroner held an inquest; and, after hearing the evidence, the jury returned a verdict of 'Death from starvation and exposure, through neglect of his master.' It appeared from the evidence that the negro was too old to work any more, being nearly seventy; and so they drove him forth into the woods to die. He had been without food for forty-eight hours, when found by Mr. Wilbank, who lives near the place, and who brought him into his premises on a wheelbarrow, gave him something to eat, and endeavoured to revive his failing energies, which had been exhausted from exposure and want of food. Every effort to save his life, however, was unavailing, and he died shortly after being brought to Mr. Wilbank's. The above statement we publish, as it was furnished us by the coroner."—*Sept.* 18, 1855.

This is the truth, then—is it not?—The slaves are generally sufficiently well-fed to be in tolerable working condition; but not as well as our free labourers generally are: slavery, in practice, affords no safety against occasional suffering for want of food among labourers, or even against their starvation any more than the competitive system; while it withholds all encouragement from the labourer to improve his faculties and his skill; destroys his self-respect; misdirects and debases his ambition, and withholds all the natural motives which lead men to endeavour to increase their capacity of usefulness to their country and the world. To all this, the *occasional suffering* of the free labourer is favourable, on the whole. The occasional suffering of the slave has no such advantage. To deceit, indolence, malevolence, and thievery, it may lead, as may the suffering—though it is much less likely to—of the free labourer; but to industry, cultivation of skill, perseverance, economy, and virtuous habits, neither the suffering, nor the dread of it as a possibility, ever can lead the slave, as it generally does the free labourer, unless it is by inducing him to run away.

CHAPTER VII.

COTTON SUPPLY AND WHITE LABOUR IN THE COTTON CLIMATE.

Mr. Russell,* although he clearly sees the calamity of the South, fully accepts the cotton planter's opinion, that, after all, the system of slavery is a necessary evil attending upon the great good of cheap cotton. He says: "If the climate had admitted of the growing of cotton on the banks of the Ohio, we should have seen that slavery possessed as great advantages over free labour in the raising of this crop as it does in that of tobacco." If this is so, it is important that it should be well understood why it is so as precisely as possible.

In his Notes on Maryland, Mr. Russell (p. 141) says: "Though a slave may, under very favourable circumstances, cultivate twenty acres of wheat and twenty acres of Indian corn, he cannot manage more than two acres of tobacco. The cultivation of tobacco, therefore, admits of the concentration of labour, and thus the superintendence and management of a tobacco plantation will be more perfect and less expensive than a corn one." And this is the only explanation he offers of the supposed advantage of slave labour in the cultivation of tobacco (and of consequence in the cultivation of cotton). The chief expense of raising Indian corn is chargeable to planting and tillage, that of tobacco to the seedbed, the transplanting and nursing of the young plants (which is precisely similar to the same operation with cabbages), the hand-weeding, the

* "North America, its Agriculture and Climate," by Robert Russell, Kilwhiss. Edinburgh: Adam and Charles Black, 1857.

hoeing after the plant has "become too large to work without injuring the leaves by the swingle-trees of a horse plough;"* "the topping," "the suckering," the selection and removal of valueless leaves, and "the worming," all of them, except hoeing, being operations which can be performed by children and child-bearing women, as they usually are in Virginia.†

The chief expense of raising cotton, as of Indian corn, is that of planting and tillage. The principal difference between the method of tillage of cotton and that of Indian corn is occasioned by the greater luxuriance of weeds in the Southern climate and the slow growth of the cotton plant in its early stages, which obliges the tillage process to be more carefully and more frequently performed. For this reason, the area of cotton cultivated by each labourer is less than of corn. The area of corn land to a hand is much over-estimated by Mr. Russell. On the other hand, the only mention he makes of the area of cotton land to a hand (being the statement of a negro) would lead to the conclusion that it is often not over three acres, and that five acres is extraordinary. Mr. De Bow says,‡ in an argument to prove that the average production per acre is over-estimated, "In the real cotton region, perhaps the average number of acres per hand is ten."

Mr. Russell observes of worming and leafing tobacco: "These operations can be done as well, and consequently as cheaply, by women and children as by full-grown men." (Page 142.) After reading Mr. Russell's views, I placed myself, through the kindness of Governor Chase, in communication with the Ohio Board of Agriculture, from which I have obtained elaborate statistics, together with reports on the subject from twelve Presidents or Secretaries of County Agricultural Societies, as well as from others. These gentle-

* De Bow, vol. iii., p. 342. † See De Bow's "Resources," art. Tobacco.
‡ Vol. i., p. 175, "Resources."

men generally testify that a certain amount of labour given to corn will be much better repaid than if given to tobacco. "Men are worth too much for growing corn to be employed in strolling through tobacco fields, looking for worms, and even women can, as our farmers think, find something better to do about the house." Children, too, are thought to be, and doubtless are, better employed at school in preparing themselves for more profitable duties, and this is probably the chief reason why coarse tobacco* cannot be cultivated with as much profit as corn in Ohio, while the want of intelligent, self-interested labour, is the reason why the corn-field, among the tall broad blades of which a man will work during much of its growth in comparative obscurity, cannot be cultivated with as much profit on soils of the same quality in Virginia as in Ohio. In short, a class of labourers, who are good for nothing else, and who, but for this, would be an intolerable burden upon those who are obliged to support them, can be put to some use in raising tobacco, and, therefore, coarse tobacco continues to be cultivated in some of the principal slaveholding counties of Virginia. But this class of labourers is of no more value in cotton culture than in corn culture. Mr. De Bow says: "The South-west, the great cotton region, is newly settled, and the number of children, out of all proportion, less than in negroes [regions ?] peopled by a natural growth of population.† Weak women and children are, in fact, not at all wanted for

* In my Notes on Eastern Virginia, it was mentioned that a tobacco planter informed me that he could not raise the finer sorts of tobacco with profit, because he could not make his slaves take pains enough with it; and in certain localities in Ohio, having a favourable soil for the production of fine or high-priced tobacco, it appears that free labour is engaged more profitably in the cultivation of tobacco than in the cultivation of corn. It is the same in parts of Connecticut and of Massachusetts. Except in these limited districts, however, it is found that the labour of Ohio, as of Connecticut and Massachusetts, is more profitably directed to the cultivation of Indian corn and other crops than of tobacco.

† "Resources," p. 175.

cotton culture, the cotton planter's inquiry being exclusively for 'prime boys,' or 'A 1 field-hands.'"

Thus in every way cotton culture more resembles corn culture than it does tobacco culture. The production of corn is larger in the aggregate, is considerably larger per man engaged in its cultivation, and is far larger per acre in Ohio than in Virginia.* I should, therefore, be inclined to reverse Mr. Russell's statement, and to say that if the climate had admitted of the growing of cotton on both banks of the Ohio, we should have seen that free-labour possessed as great advantages over slavery in the cultivation of cotton as of corn.

Mr. Russell echoes also the opinion, which every cotton planter is in the habit of urging, that the production of cotton would have been comparatively insignificant in the United States if it had not been for slave labour. He likewise restricts the available cotton region within much narrower limits than are usually given to it, and holds that the slave population must soon in a great measure be concentrated within it. As these conclusions of a scientific traveller un-

* Virginia, with 10,360,135 acres of improved land, produced, according to the last census returns,

35,254,319 bushels of corn,
56,803,227 pounds of tobacco.

Ohio, with 9,851,493 acres of improved land, produced

59,078,695 bushels of corn,
10,454,449 pounds of tobacco.

The aggregate value of these two products alone, at present New York prices, would be

Ohio. $5,127,223,565
Virginia. . . . $3,564,639,385

Actual crops per acre, on the average, as returned by the marshals for 1849-50 (Census Compilation, p. 178):

	Corn.	Tobacco.
Ohio . . .	36 bushels . . .	730 pounds.
Virginia .	18 ,, . . .	630 ,,

intentionally support a view which has been lately systematically pressed upon manufacturers and merchants both in Great Britain and the Free States, namely, that the perpetuation of slavery in its present form is necessary to the perpetuation of a liberal cotton supply, and also that the limit of production in the United States must be rapidly approaching, and consequently that the tendency of prices must be rapidly upward, the grounds on which they rest should be carefully scrutinized.

Mr. Russell says, in a paragraph succeeding the words just now quoted with regard to the supposed advantages of slave labour in raising tobacco:

> "The rich upland soils of the cotton region afford a profitable investment for capital, even when cultivated by slaves left to the care of overseers. The natural increase of the slaves, from two to six per cent., goes far to pay the interest of the money invested in them. The richest soils of the uplands are invariably occupied by the largest plantations, and the alluvial lands on the banks of the western rivers are so unhealthy for white labourers that the slaveowners occupy them without competition. Thus the banks of the western rivers are now becoming the great cotton-producing districts. Taking these facts into consideration, it appears that the quantity of cotton which would have been raised without slave labour in the United States would have been comparatively insignificant to the present supply."*

The advantages of slave-labour for cotton culture seem from this to have been predicated mainly upon the unwholesomeness to free or white labourers of the best cotton lands, especially of the alluvial lands on the banks of rivers. Reference is made particularly to "the county of Washington, Mississippi State [which] lies between the Yazoo and Mississippi rivers. * * * The soil is chiefly alluvial, though a considerable portion is swampy and liable to be flooded."†

* "North America, its Climate," etc., p. 286.

† De Bow's "Resources." See "Seaboard Slave States," pp. 463 and 586, fo further southern evidence.

Mr. Russell evidently considers that it is to this swampy condition, and to stagnant water left by floods, that the supposed insalubrity of this region is to be chiefly attributed. How would he explain, then, the undoubted salubrity of the bottom lands in Louisiana, which are lower than those of the Mississippi, exposed to a more southern sun, more swampy, and which were originally much more frequently flooded, but having been dyked and "leveed," are now inhabited by a white population of several hundred thousand. I will refer to the evidence of an expert:—

"Heat, moisture, animal and vegetable matter, are said to be the elements which produce the diseases of the South, and yet the testimony in proof of the health of the banks of the lower portion of the Mississippi river is too strong to be doubted. Here is a perfectly flat alluvial country, covering several hundred miles, interspersed with interminable lakes, lagunes, and jungles, and still we are informed by Dr. Cartwright, one of the most acute observers of the day, that this country is exempt from miasmatic disorders, and is extremely healthy. His assertion has been confirmed to me by hundreds of witnesses; and we know, from our own observation, that the population presents a robust and healthy appearance." (Statistics are given to prove a greater average length of life for the white race in the South than in the North.)—ESSAY ON THE VALUE OF LIFE IN THE SOUTH, by Dr. J. C. Nott, of Alabama.

To the same effect is the testimony of a far more trustworthy scientific observer, Darby, the surveyor and geographer of Louisiana:—

"Between the 9th of July, 1805, to the 7th of May, 1815, incredible as it may appear to many persons, I actually travelled [in Southern Alabama, Mississippi, Louisiana, and, what is now, Texas] twenty thousand miles, mostly on foot. During the whole of this period, I was not confined one month, put all my indispositions together, and not one moment by any malady attributable to climate. I have slept in the open air for weeks together, in the hottest summer nights, and endured this mode of life in the most matted woods, perhaps, in the world. During my survey of the Sabine river, myself, and the men that attended me, existed, for several weeks, on flesh and fish, without bread or salt, and without sickness of any kind. That nine-tenths of the distempers of warm climate may be guarded against, I do not harbour a single doubt.

"If climate operates extensively upon the actions of human beings, it is principally their amusements that are regulated by proximity to the tropics. Dancing might be called the principal amusement of both sexes, in Louisiana. Beholding the airy sweep of a Creole dance, the length of time that an assembly will preserve in the sport, at any season of the year, cold or warm, indolence would be the last charge that candour could lodge against such a people."*

"Copying from Montesquieu," elsewhere says Mr. Darby, himself a slaveholder, "climate has been called upon to account for stains on the human character, imprinted by the hand of political mistake. No country where Negro Slavery is established but must have parts in the wounds committed on nature and justice."

The unacclimated whites on the sea coast and on the river and bayou banks of the low country, between which and the sea coast there is much inter-communication, unquestionably suffer much from certain epidemic, contagious, and infectious pestilences. This, however, only renders the fact that dense settlements of whites have been firmly established upon them, and that they are remarkably exempt from miasmatic disease, one of more value in evidence of the practicability of white occupation of the upper bottom lands. There are grounds for doubting the common opinion that the negroes at the South suffer less from local causes of disease than whites. (See

* A writer in "Household Words," speaking of the "popular fallacy that a man cannot do a hard day's work in the climate of India," says:—

"I have seen as hard work, real bone and muscle work, done by citizens of the United Kingdom in the East, as was ever achieved in the cold West, and all upon rice and curry—not curry and rice—in which the rice has formed the real meal, and the curry has merely helped to give it a relish, as a sort of substantial Kitchener's zest, or Harvey's sauce. I have seen, likewise, Moormen, Malabars, and others of the Indian labouring classes, perform a day's work that would terrify a London porter, or coal-whipper, or a country navvy, or ploughman; and under the direct rays of a sun that has made a wooden platform too hot to stand on in thin shoes, without literally dancing with pain, as I have done many a day, within six degrees of the line."

"Seaboard Slave States," p. 647.) They may be less subject to epidemic and infectious diseases, and yet be more liable to other fatal disorders, due to such influences, than whites. The worst climate for unacclimated whites of any town in the United States is that of Charleston. (This, together with the whole of the rice coast, is clearly exceptional in respect of salubrity for whites.) It happens fortunately that the most trustworthy and complete vital statistics of the South are those of Charleston. Dr. Nott, commenting upon these, says that the average mortality, during six years, has been, of blacks alone, one in forty-four; of whites alone, one in fifty-eight. "This mortality" he adds, "is perhaps not an unfair test, as the population during the last six years has been undisturbed by emigration, and acclimated in greater proportion than at any previous period." If the comparison had been made between native negroes and native or acclimated whites alone, it would doubtless show the climate to be still more unfavourable to negroes.*

Upon the very district to which Mr. Russell refers, as offering an extreme case, I quote the testimony of a Mississippi statistician:—

"The cotton-planters, deserting the rolling land, are fast pouring in upon the 'swamp.' Indeed, the impression of the sickliness of the South

* Dr. Barton, of New Orleans, in a paper read before the Academy of Science of that city, says: "The class of diseases most fatal in the South are mainly of a '*preventible* nature,' and embraces fevers and intestinal diseases, and depends mostly on conditions under the control of man, as drainage, the removal of forest growth—of personal exposure and private hygiene. The climate further north is too rigid the greater part of the year for personal exposure to the open air, so essential to the enjoyment of health, and when the extremes are great and rapid, another class of maladies predominate—the pulmonary, as well as others arising from crowding, defective ventilation and filth—exacting preventive measures from the public authorities with as much urgency as the worst fevers of the South."

generally has been rapidly losing ground [*i. e.* among the whites of the South] for some years back, and that blessing [health] is now sought with as much confidence on the swamp lands of the Yazoo and the Mississippi as among the hills and plains of Carolina and Virginia."—(De Bow's "Resources," vol. ii., p. 43.)

Dr. Barton says:—

"In another place I have shown that the direct temperature of the sun is not near so great in the South (during the summer) as it is at the North. I shall recur to this hereafter. In fact, the climate is much more endurable, all the year round, with our refreshing breezes, and particularly in some of the more elevated parts of it, or within one hundred miles of the coast, both in and out of doors, at the South than at the North, which shows most conspicuously the folly of the annual summer migrations, to pursue an imaginary mildness of temperature, which is left at home."

Mr. Russell assumes that slave labour tends, as a matter of course, to the formation of large plantations, and that free labour can only be applied to agricultural operations of a limited scope. Of slaves, he says: "Their numbers admit of that organization and division of labour which renders slavery so serviceable in the culture of cotton." I find no reason given for this assertion, except that he did not himself see any large agricultural enterprises conducted with free labour, while he did see many plantations of fifty to one hundred slave hands. The explanation, in my judgment, is that the cultivation of the crops generally grown in the Free States has hitherto been most profitable when conducted on the "small holding" system;* the cultivation of cotton is, as a general rule, more profitable upon the "large holding" system.† Undoubtedly there is a point below which it becomes disadvantageous to

* Indian corn has been considered an exception, and there are probably larger corn fields in Indiana than cotton fields in Mississippi.

† I believe that plantations or agricultural operations devoted to a single crop are, as a general rule, profitable in proportion to their size in the Free States, unless, indeed, the market is a small one and easily overstocked, which is never the case with the cotton market.

reduce the farm in the Free States, and this varies with local circumstances. There is equally a limit beyond which it is acknowledged to be unprofitable to enlarge the body of slaves engaged in cotton cultivation under one head. If cotton were to be cultivated by free labour, it is probable that this number would be somewhat reduced. I have no doubt that the number of men on each plantation, in any case, would, on an average, much nearer approach that which would be most economical, in a free-labour cotton-growing country than in a country on which the whole dependence of each proprietor was on slaves. Is not this conclusion irresistible when we consider that the planter, if he needs an additional slave hand to those he possesses, even if temporarily, for harvesting his crop, must, in most cases, employ at least a thousand dollars of capital to obtain it?

Mr. Russell has himself observed that—

> "The quantity of cotton which can be produced on a [slave-worked] plantation is limited by the number of hands it can turn into the field during the picking or harvesting of the crop. Like some other agricultural operations, this is a simple one, though it does not admit of being done by machinery, as a certain amount of intelligence must direct the hand."

The same is true of a wheat farm, except that much more can be done by machinery, and consequently the extraordinary demand for labour at the wheat harvest is much less than it is on a cotton plantation. I have several times been on the Mississippi plantation during picking time, and have seen how everything black, with hands, was then pressed into severe service; but, after all, I have often seen negroes breaking down, in preparation for re-ploughing the ground for the next crop, acres of cotton plants, upon which what appeared to me to be a tolerable crop of wool still hung, because it had been impossible to pick it. I have seen what was confessed to be many hundred dollars' worth of cotton thus wasted on a single Red-River plantation. I much doubt if the harvest demand of the principal cotton districts of Mississippi adds five per cent. to their field-hand force. In Ohio, there is a far larger population ordinarily engaged in other pursuits which responds to the harvest demand. A temporary increase of the number of agricultural labourers thus occurs of not less than forty per cent. during the most critical period.

An analogous case is that of the vintage in the wine districts of France. In some of these the "small holding" or *parcellement* system is carried to an unfortunate extreme under the influence of what are, perhaps, injudicious laws. The parcels of land are much smaller, on an average, than the smallest class of farms ordinarily cultivated by free labour in the United States. But can any one suppose that if the slave labour system, as it exists in the United States, prevailed in those districts, that is to say, if the proprietors depended solely on themselves, their families, and their regular servants, as those of Mississippi must, at the picking time, there would not be a disastrous falling off in the commerce of those districts? Substitute the French system, unfortunate as in some respects it is, for the Mississippi system in cotton growing, and who will doubt that the cotton supply of the United States would be greatly increased?

Hop picking and cotton picking are very similar operations. The former is the more laborious, and requires the greater skill. What would the planters of Kent do if they had no one but their regular labourers to call upon at their harvest season?

I observed this advantage of the free labour system exemplified in Western Texas, the cotton fields in the vicinity of the German village of New Braunfels having been picked, when I saw them, far closer than any I had before seen, in fact, perfectly clean, having been undoubtedly gleaned, by the poor emigrants. I was told that some mechanics made more in a day, by going into the field of a slaveowner and picking side by side with his slaves, being paid by measure, than they could earn at their regular work in a week. The degree of intelligence and of practice required to pick to advantage was found to be very slight, less, very much, than in any single operation of wheat harvesters. One woman was pointed out to me who had, in the first year she had ever seen a cotton field, picked more cotton in a day than any slave in the county.

I am reminded, as this page is about to be stereotyped, by observing the letter of a cotton planter in the New Orleans Price Current, of another disadvantage for cotton production, of slave labour, or rather of the system which slavery induces. In my volume on Texas, I stated that I was informed by a merchant that the cotton picked by the free labour of the Germans was worth from one to two cents a pound more than that picked by slaves in the same township, by reason of its greater cleanliness. From the letter referred to, I make the following extracts :—

"Dear Sir: * * * There are probably no set of men engaged in any business of life who take as little pains and care to inform themselves with regard to the character and quality of their marketable produce as the cotton-planter. Not one in a thousand knows, nor cares to know, whether the cotton he sends to market is ordinary, good ordinary, or middling. Not one in a hundred spends one hour of each day at his gin in ginning season; never sees the cotton after it is gathered, unless he happens to ride near the scaffold and looks from a distance of a hundred yards, and declares the specimen very white and clean, when, perhaps, it, on the contrary, may be very leafy and dirty. * * *

"I have often seen the hands on plantations picking cotton with sacks that would hardly hold stalks, they were so torn and full of holes; these sacks dragging on the ground and gathering up pounds of dirt at every few steps. The baskets, too, were with scarcely any bottoms remaining, having been literally worn out, the cotton lying on the ground. Indeed, some overseers do not forbid the hands emptying their cotton on the ground when their sacks are full, and they some distance from their baskets. When this cotton is taken up, some dirt must necessarily come with it. When gathering in wet weather, the hands get into their baskets with muddy feet, and thus toss in some pounds of dirt, in this way making their task easier. These things are never, or rarely, seen by the proprietor; and, consequently, when his merchant writes him that his cotton is a little dusty, he says how can it be? you are surely mistaken.

"Now, sir, for all this there is one simple, plain remedy; let the planter spend his time in ginning season at his gin; let him see every load of cotton as it comes from the field and before it goes through the gin. But, says the man of leisure, the gin is a dirty, dusty place. Yes, sir, and always will be so, until you remedy the evil by staying there yourself. You say your overseer is hired to do this dirty work. *Your overseer is after quantity, sir, and the more extra weight he gets in your cotton, the more bales he will have to brag of having made at the end of the year. Don't trust him at the gin.* * * *

"Probably he has a conditional contract with his employer: *gets so many dollars for all he makes over a certain number of bales; thus having every inducement to put up as much leaf and dirt, or, if he is one of the dishonest kind, he may add stones, if they should abound in the neighbourhood.*

"Why will not the cotton-planter take pride in his own production? The merchant prides himself on his wares; the mechanic on the work of his hands. All seem to pride themselves on the result of their labour except the cotton-planter." * * *

It cannot be admitted that the absence in the Free States of that organization and division of labour in agriculture which is found on a large slave-worked plantation is a necessity attending the use of free labour. Why should it be any more impossible to employ an army of free labourers in moving the ground with an agricultural design than with the intention of constructing a canal or a road, if it were profitable to so employ the necessary capital? A railroad contractor in one of the best cotton districts of the United States told me, that having begun his work with negroes, he was substituting Irish and German labourers for them as rapidly as possible, with great advantage (and this near midsummer). But if I were convinced with Mr. Russell upon this point, I should still be inclined to think that the advantages which are possessed in a free labour state of society equally by the great hop-planters at picking time and the *petits proprietaires* at vintage, which are also found in our own new States by the wheat farmer, and which are not found under the present system anywhere at the South, for cotton picking, would of themselves be sufficient to turn the scale in favour of the free-labour cotton grower.

The error of the assumption by Mr. Russell, that large gangs of unwilling labourers are essential or important to cotton production in the United States, is, I trust, apparent. And as to the more common and popular opinion, that the necessary labour of cotton tillage is too severe for white men in the cotton-growing climate, I repeat that I do not find the slightest weight of fact to sustain it. The necessary labour and causes of fatigue and vital exhaustion attending any part, or all, of the process of cotton culture does not compare with that of our July harvesting; it is not greater than attends the cultivation of Indian corn in the usual New England method. I have seen a weakly white woman the worse for her labour in the cotton field, but never a white man, and I have seen hundreds of them at work in cotton fields under the most unfavourable circumstances, miserable, dispirited wretches, and of weak muscle, subsisting mainly, as they do, on corn bread. Mr. De Bow estimates one hundred thousand white men now engaged in the cultivation of cotton, being one ninth of the whole cotton force (numerically) of the country.* I have just seen a commercial letter from San Antonio, which estimates that the handful of Germans in Western Texas will send ten thousand bales of cotton, the production of their own labour, to market this season. If it should prove to be but half this, it must be considered a liberal contribution to the needed supply of the year, by

* Vol. i., p. 175, "Resources."

those who, following Mr. Russell, have considered Western Texas out of the true cotton region, and taking the truth of the common planters' assertion for granted, have thought Africans, working under physical compulsion, the only means of meeting the demand which could be looked to in the future of the United States.

It would not surprise me to learn that the cultivation of cotton by the German settlers in Texas had not, after all, been as profitable as its cultivation by the planters employing slaves in the vicinity. I should attribute the superior profits of the planter, if any there be, however, not to the fitness of the climate for negro labour, and its unfitness for white labour, but to the fact that his expenses for fencing, on account of his larger fields and larger estate, are several hundred per cent. less than those of the farmer; to the fact that his expenses for tillage, having mules and ploughs and other instruments to use at the opportune moment, are less than those of the farmer, who, in many cases, cannot afford to own a single team; to the fact that he has, from experience, a better knowledge of the most successful method of cultivation; to the fact that he has a gin and a press of his own in the midst of his cotton fields, to which he can carry his wool at one transfer from the picking; by which he can put it in order for market expeditiously, and at an expense much below that falling upon the farmer, who must first store his wool, then send it to the planter's gin and press and have it prepared at the planter's convenience, paying, perhaps, exorbitantly therefor; and, finally, to the fact that the planter deals directly with the exporter, while the farmer, the whole profit of whose crop would not pay his expenses in a journey to the coast, must transfer his bale or two to the exporter through two or three middle-men, carrying it one bale at a time, to the local purchaser. Merchants will never give as good prices for small lots as for large. There are reasons for this which I need not now explain. I consider, in short, that the disadvantages of the farmer in growing cotton are of the same nature as I have before explained with those which long ago made fire-wood of hand-looms, and paupers of those who could be nothing else but hand-loom weavers, in Massachusetts. Exactly how much is gained by the application of labour with the advantage of capital and combination of numbers over its isolated application as directed by individuals without capital in a slaveholding region, I cannot estimate, but no one will doubt that it is considerable. Nevertheless, in all the cotton climate of the United States, if a white farmer has made money without slaves, it will be found that it has been, in most cases, obtained exclusively from the sale of cotton. If cotton is a plant the cultivation of which by free or white labour is especially difficult, how is it that, with the additional embarrassments arising from a lack of capital, his gains are almost exclusively derived from his cotton crop ?

But I may be asked, if combination is what is needed to make cotton a source of more general prosperity at the South, why is there no such thing as a joint-stock cotton plantation in Mississippi, as there are joint-stock cotton mills in Massachusetts, the stock in which is in large part owned by those employed in them ? I ask, in reply, how is it that the common way of obtaining breadstuffs in Northern Alabama is to sow three pecks of seed wheat on hard stubble ground, plough it under with unbroken bullocks, led with a rope, and a bull-tongue plough, and finally to garner rarely so much as six bushels from an acre ? How is it that while in Ohio the spinning-wheel and hand-loom are curiosities, and homespun would be a conspicuous and noticeable material of clothing, half the white population of Mississippi still dress in homespun, and at every second house the wheel and loom are found in operation? The same influences which condemn the majority of free labourers in Alabama to hand-looms, homespun, and three hundred pounds of wheat to the acre, as the limit of production, also condemn them to isolated labour, poor soil, poor tools, bad management, "bad luck," small crops, and small profits in cotton culture.

The following passages from a letter published in the *New York Times* present convincing evidence that it is no peculiarity of the Western Texas climate, but only the exceptional social condition with which its people are favoured, that enables free white labour to be employed in increasing the cotton production of the country. I have ascertained that the author of the letter is known to the editor of the *Times*, and is esteemed a gentleman of veracity and trustworthy judgment.

"I am well acquainted with Eastern Mississippi, south of Monroe county, and there are few settlements where my name or face is unknown in the following counties, over the greater part of which I have ridden on horseback, to wit: Loundes, Oktibleha, Choctaw, Carroll, Attalla, Winston, Noxubee, Kemper, Nashoba, Leake, Scott, Newton, Lauderdale, Clarke, Smith, and Jasper. After four years' travel through these counties, transacting business with great numbers of their inhabitants, stopping at their houses, conversing much with them, and viewing their mode of living, I unhesitatingly answer that white men can and do labour in the cotton field, from Christmas to Christmas following; and that there, as elsewhere, prudence, industry, and energy find their universal reward: success and wealth.

"In the counties of Choctaw, Winston, Nashoba, Newton, and Smith, there are very few large plantations; most of those having slaves holding but two or three, while those who own none are in the majority; yet these are all cotton-growing counties, and the staple of their cotton, poor as their lands are, is equal to the average sold in the Mobile market. Where the young farmer is enterprising and go-ahead, his cotton is usually superior. * * *

"The rich lands where white labour, even in small numbers, might be profitable, are either in the hands of large planters, or too heavily timbered for a single man. The only thing now preventing any poor white man in the South from gaining a fair competence, and even attaining wealth, is his own laziness, shiftlessness, and ignorance; for the small planters in the counties I have mentioned are deplorably ignorant. * * *

"There is one case I remember, which is to the point; the man lives in Choctaw county, and was born in Georgia. He does not own a negro, but has two boys, one sixteen, the other twelve. With the assistance of these boys, and the most imperfect agricultural implements, he made twenty-two bales of cotton, year before last, plenty of corn, and sufficient small grain for himself and family, although the season was more than ordinarily bad in his neighbourhood, while many of his neighbours, with five or six slaves, did not exceed him, and some made even less. He went on to his place without ten dollars in his pocket, gave his notes for eight hundred dollars, payable in one, two, and three years' time, with interest at six per cent. per annum, and the ensuing year he purchased another one hundred and sixty acres for seven hundred and fifty dollars, also on time. This man is, however, far more intelligent and progressive in farming than those about him; he does not plant as did his grandfather, because his father did so, but endeavours to improve, and is willing to try an experiment occasionally.

"In my own county, in Alabama, there is a woman whose husband died shortly after the crop was planted, leaving her without a single servant, and no assistance except from a little son of twelve years of age; yet she went into the field, ploughed and picked her cotton, prepared her ground for the coming crop, and raised a second crop thereon.

My conclusion, from the various evidences to which I have referred, must be a widely different one from Mr. Russell's, from that which is generally thought to prevail with our leading capitalists, merchants, and manufacturers, and from that which seems to have been accepted by the Cotton Supply Associations of Liverpool and Manchester. It is this: that there is no physical obstacle in the way of our country's supplying ten bales of cotton where it now does one. All that is necessary for this purpose is to direct to the cotton-producing region an adequate number of labourers, either black or white, or both. No amalgamation, no association on equality, no violent disruption of present relations is necessary. It is not even requisite that both black and white should work in the cotton fields. It is necessary that there should be more objects of industry, more varied enterprises, more general intelligence among the people, and especially that they should become, or should desire to become, richer, more comfortable, than they are.

The simple truth is, that even if we view in the brightest light of Fourth of July patriotism, the character of the whites of the cotton-producing region, and the condition of the slaves, we cannot help seeing that, commercially speaking, they are but in a very small part a civilized people. Undoubtedly a large number of merchants have had, at times, a profitable business in supplying civilized luxuries and conveniences to the South. The same is true of Mexico, of Turkey, of Egypt, and of Russia. Silk, cloth, and calico, shoes, gloves, and gold watches, were sold in some quantity in California, before its golden coffers were forcibly opened ten years ago. The Southern supply to commerce and the Southern demand of commerce is no more what it should be, comparing the resources of the South with those of other lands occupied by an active civilized community, than is that of any half-civilized community, than was that of California. Give the South a people moderately close settled, moderately well-informed, moderately ambitious, and moderately industrious, somewhat approaching that of Ohio, for instance, and what a business it would have! Twenty double-track railroads from the Gulf to the lakes, and twenty lines of ocean steamers, would not sufficiently meet its requirements. Who doubts, let him study the present business of Ohio, and ask upon what, in the natural resources of Ohio, or its position, could, forty years ago, a prediction of its present wealth and business have been made, of its present supply and its present demand have been made, which would compare in value with the commercial resources and advantages of position possessed to-day by any one of the Western cotton States?*

* Some one can render a service to civilization by publishing precisely what feudal rights, so called, were abolished in large parts of Germany and Hungary in 1848, and what results to the commerce of the districts affected the greater freedom and impulse to industry arising therefrom has had. If I am rightly informed, trade, in many cases, both export and import, has already much more than quadrupled in value, thousands of peasants now demanding numerous articles and being able to pay for them, which before only a few score or hundred proprietors were expected to buy.

CHAPTER VIII.

THE CONDITION AND CHARACTER OF THE PRIVILEGED CLASSES OF THE SOUTH.

Since the growth of the cotton demand has doubled the value of slave labour, and with it the pecuniary inducement to prevent negroes from taking care of themselves, hypotheses and easy methods for justifying the everlasting perpetuation of slavery have been multiplied. I have not often conversed with a planter about the condition of the slaves, that he did not soon make it evident, that a number of these were on service in his own mind, naïvely falling back from one to another, if a few inquiries about matters of fact were addressed him without obvious argumentative purpose. The beneficence of slavery is commonly urged by an exposition not only of the diet, and the dwellings, and the jollity, and the devotional eloquence of the negroes, but also by demonstrations of the high mental attainments to which individuals are already found to be arriving. Thus, there is always at hand, some negro mathematician, who is not merely held to be far in advance of the native Africans, but who beats most white men in his quickness and accuracy in calculation, and who is at the same time considered to be so thoroughly trustworthy, that he is constantly employed by his master as an accountant and collecting agent; or some negro whose reputation for ingenuity and skill in the management and repair of engines, sugar-mills, cotton-presses, or other machinery, is so well established that his services are more highly valued, throughout a considerable district, than any white man's; or some negro who really manages his owner's plantation, his agricultural judgment being deferred to, as superior to that of any overseer or planter in the county. Scarcely a plantation did I visit on which some such representative black man was not acknowledged and made a matter of boasting by the owner, who, calling attention perhaps to the expression of intelligence and mien of self-confidence which distinguished his premium specimen, would cheerfully give me a history of the known special circumstances, practically constituting a special mental feeding, by which the phenomenon was to be explained. Yet it might happen that the same planter would presently ask, pointing to the brute-like countenance of a moping field-hand, what good would freedom be to such a creature? And this would be one who had been provided from childhood with food, and shelter, and clothing, with as little consideration of his own therefor as for the air he breathed; who had not been allowed to determine for himself with whom he should associate; with what tools and to what purpose he should labour; who had had no care on account of his children; who had no need to provide for old age; who had never had need to count five-and-twenty; the highest demand upon whose faculties had been to discriminate between cotton and crop-grass, and to strike one with a hoe without hitting the other; to whose intelligence, though living in a civilized land, the pen and the press, the mail and the telegraph, had contributed nothing; who had no schooling as a boy; no higher duty as a man than to pick a given quantity of cotton between dawn and dark; and of whom, under this training and these confinements, it might well be wondered that he was found able to understand and to speak the language of human intelligence any more than a horse.

Again, one would assure me that he had witnessed in his own time an obvious advance in the quality of the slaves generally; they were more active, less stupid, employed a larger and more exact vocabulary, and were less superstitious, obstinate, and perverse in their habits of mind than when he was himself a boy; but I had only to presume that, with this rapid improvement, the negroes would soon be safely allowed to take some step toward freedom, to be assured with much more apparent confidence than before, that in the special quality which originally made the negro a slave, there had been no gain; that indeed it was constantly becoming more evident that he was naturally too deficient in forecasting capacity to be able to learn how to take civilized care of himself.

As a rule, when the beneficence of slavery is argued by Southerners, an advancing intellectual as well as moral condition of the mass of negroes is assumed, and the high attainments of individuals are pointed to as evidence of what is to be expected of the mass, if the system is not disturbed. Suggest that any modification of the system would enlarge its beneficence, however, and an exception to the general rule, as regards the single quality of providence, is at once alleged, and in such a manner, that one cannot but get the impression that, in this quality, the negro is believed to be retrograding as surely as he is advancing in everything else; and this is one method by which the unconditional perpetuation of the system, as it is, is justified. Such a justification must of course involve the supposition that in the tenth generation of an unremitted training, discipline, education, and custom in abject dependence upon a voluntary provision by others, for every wish of which the gratification is permitted, *white* men would be able, as a rule, to *gain* in the quality of providence and capacity for independent self-support.

As to the real state of the case, I find, in my own observation, no reason for doubting, what must be expected of those interested, that the general improvement of the slave is usually somewhat overrated, and his forecasting ability underrated. Measures intended to prevent a man from following his natural inclinations often have the effect of stimulating those inclinations; and I believe that the system which is designed not merely to relieve the negro from having any care for himself, but, as far as practicable, to forcibly prevent him from taking care of himself, in many particulars to which he has more or less instinctive inclination, instead of gradually suppressing this inclination, to some extent stimulates it, so that the Southern negro of to-day, however depraved in his desires, and however badly instructed, is really a man of more cunning, shrewdness, reticence, and persistence, in what he does undertake for himself, than his father was. The healthful use of these qualities (which would constitute providence) is, however, in general, successfully opposed by slavery, and, as far as the slave is concerned, nothing worse than this can be said of the system.

Admitting that, in this view, slavery is not beneficent, or is no longer beneficent, or can be but for a time beneficent to the slave, the present attitude of the South still finds a mode of justification with many minds, in the broad assertion that the negro is not of the nature of mankind, therefore cannot be a subject of inhumanity. This, of course, sweeps the field, if it does anything: thus (from the Day-Book)—

"The wide-spread delusion that Southern institutions are an evil, and their extension dangerous—the notion so prevalent at the North that there is a real antagonism, or that the system of the South is hostile to Northern interests; the weakened union sentiment, and the utter debauchment, the absolute traitorism of a portion of the Northern people, not only to the Union, but to Democratic institutions, and to the cause of civilization on this continent; all these, with the minor and most innumerable mischiefs that this mighty world-wide imposture has engendered or drags in its midst, rest upon the dogma, the single assumption, the sole elementary foundation falsehood, that a negro is a black man."

This bold ground is not as often taken at the South as by desperate bidders for Southern confidence among ourselves. I have heard Christian men, however, when pushed for a justification of the sealing up of the printed Bible, of the legal disregard of marriage, of giving power to rascally traders to forcibly separate families, and so on, refer to it as a hypothesis not at all to be scouted under such circumstances. Yet, as they did so, there stood behind their chairs, slaves, in whose veins ran more Anglo-Saxon blood than of any African race's blood, and among their other slaves, it is probable there were many descendants of Nubians, Moors, Egyptians, and Indians, all interbred with white and true negro tribes, so that it would be doubtful if there remained one single absolutely pure negro, to which animal alone their argument would strictly apply. If the right or expediency of denying the means of preparing themselves for freedom to these beings could even be held to be coexistent with the evident preponderance in them of certain qualities of form, colour, etc., the number of those who are held unjustly or inexpediently in the bonds of a perpetual slavery is already quite large in the South, and is gradually but surely increasing—is increasing much more rapidly than are their means of cultivating habits which are necessary to be cultivated, before the manliest child of white men is capable of enjoying freedom.

There are but two methods of vindicating the habit of depending on the labour of slaves for the development of wealth in the land, which appear to me, on the face of them, entitled to be treated gravely. One of these, assuming the beings held in slavery to be as yet generally incompetent to take care of themselves in a civilized manner, and dangerous to the life as well as to the wealth of the civilized people who hold them in slavery, argues that it is necessary for their humane maintenance, and to prevent them from acquiring an increase of the disposition and strength of mind and will which has always been felt a source of danger to the well-being of their masters, that all the present laws for their mental repression should be rigidly maintained. It is not to be denied, I think, that there is some ground for this assumption. Inasmuch as it is also argued that the same necessity requires that these beings, and with them all these laws, should be carried on to territory now free from them, we are called upon to give a sober consideration to the argument which is based upon it. This I shall do in the last chapter. The other method to which I refer assumes that by having a well-defined class set apart for drudging and servile labour, the remainder of a community may be preserved free from the demeaning habits and traits of character which, it is alleged, servile and menial obligations and the necessity of a constant devotion to labour are sure to fix upon those who are subject to them. Hence a peculiar advantage in morals and in manners is believed to belong to the superior class of a community so divided. I am inclined to think that there is no method of justifying slavery, which is more warmly cherished by those interested to maintain it, than this. I am sure that there is none which planters are more ready to suggest to their guests.*

* From an "*Address on Climatology*," before the Academy of Science, by Dr. Barton, of New Orleans:—

"The institution of slavery operates by contrast and comparison; it elevates the tone of the superior, adds to its refinement, allows more time to cultivate the mind, exalts the standard in morals, manners, and intellectual endowments; operates as a safety-valve for the evil disposed, leaving the upper race purer, while it really preserves from degradation, in the scale of civilization, the inferior, which we see is their uniform destiny when left to themselves. The slaves constitute essentially the lowest class, and society is immeasurably benefitted by having this

No sensible man among us shuts his eyes to the ignorance, meanness, vice, and misery which accompanies our general prosperity; no class of statesmen, no politicians or demagogues, no writers deny or ignore it. It is canvassed, published, studied, struggled with, by all honest men, and this not in our closets alone, but in our churches, our legislatures, our colleges, our newspapers, our families. We are constantly urging, constantly using means for discovering it and setting it forth plainly. We commission able men to make a business of bringing it to the light, and we publish the statistics which their labours supply as legislative documents to be circu-

---

class, which constitutes the offensive fungus—the great cancer of civilized life—a vast burthen and expense to every community, under surveillance and control; and not only so, but under direction as an efficient agent to promote the general welfare and increase the wealth of the community. The history of the world furnishes no institution under similar management, where so much good actually results to the governors and the governed as this in the Southern States of North America."

"It is by the existence of slavery, exempting so large a portion of our citizens from labour, that we have leisure for intellectual pursuits."—*Governor Hammond in South. Literary Mess.*

"Would you do a benefit to the horse or the ox, by giving him a cultivated understanding, or fine feelings? So far as the *mere labourer* has the pride, the knowledge, or the aspirations of a free man, he is unfitted for his situation, and must doubly feel its infelicity. If there are sordid, servile, and laborious offices to be performed, is it not better that there should be sordid, servile, and laborious beings to perform them?"—*Chancellor Harper; Address to South Carolina Institute.*

"The relations between the North and the South are very analogous to those which subsisted between Greece and the Roman Empire, after the subjugation of Achaia by the Consul Mummius. The dignity and energy of the Roman character, conspicuous in war and in politics, were not easily tamed and adjusted to the arts of industry and literature. The degenerate and pliant Greeks, on the contrary, excelled in the handicraft and polite professions. We learn from the vigorous invective of Juvenal, that they were the most useful and capable of servants, whether as pimps or professors of rhetoric. Obsequious, dexterous, and ready, the versatile Greeks monopolized the business of teaching, publishing, and manufacturing in the Roman Empire—allowing their masters ample leisure for the service of the State, in the Senate or in the field."—*Richmond Enquirer.*

lated at the general expense, in order that our misfortune may be as well known and as exactly comprehended as possible.

From much of all this, which so painfully and anxiously concerns us, we are told that the South is free. We are told that what we bewail is seen at the South to be the result of a mistaken social system; that the South escapes that result by slavery. We do not deny, we daily acknowledge that there are mistakes in our system; we endeavour to remedy them; and we not unfrequently have to acknowledge that in doing so, we have made some of our bad things worse. Does slavery relieve all? And without compensation? We often find, upon a thorough review, that our expedients, while they have for a time seemed to produce very valuable results, have in fact corrected one evil by creating or enhancing another. We have borrowed from Peter to pay Paul. In this way we find investigation and discussion to be constantly essential to prevent errors and mistakes from being exaggerated and persevered in unnecessarily. Thus we—our honestly humane part at least—are ever calling for facts, ever publishing, proclaiming, discussing the facts of our evil. It is only those whose selfish interest is thought by themselves to be served by negligence, who resist investigation and publication, who avoid discussion. Thus we come to habitually associate much activity of discussion, much consideration, much publication with improvement—often no doubt erroneously—still it is natural and rational that when we find no discussion of facts, no publication, no consideration, where we find general consideration and general discussion practically prevented by a forcible resistance to publication, we cannot but suspect there is something sadly needing to be made better. And this last we do find to be the case at the South, and with regard to slavery. Why, if their system has such tangible evidence of its advantages within the personal knowledge of any citizen, do they object to its alleged disadvantages being set forth for consideration, and, if it should happen, discussion? True, we may be wrong, we may be mistaken in supposing that this, our constant publication and challenge to discussion is a good thing. Perhaps if we were better, we should talk less, know less of what evil remained to be gradually grown out of. It might be found that the constant consideration of our evil had had a bad effect upon us. But I have not found that the people of the South are inclined to shut their eyes, and close their ears, and bar their imaginations to the same evil. With the misery which prevails among us, Southerners generally appear to be, indeed, more familiar than the most industrious of our home philanthropists. Great as it is, it is really over-estimated at the South—over-estimated in the aggregate at least; for it is perhaps impossible to overestimate the sufferings of individuals. South of Virginia, an intelligent man or woman is rarely met who does not maintain, with the utmost apparent confidence, that the people who do the work of the North are, on the whole, harder driven, worse fed, and more destitute of comfort than are the slaves at the South, taking an average of both classes; and this I heard assumed by gentlemen, the yearly cost of maintaining whose own slaves, according to their statement to me, would not equal the average monthly expenses of an equal number of the poorest class of labourers I have ever known at the North. I have heard it assumed by planters, who not only did not themselves enjoy, but who never imagined or aspired to a tithe of the comfort to which most journeymen mechanics whom I have known are habituated. I have heard it assumed by gentlemen, nine-tenths of whose neighbours for a hundred miles around them lived in a manner which, if witnessed at the North, would have made them objects of compassion to the majority of our day-labourers.

A gentleman coming up the Mississippi, just after a recent "Southern Commercial Convention" at Memphis, says:

"For three days I have been sitting at a table three times a day opposite four of the fire-eaters. * * * It was evident that they were sincere: for they declared to one another the belief that Providence was directing the South to recommence the importation of Africans, that she might lead the world to civilization and Christianity through its dependence upon her soil for cotton. All their conversation was consistent with this. They believed the South the centre of Christianity and the hope of the world, while they had not the slightest doubt that the large majority of the people of the North were much more to be pitied than their own negroes. Exclusive of merchants, manufacturers, lawyers, and politicians, they evidently imagined the whole population of the North to be quite similar to the poor white population of the South. Yet they had travelled in the North, it appeared. I could only conclude that their observation of northern working men had been confined to the Irish operatives of some half-finished western railroad, living in temporary shanties along the route."

I have even found that conservative men, who frankly acknowledged the many bad effects of slavery, and confessed the conviction that the Northern Slave States were ruined by it; men who expressed admiration of Cassius Clay's course, and acknowledged no little sympathy with his views, and who spoke with more contempt of their own fanatics than of the Abolitionists themselves; that such men were inclined to apologize for slavery, and for their own course in acting politically for its extension and perpetuation, by assuming certain social advantages to exist where it prevailed. "There is a higher tone in Southern society than at the North," they would say, "which is, no doubt, due to the greater leisure which slavery secures to us. There is less anxiety for wealth, consequently more honesty. This also leads to the habit of more generous living and of hospitality, which is so characteristic of the South."

I think that there is a type of character resulting in a secondary way from slavery, of which Mr. Clay is himself a noble example, which attracts admiration and affection in a rare manner. I shall explain this secondary action of slavery by-and-by. I have come to the conclusion that whatever may be the good results of slavery in the way I shall then describe, this so constantly asserted, so generally conceded, of inducing a "higher tone" of breeding, and especially of nourishing the virtue of hospitality, is chimerical.

Some reader may at once be inclined to say that the Southerners whom he has met are unquestionably better bred people than are common at the North, and that they state as their experience that they do not find that hospitality, that honesty, that guilelessness of dealing one with another among the people of the North, to which they are accustomed at home. It would remain a question, whether the Southerners whom the reader has met are of a common or an exceptional class; whether it is to slavery, or to some other circumstance, they owe their breeding; whether this other circumstance is dependent on slavery, or whether it may exist (and, if so, whether, when it does exist, it produces the same fruit) quite independently of slavery. It cannot be said that there are no gentlemen and gentlewomen of first water in free countries. A comparison, then, must be a comparison of numbers. I shall, by-and-by, offer the reader some assistance in making a comparison of this kind. And if, as we hear, free-labour society is still an experiment, and one of the results of that experiment is to be found in the low condition of portions of our community, and it is by comparing this result with the condition of the whites of the South that we must judge of the success of the experiment; it may again be a question of numbers. As to experience of hospitality, that is not a question of quantity or of quality merely. I should wish to ask the reader's Southern authorities, "Where and with whom has your experience been, North and South?" And if with a similar class and in similar circumstances, I should wish to ask further, "What do you mean by hospitality?"

I think that the error which prevails in the South, with regard to the general condition of our working people, is much strengthened by the fact, that a different standard of comfort is used by most persons at the South from that known at the North, and that used by Northern writers. People at the South are content and happy with a condition which few accept at the North unless with great complaint, or with expressions of resignation such as are the peculiar property of slaves at the South. If, reader, you had been travelling all day through a country of the highest agricultural capability, settled more than twenty years ago, and toward nightfall should be advised by a considerate stranger to ride five miles further, in order to reach the residence of Mr. Brown, because Mr. Brown, being a well-to-do man, and a right good fellow, had built an uncommonly good house, and got it well furnished, had a score of servants, and being at a distance from neighbours, was always glad to entertain a respectable stranger—after hearing this, as you continued your ride somewhat impatiently in the evening chill, what consolations would your imagination find in the prospect before you? My New England and New York experience would not forbid the hope of a private room, where I could, in the first place, wash off the dust of the road, and make some change of clothing before being admitted to a family apartment. This family room would be curtained and carpeted, and glowing softly with the light of sperm candles or a shaded lamp. When I entered it, I could expect that a couch or an arm-chair, and a fragrant cup of tea, with refined sugar, and wholesome bread of wheaten flour, leavened, would be offered me. I should think it likely that I could then have the snatch of Tannhäuser or Trovatore, which had been running faintly in my head all day, fingered clearly out to my entire satisfaction upon a pianoforte. I should then look with perfect confidence to being able to refer to Shakespeare, or Longfellow, or Dickens, if anything I had seen or thought during the day had haply led me to wish to do so. I should expect, as a matter of course, a clean, sweet bed, where I could sleep alone and undisturbed, until possibly in the morning a jug of hot water should be placed at my door, to aid the removal of a traveller's rigid beard. I should expect to draw a curtain from before a window, to lift the sash without effort, to look into a garden and fill my lungs with fragrant air; and I should be certain when I came down of a royal breakfast. A man of these circumstances in this rich country, he will be asking my opinion of his fruits. A man of his disposition cannot exist in the country without ladies, and ladies cannot exist in the country without flowers; and might I not hope for the refinement which decks even the table with them? and that the breakfast would be a meal as well as a feed—an institution of mental and moral sustenance as well as of palatable nourishment to the body? My horse I need hardly look after, if he be a sound brute;—good stables, litter, oats, hay, and water, grooming, and discretion in their use, will never be wanting in such a man's house in the country.

In what civilized region, after such advice, would such thoughts be preposterous, unless in the Slave States? Not but that such men and such houses, such family and home comforts may be found in the South. I have found them—a dozen of them, delightful homes. But then in a hundred cases where I received such advice, and heard houses and men so described, I did not find one of the things imagined above, nor anything ranging with them. In my last journey of nearly three months between the Mississippi and the Upper James River, I saw not only none of those things, received none of those attentions, but I saw and met nothing of the kind. Nine times out of ten, at least, after such a promise, I slept in a room with others, in a bed which stank, supplied with but one sheet, if with any; I washed with utensils common to the whole household; I found no garden, no flowers, no fruit, no tea, no cream, no sugar, no bread; (for corn pone—let me assert, in parenthesis, though possibly, as tastes differ, a very good thing of its kind for ostriches—is not bread: neither does even flour, salt, fat, and water, stirred together and warmed, constitute bread;) no curtains, no lifting windows (three times out of four absolutely no windows), no couch—if one reclined in the family room it was on the bare floor—for there were no carpets or mats. For all that, the house swarmed with vermin. There was no hay, no straw, no oats (but mouldy corn and leaves of maize), no discretion, no care, no honesty, at the —— there was no stable, but a log-pen; and besides this, no other out-house but a smoke-house, a corn-house, and a range of nigger houses.

In nine-tenths of the houses south of Virginia, in which I was obliged, making all reasonable endeavour to find the best, to spend the night, there were none of these things. And most of these had been recommended to me by disinterested persons on the road as being better than ordinary—houses where they "sot up for travellers and had things." From the banks of the Mississippi to the banks of James, I did not (that I remember) see, except perhaps in one or two towns, a thermometer, nor a book of Shakespeare, nor a pianoforte or sheet of music; nor the light of a carcel or other good centre-table or reading-lamp, nor an engraving or copy of any kind, of a work of art of the slightest merit. I am not speaking of what are commonly called "poor whites;" a large majority of all these houses were the residences of shareholders, a considerable proportion cotton-planters.

Those who watch the enormous export of cotton from the South, and who are accustomed to reckon up its value, as it goes forward, million on million, hundred million on hundred million, year after year, say that it is incomprehensible, if it be not incredible, that the people of the South are not rich and living in luxury unknown elsewhere. It is asking too much that such statements as I have made should be received without any explanation. I have found this to be so, and so far as the explanation appears in the attendant social phenomena of the country, I shall endeavour to set it forth, sustaining the accuracy of my report by the evidence of competent Southern witnesses.

William H. Gregg, Esq., a distinguished citizen of Charleston, South Carolina, in a report to the directors of the Graniteville Manufacturing Company of that State, describes at length the condition of the operatives of the company, whom he states to have been drawn originally "from the poor of Edgefield, Barnwell and Lexington districts." These are cotton-growing districts of South Carolina, better supplied than usual with the ordinary advantages of civilized communities. For instance, by reference to the census returns, I find that they are provided with public schools at the rate of one to less than thirty square miles, while within the State, inclusive of its several towns, there is but one public school, on an average, to every forty square miles. There are churches within these districts, one to about seventeen square miles; throughout the State, including Charleston and its other cities, one to every twenty-five square miles. In Georgia the average is one to thirty-two square miles. With the condition of the newer cotton States, in these respects, that of Edgefield,

Barnwell, and Lexington, would be found to compare still more favourably for the poor. In Lexington there is even a theological seminary. What, nevertheless, there is not generally available to the people at large, Mr. Gregg indicates by his statement of what advantages they possess who have come to Graniteville.

"When they were first brought together, the *seventy-nine* out of a hundred grown girls who could neither read nor write were a by-word around the country; that reproach has long since been removed. We have night, Sunday, and week-day schools. Singing-masters, music-teachers, writing-masters, and itinerant lecturers all find patronage in Graniteville where the people can easily earn all the necessaries of life, and are in the enjoyment of the usual luxuries of country life." * * *

"To get a steady supply of workmen, a population must be collected *which will regard themselves as a community;* and two essential elements are necessary to the building up, moral growth, and stability of such a collection of people, namely, a church and a school-house." * * *

"I can safely say that it is only necessary to make *comfortable homes* in order to procure families, that will afford labourers of the best kind. A large manufacturing establishment located anywhere in the State, away from a town and in a healthy situation, will soon collect around it a population who, however poor, with proper moral restraints thrown around them, will soon develope all the elements of good society. Self-respect and attachment to the place will soon find their way into the minds of such, while intelligence, morality, and well directed industry, *will not fail to acquire position.*"

What the poor people of Edgefield, Barnwell, and Lexington districts needed was, in the first place, to be led "to regard themselves as a community;" for this purpose the nuclei of "a church and a schoolhouse" are declared to be essential, to which must be added, such other stimulants to improvement as "singing and writing schools, itinerant lecturers," etc., etc. In short, the power of obtaining, as the result of their labour, "the necessaries of life," "the usual luxuries of country life," or, in two words, which cover and include church, school, music and lecture, as well as bread, cleanliness, luxuries and necessities, "comfortable homes." It was simply by making possible to them what before had not been possible, the essential conditions of a comfortable civilized home, that Mr. Gregg was enabled in a few years to announce, as he did, that, "from extreme poverty and want, they have become a thrifty, happy, and contented people."

The present system of American slavery, notwithstanding the enormous advantages of wealth which the cotton monopoly is supposed to offer, prevents the people at large from having "comfortable homes," in the sense intended by Mr. Gregg. For nine-tenths of the citizens, comfortable homes, as the words would be understood by the mass of citizens of the North and of England, as well as by Mr. Gregg, are, under present arrangements, out of the question.

Examine almost any rural district of the South, study its history, and this will be as evident as it was to Mr. Gregg in the case of those to which his attention was especially called. These, to be sure, contained, probably, a large proportion of very poor soil. But how is it in a district of entirely rich soil? Suppose it to be of twenty square miles, with a population of six hundred, all told, and with an ordinarily convenient access by river navigation to market. The whole of the available cotton land in this case will probably be owned by three or four men, and on these men the demand for cotton will have had, let us suppose, its full effect. Their tillage land will be comparatively well cultivated. Their houses will be comfortable, their furniture and their food luxurious. They will, moreover, not only have secured the best land on which to apply their labour, but the best brute force, the best tools, and the best machinery for ginning and pressing, all superintended by the best class of overseers. The cotton of each will be shipped at the best season, perhaps all at once, on a boat, or by trains expressly engaged at the lowest rates of freight. It will everywhere receive special attention and care, because it forms together a parcel of great value. The merchants will watch the markets closely to get the best prices for it, and when sold the cash returns to each proprietor will be enormously large. As the expenses of raising and marketing cotton are in inverse ratio to the number of hands employed, planters nearly always immediately reinvest their surplus funds in slaves; and as there is a sufficient number of large capitalists engaged in cotton-growing to make a strong competition for the limited number of slaves which the breeding States can supply, it is evident that the price of a slave will always be as high as the product of his labour, under the best management, on the most valuable land, and with every economical advantage which money can procure, will warrant.

But suppose that there are in the district besides these three or four large planters, their families and their slaves, a certain number of whites who do not own slaves. The fact of their being non-slaveholders is evidence that they are as yet without capital. In this case one of two tendencies must soon be developed. Either being stimulated by the high price of cotton they will grow industrious, will accumulate capital and purchase slaves, and owning slaves will require a larger amount of land upon which to work them than they require for their own labour alone, thus being led to buy out one of the other planters, or to move elsewhere themselves before they have acquired an established improvement of character from their prosperity; or, secondly, they will not purchase slaves, but either expend currently for their own comfort, or hoard the results of their labour. If they hoard they will acquire no increase of comfort or improvement of character on account of the demand. If they spend all their earnings, these will not be sufficient, however profitable their cotton culture may be supposed, to purchase luxuries much superior to those furnished to the slaves of the planters, because the local demand, being limited to some fifty white families, in the whole district of twenty square miles, is not enough to draw luxuries to the neighbourhood, unless they are brought by special order, and at great expense from the nearest shipping port. Nor is it possible for such a small number of whites to maintain a church or a newspaper, nor yet a school, unless it is one established by a planter, or two or three planters, and really of a private and very expensive character.

Suppose, again, another district in which either the land is generally less productive or the market less easy of access than in the last, or that both is the case. The stimulus of the cotton demand is, of course, proportionately lessened. In this case, equally with the last, the richest soils, and those most convenient to the river or the railroad, if there happens to be much choice in this respect, will assuredly be possessed by the largest capitalists, that is, the largest slaveholders, who may nevertheless be men of but moderate wealth and limited information. If so, their standard of comfort will yet be low, and their demand will consequently take effect very slowly in increasing the means of comfort, and rendering facilities for obtaining instruction more accessible to their neighbours. But suppose, notwithstanding the disadvantages of the district in its distance from market, that their sales of cotton, the sole export of the district, are very profitable, and that the demand for cotton is constantly increasing. A similar condition with regard to the chief export of a free labour community would inevitably tend to foster the intelligence and industry of a large number of people. It has this effect with only a very limited number of the inhabitants of a plantation district consisting in large part as they must of slaves. These labourers may be driven to work harder, and may be furnished with better tools for the purpose of increasing the value of cotton which is to be exchanged for the luxuries which the planter is learning to demand for himself, but it is for himself and for his family alone that these luxuries will be demanded. The wages—or means of demanding home comfort—of the workmen are not at all influenced by the cotton demand: the effect, therefore, in enlarging and cheapening the local supply of the means of home comfort will be almost inappreciable, while the impulse generated in the planter's mind is almost wholly directed toward increasing the cotton crop through the labour of his slaves alone. His demand upon the whites of the district is not materially enlarged in any way. The slave population of the district will be increased in number, and its labour more energetically directed, and soon the planters will find the soil they possess growing less productive from their increasing drafts upon it. There is plenty of rich unoccupied land to be had for a dollar an acre a few hundred miles to the West, still it is no trifling matter to move all the stock, human, equine, and bovine, and all the implements and machinery of a large plantation. Hence, at the same time, perhaps, with an importation from Virginia of purchased slaves, there will be an active demand among the slaveholders for all the remaining land in the district on which cotton can be profitably grown. Then sooner or later, and with a rapidity proportionate to the effect of the cotton demand, the white population of the district divides, one part, consisting of a few slaveholders, obtains possession of all the valuable cotton land, and monopolizes for a few white families all the advantages of the cotton demand. A second part removes with its slaves, if it possess any, from the district, while a third continues to occupy the sand hills, or sometimes perhaps takes possession of the exhausted land which has been vacated by the large planters, because they, with all their superior skill and advantages of capital, could not cultivate it longer with profit.*

The population of the district, then, will consist of the large landowners and slaveowners, who are now so few in number as to be unnoticeable either as producers or consumers; of their slaves, who are producers but not consumers (to any important extent), and of this forlorn hope of poor whites, who are, in the eyes of the commercial world, neither producers nor consumers. The contemplation from a distance of their condition, is a part of the price which is paid by those who hold slavery to be justifiable on the ground that it maintains a race of gentlemen. Some occasionally flinch for a moment, in observing it, and vainly urge that something should be done to render it less appalling. Touching their ignorance, for instance, said Governor Seabrooke of South Carolina, addressing the Legislature of that State, years ago:—

"Education has been provided by the Legislature, but for one class of the citizens of the State, which is the wealthy class. For the middle and poorer classes of society it has done nothing, since no organized system has been adopted for that purpose. You have appropriated seventy-five thousand dollars annually to free schools; but, under the present mode of applying it, that liberality is really the profusion of the prodigal, rather than the judicious generosity which confers real benefit. The few who are educated at public expense in those excellent and truly useful institu-

---

* The business committee of the South Carolina State Agricultural Society reported, Aug. 9, 1855:—

"Our old fields are enlarging, our homesteads have been decreasing fearfully in number. * * * We are not only losing some of our most energetic and useful citizens to supply the bone and sinew of other States, but we are losing our slave population, which is the true wealth of the State, our stocks of hogs, horses, mules, and cattle are diminishing in size and decreasing in number, and our purses are strained for the last cent to supply their places from the North-western States."

tions, the Arsenal and Citadel Academies [military schools], form almost the only exception to the truth of this remark. Ten years ago, twenty thousand adults, besides children, were unable to read or write, in South Carolina. Has our free-school system dispelled any of this ignorance? Are there not any reasonable fears to be entertained that the number has increased since that period?"

Since then, Governor Adams, in another message to the South Carolina Legislature, vainly urging the appointment of a superintendent of popular education, said :—

"Make, at least, this effort, and if it results in nothing—if, in consequence of insurmountable difficulties in our condition, no improvement can be made on the present system, and the poor of the land are hopelessly doomed to ignorance, poverty, and crime—you will, at least, feel conscious of having done your duty, and the public anxiety on the subject will be quieted."

It is not unnatural that there should be some anxiety with at least that portion of the public not accustomed to look at public affairs in the large way of South Carolina legislators, when the travelling agent of a religious tract society can read from his diary in a church in Charleston, such a record as this :—

"Visited sixty families, numbering two hundred and twenty-one souls over ten years of age; only twenty-three could read, and seventeen write. Forty-one families destitute of the Bible. Average of their going to church, once in seven years. Several, between thirty and forty-five years old, had heard but one or two sermons in their lives. Some grown-up youths had never heard a sermon or prayer, until my visit, and did not know of such a being as the Saviour; and boys and girls, from ten to fifteen years old, did not know who made them. All of one family rushed away when I knelt to pray, to a neighbour's, begging them to tell what I meant by it. Other families fell on their faces, instead of kneeling."*

The following is written by a gentleman, "whose name," says the editor of De Bow's "Review," "has long been illustrious for the services he has rendered to the South."

"All of you must be aware of the condition of the class of people I allude to. What progress have they made in the last hundred years, and

* De Bow's "Review," vol. xviii. p. 790.

what is to be their future condition, unless some mode of employment be devised to improve it? A noble race of people! reduced to a condition but little above the wild Indian of the forest, or the European gipsy, without education, and, in many instances, unable to procure the food necessary to develop the natural man. They seem to be the only class of people in our State who are not disposed to emigrate to other countries, while our wealthy and intelligent citizens are leaving us by scores, taking with them the treasures which have been accumulated by mercantile thrift, as well as by the growth of cotton and the consequent exhaustion of the soil."

Says Governor Hammond, also of South Carolina, in an address before the South Carolina Institute:—

"According to the best calculations which, in the absence of statistic facts, can be made, it is believed that, of the 300,000 *white* inhabitants of South Carolina, there are not less than 50,000, whose industry, such as it is, and compensated as it is, is not, in the present condition of things, and does not promise, hereafter, to be, adequate to procure them, honestly, such a support as every white person in this country is and feels himself entitled to.

"Some cannot be said to work at all. They obtain a precarious subsistence by occasional jobs, by hunting, by fishing, sometimes by plundering fields or folds, and, too often, by what is, in its effects, far worse—trading with slaves, and seducing them to plunder for their benefit."

In another part of the same address, Governor Hammond says, that " $18 or, at the most $19, will cover the whole necessary annual cost of a full supply of wholesome and palatable food, purchased in the market;" meaning, generally, in South Carolina. From a comparison of these two extracts, it will be evident that $19 per annum is high wages for the labour of one-sixth of all the white population of South Carolina—and that one-sixth exclusive of the classes not obliged to labour for their living.

South Carolina affords the fairest example of the tendency of the Southern policy, because it is the oldest cotton State, and because slavery has been longest and most strongly and completely established there. But the same laws are seen in operation leading to the same sure results everywhere. Some carefully compiled statistics of the seaboard district of Georgia will be found in Appendix (D), showing the comparative condition of the people in the rich sea-island counties, and those in their rear, the latter consisting in large proportion of poor or worn-out lands. I recapitulate here the more exact of these statistics:—

Population.—A large majority of the whole white population resides within the barren counties, of which the slave population is less than one-fourteenth that of the aggregate slave population of the whole.

Wealth.—The personal estate of the whites of these upper counties is, on an average, less than one-sixth that of the others.

Education.—As the wealthy are independent of public schools, the means of education are scarcely more available for those who are not rich in one than the other, the school-houses being, on an average, ten and a half miles apart in the less populous, thirteen and three-quarters miles apart in the more populous.

Religion.—It is widely otherwise as to churches. In the planting counties, there is a house of worship for every twenty-nine white families; in the poor white counties, one for every one hundred and sixty-two white families. Notwithstanding the fact, that to accommodate all, the latter should be six times as large, their average value is less than one-tenth that of the others; the one being eight hundred and ninety-eight dollars, the other eighty-nine dollars.

Commerce.—So wholly do the planters, in whose hands is the wealth, depend on their factors for direct supplies from without, the capital invested in trade, in the coast counties, is but thirty-seven and a half cents to each inhabitant, and in the upper counties it is but one dollar and fifty cents. From the remarks on temperance it would seem that the most of this capital must be held in the form of whiskey. One "store" in Liberty county, which I myself entered, contained, so far as I could see, nothing but casks, demijohns, decanters, a box of coffee, a case of tobacco, and some powder and lead; and I believe that nine-tenths of the stock in trade referred to in these statistics is of this character. It was mentioned to me by a gentleman who had examined this district with a commercial purpose, that, off the plantations, there was no money in the country—almost literally, no money. The dealings even of the merchants or tradesmen seemed to be entirely by barter. He believed there were many full-grown men who had never seen so much as a dollar in money in their lives.

The following is a graphic sketch by a native Georgian of the present appearance of what was once the most productive cotton land of the State:—

"The classic hut occupied a lovely spot, overshadowed by majestic hickories, towering poplars, and strong-armed oaks. The little plain on which it stood was terminated, at the distance of about fifty feet from the door, by the brow of a hill, which descended rather abruptly to a noble spring, that gushed joyously forth from among the roots of a stately beech, at its foot. The stream from this fountain scarcely burst into view, before it hid itself in the dark shade of a field of cane, which overspread the dale through which it flowed, and marked its windings, until it turned from sight, among vine-covered hills, at a distance far beyond that to which the eye could have traced it, without the help of its evergreen belt. A remark of the captain's, as we viewed this lovely country, will give the reader my apology for the minuteness of the foregoing description: 'These lands,' said he, 'will never wear out. Where they lie level, they will be just as good, fifty years hence, as they are now.' Forty-two years afterwards, I visited the spot on which he stood when he made the remark. The sun poured his whole strength upon the bald hill which once supported the sequestered school-house; many a deep-washed gully met at a sickly bog, where had gushed the limpid fountain; a dying willow rose from the soil which had nourished the venerable beech; flocks wandered among the dwarf pines, and cropped a scanty meal from the vale where the rich cane had bowed and rustled to every breeze, and all around was barren, dreary, and cheerless."*

I will quote from graver authority: Fenner's Southern Medical Reports:—

"The native soil of Middle Georgia is a rich argillaceous loam, resting on a firm clay foundation. In some of the richer counties, nearly all the lands have been cut down, and appropriated to tillage; a large maximum of which have been worn out, leaving a desolate picture for the traveller to behold. Decaying tenements, red, old hills, stripped of their native growth and virgin soil, and washed into deep gullies, with here and there patches of Bermuda grass and stunted pine shrubs, struggling for subsistence on what was once one of the richest soils in America."

Let us go on to Alabama, which was admitted as a State of the Union only so long ago as 1818.

In an address before the Chunnenuggee Horticultural Society, by Hon. C. C. Clay, Jr., reported by the author in De Bow's "Review," December, 1855, I find the following passage. I need add not a word to it to show how the political experiment of the Carolinas, and Georgia, is being repeated to the same cursed result in young Alabama. The author, it is fair to say, is devoted to the sustentation of Slavery, and would not, for the world, be suspected of favouring any scheme for arresting this havoc of wealth, further than by chemical science:—

"I can show you, with sorrow, in the older portions of Alabama, and in my native county of Madison, the sad memorials of the artless and exhausting culture of cotton. Our small planters, after taking the cream off their lands, unable to restore them by rest, manures, or otherwise, are going further west and south, in search of other virgin lands, which they may and will despoil and impoverish in like manner. *Our wealthier planters, with greater means and no more skill, are buying out their poorer neighbours, extending their plantations, and adding to their slave force. The wealthy few,*

* "Georgia Scenes," by the Rev. and Hon. Judge Longstreet, now President of the University of Mississippi. Harper's edition, p. 76.

who are able to live on smaller profits, and to give their blasted fields some rest, are thus pushing off the many, who are merely independent.

"Of the twenty millions of dollars annually realized from the sales of the cotton crop of Alabama, nearly all not expended in supporting the producers is reinvested in land and negroes. Thus the white population has decreased, and the slave increased, almost *pari passu* in several counties of our State. In 1825, Madison county cast about 3,000 votes; now she cannot cast exceeding 2,300. *In traversing that county one will discover numerous farm-houses, once the abode of industrious and intelligent freemen, now occupied by slaves, or tenantless, deserted, and dilapidated; he will observe fields, once fertile, now unfenced, abandoned, and covered with those evil harbingers—fox-tail and broom-sedge; he will see the moss growing on the mouldering walls of once thrifty villages; and will find 'one only master grasps the whole domain' that once furnished happy homes for a dozen white families. Indeed, a country in its infancy, where, fifty years ago, scarce a forest tree had been felled by the axe of the pioneer, is already exhibiting the painful signs of senility and decay, apparent in Virginia and the Carolinas; the freshness of its agricultural glory is gone; the vigour of its youth is extinct, and the spirit of desolation seems brooding over it.*"

What inducement has capital in railroads or shops or books or tools to move into districts like this, or which are to become like this? Why, rather, I shall be asked, does it not withdraw more completely? Why do not all, who are able, remove from a region so desolate? Why was not its impoverishment more complete, more simultaneous? How is it that any slaveholders yet remain? The "venerable Edmund Ruffin," president of the Virginia State Agricultural Society, shall answer:*

"The causes are not all in action at once, and in equal progress. The labours of exhausting culture, also, are necessarily suspended as each of the cultivators' fields is successively worn out. And when tillage so ceases, and any space is thus left at rest, nature immediately goes to work to recruit and replace as much as possible of the wasted fertility, until another destroyer, after many years, shall return, again to waste, and in much shorter time than before, the smaller stock of fertility so renewed. Thus the whole territory, so scourged, is not destroyed at one operation. But though these changes and partial recoveries are continually, to some extent

* Address before the South Carolina Institute.

counteracting the labours for destruction, still the latter work is in general progress. It may require (as it did in my native region) more than two hundred years, from the first settlement, to reach the lowest degradation. But that final result is not the less certainly to be produced by the continued action of the causes."

As to the extent to which the process is carried, Mr. Gregg says :*

"I think it would be within bounds to assume that the planting capital withdrawn within that period [the last twenty-five years] would, judiciously applied, have drained every acre of swamp land in South Carolina, besides resuscitating the old, worn-out land, and doubling the crops—thus more than quadrupling the productive power of the agriculture of the State."

It would be consoling to hope that this planters' capital in the new region to which it is driven were used to better results. Does the average condition of the people of western Louisiana and Texas, as I have exhibited it to the reader in a former chapter, justify such a hope? When we consider the form in which this capital exists, and the change in the mode of its investment which is accomplished when it is transferred from South Carolina, we perceive why it does not.

If we are told that the value of one hundred thousand dollars has been recently transferred from Massachusetts to a certain young township of Illinois, we reasonably infer that the people of this township will be considerably benefited thereby. We think what an excellent saw mill and grist mill, what an assortment of wares, what a good inn, what a good school, what fine breeding stock, what excellent seeds and fruit trees, what superior machinery and implements, they will be able to obtain there now; and we know that some of these or other sources of profit, convenience, and comfort to a neighbourhood, are almost certain to exist in all capital so transferred. In the capital transferred from South Caro-

* Fifth Annual Report to Directors of Graniteville Company.

lina, there is no such virtue—none of consequence. In a hundred thousand dollars of it there will not be found a single mill, nor a waggon load of "store goods;" it will hardly introduce to the neighbourhood whither it goes a single improvement, convenience, or comfort. At least ninety thousand dollars of it will consist in slaves, and if their owners go with them it is hard to see in what respect their real home comfort is greater.

We must admit, it is true, that they are generally better satisfied, else this transfer would not be so unremitting as it is. The motive is the same at the North as at the South, the prospect of a better interest from the capital, and if this did not exist it would not be transferred. Let us suppose that, at starting, the ends of the capitalist are obtained equally in both cases, that a sale of produce is made, bringing in cash twenty thousand dollars; suppose that five thousand dollars of this is used in each case for the home comfort of the owners, and that as much immediate comfort is attainable with it in the one case as in the other. What, then, is done with the fifteen thousand dollars? At the South, it goes to pay for a further transfer of slaves purchased in the East, a trifle also for new tools. At the North, nearly all of it will go to improvement of machinery of some kind, machinery of transfer or trade, if not of manufacture, to the improvement of the productive value of whatever the original capital had been invested in, much of it to the remuneration of talent, which is thus enabled to be employed for the benefit of many people other than these capitalists—for the home comfort of many people. If five thousand dollars purchased no more comfort in the one case than the other, at starting, in a few years it will purchase double as much. For the fifteen thousand dollars which has gone East in the one case to pay for more labour, will, in the other, have procured good roads and cheap transportation of comforts, or shops and machinery, and thus the cheap manufacture of comforts on the spot where they are demanded. But they who sell the reinforcement of slaves, and to whom comes the fifteen thousand dollars, do they have no increase of home comfort? Taking into consideration the gradual destruction of all the elements of home comfort which the rearing and holding of those slaves has occasioned in the district from which they are sold, it may be doubtful if, in the end, they do. Whither, then, does this capital go? The money comes to the country from those who buy cotton, and somebody must have a benefit of it. Who? Every one at the South says, when you ask this, it is the Northern merchant, who, in the end, gets it into his own hands, and it is only him and his whom it benefits. Mr. Gregg apparently believes this. He says, after the sentence last quoted from him, describing the transfer of capital to the West from South Carolina:—

"But this is not all. Let us look for a moment at the course of things among our mercantile classes. We shall not have to go much further back than twenty-five years to count up twenty-five millions of capital accumulated in Charleston, and which has left us with its enterprising owners, who have principally located in northern cities. This sum would build factories enough to spin and weave every pound of cotton made in the State, besides making railroads to intersect every portion of the up-country, giving business facilities to the remotest points."

How comes this capital, the return made by the world for the cotton of the South, to be so largely in the hands of Northern men? The true answer is, that what these get is simply their fair commercial remuneration for the trouble of transporting cotton, transporting money, transporting the total amount of home comfort, little as it is, which the South gets for its cotton, from one part of the country to the other (chiefly cotton to the coast, and goods returned instead of money from the coast to the plantations), and for the enormous risks and advances of capital which are required in dealing with the

South. Is this service over paid? If so, why do not the planters transfer capital and energy to it from the plantations? It is not so. Dispersed and costly labour makes the cost of trade or transfer enormous (as it does the cost of cotton producing). It is only when this wealth is transferred to the Free States or to Europe that it gives great results to human comfort and becomes of great value. The South, as a whole, has at present no advantage from cotton, even planters but little. The chief result of the demand for it, as far as they are concerned, is to give a fictitious value to slaves.

Throughout the South-west I found men, who either told me themselves, or of whom it was said by others, that they settled where I found them, ten or fifteen years ago, with scarcely any property beyond half a dozen negroes, who were then indeed heavily in debt, but who were now quite rich men, having from twenty to fifty negroes. Nor is this at all surprising, when it is considered that cotton costs nothing but labour, the value of the land, however rich, being too inconsiderable to be taken into account, and that the price of cotton has doubled in ten years. But in what else beside negroes were these rich men better off than when they called themselves poor? Their real comfort, unless in the sense of security against extreme want, or immunity from the necessity of personal labour to sustain life, could scarcely have been increased in the least. There was, at any rate, the same bacon and corn, the same slough of a waggon channel through the forest, the same bare walls in their dwellings, the same absence of taste and art and literature, the same distance from schools and churches and educated advisers, and—on account of the distance of tolerable mechanics, and the difficulty of moving without destruction, through such a rough country, anything elaborate or finely finished—the same make-shift furniture. There were, to be sure, ploughs and hoes, and gins and presses, and there were scores of very "likely negroes." Whoever sold such of these negroes as had been bought must have been the richer, it will be said. But let us see.

The following picture of the condition of Virginia, the great breeding ground of slaves, is drawn by the last governor of that State, Henry A. Wise. It was addressed to a Virginia audience, who testified to its truthfulness.

"You have had no commerce, no mining, no manufactures.

"You have relied alone on the single power of agriculture—and such agriculture! Your sedge-patches outshine the sun. Your inattention to your only source of wealth has scared the very bosom of mother earth. Instead of having to feed cattle on a thousand hills, you have had to chase the stump-tailed steer through the sedge-patches to procure a tough beef-steak.

"The present condition of things has existed too long in Virginia. The landlord has skinned the tenant, and the tenant has skinned the land, until all have grown poor together. I have heard a story—I will not locate it here or there—about the condition of the prosperity of our agriculture. I was told by a gentleman in Washington, not long ago, that he was travelling in a county not a hundred miles from this place, and overtook one of our citizens on horseback, with, perhaps, a bag of hay for a saddle, without stirrups, and the leading line for a bridle, and he said: 'Stranger, whose house is that?' 'It is mine,' was the reply. They came to another. Whose house is that?' 'Mine, too, stranger.' To a third: 'And whose house is that?' 'That's mine, too, stranger; but don't suppose that I'm so darned poor as to own all the land about here.'"

But more to the purpose is the following statement of "the venerable Edmund Ruffin," President of the Virginia Agricultural Society.

"A gang of slaves on a farm will increase to four times their original number in thirty or forty years. If a farmer is only able to feed and maintain his slaves, their increase in value may double the whole of his capital originally invested in farming before he closes the term of an ordinary life. But few farms are able to support this increasing expense, and also furnish the necessary supplies to the family of the owner; whence very many owners of large estates, in lands and negroes, are throughout their lives too poor to enjoy the comforts of life, or to incur the expenses necessary to improve their unprofitable farming. A man so situated may be said to be a slave to his own slaves. If the owner is industrious and frugal, he may be able to support the increasing numbers of his slaves, and to bequeath them undiminished to his children. But the income of few persons increases as fast as their slaves, and, if not, the consequence must be that some of them will be sold, that the others may be supported, and the sale of more is perhaps afterwards compelled to pay debts incurred in striving to put off that dreaded alternative. The slave at first almost starves his master, and at last is eaten by him—at least, he is exchanged for his value in food."

A large proportion of the negroes sold to these South-western planters, then, had probably been bought by traders at forced sales in the older States, sales forced by merchants who had supplied the previous owners of the negroes, and who had given them credit, not on account of the productive value of their property as then situated, but in view of its cash value for sale, that is, of the value which it would realize when applied to cotton on the new soils of the South-west.

The planters of the South-west are then, in fact, supplying the deficit of Eastern production, taking their pay almost entirely in negroes. The free West fills the deficit of the free Eastern cereal production, but takes its pay in the manufactured goods, the fish, the oil, the butter, and the importations of the free East.

Virginia planters owning twenty to forty slaves, and nominally worth as many thousand dollars, often seem to live generously; but according to Northern standards, I do not think that the comforts and advantages for a rationally happy life, which they possess, compare with those of the average of Northern farmers of half that wealth. When they do, they must be either supplying slaves for the new cotton fields or living on credit—credit based on an anticipation of supplying that market.

Of course it cannot be maintained that no one, while living at the South, is actually richer from the effects of the cotton demand. There are a great many very wealthy men at the South, and of planters, as well as land dealers, negro dealers, and general merchants, but, except in or near those towns which are, practically, colonies of free labour, having constant direct communication and intimate relationship with free countries, the wealth of these more fortunate people secures to them but a small proportion of the advantages which belong to the same nominal wealth anywhere in the Free States, while their number is so small that they must be held of no account at all in estimating the condition of the people, when it is compared with the number of those who are exceedingly destitute, and at whose expense, quite as much as at the expense of their slaves, the wealth of the richer class has been accumulated.

This cannot be rightly deemed extravagant or unjust language. I should not use it if I did not feel satisfied that it was warranted, not only by my own personal observations, but by the testimony of persons whose regard for the pride of the South, whose sympathy with wealthy planters, and whose disposition not to underrate the good results of slavery, if not more sincere than mine, is more certain not to be doubted. I quote, for instance, a single passage from the observations of Mr. Russell, an English gentleman, who, travelling with a special view of studying the agricultural condition and prospects of the country, was, nevertheless, so much limited in time that he was obliged to trust in a great degree to the observations of planters for his facts.

"In travelling through a fertile district in any of the Southern States, the appearance of things forms a great contrast to that in similar districts in the Free States. During two days' sail on the Alabama river from Mobile to Montgomery, I did not see so many houses standing together in any one spot as could be dignified with the appellation of village :* but I may possibly have passed some at night. There were many places where cotton was shipped and provisions were landed, still there were no signs of enterprise to indicate that we were in the heart of a rich cotton region. * * * The planters supply themselves directly through agents in the large towns, and comparatively little of the money drawn for the cotton crop is spent in the Southern States. Many of the planters spend their incomes by travelling with their families in the Northern States or in Europe during the summer, and a large sum is required to pay the hog-raiser in Ohio, the mule-breeder in Kentucky, and, above all, the Northern capitalists who have vast sums of money on mortgage over the estates. *Dr. Cloud, the editor of the Cotton Plant* [Alabama], assured me that after all these items are paid out of the money received for the whole cotton crop and sugar crops of the South, there did not remain one-fourth part of it to be spent in the Southern States. Hence, the Slave States soon obtain a comparatively stationary condition, and, further, the progress they make is in proportion to the increase of freemen, whose labour is rendered comparatively unproductive, seeing that the most fertile land is occupied by slaveholders."†

I questioned the agent of a large land speculation in Mississippi, a Southerner by birth, with regard to the success of small farmers. In reply he made the following statement, allowing me to take notes of it, understanding they were for publication :—

"The majority of our purchasers have been men without capital. To such we usually sell one hundred and sixty acres of land, at from two to three dollars an acre, the agreement being to pay in one, two, and three years, with six per cent. interest. It is very rare that the payments are made when due, and much the largest proportion of this class fail even to pay their interest punctually. Many fail altogether, and quit their farms in about ten years. When crops are generally good, and planters in the same neighbourhood make seven bales to a hand, poor people will not make over two bales, with their whole family. There is ——— ———, in ——— county, for instance. We sold him one hundred and sixty acres of land in 1843. He has a family of good-sized boys—young men now. For

* Mr. Russell uses the language of England. There are several collections of houses on this river bank, the inhabitants of which would consider it an insult if they should hear such a humble term as "village" applied to their pseudo towns and cities.

† "North America ; its Agriculture and Climate," p. 290.

ten years he was never able to pay his interest. He sold from two to four bales a year, but he did not get much for it, and after taking out the cost of bagging and rope, and ginning and pressing, he scarcely ever had two hundred dollars a year coming to him, of which he had to pay his store bills, chiefly for coffee and molasses, sometimes a little clothing—some years none at all. They made their own cloth mostly in the house, but bought sheeting sometimes. He has made one payment on the principal, from a sale of hogs. Almost the only poor people who have kept up to their agreement have been some near ——, since the cotton factory was started there. It is wonderful what a difference that has made, though it's but a picayune affair. People who have no negroes in this country generally raise corn enough to bread them through the year, and have hogs enough ranging in the swamps to supply them with bacon. They do not often buy anything except coffee and molasses and tobacco. They are not generally drunkards, but the men will spend all the money they may have and get gloriously drunk once or twice a year, at elections or at court time, when they go to the county town. I think that two bales of cotton a year is as much as is generally made by people who do not own negroes. They are doing well if they net over fifty dollars a year from their labour, besides supplying themselves with corn. A real smart man, who tends his crop well, and who knows how it ought to be managed, can make five bales, almost always. Five bales are worth two hundred and fifty dollars, but it's very rare that a white man makes that. They have not got the right kind of tools, and they don't know how. Their crops are never half tended. If folks generally tended their crops as some do, there would be more than twice as much cotton raised as there is."

With regard to the enlargement of estates by successful planters, having stated what were my impressions, the same gentleman replied that I was entirely right, and gave an instance, as follows, from his personal knowledge:—

"J. B. moved into —— county within my recollection. He has bought out, one after another, and mainly since 1850, more than twenty small landowners, some of them small slaveholders, and they have moved away from the vicinity. I do not know how many negroes he has now, but several hundred, certainly. His surplus must have averaged twenty thousand dollars a year for several years, and, as far as I know, the whole is expended in purchasing negroes or land. He spends no money for anything else in the county, I am sure. It is a common thing to hear a man say, 'J. B. has bought up next to me, and I shall have to quit soon.' He never gets the land alongside of a man that within two years he does not buy him out. In the last ten years I know of but one exception, and that is a man who has shot two of B.'s niggers who were stealing his corn.

This man swears he won't sell at any price, and that he will shoot any of J. B.'s niggers whom he catches coming on his place. B.'s niggers are afraid of him, and let him alone. J. B. will pay more for land than its worth to anybody else, and his negroes are such thieves that nobody can live in comfort on any place adjoining one of his. There are two other men in the county who are constantly buying up the land around there. The white population of the county is diminishing, and the trade of the place [the county town] is not so good as it was ten years ago."

The following is an extract from a letter written by a worthy farmer of Illinois, whose name and address is in my possession, and who is deemed by those who have known him for many years a sound trustworthy man :—

"What might be made of this country if the people were free, and the labourer everywhere owned the land, one may speculate upon; and when he sees the homes of Yankees who go thither often with small means, and make old worn-out places blossom and bloom, he begins to suspect that there is something in men as well as in climate.

"I now come to speak of the wealth of the people of the South-western Slave States, and, for fear I may be thought to exaggerate, I here say I will not tell the whole truth. I'll keep some back for another time. Now, men who go through on boats and cars, and stop in cities and large hotels, know nothing to what I do—I who have gone among the people of every class, I who have stayed with them hundreds of nights, Sundays and all, and gone to meetings and frolics, and travelled hours in the woods, where sometimes there was a road, and sometimes not, trying to find a place to stay over night—and, having visited more than a thousand plantations, and slept and eat in I know not how many hovels, and talked with them all, and, if I choose, can talk precisely as they do, and they wouldn't suspect I was born up North—I say, I think I ought to know something about them.

"The impression which one gets on going South is the general dilapidation or carelessness which appears, even upon some of the best plantations. The nice white houses so common at the North, even in the remotest agricultural districts, with green blinds, with clean door-yards, and well-kept shrubbery, snug barns, green meadows, and corner school-houses, are nowhere seen. The furniture of the houses is of the commonest description; and to make short work with it, I estimate that there are not decent chairs enough in the whole South to give half a set to each family. For there are to-day, and there have been for every day for more than ten years past, more than 30,000 people in Tennessee alone, who have not a foot of land or a bit of work to do. I am speaking of whites, and not of negroes at all. A bushel of corn-meal, a side of bacon, and a little coffee, will be all that a family of this class can ever expect to get beforehand, and it is often they get neither coffee nor bacon. If they have a cow, and she 'comes up,' they may have milk, but as for butter, some have heard of it, some have seen it, few have eaten it. And the fact is, many, yes, many who own from two to five slaves, are little better off. I stayed with a man who had fifteen slaves and 400 acres of land, where he had lived forty years, and his house was not worth fifty cents; what my fare was you may guess. I have seen hundreds of families living in log cabins, ten or twelve feet square, where the children run around as naked as ever they were born, and a bedstead or chair was not in the house, and never will be. I have seen the children eat wheat and grass, growing in the field. I have seen them eat dirt. I saw children here on my own place, in Southern Illinois, last year, eat dirt, they were so hungry. Southern Illinois has been a city of refuge for the poor people of the Slave States. Folks thought Humboldt told a big story when he gave an account of the clay-eating Indians of South America. Of course where poverty is so general, and where the slaves are few, the slaves cannot fare much worse than their masters. It is generally said by the people of the Slave States that they prefer corn bread, but, place the two kinds before them, and you will see which they like best. No class of people like corn bread, and no people, as a general thing, are worth much who can get nothing else.

"For the most part, the people of these regions manufacture all their every-day clothing, and their garments look as though they were made for no other purpose than to keep them warm and to cover their nakedness; beauty of colouring and propriety in fitting are little regarded. Every man who is not rich is a shoemaker. Blacksmith-shops are innumerable, and yet I have sent a boy over eighty miles from shop to shop, and then did not get a horse shod. Men call themselves gunsmiths, but they only stock guns. There are carpenters, and cabinet-makers, and chair-makers, and all this working badly with poor tools. The sum is, there is no real discipline of mind among them, no real ingenuity, no education, no comfortable houses, no good victuals, nor do they know how to cook; and when I go among them, what troubles me most is, they have *no grass, no clover, no hay.*

"And yet, as fine and well-disposed men, and as anxious to improve, are to be found in the South-western States as are to be found anywhere. They are as honest as men ever are, and they will treat a stranger the best they know how. The trouble is, the large slaveholders have got all the good land. There can be no schools, and if the son of a poor man rises above his condition there is no earthly chance for him. He can only hope to be a slave-driver, for an office is not his, or he must leave and go to a Free State. *Were there no Free States, the white people of the South would to-day be slaves.*"

I will here call upon just one more witness, whose evidence I cite at this point, not merely because, in very few words, having reference to the very heart of the planter's prosperity, it practically endorses all I have said, but for another reason which will presently appear.

First as to the non-slaveholders :—

"I am not aware that the relative number of these two classes has ever been ascertained in any of the States, but I am satisfied that the non-slaveholders far outnumber the slaveholders, perhaps by three to one.* In the more southern portion of this region ['the South-west,' of which Mississippi is the centre], the non-slaveholders possess generally but very small means, and the land which they possess is almost universally poor, and so sterile that a scanty subsistence is all that can be derived from its cultivation, and the more fertile soil, being in the hands of the slaveholders, must ever remain out of the power of those who have none. * * * And I lament to say that I have observed of late years that an evident deterioration is taking place in this part of the population, the younger portion of it being less educated, less industrious, and, in every point of view, less respectable than their ancestors."—J. O. B. De Bow, *Resources of the South and West,* vol. ii. p. 106.

Again as to the cotton-planters and slaveholders :—

"If one unacquainted with the condition of the South-west were told that the cotton-growing district alone had sold the crop for fifty million dollars for the last twenty years he would naturally conclude that this must be the richest community in the world. * * * But what would be his surprise when told that so far from living in palaces, many of these planters dwell in habitations of the most primitive construction, and these so inartificially built as to be incapable of defending the inmates from the winds and rains of heaven. That instead of any artistical improvement, this rude dwelling was surrounded by cotton fields, or probably by fields exhausted, washed into gullies, and abandoned; that instead of canals, the navigable streams remain unimproved, to the great detriment of transportation; that the common roads of the country were scarcely passable; that the edifices erected for the purposes of learning and religion were frequently built of logs and covered [roofed] with boards."—J. O. B. De Bow, *Resources of the South,* vol. ii. p. 113.

* It was not long since estimated in the Legislature of Kentucky as seven to one in that State.

Do a majority of Northern working men dwell in habitations having no more elements of comfort, even taking difference of climate into consideration, than Mr. De Bow ascribes to the residences of the slaves' owners? No Northern man can for a moment hold such an opinion. What, then, becomes of the theory by which the planters justify slavery to themselves and recommend it to us? If the ennobling luxuries which the institution of slavery secures to the "superior class," and by which it is supposed to be "qualified for the higher duties of citizenship," are, at the most, sugar, instead of molasses, in its coffee; butter, with its pone; cabbage, with its bacon, and two sheets to its bed—and the traveller who goes where I travelled, month after month, with the same experience, cannot help learning to regard these as luxuries indeed,—if "freedom from sordid and petty cares," and "leisure for intellectual pursuits," means a condition approaching in comfort that of the keeper of a light-ship on an outer bar, what is the exact value of such words as "hospitality," "generosity," and "gallantry?" What is to be understood from phrases in such common use as "high toned," "well bred," "generous," "hospitable," and so on, when used in argument to prove the beneficence of slavery and to advocate its extension?

From De Bow's Review.

"Mr. Frederick Law Olmsted, after signalizing himself by two very wordy volumes, abounding in bitterness and prejudice of every sort, and misrepresentations upon the 'Seaboard Slave States,' finding how profitable such literature is in a pecuniary point of view, and what a run is being made upon it thoughout the entire limits of abolitiondom, vouchsafes us now another volume, entitled a 'Journey through Texas, or a Saddle-trip on the South-western Frontier.' Here, again, the opportunity is too tempting to be resisted to revile and abuse the men and the society whose open hospitality he undoubtedly enjoyed, and whom we have no doubt, like every other of his tribe travelling at the South, he found it convenient at the time to flatter and approve. We have now grown accustomed to this, and it is not at all surprising that here and there it is producing its effect in some violent exhibition of feeling like that displayed by our worthy old friend Dr. Brewer, of Montgomery county, Maryland, who persistently refuses, on all occasions, to allow a Yankee even to cross his fields, or like that of John Randolph, who said in the House, 'Mr. Speaker, I would not allow one of my servants to buy as much as a toot-horn from one of these people.' * * *

"Somewhat further on, the parties rest for the night. 'For this the charge was $1.25 each person, including breakfast and horse-feed.' At the end of every page or two our tourist repeats these growlings over the enormous exactions. It is the refrain from one cover of the book to the other. What a series of martyrdoms. Could such a journey by any possibility be made 'to pay?' Perhaps, friend traveller, you have heard of the lavish hospitality of the South, and imagined that people there moved out upon the high road for the sole purpose of sharing the society which gentlemen, like yourself, could furnish, believing every arrival to be an act of special providence! When you offered to pay the woman on Red River, and 'feared she was offended by your offering her money for her hospitality,' you paid the highest compliment to the South; for heaven knows you would have had no such apprehension on the banks of the Connecticut."

I cannot but be gratified that so much importance should have been attached to my earlier volumes as to induce the Superintendent of the Census to devote to their consideration a leading article in the first economico-political review of the country; and I can feel nothing but regret that he should be obliged to attribute to an unworthy motive even those of my labours the result of which he does me the honour to designate as valuable and trustworthy. I have often had occasion to refer to Mr. De Bow, and, I believe, have always done so in a manner consistent with the respect which I feel for the class of men among whom he has had the honourable ambition to rank himself. That a man, while occupying a position which properly belongs to the most able and just-minded statistician in the country, should think it proper to write under his own name in the manner of which the above extracts are a sample, about a work which assumes to relate calmly and methodically, the result of a personal study of the condition of the people of a certain State, is a note-worthy circumstance in illustration of the present political history of our country. I cite them now, however, chiefly to show what need there is for a discussion upon which I propose to enter, myself, little further than is necessary to enable me to clearly set forth certain facts in their more important significance, the right of publishing which can hardly be denied me, in view of the insinuations made by Mr. De Bow, who in this follows what has got to be a general custom of Southern reviewers and journalists towards travellers with whose expressed judgments upon any matter observed within the slave States they differ. There are numerous homes in the South the memory of which I cherish tenderly. There are numbers of men in the South for whom I have a warm admiration, to whom I feel grateful, whose respect I wish not to lose. There are others for whom I have a quite different feeling. Of a single individual of neither class have I spoken in these two volumes, I believe, by his true name, or in such a manner that he could be recognized, or his home pointed out by any one who had not been previously familiar with it and with him, being, as a rule, careful to so far differ from the actual order of the events of my journey in narrating them, that facts of private life could not be readily localized. From this rule I do not intend now to depart further than is necessary to exhibit the whole truth of the facts to which I have referred, but since the charge of ingratitude and indelicacy is publicly made against me, as it has frequently been of late against better men on similar grounds, I propose to examine those grounds in the light of certain actual experiences of myself and others, and let it be judged whether there must always exist a peculiar moral obligation upon travellers to be mealy-mouthed as to the habits of the people of the South, either on account of hospitality or in reciprocation of the delicate reserve which, from the tenor of Mr. De Bow's remarks, it might be supposed was habitually exercised in the South with regard to the habits of their own people. These experiences shall be both special and general. What immediately follows is of the former class, but, in the end, it will be found to have a general significance.

On a hot morning in July a Northern traveller left the town of Lynchburg, the chief market-town of Virginia tobacco, and rode eastwardly towards Farmville. Suddenly taken severely ill, and no house being in sight, he turned from the road into the shade of the wood, dismounted, reclined against a sturdy trunk, took an anodyne, which he fortunately had with him, and at length found relief in sleep. Late in the day he awoke, somewhat recovered, but with a sharp headache and much debilitated. He managed, however, to mount, and rode slowly on to find a shelter for the night. In half an hour the welcome sight of an old plantation mansion greeted his eyes. There was a large court, with shade trees and shrubbery between the road and the house, and in the corner of this court, facing the road, a small warehouse or barn, in and around which were a number of negroes moving casks of tobacco. A white man, evidently their owner, was superintending their labour, and to him the traveller applied for lodging for the night.

"We don't take in strangers."

The traveller informed the planter of his illness and inability to ride further.

"You'll have to try to ride as far as the next house, sir; we don't take in travellers here," was the reply.

"Really I don't feel able. I should not like to put you to inconvenience, sir, but I am weak and faint. My horse, too, has eaten nothing since early in the morning."

"Sorry for you, but we have no accommodation for travellers here," was the only reply, and the planter stepped to the other side of a tobacco cask.

The traveller rode on. About half an hour afterwards he came in sight of another house. It was at a distance from the road, and to reach it he was obliged to let down and put up again three different sets of fence-bars. The owner was not at home, and his wife said that they were not accustomed to take in strangers. "It was not far to the next house," she added, as the traveller hesitated.

He reached, at length, the next house, which proved to be the residence of another large tobacco planter, who sat smoking in its verandah, as the traveller rode near and made his petition.

"We don't take in travellers," was again his answer.

The sick man stated his special claims to kindness, and the planter good-naturedly inquired the particulars, asked how far he had ridden, where he got his horse and his dog, whither he was bound, and so on (did not ask where he was born or what were his politics). The traveller again stated that he was ill, unable to ride further, and begged permission to remain for the night under the planter's roof, and again the planter carelessly replied that they didn't take in travellers; anon, asked how crops were looking further west, and talked of guano, the war news, and the prospect for peaches. It became dusk while the traveller lingered, and the negroes came in with their hoes over their shoulders from the fields across the road, but the planter continued chatting and smoking, not even offering the traveller a cigar, till at length the latter said, "If you really cannot keep me to-night, I must go on, sir; I cannot keep my horse much longer, I fear."

"It is not far to the next house."

"But I have already called at three houses to-night, sir."

"Well, you see, since the railroad was done, people here don't reckon to take in travellers as they once did. So few come along they don't find their account in being ready for them."

The traveller asked for a drink of water, which a negro brought in a calabash, bade good night to the planter, and rode on through the woods. Night presently set in; the road crossed a swamp and was difficult to follow, and for more than an hour he rode on—seeing no house—without stopping. Then crossing water, he deliberated whether he should not bivouac for the night where he was. He had with him a few biscuits and some dried figs. He had not eaten hitherto, hoping constantly to come to a habitation where it might happen he could get a cup of tea, of which he felt more particularly in need. He stopped, took some nourishment, the first he had tasted in fifteen hours, and taking also a little brandy, gained strength and courage to continue his journey. A bright light soon cheered him, and after a time he made his way to a large white house, in the rear of which was an old negro woman stirring the contents of a caldron which stood over the fire, by which he had been guided. The old woman had the appearance of a house servant, and he requested her to ask her master if he would favour him with lodging for the night.

"Her master did not take in travellers," she said, "besides, he was gone to bed;" and she stirred on, hardly looking at the traveller till he put his hand in his pocket, and, holding forth silver, said—

"Now, aunty, mind what I tell you. Do you go in to your master, and say to him, 'There is a gentleman outside who says he is sick, and that his horse is tired and has had nothing to eat to-day; that he is a stranger and has been benighted, don't know the roads, is not well enough to ride further, and wants to know if you won't be so kind as to let him stay here to-night.' "

"Yes, massa, I'll tell him; 'twon't do no good, though, and he'll be almighty cross."

She went in, returned after a few minutes, seized her paddle, and began stirring before she uttered the words—

"Says yer ken go on to de store, he reckon."

It was after ten o'clock when the traveller reached the next house. It stood close upon the road, and the voice of a woman answered a knock upon the door, and, in reply to the demand, said it was not far to the store, and she reckoned they accommodated travellers there.

Finally, at the store, the traveller succeeded in getting admittance, was comfortably lodged and well entertained by an amiable family. Their kindness was of such a character that he felt, in the position of an invited guest, unable to demand and unwilling to suggest any unvolunteered service. There was no indication that the house was an inn, yet the traveller's experience left him little room to hesitate to offer money, nor was there the slightest hesitation on the part of the storekeeper in naming the amount due for the entertainment he had, or in taking it.

If the reader will accept the traveller's judgment of himself, he will assume that there was nothing in his countenance, his dress, his language, or his bearing, by which he could readily be distinguished from a gentleman of Southern birth and education, and that he was not imagined to be anything else, certainly not on his first inquiry, at any one of the plantations where he was thus refused shelter.

So far as this inhospitality (for this is, I think, what even the Southern reader will be inclined to call it) needed explanation, it was supposed to be sufficiently given in the fact that the region had, by the recent construction of a railroad through it, approximated the condition of a well-settled and organized community, in which the movements of travellers are so systematized, that the business of providing for their wants, as a matter of pecuniary profit, can no longer be made a mere supplement of another business, but becomes a distinct occupation.

This, then, but a small part of the whole land being thus affected by railroads, was an exception in the South. True; but what is the rule to which this is the exception?

Mr. De Bow says, that the traveller would have had no apprehension that the offer of money for chance entertainment for the night furnished him at a house on the banks of the Connecticut, would give offence; yet in the Connecticut valley, among people having no servants, and not a tithe of the nominal wealth of the Red River planter, or of one of these Virginia planters, such has been a frequent experience of the same traveller. Nor has he ever, when calling benighted at a house, anywhere in the State of Connecticut, far from a public-house, escaped being invited with cordial frankness to enjoy such accommodation as it afforded; and this, he is fully convinced, without any thought in the majority of cases of pecuniary remuneration. In several instances a remuneration in money has been refused in a manner which conveyed a reproof of the offer of it as indelicate; and it thus happens that it was a common experience of that, of the possibility of which Mr. De Bow is unable to conceive, that led in no small degree to the hesitation upon which this very comment was made.

This simple faith in the meanness of the people of the North, and especially of New England, is no eccentricity of Mr. De Bow's. It is in accordance with the general tone of literature and of conversation at the South, that penuriousness, disingenuousness, knavish cunning, cant, cowardice, and hypocrisy are assumed to be the prevailing traits by which they are distinguished from the people of the South—not the poor people of New England from the planters of the South, but the people generally from the people generally. Not the tone of the political literature and of the lower class of the South, but of its wealthy class, very generally, really of its "better class." Mr. De Bow is himself the associate of gentlemen as well informed and as free from narrow prejudices as any at the South. No New England man, who has travelled at the South, would be surprised, indeed, if, at a table at which he were a guest, such an assumption as that of Mr. De Bow should be apparent in all the conversation, and that the gist of it should be supposed to be so well understood and generally conceded, that he could not be annoyed thereat.

I need hardly say that this reference to Mr. De Bow is continued, not for the purpose of vindicating the North any more than myself from a mistaken criticism. I wish only to demonstrate how necessary it must soon be to find other means for saving the Union than these commonplace flatteries of Southern conceit and apologies for Southern folly, to which we have not only become so accustomed ourselves, as to hardly believe our eyes when we are obliged to meet the facts (as was my own case), but by which we have so successfully imposed upon our friends, that a man like Mr. De Bow actually supposes that the common planters of the teeming and sunny South, are, as a rule, a more open-handed, liberal, and hospitable class than the hard-working farmers of the bleak and sterile hills of New England; so much so, that he feels warranted not merely in stating facts within his personal knowledge, illustrating the character of the latter and arguing the causes, but in incidentally referring to their penuriousness as a matter of proverbial contempt. Against this mistake, which,

I doubt not, is accomplishing constant mischief to our nation, I merely oppose the facts of actual experience. I wish to do so with true respect for the good sense of the South.

Presenting myself, and known only in the character of a chance traveller, most likely to be in search of health, entertainment, and information; usually taken for and treated as a Southerner, until I stated that I was not one, I journeyed nearly six months at one time (my second journey) through the South. During all this journey, I came not oftener than once a week, on an average, to public-houses, and was thus generally forced to seek lodging and sustenance at private houses. Often it was refused me; not unfrequently rudely refused. But once did I meet with what Northern readers could suppose Mr. De Bow to mean by the term (used in the same article), "free road-side hospitality." Not once with the slightest appearance of what Noah Webster defines hospitality—the "practice of receiving or entertaining strangers without reward."

Only twice, in a journey of four thousand miles, made independently of public conveyances, did I receive a night's lodging or a repast from a native Southerner, without having the exact price in money which I was expected to pay for it stated to me by those at whose hands I received it.

If what I have just narrated had been reported to me before I travelled in the manner I did in my second journey at the South, I should have had serious doubts of either the honesty or the sanity of the reporter. I know, therefore, to what I subject myself in now giving my own name to it. I could not but hesitate to do this, as one would be cautious in acknowledging that he believed himself to have seen the sea-serpent, or had discovered a new motive power. By drawing out the confidence of other travellers, who had chanced to move through the South in a manner at all similar, however, I have had the satisfaction of finding that I am not altogether solitary in my experience. Even this day I met one fresh from the South-west, to whom, after due approach, I gave the article which is the text of these observations, asking to be told how he had found it in New England and in Mississippi. He replied:

"During four winters, I have travelled for a business purpose two months each winter in Mississippi. I have generally spent the night at houses with whose inmates I had some previous acquaintance. Where I had business transactions, especially where debts were due to me, which could not be paid, I sometimes neglected to offer payment for my night's lodging, but in no other case, and never in a single instance, so far as I can now recollect, where I had offered payment, has there been any hesitation in taking it. A planter might refrain from asking payment of a traveller, but it is universally expected. In New England, as far as my limited experience goes, it is not so. I have known New England farmers' wives take a small gratuity after lodging travellers, but always with apparent hesitation. I have known New England farmers refuse to do so. I have had some experience in Iowa; money is there usually (not always) taken for lodging travellers. The principal difference between the custom at private houses there and in Alabama and Mississippi being, that in Iowa the farmer seems to carefully reckon the exact value of the produce you have consumed, and to charge for it at what has often seemed to me an absurdly low rate; while in Mississippi, I have usually paid from four to six times as much as in Iowa, for similar accommodations. I consider the usual charges of planters to travellers extortionate, and the custom the reverse of hospitable. I knew of a Kentucky gentleman travelling from Eutaw to Greensboro' [twenty miles] in his own conveyance. He was taken sick at the crossing of the Warrior River. It was nine o'clock at night. He averred to me that he called at every plantation on the road, and stated that he was a Kentuckian, and sick, but was refused lodging at each of them."

This the richest county of Alabama, and the road is lined with valuable plantations!

The following is an extract from a letter dated Columbus, Mississippi, November 24, 1856, published in the London *Daily News*. It is written by an Englishman travelling for commercial purposes, and tells what he has learned by experience of the custom of the country:

"It is customary in travelling through this country, where towns are few and taverns scarce and vile, to stop at the planters' houses along the road, and pay for your bed and board in the morning just as if you had stayed at an inn. The custom is rather repugnant to our Old World notions of hospitality, but it appears to me an excellent one for both the host and his guest. The one feels less bored by demands upon his kindness, as soon as it ceases to be merely a kindness to comply with them, and the other has no fear about intruding or being troublesome when he knows he will have to pay for his entertainment. It is rarely, however, that the *entrée* can be obtained into the houses of wealthy planters in this way. They will not be bothered by your visits, and, if you apply to them, have no hesitation in politely passing you on to such of their neighbours as have less money or more generosity."

The same writer afterwards relates the following experience:—

"About nineteen miles from Canton, I sought lodging at nightfall at a snug house on the roadside, inhabited by an old gentleman and his two daughters, who possessed no slaves and grew no cotton, and whose two sons had been killed in the Mexican war, and who, with the loudest professions of hospitality, cautiously refrained from giving himself any personal trouble in support of them. He informed me that there was corn in the husk in an almost inaccessible loft, there was fodder in an un-get-at-able sort of a cage in the yard, water in a certain pond about half a mile off, and a currycomb in a certain hole in the wall. Having furnished me with this intelligence, he left me to draw my own conclusions as to what my conduct ought to be under the circumstances."

A naturalist, the author of a well-known standard work, who has made several tours of observation in the Slave States, lately confided to me that he believed that the popular report of Southern hospitality must be a popular romance, for never, during all his travels in the South, had he chanced to be entertained for a single night, except by gentlemen to whom he was formally presented by letter, or who had previously been under obligations to him, without paying for it in money, and to an amount quite equal to the value received. By the wealthier, a night's entertainment had been frequently refused him, under circumstances which, as must have been evident to them, rendered his further progress seriously inconvenient. Once, while in company with a foreign naturalist—a titled man—he had been dining at the inn of a small county-town, when a certain locally distinguished judge had seen fit to be eloquent at the dinner-table upon the advantages of slavery in maintaining a class of "high-toned gentlemen," referring especially to the proverbial hospitality of Southern plantations, which he described as quite a bewilderment to strangers, and nothing like which was to be found in any country unblessed with slavery, or institutions equivalent to it. It so happened that the following night the travellers, on approaching a plantation mansion in quest of lodging, were surprised to find that they had fallen upon the residence of this same judge, who recognized them, and welcomed them and bade them be at home. Embarrassed by a recollection of his discourse of hospitality, it was with some difficulty that one of them, when they were taking leave next morning, brought himself to inquire what he might pay for the entertainment they had received. He was at once relieved by the judge's prompt response, "Dollar and a quarter apiece, I reckon."

It is very true that the general custom of the South which leads a traveller to ask for a lodging at any private house he may chance to reach near nightfall, and to receive a favourable answer not merely as a favour but as a matter of business, is a convenient one, is one indeed almost necessary in a country so destitute of villages, and where, off certain thoroughfares of our merchants, there are so few travellers. It is a perfectly respectable and entirely sensible custom, but it is not, as is commonly represented to be, a custom of hospitality, and it is not at all calculated to induce customs of hospitality with the mass of citizens. It is calculated to make inhospitality of habit and inhospitality of character the general rule; hospitality of habit and of character the exception. Yet the common misapplication of the word to this custom is, so far as I can ascertain, the only foundation of the arrogant assumption of superiority of character in this respect of the Southerners over ourselves—the only ground of the claim that slavery breeds a race of more generous and hospitable citizens than freedom.

The difficulty of giving anything like an intelligent and exact estimate of the breeding of any people or of any class of people is almost insurmountable, owing to the vagueness of the terms which must be used, or rather to the quite different ideas which different readers will attach to these terms. The very word which I have employed to designate my present subject has itself such a varied signification that it needs to be defined at the outset. I mean to employ it in that sense wherein, according to Webster, it covers the ground of "nurture, instruction, and the formation of manners." It is something more than "manners and customs," then, and includes, or may include, qualities which, if not congenital, are equally an essential part of character with those qualities which are literally in-bred of a man. Such qualities are mainly the result of a class of circumstances, of the influence of which upon his character and manners a man, or a child growing to a man, is usually unconscious, and of which he cannot be independent if he would.

The general difficulty is increased in dealing with the people of the Slave States, because among themselves all terms defining social rank and social characteristics are applied in a manner which can be understood only after considerable experience; and also because the general terms of classification, always incomplete in their significance, fail entirely with a large class of Southerners, whose manners have some characteristics which would elsewhere be thought "high bred," if they had not other which are elsewhere universally esteemed low and ruffianly.

There are undoubted advantages resulting from the effects of slavery upon the manners of some persons. Somewhat similar advantages I have thought that I perceived to have resulted in the Free States, where a family has been educated under favourable influences in a frontier community. There is boldness, directness, largeness, confidence, with the effect of the habitual sense of superiority to most of the community; not superiority of wealth, and power from wealth merely, but of a mind well stocked and refined by such advantages of education as only very unusual wealth, or very unusual individual energy, rightly directed, can procure in a scattered and frontier community. When to this is added the effect of visits to the cultivated society of denser communities; when refined and polished manners are grafted on a natural, easy abandon; when there is high culture without effeminacy either of body or mind, as not unfrequently happens, we find a peculiarly respectable and agreeable sort of men and women. They are the result of frontier training under the most favourable circumstances. In the class furthest removed from this on the frontier—people who have grown up without civilized social restraints or encouragements, and always under what in a well-conditioned community would be esteemed great privations—happens, on the other hand, the most disagreeable specimen of mankind that the world breeds; men of a sort almost peculiar to America and Australia; border ruffians, of whom the "rowdies" of our eastern towns are tame reflections. Cooper has well described the first class in many instances. I know of no picture of the latter which represents them as detestable as I have found them.

The whole South is maintained in a frontier condition by the system which is apologized for on the ground that it favours good breeding. This system, at the same time, tends to concentrate wealth in a few hands. If there is wisdom and great care in the education of a family thus favoured, the result which we see at the North, under the circumstances I have described, is frequently reproduced. There are many more such fruits of frontier life at the South than the North, because there is more frontier life. There is also vastly more of the other sort, and there is everything between, which degrees of wealth and degrees of good fortune in education would be expected to occasion. The bad breed of the frontier, at the South, however, is probably far worse than that of the North, because the frontier condition of the South is everywhere permanent. The child born to-day on the Northern frontier, in most cases, before it is ten years old, will be living in a well organized and tolerably well provided community; schools, churches, libraries, lecture and concert halls, daily mails and printing presses, shops and machines in variety, having arrived within at least a day's journey of it; being always within an influencing distance of it. There are improvements, and communities loosely and gradually cohering in various parts of the South, but so slowly, so feebly, so irregularly, that men's minds and habits are knit firm quite independently of this class of social influences.

There is one other characteristic of the Southerner, which is far more decided than the difference of climate merely would warrant, and which is to be attributed not only to the absence of the ordinary restraints and means of discipline of more compact communities in his education, but unquestionably also to the readiness and safety with which, by reason of slavery, certain passions and impulses may be indulged. Every white Southerner is a person of importance;

must be treated with deference. Every wish of the Southerner is imperative; every belief undoubted; every hate, vengeful; every love, fiery. Hence, for instance, the scandalous fiend-like street fights of the South. If a young man feels offended with another, he does not incline to a ring and a fair stand-up set-to, like a young Englishman; he will not attempt to overcome his opponent by logic; he will not be content to vituperate, or to cast ridicule upon him; he is impelled straightway to strike him down with the readiest deadly weapon at hand, with as little ceremony and pretence of fair combat as the loose organization of the people against violence will allow. He seems crazy for blood. Intensity of personal pride—pride in anything a man has, or which connects itself with him, is more commonly evident. Hence, intense local pride and prejudice; hence intense partisanship; hence rashness and over-confidence; hence visionary ambition; hence assurance in debate; hence assurance in society. As self-appreciation is equally with deference a part of what we call good breeding, and as the expression of deference is much more easily reduced to a matter of manners and forms, in the commonplace intercourse of society, than self-appreciation, this characteristic quality of the Southerner needs to be borne in mind in considering the port and manners he commonly has, and judging from them of the effects of slavery.

It must be also considered that the ordinary occupations and amusements of people of moderate wealth at the North are seldom resorted to at the South, that public entertainments of any kind, for instance, are impracticable to a sparse population; consequently that where men of wealth are socially disposed, all intercourse with others is highly valued, prepared for, and made the most of. Hence, with these, the act of social intercourse is more highly esteemed, and is much more frequently carried to a nice perfection of manner than it usually is with men otherwise of corresponding education, and habits at the North.

In a Northern community a man who is not greatly occupied with private business is sure to become interested in social enterprises and to undertake duties in them which will demand a great deal of time and strength. School, road, cemetery, asylum, and church corporations; bridge, ferry, and water companies; literary, scientific, art, mechanical, agricultural and benevolent societies; all these things are managed chiefly by the unpaid services of gentlemen during hours which they can spare from their private interests. In the successful operations of such enterprises they find much of the satisfaction of their life. So, too, our young men, who are not obliged to devote their thoughts chiefly to business success, are members and managers of reading rooms, public libraries, gymnasiums, game clubs, boat clubs, ball clubs, and all sorts of clubs, Bible classes, debating societies, military companies; they are planting road-side trees, or damming streams for skating ponds, or rigging diving-boards, or getting up firework displays, or private theatricals; they are always doing something, not conversing for the entertainment of the moment. Planters, the details of whose business fall into the hands of overseers, and young men of fortune, at the South, have, when at home on the plantation, none of these occupations. Their talents all turn into two channels, politics and sociality; the very paucity of society making it the more esteemed and the more carefully used. Social intercourse at the North is a relaxation from the ordinary bent of men's talents; at the South, it is that to which mainly their talents are bent. Hence, with men who are otherwise on a par, in respect of natural advantages and education, the Southerner will have a higher standard of manners than the Northerner, because, with him, social intercourse is the grand resource to which all other possible occupations of his mind become subordinate. The Northerner, being troubled by no monotony, unquestionably too much neglects at present this, the highest and final art of every type of civilization. In making this comparison, however, it must not be forgotten that it is made between men who are supposed to be equal in all respects, except in the possession of this advantage, and who are equally at leisure from any necessary habitual occupation for a livelihood.

Having conceded to the South certain elements of advantage in this respect, for a single class, it still remains to inquire where is the greatest weight of advantage for this class, and for all classes of our citizens. In attempting to make such a general comparison, I shall begin at the bottom of the social ladder, and return to the class who can in a great degree choose how they will be occupied.

In the North at the Revolution we scarcely had a distinct class corresponding to the lowest white class of Virginia, as described by Jefferson, our labourers being less ignorant and coarse in their habits, and associating much more familiarly with their betters. We have now a class more nearly corresponding to it furnished by the European peasant immigration. It is, however, a transient class, somewhat seldom including two generations, and, on an average, I trust, not one. It is therefore practically not an additional class, but, overlooking the aged and diseased, a supplement to our lowest normal class. Out of twenty Irish emigrants, landing in New York, perfectly destitute, of whose history I have been intimately cognizant, only two, both of whom were over fifty years of age, have lived out five years here without beginning to acquire wealth and becoming superior in their ambition and habits to the lowest order, which I believe to include a majority of the whites in the plantation districts of the

South.* Our lowest class, therefore, has a higher standard than the lowest class of the Slave States. This, I understand, is made very evident where the two come together at the West, as in southern Illinois. The very poorest and lowest New England women who go there are frequently offended by the inconsiderate rudeness and coarseness of the women immigrating from the South, and shocked by their "shiftless," comfortless, vagrant habits, so much so that families have often removed, after having been once established, to escape being bored and annoyed by their Southern-born neighbours.

Referring to the lowest class, North and South, as the fourth, I class as third, the lowest rank in society, North or South, in which regard is had by its members to the quality of their associates from other than moral motives, or the prejudices of locality, race, sectarianism, and politics. In other words, that in which there is a distinct social selectiveness and pride. I think that everywhere in the Free States men of this class would almost universally feel their position damaged—be a little ashamed—if obliged to confess that they did not take a newspaper, or were unable to read it with a clear understanding of the intelligence it was intended to communicate. Allusions to the main facts of American history, to any clause of the Bible, to the provisions of the Constitution, and the more important laws, State and National, would be understood in most cases by those whom I refer to as the third class in Northern society. In few families of this class would you fail to find some volumes of the English poets, or some works of great novelists or renowned travellers. No-

* I fear that it must be confessed that this general rule has now a multitude of exceptions in our large towns, where, in New York, especially, we seem taking some pains to form a permanent lower class. With the present great and apparently permanent falling off in the European emigration, it can hardly last, however.

thing like this would you find, however, in a grade of society distinctly superior to the lowest at the South.

The ratio of the number of the citizens who cannot read at all to the whole, appears, by the census returns, to be only three times larger at the South than at the North. I believe it to be much greater at the South than these returns indicate.* The comparative education of the third class "North" and of the third class "South," however, cannot be at all judged from these statistics, supposing them correct. Those who can read and who do not read, or whose reading is confined within extremely narrow limits, are a much larger number at the South than at the North, owing to the much poorer supply of books and newspapers which commerce can afford to put within the reach of the former. The census returns two million newspapers, for instance, printed annually in Virginia, one hundred and fifteen million in New York. There is a post-office to every fourteen square miles in New York, one to forty-seven square miles in Virginia; over five hundred publishers and booksellers in New York, but forty in Virginia. Thirty thousand volumes in public libraries in Virginia, eight hundred thousand in New York. The area occupied by the population of Virginia being much the largest, it may be inferred that with the disposition and the ability to read anything in particular, the Virginian of the third class will have to travel more than thirty times as far as the New Yorker to procure it. The same proposition will hold good in regard to most other means of cultivation, and the third

* The ratio of white illiterate to white population, per cent., as returned, is, {Free States, 3·36; Slave „ 8·27} of the native population, over twenty years old, it is, {Free States, 4·12; Slave „ 17·23} (Census Compendium, pp. 152, 153). The ability to merely read and write may itself be of little value, but the fact of a child's having had the painstaking necessary to so far instruct him is in some degree a means of measuring his other inherited wealth, and thus his breeding.

class of the South generally has seemed to me to be as much more narrow-minded, rude, coarse, "dangerous," and miserable, than the third class of the Free States, as the most sanguine friend of popular education could anticipate from these facts.

The great difference in character between the third class of the South and that of the North, as indicated by their respective manners, is found in the much less curiosity and ready intelligent interest in matters which have not an immediate personal bearing in that of the South. Apathetic carelessness rather than simple indifference, or reckless incivility as to your comfort, is what makes the low Southerner a disagreeable companion. It is his impertinent shrewdness which makes you wish to keep the Yankee at a distance. The first seems without object, spiritless; the latter keen to better himself, if with nothing else, with information which he can draw from you, and by gaining your good opinion.

The next or second class would include, both North and South, those with whose habits and character I am most familiar, and of whom I can speak with the best right to confidence. It would include in New England and New York the better educated farmers—these owning, I should say, half the agricultural land—the permanently established manufacturers and merchants of moderate capital; most of the shopkeepers and the better-educated master mechanics and artisan foremen; most of the preachers, physicians, and lawyers (some ranking higher). It would correspond most nearly to what in England would be called the lower-middle class, but any higher grade being very ill-defined, existing distinctly but in few localities, and rarely recognized as existing at all, it is in a great measure free from the peculiar vulgarity of its English parallel.

The number of those at the South who correspond in

education and refinement of manners and habits to the average of this class of the North, it will be evident, from a similar mode of reasoning to that before employed, must be very much smaller relatively, either to the territory or the whole white population of their respective regions.

In the comparison commonly made by Southern writers between the condition of the people of a sparsely-settled country and another, it is usually assumed that the advantages of the latter are confined exclusively to towns, and to large and crowded towns. By contrasting the evils which concentrate in such towns with the favourable circumstances of localities where at least wood, water, and air are abundant, and corn enough to support life can usually be got by any one with a little occasional labour, an argument of some force to ignorant people is easily presented. The advantages possessed by a people living in moderately well-occupied rural districts, who are even more free from the evils of great towns than their own people, are entirely overlooked by most Southern writers. Such is the condition, however, of more white people in the Free States than the whole white population of the Slave States. A majority of our farmers' daughters can walk from their dwellings to schools of a quality such as at the South can be maintained not twice in five hundred square miles. These schools are practically a part of their homes. Probably, in more than half the families of the South, the children of which are instructed to the least degree which would be considered "respectable," among this second class of the North, private governesses are obliged to be employed, or the children must be for many years at boarding-schools. We all know that the young women who go to the South, to meet the demand thus occasioned for home education, are not generally, though they may be in cases, our own most esteemed and successful instructresses; and we also know from their report that their skill and labour has necessarily to be long chiefly employed in laying those simple foundation habits of *instructability*, which our Northern children acquire imperceptibly from association with those of the neighbourhood slightly in advance of them. Churches and the various sub-organizations centreing in them, in which class distinctions are much lost sight of, to the great advantage of the manners of the lower classes, and little chance of injury to the higher; libraries; literary societies; lecture arrangements; dramatic and musical, art and scientific entertainments, and also highly educated professional men, with whom, for various purposes, many persons are brought often in contact, are correspondingly more frequent at the North, correspondingly more accessible; in other words, the advantages to be derived from them are cheaper, and so more influential on the manners of the people at large.

The common opinion has been that the Southerners or planters of the class now under consideration, are more social, more generous, more heartily kind and genial than Northerners. According to my experience, the reverse of all this is true, as a general rule. Families live so isolatedly at the South, that any social contact, out of the family, is of course much more eventful and stimulating than it is ordinarily at the North, and this accounts for the common opinion. I could not but think, however, that most persons at the South looked to the voluntary good offices and conversation of others, both within and without their families, for their enjoyment of the world, much less than most at the North. It may be that when in towns they attach a greater value to, and are more careful to make use of the opportunities for social gathering afforded by towns, than are Northerners. In towns they attach more consequence to forms, are more scrupulous in matters of etiquette, more lavish in expenditure for dress, and for certain other things which are the signs of luxury rather than luxury itself, such as plate and fancy brands of wines. They make less show of fine art and less pretence of artistic judgment; more of respect and regard for their associates, and of indifference or superiority to all others.

As to manner or deportment simply, with the same impulse and intention, that of the Southerner will habitually, under ordinary circumstances, be best, more true, more composed, more dignified. I have said that the second class at the North is without the pervading vulgarity of the class to which it most nearly corresponds in England, the reason being that those which constitute it seldom wish or attempt to appear to belong to a superior class, not clearly recognizing a superior class. Individuals, however, very generally have a strong desire to be thought better informed, more ingenious, more witty, as well as more successful in their enterprises than they are, and this stamps them with a peculiar quality of manners vulgarly called "smartness," the absence of which makes Southern men and women generally much more agreeable companions than Northerners of the same degree of education and accomplishments in other respects. Not but that snobs abound; of these it will be more convenient to speak under the next division, however.

The traditional "old family," stately but condescending, haughty but jovial, keeping open house for all comers on the plantations of Virginia or South Carolina, is not wholly a myth.

There really was something which, with some sort of propriety, could be termed a gentry in Carolina and Virginia in their colony days; yet of the names which are now thought to have belonged to it, as descended of brave, loyal, and adventurous cavaliers, some I once saw in London upon an old freight-list of a ship outward bound for Virginia, with the addition of tinker and tailor, poacher and pickpocket, all to be sold for life, or a term of years, to the highest bidder when they should arrive. A large majority of the fathers of Virginia were unquestionably of this class.

What was properly to be termed the gentry in Virginia and South Carolina previous to the Revolution, was very small in number. A large proportion of the families who composed it, and who remained after the Revolution in the country (for many were Tories) have since passed in all their branches through a poverty-stricken period, very dissipating in its influence upon hereditary breeding, novelists and dramatic old servants to the contrary notwithstanding. Many of those who have retained wealth and family pride in succession to the present time, have undeniably, from various causes, degenerated wofully in breeding. Coarse tastes and brutal dispositions cannot be disguised under a cavalier address, and the most assured readiness in the established forms of polite society. Of the real "old families" which remain at all "well bred" in their qualities, habits, and manners, by reason of their lineage, I think it will be difficult for most readers who have not studied the matter at all to form a sufficiently small estimate; call them a dozen or a hundred, what does it matter in a region much larger than the old German empire? Associating with these are a few hundred more new or recuperated families, in which there is also the best breeding, and in certain few parts or districts of the South, to be defined and numbered without difficulty, there is a wealthy, distinct, generous, hospitable, refined, and accomplished first class, clinging with some pertinacity, although with too evident an effort, to the traditional manners and customs of an established gentry.

There was a gentry in the North as well as in Virginia and Carolina in the colony period, though a less important and numerous one. As the North has been much more prosperous, as the value of its property has much more rapidly increased than that of the South, the advantages of wealth have, I believe, been more generally retained in families, and probably the number of those who could trace their breeding in an uninterrupted parental influence from the colonial gentry, is now larger at the North than the South.

Including new families, in whose habits and manners and conversation the best bred people of Europe would find nothing more offensive and inharmonious with themselves than might be ascribed to local fashion or a desire to avoid appearances which, though perfectly proper in an aristocratic society, would be snobbish in a republic, there is unquestionably at this time a very much larger number of thoroughly well-bred people in the Free than in the Slave States. It is equally certain that the proportion of such people to the whole population of whites is larger at the North than the South.

The great majority of wealthy planters who at the present day assume for themselves a special social respectability and superiority to the class I have defined as the second, are, as a general rule, not only distinguished for all those qualities which our satirists and dramatists are accustomed to assume to be the especial property of the newly rich of the Fifth Avenue, but, as far as I have had opportunity to observe both classes, are far more generally and ridiculously so than the would-be fashionable people of New York, or of any other part of the United States. It is a part of the *rôle* they undertake to act, to be hospitable and generous, as it was lately that of our fops to be sleepy and critical. They are not hospitable and generous, however; they know not the meaning of these terms. They are absurdly ostentatious in entertainment, and extravagant in the purchase of notoriety; possibly they have more tact in this than our Potiphars, but such has not been my personal observation.

CHAPTER IX.

THE DANGER OF THE SOUTH.

BEFORE the advent of modern science, any idea of systematic laws of human improvement would have been deemed alike impossible and absurd; but the constant observation of facts, the exact statistics recorded, the progress of science in all departments, has made it possible to conceive of, and probable that there actually exist *uniform laws of social movement*, based upon any given condition of society. If the *elementary social* condition be different in regard to religion, government, arts, science, industry, the resulting movements of society will be different. Hence, when we have ascertained by accurate observation upon and record of the social phenomena, that the social movement is uniformly in a certain direction, and that certain results uniformly follow, we shall know in what *elements* the conditions of society must be changed, in order to change the results. Hence, when this law of social movements is ascertained, the philanthropist, legislator, and jurist will know precisely what must be done, and how, in order to remove the evils, or reform the wrongs, or produce the results they desire. They will know that *certain elementary conditions of society* must be changed, and they well know that by removing temptations, or laying restraints, or enlightening the mind, or changing the course of industry, or producing new arts, they will change the social tendency, and thus change the results. * * * Society, or that part of it which thinks and acts, can change the results by changing the elementary conditions which produce them. When you know exactly what the change ought to be, it is not very difficult to produce it; nor does it follow that because a thousand crimes must be committed in Ohio, that a thousand particular individuals *must* commit them. It is true that the individual frequently acts from motives, but is it not just as true that the individual frequently seeks these motives, and presents them to himself?"—*From the Report of the Ohio State Commissioner of Statistics*, 1859.

"If there is a first principle in intellectual education it is this—that the discipline which does good to the mind is that in which the mind is active, not that in which it is passive. The secret for developing the faculties is to give them much to do, and much inducement to do it."—*Mill's Political Economy.*

The field-hand negro is, on an average, a very poor and very bad creature, much worse than I had supposed before I had seen him and grown familiar with his stupidity, indolence, duplicity, and sensuality. He seems to be but an imperfect man, incapable of taking care of himself in a civilized manner, and his presence in large numbers must be considered a dangerous circumstance to a civilized people.

A civilized people, within which a large number of such creatures has been placed by any means not within its own control, has claims upon the charity, the aid, if necessary, of all other civilized peoples in its endeavours to relieve itself from the danger which must be apprehended from their brutal propensities, from the incompleteness of their human sympathies—their inhumanity—from their natural love of ease, and the barbaric want of forethought and providence, which would often induce desperate want among them. Evidently the people thus burthened would have need to provide systematically for the physical wants of these poor creatures, else the latter would be liable to prey with great waste upon their substance. Perhaps the very best thing to do would be to collect them into small herds, and attach each herd to a civilized family, the head of which should be responsible for its safe keeping. Such a superintendent should of course contrive, if possible, to make his herd contribute in some way to the procuring of its necessary sustenance; and if, besides this, he even turned their feeble abilities to such good account by his superior judgment, that they actually procured a considerable surplus of food and clothing for the benefit of others, should not Christendom applaud and encourage his exertions, even if a certain amount of severity and physical constraint had been found necessary to accomplish this success?

Let us endeavour to assume a similar difficulty for ourselves. Let us suppose that a large part—the proportion varying with the locality—of our own community should next year suffer from some new malady, the result of which should in no case be fatal, but which should, like the *goître* of Savoy, leave all who were affected by it permanently injured in their intellects, with diminished bodily activity, and fiercer animal propensities. (I take this method of stating the case, because some of us who only see the negro as he exists at the North might find it difficult to imagine him as he is known to the planters.)

Suppose, further, that this malady should be confined to certain families, as if its seed had been received hundreds of years ago by numerous individuals, and only their descendants (but all of these to the most distant trace of the blood) now suffered from it. Also, that some of our doctors should be of the opinion that the effects of the malady upon the intellect would descend to the children, and to all descendants of those who suffered. Suppose that these unfortunates should be subject to certain hallucinations, that they should be liable to think themselves sane and able to take care of themselves, and that when possessed with these ideas that they should be quite cunning and dangerous in attempting to exercise the usual prerogatives of sane men.

What should we do with them?

Finding them in a degree tractable; and sensible enough, after all, to yield readily, if not cheerfully, to superior force, we might herd them together on a sort of farm-hospitals, and let them earn their living, giving especially capable men charge of many, and rewarding them with good salaries, and ordinary small farmers, smaller numbers, with smaller compensations for overseeing them?

Of course, we should place every possible legislative guard and check upon these superintendents and overseers to secure fair and honest dealing, to prevent them from making perquisites for themselves at the expense of a reasonable comfort in their institutions. Careful instructions to secure economical sustenance, and how to turn such labour as could be got from the unfortunates to the best account, in defraying the cost of their keeping, would also be framed by talented men and furnished each keeper.

And having regard to national wealth, to the temporal good of the commonwealth, this is about all that common sense would lead us to do, at least through the agency of government.

Is this all, reader?

You have too much overlooked our small matters of State, if you think so. We have a few crazy people, a few fools, not enough to be a matter of much consideration to our statesmen or legislators, yet we have a State system in our dealing with them, such as it is, and such as it is it puts our dealing with them on a little different footing than would the system I have above imagined. What I have imagined is not quite all we have for some time been in the habit of doing when we did anything with this class. And judging from what we have done, it does not seem as if it would be all that we should do in such an emergency as I have supposed, engaging as it would all the talent of the country to diminish as much as possible the necessary results of the calamity.

We should, it appears, call upon our learned doctors eagerly to study; we should each of us eagerly observe for ourselves whether the fearful infirmity by which so many were incapacitated for their former usefulness, were not only absolutely incurable, but also absolutely not possible to be alleviated. And if our observation should satisfy us, if our doctors could not deny that, with judicious treatment, a considerable alleviation could be effected, so much so indeed, that with a very large part a close approximation to the normal condition of sane and capable mankind could be obtained, there are doubtless those amongst us who would think this a dangerous and an infidel presumption. Just as every year some miserable wretch is found in our dark places to have a crazy father or brother whom he keeps in a cage in his garret, and whose estate he takes care of, and who is of the opinion that it will be of no use, but, on the contrary, a manifest defiance of Divine Providence, and most dangerous to life and property to let this unfortunate out of his cage, to surround him with comforts, and contrive for him cheerful occupation, as our State requires shall be done. But would the average common sense and humanity of the people of the Free States allow them to refuse all reduction from their usual annual incomes; refuse to suffer all necessary addition to their usual taxes; refuse to burden their minds with the difficulties of the all-absorbing problem, in order to initiate a remedial system? Our worst and most cowardly legislature would never dare adjourn leaving this duty incompletely performed. There are thousands on thousands of our citizens who would not only spare from their incomes, but would divide their estates for such a purpose. There is not a county that would not submit to the highest war taxes for it.

Suppose that the doctors and that the universal observation of the community should determine that the defective class were not only capable of being improved, but that so far as their limited intellects permitted, the laws of improvement were the same for them as for healthy men; that they were found to be influenced by a liking for food and drink, for the society of each other and of sane men, for the admiration and respect of each other and of sane men, for their ease, for dancing, for music and other amusements; and that their imperfect natures could be acted upon, drawn out, and enlarged by means of these likings. Suppose that it were found that nearly all of them had still some knowledge of religion, that although they were inclined sometimes to consider sane men as their enemies, they were yet, in most cases, by judicious play upon their inclinations and disinclinations, capable of being trained quite beyond the most sagacious of our domestic animals, even to read intelligently. Should we, because there were so many of them, go back two hundred years in our civilization, denying ourselves the addition which this capacity would give to their powers of usefulness, and consequently of economy of maintenance; denying them the advantages for improvement which we now in every State give to our hopelessly insane, to our blind and mute, to our fools, to our worst and most dangerous criminals.

Why do we not pass laws forbidding criminals and maniacs to read? Our fathers did not allow them to read when negroes were introduced in Virginia. But every man among us whom we call well informed, now knows that it is a profitable business for the State, which has so little profitable business, even to provide teachers and books for a portion of her criminals, to allow books and encourage reading with all. To provide books, to provide physicians, to provide teachers, to provide halls and gardens of recreations, as stimulants to healthful thought for our madmen and our fools; to this the State is impelled equally by considerations of safety and of economy. Even Kentucky has its State institution for the development of manhood in fools born of white women.

Does not every such man know, too, that, given an improvable mind with a sound body, possessed of the natural instincts, the usual desires, appetites, aversions, no matter if at starting the being is even what we call an idiot, a drivelling imbecile, disgusting all who see him, a sheer burden upon society, the process of making him clean in his habits, capable of labouring with a good and intelligent purpose, and of associating inoffensively with others, is just as certain in its principles and in its progress—infinite progress—as the navigation of a ship or the building of a house?

This is even so with a cretin, whose body is deformed beyond remedy, whose brain is contracted, whose face is contorted, whose limbs are half paralyzed, whose every organ is defective, and who has inherited these conditions from goitrous parents and grandparents.

Dr. Seguin says: "The idiot wishes for nothing; he wishes only to remain in his vacuity."

Even so thinks Dr. Cartwright of the negro; and surely nothing worse can be thought of him.

But Dr. Seguin adds: "To treat successfully this ill-will [indisposition to take care of himself], the physician wills that the idiot should act *and think himself, of himself, and, finally, by himself.* The incessant volition of the moral physican urges incessantly the idiot into the sphere of activity of thinking, of labour, of duty, and affectionate feelings."

Is there no such law of progression of capacity for the black imbeciles? All the laws of the South have the contrary aims: to withdraw them as much as possible from the sphere of self-willed activity, thought, labour—to prevent the negro from thinking by himself, of himself, for himself; and the principle on which these laws are based is thus defined by Mr. De Bow:—

"The Almighty has thought well to place certain of His creatures in certain *fixed positions* in this world of ours, for what cause He has not seen fit to make quite clear to our limited capacities; and why an ass is not a man, and a man is not an ass, will probably for ever remain a mystery." "God made the world; God gave thee thy place, my hirsute brother, and, according to all earthly possibilities and probabilities, it is thy destiny there to remain, bray as thou wilt. From the same great power have our sable friends, Messrs. Sambo, Cuffee, & Co., received their position also. . . . Alas, my poor black brother! thou, like thy hirsute friend, must do thy braying in vain."*

Are there laws on our statute-books to prevent asses from being taught to read?

The *Richmond Examiner* says—

"These immigrants do not, like our ancestors, fly from religious and political persecution; they come merely as animals in search of a richer and fresher pasture. They come to gratify physical want—for moral, intellectual, or religious wants they have not acquired. They will settle in large masses, and, for ages to come, will practise and inculcate a pure (or rather impure) materialism. Mormonism is a fit exponent, proof, and illustration of our theory. The mass of them are sensual, grovelling, low-minded agrarians, and nine-tenths of them would join the Mormons, or some such brutal, levelling sect, if an opportunity offered to do so.

"European writers describe a large class of population throughout England and the Continent as being distinguished by restless, wandering, nomadic habits, and by a peculiar conformation of the skull and face. Animal and sensual nature largely predominates, with them, over the moral and intellectual. It is they who commit crimes, fill prisons, and adorn the gallows. They will not submit to the restraints of law or religion, nor can they be educated. From their restless and lawless habits, we should infer they composed a large part of the northern immigration."

If all this were true, and were felt by us to be true, should we think it necessary to put the minds of these beings in fetters? Should we hold it to be dangerous if one should undertake to strengthen their intellects, to give them larger ideas?

If all the slaves in the United States were "real Congo niggers," which not one in a thousand is, and if all real Congo niggers were as incapable, and as beastly, and as savage in their propensities as the very worst of them are asserted to be, would the method of dealing with them which

* "Resources," vol. ii., pp. 197, 198.

the legislation of the Slave States, and which a large part of the labour of the Congress and Executive of our nation is directed to the purpose of perpetuating, be felt to be strictly in accordance with sound and well-established economico-political principles? The purpose of that legislation is avowed to be merely to secure safety with economy. Would a project for establishing an institution planned upon the principles of the ancient Bedlam and the ancient Bridewell be felt to-day to be completely justified among us, by the statement that highwaymen and maniacs will endanger life and the security of our property if they are not somehow taken care of?

If there had been no Mettray with its Demetz, no Norfolk Island with its Machonochie, no Hanwell with its Connolly, no Abendberg with its Guggenbuhl; if the courage, devotion, and labour of Pinel, Sicard, and Seguin had been in vain; if there had been no progress in the science of civilized society since the days of Howard, we might listen with merely silent sadness to such an excuse for debilitating the weak, for holding down the fallen; for permitting brutal keepers to exasperate the mad, and mercenary nurses to stupefy the idiotic; we might, if we saw it to be necessary to preserve a civilized community from destruction, even give its object our aid; but with the knowledge which in our time is everywhere else acted upon, it is impossible for us not to feel that such an argument is a specious and a fallacious one, and that no State can long act upon it with safety, much less with economy.

And surely the system by which intellectual demands and ambition are repressed in the negro is as little calculated to produce the security which is its object, as it is to turn his physical abilities to the most profitable use for his owner. How far it fails in this respect, the extra-legal measures of safety and the semi-instinctive habits of unconscious precaution which pervade Southern society evince. I say unconscious precaution, because Southerners themselves seem to have generally a very inadequate idea of the influence of slavery upon their habits in this way, and this is very natural.

"Every habit breeds unconsciousness of its existence in the mind of the man whom it controls, and this is more true of habits which involve our safety than of any others. The weary sailor aloft, on the look-out, may fall asleep; but, in the lurch of the ship, his hands will clench the swaying cordage only the more firmly, that they act in the method of instinct. A hard-hunted fugitive may nod in his saddle, but his knees will not unloose their hold upon his horse. Men who live in powder-mills are said to lose all conscious feeling of habitual insecurity; but visitors perceive that they have acquired a constant softness of manner and of voice.

"If a labourer on a plantation should insolently contradict his master, it may often appear to be no more than a reasonable precaution for his master to kill him on the spot; for, when a slave has acquired such boldness, it may be evident that not merely is his value as property seriously diminished, but that the attempt to make further use of him at all, as property, involves in danger the whole white community. 'If I let this man live, and permit him the necessary degree of freedom to be further useful to me, he will infect with his audacity all my negro property, which will be correspondingly more difficult to control, and correspondingly reduced in value. If he treats me with so little respect now, what have I to anticipate when he has found other equally independent spirits among the slaves? They will not alone make themselves free, but will avenge upon me, and my wife, and my daughters, and upon all our community, the injustice which they will think has been done them, and their women, and children.' Thus would he reason, and shudder to think what might follow if he yielded to an impulse of mercy.

"To suppose, however, that the master will pause while he thus weighs the danger exactly, and then deliberately act as, upon reflection, he considers the necessities of the case demand, is absurd. The mere circumstance of his doing so would nourish a hopeful spirit in the slave, and stimulate him to consider how he could best avoid all punishment. Hence the instinct-like habit of precaution with individuals, and hence the frenzy which often seizes whole communities.

"But 'planters sleep unguarded, and with their bedroom doors open.' So, as it was boasted, did the Emperor at Biarritz, and with greater bravery, because the assassin of Napoleon would be more sure, in despatching him, that there would be no one left with a vital interest to secure punishment for such a deed: and because, if he failed, Napoleon dare never employ such exemplary punishment for his enemies as would the planters for theirs. The emperors of the South are the whole free society of the South, and it is a society of mutual assurance. Against a slave who has the disposition to become an assassin, his emperor has a body-guard, which, for general effectiveness, is to the Cent Garde as your right hand is to your right hand's glove.

"It is but a few months since, in Georgia or Alabama, a man treated another precisely as Mr. Brooks treated Mr. Sumner—coming up behind him, with the fury of a madman, and felling him with a bludgeon; killing him by the first blow, however, and then discharging vengeance by repeated strokes upon his senseless body.* The man thus pitifully

* The late Mr. Brooks' character should be honestly considered, now that personal enmity toward him is impossible. That he was courteous, accomplished, warm-hearted, and hot-blooded, dear as a friend and fearful as an enemy, may be believed by all; but, in the South, his name is yet never mentioned without the term gallant or courageous, spirited or noble, is also attached to it; and we are obliged to ask, why insist on this? The truth is, we include a habit of mind in these terms which slavery has rendered, in a great degree, obsolete in the South. The

abused had been the master of the other, a remarkably confiding and merciful master, it was said—too much so. 'It never does to be too slack with niggers.' By such indiscretion he brought his death upon him. But did his assassin escape? He was roasted, at a slow fire, on the spot of the murder, in the presence of many thousand slaves, driven to the ground from all the adjoining counties, and when, at length, his life went out, the fire was intensified until his body was in ashes, which were scattered to the winds and trampled under foot. Then 'magistrates and clergymen' addressed appropriate warnings to the assembled subjects. It was not thought indiscreet to leave doors open again that night.

"Will any traveller say that he has seen no signs of discontent, or insecurity, or apprehension, or precaution; that the South has appeared quieter and less excited, even on the subject of slavery, than the North; that the negroes seem happy and contented, and the citizens more tranquilly engaged in the pursuit of their business and pleasure? Has that traveller been in Naples? Precisely the same remarks apply to the appearance of things there at this moment [the moment of this writing—it was in 1857].

---

man who has been accustomed from childhood to see men beaten when they have no chance to defend themselves; to hear men accused, reproved, vituperated, who dare not open their lips in self-defence or reply; the man who is accustomed to see other men whip women without interference, remonstrance, or any expression of indignation, must have a certain quality, which is an essential part of personal honour with us, greatly blunted, if not entirely destroyed. The same quality which we detest in the assassination of an enemy, is essentially constant in all slavery. It is found in effecting one's will with another, when he cannot, if he would, defend himself. Accustomed to this in every hour of their lives, Southerners do not feel magnanimity and the "fair-play" impulse to be a necessary part of the quality of "spirit," courage, and nobleness. By spirit they apparently mean only passionate vindictiveness of character, and by gallantry mere intrepidity.

"The massacre of Hayti opened in a ball-room. Mr. Cobden judged there was not the smallest reason in the French king's surrounding himself with soldiers the day before the hidden force of insubordination broke forth and cast him forth from his kingdom. It is true, however, that the tranquillity of the South is the tranquillity of Hungary and of Poland, rather than of France or the Two Sicilies; the tranquillity of hopelessness on the part of the subject race. But, in the most favoured regions, this broken spirit of despair is as carefully preserved by the citizens, and with as confident and unhesitating an application of force, when necessary to teach humility, as it is by the army of the Czar, or the omnipresent police of the Kaiser. In Richmond, and Charleston, and New Orleans, the citizens are as careless and gay as in Boston or London, and their servants a thousand times as childlike and cordial, to all appearance, in their relations with them as our servants are with us. But go to the bottom of this security and dependence, and you come to police machinery such as you never find in towns under free government: citadels, sentries, passports, grape-shotted cannon, and daily public whippings for accidental infractions of police ceremonies. I happened myself to see more direct expression of tyranny in a single day and night at Charleston, than at Naples [under Bomba] in a week; and I found that more than half the inhabitants of this town were subject to arrest, imprisonment, and barbarous punishment, if found in the streets without a passport after the evening 'gun-fire.' Similar precautions and similar customs may be discovered in every large town in the South.

"Nor is it so much better, as is generally imagined, in the rural districts. Ordinarily there is no show of government any more than at the North: the slaves go about with as much apparent freedom as convicts in a dockyard. There is, however, nearly everywhere, always prepared to act, if not always in service, an armed force, with a military organization, which is invested with more arbitrary and cruel power than any police in Europe. Yet the security of the whites is in a much less degree contingent on the action of the 'patrols' than upon the constant, habitual, and instinctive surveillance and authority of all white people over all black. I have seen a gentleman, with no commission or special authority, oblige negroes to show their passports, simply because he did not recognize them as belonging to any of his neighbours. I have seen a girl, twelve years old, in a district where, in ten miles, the slave population was fifty to one of the free, stop an old man on the public road, demand to know where he was going, and by what authority, order him to face about and return to his plantation, and enforce her command with turbulent anger, when he hesitated, by threatening that she would have him well whipped if he did not instantly obey. The man quailed like a spaniel, and she instantly resumed the manner of a lovely child with me, no more apprehending that she had acted unbecomingly, than that her character had been influenced by the slave's submission to her caprice of supremacy; no more conscious that she had increased the security of her life by strengthening the habit of the slave to the master race, than is the sleeping seaman that he tightens his clutch of the rigging as the ship meets each new billow.

"There is no part of the South in which the people are more free from the direct action of slavery upon the character, or where they have less to apprehend from rebellion, than Eastern Tennessee. Yet, after the burning of a negro near Knoxville, a few years ago, the deed was justified, as necessary for the maintenance of order among the slaves, by the editor of a newspaper (the *Register*), in the following terms:—'It was,' he observed, 'a means of absolute, necessary self-defence, which could not be secured by an ordinary resort to the laws. Two executions on the gallows have occurred in this county within a year or two past, and the example has been unavailing. Four executions by hanging have taken place, heretofore, in Jefferson, of slaves guilty of similar offences, and it has produced no radical terror or example for the others designing the same crimes, and hence any example less horrible and terrifying would have availed nothing here.'

"The other local paper (the *Whig*), upon the same occasion, used the following language:—

"'We have to say in defence of the act, that it was not perpetrated by an excited multitude, but by one thousand citizens —good citizens at that—who were cool, calm, and deliberate.'

"And the editor, who is a Methodist preacher, presently adds, after explaining the enormity of the offence with which the victim was charged—"We unhesitatingly affirm that the punishment was unequal to the crime. Had we been there we should have taken a part, and even suggested the pinching of pieces out of him with red-hot pincers—the cutting off of a limb at a time, and then burning them all in a heap. The possibility of his escaping from jail forbids the idea of awaiting the tardy movements of the law.' [Although one thousand trusty citizens volunteered to guard him at the stake.]

"How much more horrible than the deed are these apologies for it. They make it manifest that it was not accidental in its character, but a phenomenon of general and fundamental significance. They explain the paralytic effect upon the popular conscience of the great calamity of the South. They indicate a necessary tendency of people living under such circumstances to return in their habits of thought to the dark ages of mankind. For who, from the outside, can fail to see that the real reason why men in the middle of the nineteenth century, and in the centre of the United States, are publicly burned at the stake, is one much less heathenish, less disgraceful to the citizens than that given by the more zealous and extemporaneous of their journalistic exponents—the desire to torture the sinner proportionately to the measure of his sin. Doubtless, this reverend gentleman expresses the utmost feeling of the ruling mind of his community. But would a similar provocation have developed a similar avenging spirit in any other nominally Christian or civilized people? Certainly not. All over Europe, and in every Free State—California, for significant reasons, temporarily excepted—in similar cases, justice deliberately takes its course; the accused is systematically assisted in defending or excusing himself. If the law demands his life, the infliction of unnecessary suffering, and the education of the people in violence and feelings of revenge, is studiously avoided. Go back to the foundation of the custom which thus neutralizes Christianity among the people of the South, which carries them backward blindly against the tide of civilization, and what do we find it to be? The editor who still retains moral health enough to be suspected—as men more enlightened than their neighbours usually are—of heterodoxy, answers. To follow the usual customs of civilization elsewhere would not be felt safe. To indulge in feelings of humanity would not be felt safe. To be faithful to the precepts of Christ would not be felt safe. To act in a spirit of cruel, inconsiderate, illegal, violent, and pitiless vengeance, must be permitted, must be countenanced, must be defended by the most conservative, as a 'means of absolute, necessary self-defence.' To educate the people practically otherwise would be felt to be suicidal. Hence no free press, no free pulpit, no free politics can be permitted in the South. Hence every white stripling in the South may carry a dirk-knife in his pocket, and play with a revolver before he has learned to swim."*

I happened to pass through Tennessee shortly after this tragedy, and conversed with a man who was engaged in it—a mild, common-sense native of the country. He told me that there was no evidence against the negro but his own confession. I suggested that he might have been crazy. "What if he was?" he asked with a sudden asperity. What if he was, to be sure? The slaves who were brought together to witness his torture were not insane. They were at least capable of instruction. That day they were given a lesson; were taught to know their masters better; were taught that when ordinary and legal discipline failed, resort would be had to more potent means of governing them. A better informed man, having regard to the ignorance of a stranger, might have answered me: "It was of no consequence, practically, whether he were sane or mad. We do not wish our slaves to study the right and the wrong of every exciting occurrence. To say that being mad the negro was not responsible, therefore not guilty of a crime, therefore not to be punished, would be proclaiming to them that only that which is wrong is to be dreaded. Whatever offends us, whatever is against our will and pleasure, is what a slave must be made to dread."

Constantly, and everywhere throughout the South, are there occurrences of this significance; I do not say as horrible, though I can answer for it, that no year in the last ten has passed without something as bad;† but constantly and everywhere of the same nature, of the same impulse, the

* From the Introduction to "The Englishman in Kansas," (by the author of this work).

† That slaves have ever been burned alive has been indignantly denied. The late Judge Jay told me that he had evidence in his possession of negro burnings every year in the last twenty.

same reasoning, the same purposes, the same disregard of principles of society, which no people can ever set aside and not have reason to feel their situation insecure. It is false, it is the most dangerous mistake possible to assume that this feeling of insecurity, this annihilation of the only possible basis of security in human society, is, in the slightest degree, the result of modern agitation. It is the fundamental law of slavery, as distinctly appears in the decision of Justice Ruffin, of North Carolina, in the case of the State *v.* Mann.* The American system of slavery from its earliest years (as shown p. 496, "Seaboard Slave States"), and without cessation to the present time, has had this accompaniment. Less in the last twenty years, if anything, than before. Would it not be more just to say that this element of the present system was the cause of agitation? Must not the determined policy of the South to deal with slavery on the assumption that it is, in its present form, necessary, just, good, and to be extended, strengthened, and perpetuated indefinitely, involve constant agitation as a necessary incident of the means used to carry it out? I do not say with you or with me, reader, but with a goodly number of any civilized community? Do you not, who wish to think otherwise, consider that it will always require what you must deem a superior mind not to be overcome by incidents necessary to the carrying out of this determination? And will not such agitation give renewed sense of danger, and occasion renewed demands for assurance from us?

I have remarked before that in no single instance did I find an inquiry of the owner or the overseer of a large plantation about the poor whites of its vicinity fail to elicit an expression indicating habitual irritation with them. This equally with the polished and tranquil gentleman of South Carolina and the rude pioneer settler of Texas, himself born a

* 2 Devereaux's North Carolina Reports, 263.

dirt-eating sand-hiller. It was evident in most cases, and in one it was distinctly explained to me by a Louisianian planter, that the reason of this was not merely the bad effect upon the discipline of the plantation, which was had by the intercourse between these people and the slaves, but that it was felt that the contrast between the habits of the former—most of the time idle, and when working, working only for their own benefit and without a master—constantly offered suggestions and temptations to the slaves to neglect their duty, to run away and live a vagabond life, as these poor whites were seen to. Hence, one of the acknowledged advantages of very large and isolated plantations, and hence, in part, the desire of every planter to get possession of the land of any poor non-slaveholding neighbour.

As few Southern writers seem to have noticed this, I suppose that few Southerners are aware how universal with planters is this feeling. My attention being early directed to the causes of the condition of the poor whites, I never failed to make inquiries of planters, and of intelligent men especially, about those in their neighbourhood; and being soon struck by the constant recurrence of similar expressions with regard to them, I was the more careful to introduce the subject at every proper opportunity, and, I repeat, always with the same result. I am afraid that the feeling of the South to the North is (more or less defined in individual minds) of the same nature, and that the contiguity of a people whose labourers take care of themselves, and labour industriously without being owned, can never be felt to be safe by slaveholders. That it must always be looked upon with apprehension, with a sense of danger, more or less vague, more or less well defined, but always sufficient to lead to efforts intended to counteract its natural influence—its influence not so much with slaves, certainly not alone with the slaves, but also with that important element of population which reaps no profit from the good behaviour of the slaves.

In De Bow's "Review" for January, 1850, will be found the following passage in an article discussing the practicability of employing the non-slaveholding whites in factories, the argument being that there will be less danger of their becoming "Abolitionists" under such circumstances than at present exists:—

"The great mass of our poor white population begin to understand that they have rights, and that they, too, are entitled to some of the sympathy which falls upon the suffering. They are fast learning that there is an almost infinite world of industry opening before them by which they can elevate themselves and their families from wretchedness and ignorance to competence and intelligence. It is this great upheaving of our masses that we have to fear, so far as our institutions are concerned."

It is, in the nature of things, while slaveholders refuse the slightest concession to the spirit of the age—while, in their legislation, they refuse to recognize, in the slightest degree, the principles of social science under which we live, and must live, and which every civilized people has fully adopted, that they should endeavour to make it appear the fault of others that they do not feel assured of safety and at ease with themselves; that they should try to make their own ignorant people believe that it is from without all danger is to be apprehended—all assurance of safety to be clamoured for—that they should endeavour to make themselves believe it.*

* The real object of the systematic mail robbery which is maintained throughout the South, and of the censorship of the press which is otherwise attempted, was once betrayed by a somewhat distinguished Southern editor, Duff Green, in the *United States Telegraph*, in the following words:—

"The real danger of this [slave insurrection] is remote. We believe we have most to fear from the organized action upon the consciences and fears of the slaveholders themselves; from the insinuation of their dangerous heresies into our schools, our pulpits, and our domestic circles. It is only by alarming the consciences of the weak and feeble, and diffusing among our people a morbid sensibility on the question of slavery, that the Abolitionists can accomplish their object."

Those who seriously propose to stop all agitation on the subject of slavery, by causing the Abolitionists to refrain from proceedings which cause apprehension at the South, by silencing all who entertain sentiments the utterance of which is deemed a source of "danger to Southern institutions," by refraining themselves from all proceedings which will be looked upon with alarm by their fellow-citizens of the Slave States, can know very little of what would be required before the South were satisfied. The destruction of some million dollars' cost in school and text books would be one of the first things, and yet but a small item in the undertaking. Books which directly comment upon slavery are considered comparatively safe, because their purpose being defined, they can be guarded against. As is well understood, it is the insidious attacks of a free press that are most feared. But is it well understood what are felt to be "insidious attacks?" Some idea may be formed from the following passages which I take, not from the heated columns of a daily newspaper, but from the cool pages of the deliberate De Bow's "Review." The apprehension they express is not of to-day; in the first article from which I quote (which was published in the middle of Mr. Pierce's presidential term), reference is made to warnings of the same character which have been sounded from time to time before; and this very number of the "Review" contains a testimonial from fifty-five Southern senators and representatives in Congress to the "ability and accuracy" of its "exposition of the working of the system of polity of the Southern States."

"Our text books are abolition books. They are so to the extent of their capacity." . . . "We have been too careless and indifferent to the import of these things."

"And so long as we use such works as 'Wayland's Moral Science,' and the abolition geographies, readers, and histories, overrunning, as they do, with all sorts of slanders, caricatures, and blood-thirsty sentiments, let us never complain of their [northern Church people's] use of that transitory romance ['Uncle Tom's Cabin']. They seek to array our children, by false ideas, against the established ordinance of God; and it sometimes takes effect. A professor in one of our Southern seminaries, not long since placed in the hands of a pupil 'Wayland's Moral Science,' and informed her that the chapter on slavery was heretical and unscriptural, and that she would not be examined on that chapter, and need not study it, *Perhaps* she didn't. But on the day of examination she wished her teacher to tell her 'if that chapter was heretical how she was to know but they were all so?' We might enumerate many other books of similar character and tendencies. But we will refer to only one more—it is 'Gilbert's Atlas'—though the real author's name does not appear on the title page. On the title page it is called 'Appleton's Complete Guide of the World;' published by D. Appleton & Co., New York. This is an elegant and comprehensive volume, endorsed by the Appletons and sent South, containing hidden lessons of the most fiendish and murderous character that enraged fanaticism could conceive or indite.* It is a sort of literary and scientific infernal machine. And whatever the design may have been, the tendency is as shocking as the imagination can picture. . . . This is the artillery and these the implements England and our own recreant sister States are employing to overturn the order of society and the established forms of labour that date back beyond the penning of the decalogue. . . . This book, and many other Northern school-books scattered over the country, come within the range of the statutes of this State, which provide for the imprisonment for life or the infliction of the penalty of death upon any person who shall 'publish or distribute' such works; and were I a citizen of New Orleans, this work should not escape the attention of the grand jury. But need I add more to convince the sceptical of the necessity there is for the production of our own text-books, and, may I not add, our own literature? Why should the land of domestic servitude be less productive in the great works of the mind now than when Homer evoked the arts, poetry, and eloquence into existence? Moses wrote the Genesis of Creation, the Exodus of Israel, and the laws of mankind? and when Cicero, Virgil, Horace, St. John, and St. Paul became the instructors of the world?† . . . They will want no cut-throat literature, no fire-brand moral science . . . nor Appleton's 'Complete Atlas,' to encourage crimes that would blanch the cheek of a pirate, nor any of the ulcerous and polluting agencies issuing from the hot-beds of abolition fanaticism."

---

* Elsewhere the Messrs. Appleton are spoken of as "the great Abolition publishers of New York."

† Note the argument, I pray you, reader. Why, indeed? Why is there not a Feejee Iliad? Are not the Feejees heathen, as Homer was? Why should not the Book of Mormon be as good a thing as the Psalms of David? Was not Joseph Smith also a polygamist?

From an article on educational reform at the South, in the same "Review," 1856, I take the following indications of what, among other Northern doings, are considered to imperil the South:—

"'Lovell's United States Speaker,' the 'National Reader,' the 'Young Ladies' Reader,' 'Columbian Orator,' 'Scott's Lessons,' the 'Village Reader,' and numerous others, have been used for years, and are all, in some respects, valuable compilations. We apprehend, however, there are few parents or teachers who are familiar with the whole of their contents, or they would demand expurgated editions for the use of their children. *The sickly sentimentality of the poet Cowper*, whose ear became so 'pained,' and his soul 'sick with every day's report of wrong and outrage,' that it made him cry out in agony for 'a lodge in some vast wilderness,' where he might commune with howling wolves and panthers on the blessings of *liberty* (?), stamps its infectious poison upon many of the pages of these works." . . .

"From the American First Class Book, page 185, we quote another more modern sentiment, which bears no less higher authority than the name of the great Massachusetts statesman, Mr. Webster:"

Having burnt or expurgated Webster and Cowper, is it to be imagined that the leaders of opinion in the South would yet be willing to permit familiar intercourse between themselves and a people who allowed a book containing such lines as these to circulate freely?—

"What is a man
If his chief good and market of his time
Be but to sleep and feed? A beast, no more.
Sure, He that made us with such large discourse,
Looking before and after, gave us not
That capability and Godlike reason,
To rust unused."

What a dangerous sentiment to come by any chance to a slave! Is it not? Are you, then, prepared to burn your Shakespeare? I will not ask if you will have another book "expurgated," of all passages the tendency of which is to set the bondmen free.

If the security of life and property at the South must for ever be dependent on the thoroughness with which the negro population is prevented from acquiring knowledge; from thinking of themselves and for themselves, it will never be felt to be greater than it is to-day. Efforts made to increase this security will of themselves occasion agitation, and agitation must counteract those efforts. Knowledge, knowledge of what is going on elsewhere, of the condition of men elsewhere, of what is thought elsewhere, must have increased currency with every class of mankind in all parts of this continent, as it increases in population, and the movements of its population increase in activity and importance. No human laws, embargoes, or armies and navies can prevent it. Do our utmost, we cannot go back of the steam-engine, the telegraph, the cotton-gin, and the cylinder press. The South has admitted steamboats and railroads. It was not practicable to stop with these, and bar out all the rest that is peculiar to the nineteenth century. Is it practicable to admit the machinery of modern civilized life, and not stir up its free people? Is it practicable to stir up its intermediate class, and keep its lowest torpid? Assuredly the security which depends upon preventing either of these steps can never be permanently increased; spite of all possible further extension of slave territory, and dispersion and disconnection of plantations, it must gradually lessen. As it lessens, the demand upon the nation to supply new grounds of security must increase—increase continually, until at length, this year, next year, or another, they conclusively and hopelessly fail. It may cost us much or it may cost us little to reach that point, but it is inevitably to be reached. It may be after long and costly civil war, or longer and more costly foreign wars, or it may be peaceably, sensibly, and soon, but it must come. The annexation of Cuba, international fugitive slave laws,* the African slave trade, judgments of the Supreme Court, and whatever else may be first asked and given, will not prevent it—nothing the North will do, nothing the North can do, will prevent it. The proximity of a people who cannot hold labour in contempt; who cannot keep labourers in ignorance and permanent dependence each upon another man; who cannot have an effective censorship of the press, or a trustworthy army of *mouchards*, prevents, and must always prevent, the South from standing with the slightest confidence of safety on that policy which it proclaims to be its only ground of safety. Nothing but a reversal of the current of our Northern history for half a century, nothing, in fact, but the enslavement of labour at the North, could in the nature of things, give that security, even temporarily, to the capitalists of labour at the South which they need.† Some demand of the South upon the na-

* From the *Columbia* (S. C.) *Times*, quoted without dissent in the conservative South Carolina paper, the *Charleston Mercury*:—

"The loss that the South annually sustains by the running of slaves into Canada, is of sufficient importance to justify her public men in insisting upon some action of the Government of the United States in the premises. And we confess our surprise that Southern statesmen have submitted with so much patience to the annual robbery of thousands of dollars' worth of property to which she has as good a right as the land they cultivate. The time is propitious for the acquisition of all disputed rights from European powers. They cannnot afford to break just now with the United States. Let our public men move in the matter, and we question not but that the President and the American Minister at St. James's will give the movement a cordial support. Besides, this is a golden moment which may never return. Before we get another sound man in the presidential chair, peace may be made in Europe, and the European powers be less inclined to look with favour upon the demands of America."

† "While it is far more obvious that negroes should be slaves than whites, for they are only fit to labour, not to direct; yet the principle of slavery is itself right, and does not depend upon difference of complexion. Difference of race, lineage, of language, of habits, and customs, all tend to render the institution more natural and durable; and although slaves have been generally whites, still the masters and slaves have generally been of different national descent. Moses and Aristotle, the earliest historians, are both authorities in favour of this difference of race, but not of colour."—*Richmond Enquirer.*

tion, acquiescence in which it holds essential to its safety, must then at length be distinctly refused. And when, ten or twenty years hence, if so be, this shall come to pass, what then is to happen to us?

Dissolution?

This is what many Southern politicians avow, whenever they contemplate such a contingency.

Why?

Because it is known that the people of the North are unwilling that the Union should be dissolved, whereas they have no indisposition to the only course which it will then be possible for the South to adopt, for the sake of increasing the security of its citizens, against insurrectionary movements of its slaves. This plainly would be to arrange a systematic opportunity and method for the slaves to labour, whenever they chose, and as much as they might choose, in an orderly, peaceable, and wise way, for their own release and improvement, each man for himself and those most dear to him; each man by himself, independently, openly, with no occasion for combination, secrecy, plots, or conspiracy. To prepare, for those disposed to avail themselves of it, a field, either here or elsewhere, in which their capability and Godlike reason, such as it may be, little or great, need not be forced by law to rust unused, or brighten *only* to the material advantage of a master. This I must think to be consciously, even now, the only final course of safety before every reflective Southern mind. This, or——dissolution, and the chances of war.

[The above was written before Mr. Lincoln was spoken of as a candidate for the Presidency.]

APPENDIX.

(A.)

THE CONDITION OF VIRGINIA.—STATISTICS.

1.

The *Richmond Enquirer*, a strong and influential pro-slavery newspaper of Virginia, in advocating some railroad projects, thus describes the progress of the State relatively to that of some of the Free States, since the Revolution. (Dec. 29, 1852.)

"Virginia, anterior to the Revolution, and up to the adoption of the Federal Constitution, contained more wealth and a larger population than any other State of this Confederacy. * * *

"Virginia, from being first in point of wealth and political power, has come down to the fifth in the former, and the fourth in the latter: New York, Pennsylvania, Massachusetts, and Ohio stand above her in wealth, and all, but Massachusetts, in population and political power. Three of these States are literally chequered over with railroads and canals; and the fourth (Massachusetts) with railroads alone. * * *

"But when we find that the population of the single city of New York and its environs exceeds the whole free population of Eastern Virginia, and the valley between the Blue Ridge and Alleghany, we have cause to feel deeply for our situation. Philadelphia herself contains a population far greater than the whole free population of Eastern Virginia. The little State of Massachusetts has an aggregate wealth exceeding that of Virginia by more than one hundred and twenty-six millions of dollars—a State, too, which is incapable of subsisting its inhabitants from the production of its soil. And New York, which was as much below Massachusetts, at the adoption of the Federal Constitution, in wealth and power, as the latter was below Virginia, now exceeds the wealth of both. While the aggregate wealth of New York, in 1850, amounted to $1,080,309,216, that of Virginia was $436,701,082—a difference in favour of the former of $643,608,134. The unwrought mineral wealth of Virginia exceeds that of New York. The climate and soil are better; the back country, with equal improvements, would contribute as much."

The same journal adds, on another occasion:—

"In no State of the Confederacy do the facilities for manufacturing operations exist in greater profusion than in Virginia. Every condition essential to success in these employments is found here in prodigal abundance, and in a peculiarly convenient combination. First, we have a limitless supply of water power—the cheapest of motors—in localities easy of access. So abundant is this supply of water power that no value is attached to it distinct from the adjacent lands, except in the vicinity of the larger towns. On the Potomac and its tributaries; on the Rappahannock; on the James and its tributaries; on the Roanoke and its tributaries; on the Holston, the Kanawha, and other streams, numberless sites may now be found where the supply of water power is sufficient for the purposes of a Lawrence or a Lowell. Nor is there any want of material for building at these localities; timber and granite are abundant; and, to complete the circle of advantages, the climate is genial and healthful, and the soil eminently productive. * * * Another advantage which Virginia possesses, for the manufacture of cotton, is the proximity of its mills to the raw material. At the present prices of the staple, the value of this advantage is estimated at 10 per cent."

The *Lynchburg Virginian*, another newspaper of respectability, having a similar purpose in hand, namely, to induce capitalists to invest their money in enterprises that shall benefit the State, observes that—

"The coal fields of Virginia are the most extensive in the world, and her coal is of the best and purest quality. Her iron deposits are altogether inexhaustible, and in many instances so pure that it is malleable in its primitive state; and many of these deposits in the immediate vicinity of extensive coal-fields. She has, too, very extensive deposits of copper, lead, and gypsum. Her rivers are numerous and bold, generally with fall enough for extensive water power.

"A remarkable feature in the mining and manufacturing prospects of Virginia is, the ease and economy with which all her minerals are mined; instead of being, as in England and elsewhere, generally imbedded deep within the bowels of the earth, from which they can be got only with great labour and at great cost, ours are found everywhere on the hills and slopes, with their ledges dipping in the direction of the plains below. Why, then, should not Virginia at once employ at least half of her labour and capital in mining and manufacturing? Richmond could as profitably manufacture all cotton and woollen goods as Lowell, or any other town in New England. Why should not Lynchburg, with all her promised facility of getting coal and pig metal, manufacture all articles of iron and steel just as cheaply, and yet as profitably, as any portion of the Northern States? Why should not every town and village on the line of every railroad in the State, erect their shops, in which they may manufacture a thousand articles of daily consumption, just as good and cheap as they may be made anywhere? * * *

"Dependent upon Europe and the North for almost every yard of cloth, and every coat, and boot, and hat we wear; for our axes, scythes, tubs, and buckets—in short, for everything except our bread and meat! —it must occur to the South that if our relations with the North should ever be severed—and how soon they may be, none can know (may God avert it long!)—we would, in all the South, not be able to clothe ourselves. We could not fell our forests, plough our fields, nor mow our meadows. In fact, we would be reduced to a state more abject than we are willing to look at even prospectively. And yet, with all these things staring us in the face, we shut our eyes, and go on blindfold."

At the Convention for the formation of the Virginia State Agricultural Society, in 1852, the draft of an address to the farmers of the State was read, approved, and once adopted by the Convention. The vote by which it was adopted was soon afterwards reconsidered, and it was again approved and adopted. A second time it was reconsidered; and finally it was rejected, on the ground that there were admissions in it that would feed the fanaticism of the Abolitionists. No one argued against it on the ground of the falsity or inaccuracy of these admissions. Twenty of the most respectable proprietors in the State, immediately afterwards, believing it to contain "matter of grave import," which should not be suppressed for such a reason, united in requesting a copy of it for publication. In the note of these gentlemen to the author, they express the belief that Virginia now "possesses the richest soil, most genial climate, and cheapest labour on earth." The author of the address, in his reply, says: "Fanaticism is a fool for whose vagaries I am not responsible. I am a pro-slavery man—I believe it, at this time, impossible to abolish it, and not desirable if it were possible."

The address was accordingly published, and I make the following extracts from it:—

"ADDRESS TO THE FARMERS OF VIRGINIA.

"'The Southern States stand foremost in agricultural labour, though they hold but the third rank in population.' At the head of these Southern States, in production, in extent of territory, in climate, in soil, and in population, stands the Commonwealth of Virginia. She is a nation of farmers. Eight-tenths of her industry is expended upon the soil; but less than one-third of her domain is in pasturage, or under the plough.

"Out of somewhat more than thirty-nine millions of acres, she tills but little over ten millions of acres, or about twenty-six and a quarter per cent., whilst New York has subdued about forty-one per cent., or twelve and a quarter out of her twenty-nine and a half millions of acres: and Massachusetts, with her sterile soil and inhospitable climate, has reclaimed from the forest, the quarry, and the marsh, about forty-two and a half per cent., or two and one-eighth out of her little territory of five millions of acres. Yet, according to the census of 1840, only six-tenths of the labour of New York, and four-tenths of that of Massachusetts, or, relatively, one-fifth and two-fifths less than our own, is expended upon agriculture. * * *

"The live stock of Virginia are worth only three dollars and thirty-one cents for every arable acre; but in New York they are worth six dollars and seven cents, and in Massachusetts four dollars and fifty-two cents.

"The proportion of hay for the same quantity of land is, for Virginia, eighty-one pounds; for New York, six hundred and seventy-nine pounds; for Massachusetts, six hundred and eighty-four pounds. * *

"With access to the same markets, and with hundreds of mechanics of our own, who can vie with the best Northern manufacturers, we find that our implements are inferior, that the New York farmer spends upon his nearly three times as much as we do upon ours, and the Massachusetts farmer more than double. * * *

"Manure is indispensable to good husbandry. Judging from the history of agriculture in all other countries, we may safely say, that farming can never attain to continued perfection where manure is not put on with an unsparing hand. By far the larger part of this can only be made by stock, which should, at the same time, be made the source of profit, at least sufficient to pay the cost of their keep, so that, *other things being equal*, it is a safe rule to estimate the condition of a farming district by the amount of live stock it may possess, and the provision made for their sustenance. Applied in this instance, we see that the New York farmer has invested in live stock two dollars and seventy-six cents, and the Massachusetts farmer one dollar and twenty-one cents per acre more than the Virginia farmer. In pasturage we cannot tell the difference. It is well, perhaps, for the honour of the State, that we cannot. But in hay, New York has five hundred and ninety-eight pounds, and Massachusetts six hundred and three pounds more per acre than we have. This, however, does not present the true state of the case. Land-locked by mountain barriers, as yet impassable for the ordinary agricultural staples, or debarred from their production by distance and prohibitory rates of transportation, most of the wealth and exports of many considerable portions of our State consists of live stock alone. What proportion these parts bear to the whole, we have been unable definitely to ascertain; but it is, no doubt, so great as to warrant us in assuming a much more considerable disparity than the statistics show in the live stock of the whole Atlantic slope, as compared with New York and Massachusetts. And we shall appreciate, still more highly, the skill of the Northern farmer, if we reflect that a readier market for every, the most trivial, product of his farm, operates as a constant temptation to break up his rotation and diminish his stock.

"In the above figures, carefully calculated from the data of authentic documents,* we find no cause for self-gratulation, but some food for meditation. They are not without use to those who would improve the future by the past. They show that we have not done our part in the bringing of land into cultivation; that, notwithstanding natural advantages which greatly exceed those of the two States drawn into parallel with Virginia, we are yet behind them both—that with forty and sixty per cent. respectively of their industry devoted to other pursuits, into which it has been lured by prospects of greater gain, they have done more than we have done. * * *

"Whilst our population has increased for the last ten years, in a ratio of 11·66, that of New York has increased in a ratio of 27·52, and that of Massachusetts at the still heavier and more startling rate of 34·81. With a territorial area thirty per cent. larger than New York, we have but little more than one-third of her Congressional representation; and Massachusetts, only one-eighth our size, comes within two of our number of representatives, we being cut down to thirteen, while she rises to eleven. And thus we, who once swayed the councils of the Union, find our power gone, and our influence on the wane, at a time when both are of vital importance to our prosperity, if not to our safety. As other States accumulate the means of material greatness, and glide past us on the road to wealth and empire, we slight the warnings of dull statistics, and drive lazily along the field of ancient customs, or stop the

* Abstract of the Seventh Census, and the able work of Professor Tucker, on the "Progress of the United States in Population and Wealth."

plough, to speed the *politician*—should we not, in too many cases, say with more propriety, the *demagogue*?

"State pride is a good thing; it is one mode in which patriotism is manifested. But it is not always a wise one. Certainly not, when it makes us content on small grounds. And when it smothers up improvement in self-satisfaction, it is a most pernicious thing. We have much to be proud of in Virginia. In intellect and fitness to command, in personal and social qualities, in high tone and noble bearing, in loyalty, in generosity, and magnanimity, and disinterestedness, above all, in moral purity, we once stood—let us hope, still stand—pre-eminent among our sister States. But the possession and practice of these virtues do not comprise our whole duty as men or as citizens. The great decree which has gone forth ordaining that we shall 'increase, and multiply, and replenish the earth,' enjoins upon us quite other duties, which cannot be neglected with impunity; so we have found out by experience—for we *have* neglected these duties. And when we contemplate our field of labour, and the work we have done in it, we cannot but observe the sad contrast between capacity and achievement. With a wide-spread domain, with a kindly soil, with a climate whose sun radiates fertility, and whose very dews distil abundance, we find our inheritance so wasted that the eye aches to behold the prospect."

2.

The Census of 1850 gives the following values to agricultural land in the adjoining States of Virginia and Pennsylvania.

	In Virginia.	In Pennsylvania.
No. of acres improved land in farms,	10,360,135	8,626,619
,, unimproved,	15,792,176	6,294,728
Cash value of farms,	$216,401,543—$8 an acre.	$407,876,099—$25 an acre.

Considering that, at the Revolution, Virginia had nearly twice the population of Pennsylvania, was in possession of much more wealth or disposable capital, and had much the best natural facilities for external commerce and internal communication, if her political and social constitution had been and had continued equally good, and her people equally industrious and enterprising with those of Pennsylvania, there is no reason why the value of her farms should not have been, at this time, at least equal to those of Pennsylvania. Were it so, it appears that Virginia, in that particular alone, would now be richer than she is by four hundred and thirty millions of dollars.

If it should be thought that this difference between the value of land in Virginia and Pennsylvania is in some degree due to more fertile soils in the latter, a similar comparison may be made with the other adjoining Free State, and old State of New Jersey, the climate of which, owing to its vicinity to the ocean, differs imperceptibly from that of Virginia, while its soil is decidedly less fertile, taking both States on an average. The average value of farming-land in New Jersey is recorded at $44.

Give this value to the Virginia farms, and the difference between it and their present value would buy, at a large valuation, all the slaves now in the State, send them to Africa, provide each family of them five hundred dollars to start with when they reached there, and leave still a surplus which, divided among the present white population of the State, would give between two and three thousand dollars to each family.

Some Southern writers have lately objected to comparisons of density of population, as indications of the prosperity of communities. Between two adjoining communities, however, where there are no restrictions upon the movements of the populations, and when the people are so ready to move as both those of Pennsylvania, and New Jersey, and of Virginia have shown themselves to be, the price of land must indicate with considerable exactness the comparative value or desirableness of it, all things considered, to live upon. The Virginians do not admit, and have no occasion to do so, that Pennsylvania and New Jersey have any advantage over Virginia, in soil, in climate, or in any natural quality.

3.

In intellectual productions, the same general comparative barrenness is noticeable.

From the Richmond Whig.

"We receive nearly all our books from Northern or foreign authors—gotten up, printed by Northern or foreign publishers—while we have among us numberless men of ripe scholarship, profound acquirements, elegant and forcible writers—men willing to devote themselves to such labour, *only a Southern book is not patronized.* The North usually scowls at it, ridicules it, or damns it with faint praise; and the South takes on a like hue and complexion and neglects it. We have printers and publishers able, willing, and competent to publish, but, such is the *apathy* on the part of Southern people, that it involves hazard to Southern publishers to put them out. Indeed, until recently, almost all the publications, even of Southern books, issued (and that was their only hope of success) from Northern houses. The last chance now of getting a Southern book sold, is to manage to secure the favourable notice of the Northern press, and then the South buys it. Our magazines and periodicals languish for support."

Mr. Howison, "The Virginia Historian," observes:

"The question might be asked, Where is the literature of Virginia? and it would not be easily answered. It is a melancholy fact, that her people have never been a reading people. In the mass they have shown an indifference to polite literature and education in general, depressing to the mind that wishes to see them respectable and happy."

"It is with pain," says the same authority, "that we are compelled to speak of the horrible cloud of ignorance that rests on Virginia," and he computes that (1848) there are in the State 166,000 youth, between seven and sixteen years of age, and of these 126,000 attend no school at all, and receive no education except what can be imparted by poor and ignorant parents. Besides these, he reckons 449,087 slaves and 48,852 free negroes, with few exceptions, wholly uneducated.

"The policy which discourages further extension of knowledge among them is necessary: but the fact remains unchanged, that they exist among us, *a huge mass of mind, almost entirely unenlightened.* We fear that the most favourable estimates will leave, in our State, 683,000 rational beings who are destitute of the merest rudiments of knowledge."

APPENDIX (B.)

THE SLAVE TRADE IN VIRGINIA.

From Chambers's Journal.

"The exposure of ordinary goods in a store is not more open to the public than are the sales of slaves in Richmond. By consulting the local newspapers, I learned that the sales take place by auction every morning in the offices of certain brokers, who, as I understood by the terms of their advertisements, purchased or received slaves for sale on commission.

"Where the street was in which the brokers conducted their business, I did not know; but the discovery was easily made. Rambling down the main street in the city, I found that the subject of my search was a narrow and short thoroughfare, turning off to the left, and terminating in a similar cross thoroughfare. Both streets, lined with brick houses, were dull and silent. There was not a person to whom I could put a question. Looking about, I observed the office of a commission agent, and into it I stepped. Conceive the idea of a large shop with two windows, and a door between; no shelving or counters inside; the interior a spacious, dismal apartment, not well swept; the only furniture a desk at one of the windows, and a bench at one side of the shop, three feet high, with two steps to it from the floor. I say, conceive the idea of this dismal-looking place, with nobody in it but three negro children, who, as I entered, were playing at auctioneering each other. An intensely black little negro, of four or five years of age, was standing on the bench, or block, as it is called, with an equally black girl, about a year younger, by his side, whom he was pretending to sell by bids to another black child, who was rolling about the floor.

"My appearance did not interrupt the merriment. The little auctioneer continued his mimic play, and appeared to enjoy the joke of selling the girl, who stood demurely by his side.

"'Fifty dolla for de gal—fifty dolla—fifty dolla—I sell dis here fine gal for fifty dolla,' was uttered with extraordinary volubility by the woolly-headed urchin, accompanied with appropriate gestures, in imitation, doubtless, of the scenes he had seen enacted daily on the spot. I spoke a few words to the little creatures, but was scarcely understood; and the fun went on as if I had not been present: so I left them, happy in rehearsing what was likely soon to be their own fate.

"At another office of a similar character, on the opposite side of the street, I was more successful. Here, on inquiry, I was respectfully informed, by a person in attendance, that the sale would take place the following morning at half-past nine o'clock.

"Next day I set out accordingly, after breakfast, for the scene of operations, in which there was now a little more life. Two or three persons were lounging about, smoking cigars; and, looking along the street, I observed that three red flags were projected from the doors of those offices in which sales were to occur. On each flag was pinned a piece of paper, notifying the articles to be sold. The number of lots was not great. On the first was the following announcement:—'Will be sold this morning, at half-past nine o'clock, a Man and a Boy.'

"It was already the appointed hour; but as no company had assembled, I entered and took a seat by the fire. The office, provided with a few deal forms and chairs, a desk at one of the windows, and a block accessible by a few steps, was tenantless, save by a gentleman who was arranging papers at the desk, and to whom I had addressed myself on the previous evening. Minute after minute passed, and still nobody entered. There was clearly no hurry in going to business. I felt almost like an intruder, and had formed the resolution of departing, in order to look into the other offices, when the person referred to left his desk, and came and seated himself opposite to me at the fire.

"'You are an Englishman,' said he, looking me steadily in the face; 'do you want to purchase?'

"'Yes,' I replied, 'I am an Englishman; but I do not intend to purchase. I am travelling about for information, and I shall feel obliged by your letting me know the prices at which negro servants are sold.'

"'I will do so with much pleasure,' was the answer; 'do you mean field-hands or house-servants?'

"'All kinds,' I replied; 'I wish to get all the information I can.'

"With much politeness, the gentleman stepped to his desk, and began to draw up a note of prices. This, however, seemed to require careful consideration; and while the note was preparing, a lanky person, in a wide-awake hat, and chewing tobacco, entered, and took the chair just vacated. He had scarcely seated himself, when, on looking towards the door, I observed the subjects of sale—the man and boy indicated by the paper on the red flag—enter together, and quietly walk to a form at the back of the shop, whence, as the day was chilly, they edged themselves towards the fire, in the corner where I was seated. I was now between the two parties—the white man on the right, and the old and young negro on the left—and I waited to see what would take place.

"The sight of the negroes at once attracted the attention of Wide-awake. Chewing with vigour, he kept keenly eyeing the pair, as if to see what they were good for. Under this searching gaze, the man and boy were a little abashed, but said nothing. Their appearance had little of the repulsiveness we are apt to associate with the idea of slaves. They were dressed in a gray woollen coat, pants, and waistcoat, coloured cotton neckcloths, clean shirts, coarse woollen stockings, and stout shoes. The man wore a black hat; the boy was bareheaded. Moved by a sudden impulse, Wide-awake left his seat, and rounding the back of my chair, began to grasp at the man's arms, as if to feel their muscular capacity. He then examined his hands and fingers; and, last of all, told him to open his mouth and show his teeth, which he did in a submissive manner. Having finished these examinations, Wide-awake resumed his seat, and chewed on in silence as before.

"I thought it was but fair that I should now have my turn of investigation, and accordingly asked the elder negro what was his age. He said he did not know. I next inquired how old the boy was. He said he was seven years of age. On asking the man if the boy was his son, he said he was not—he was his cousin. I was going into other particulars, when the office-keeper approached, and handed me the note he had been preparing; at the same time making the observation that the market was dull at present, and that there never could be a more favourable opportunity of buying. I thanked him for the trouble which he had taken; and now submit a copy of his price-current:

Best Men, 18 to 25 years old	1200 to 1300	dollars.
Fair do. do. do.	950 to 1050	,,
Boys, 5 feet	850 to 950	,,
Do., 4 feet 8 inches	700 to 800	,,
Do., 4 feet 5 inches	500 to 600	,,
Do., 4 feet	375 to 450	,,
Young Women	800 to 1000	,,
Girls, 5 feet	750 to 850	,,
Do., 4 feet 9 inches	700 to 750	,,
Do., 4 feet	350 to 450	,,

(Signed) ——————

Richmond, Virginia.

"Leaving this document for future consideration, I pass on to a history of the day's proceedings. It was now ten minutes to ten o'clock, and Wide-awake and I being alike tired of waiting, we went off in quest of sales further up the street. Passing the second office, in which also nobody was to be seen, we were more fortunate at the third. Here according to the announcement on the paper stuck to the flag, there were to be sold, 'A woman and three children; a young woman, three men, a middle-aged woman, and a little boy.' Already a crowd had met, composed, I should think, of persons mostly from the cotton-plantations of the South. A few were seated near a fire on the right-hand side, and others stood round an iron stove in the middle of the apartment. The whole place had a dilapidated appearance. From a back window, there was a view into a ruinous court-yard; beyond which, in a hollow, accessible by a side lane, stood a shabby brick house, on which the word *Jail* was inscribed in large black letters on a white ground. I imagined it to be a depôt for the reception of negroes.

"On my arrival, and while making these preliminary observations, the lots for sale had not made their appearance. In about five minutes afterwards, they were ushered in, one after the other, under the charge of a mulatto, who seemed to act as principal assistant. I saw no whips, chains, or any other engine of force. Nor did such appear to be required. All the lots took their seats on two long forms near the stove; none showed any signs of resistance; nor did any one utter a word. Their manner was that of perfect humility and resignation.

"As soon as all were seated, there was a general examination of their respective merits, by feeling their arms, looking into their mouths, and investigating the quality of their hands and fingers—this last being evidently an important particular. Yet there was no abrupt rudeness in making these examinations—no coarse or domineering language was employed. The three negro men were dressed in the usual manner—in gray woollen clothing. The woman, with three children, excited my peculiar attention. She was neatly attired, with a coloured handkerchief bound around her head, and wore a white apron over her gown. Her children were all girls, one of them a baby at the breast three months old, and the others two and three years of age respectively, rigged out with clean white pinafores. There was not a tear or an emotion visible in the whole party. Everything seemed to be considered as a matter of course; and the change of owners was possibly looked forward to with as much indifference as ordinary hired servants anticipate a removal from one employer to another.

"While intending purchasers were proceeding with personal examinations of the several lots, I took the liberty of putting a few questions to the mother of the children. The following was our conversation:—

"'Are you a married woman?'

"'Yes, sir.'

"'How many children have you had?'

"'Seven.'

"'Where is your husband?'

"'In Madison county.'

"'When did you part from him?'

"'On Wednesday—two days ago.'

"'Were you sorry to part from him?'

"'Yes, sir,' she replied, with a deep sigh; 'my heart was a'most broke.'

"'Why is your master selling you?'

"'I don't know—he wants money to buy some land—suppose he sells me for that.'

"There might not be a word of truth in these answers, for I had no means of testing their correctness; but the woman seemed to speak unreservedly, and I am inclined to think that she said nothing but what, if necessary, could be substantiated. I spoke, also, to the young woman who was seated near her. She, like the others, was perfectly black, and appeared stout and healthy, of which some of the persons present assured themselves by feeling her arms and ankles, looking into her mouth, and causing her to stand up. She told me she had several brothers and sisters, but did not know where they were. She said she was a house-servant, and would be glad to be bought by a good master—looking at me, as if I should not be unacceptable.

"I have said that there was an entire absence of emotion in the looks of men, women, and children, thus seated preparatory to being sold. This does not correspond with the ordinary accounts of slave-sales, which are represented as tearful and harrowing. My belief is, that none of the parties felt deeply on the subject, or at least that any distress they experienced was but momentary—soon passed away, and was forgotten. One of my reasons for this opinion rests on a trifling incident which occurred. While waiting for the commencement of the sale, one of the gentlemen present amused himself with a pointer dog, which, at command, stood on its hind legs, and took pieces of bread from his pocket. These tricks greatly entertained the row of negroes, old and young; and the poor woman, whose heart three minutes before was almost broken, now laughed as heartily as any one.

"'Sale is going to commence—this way, gentlemen,' cried a man at the door to a number of loungers outside; and all having assembled, the mulatto assistant led the woman and her children to the block, which he helped her to mount. There she stood, with her infant at the breast, and one of her girls at each side. The auctioneer, a handsome, gentlemanly personage, took his place, with one foot on an old deal chair with a broken back, and the other raised on the somewhat more elevated block. It was a striking scene.

"'Well, gentlemen,' began the salesman, 'here is a capital woman and her three children, all in good health—what do you say for them? Give me an offer. (Nobody speaks.) I put up the whole lot at 850 dollars—850 dollars—850 dollars (speaking very fast)—850 dollars. Will no one advance upon that? A very extraordinary bargain, gentlemen. A fine, healthy baby. Hold it up. (Mulatto goes up the first step of the block; takes the baby from the woman's breast, and holds it aloft with one hand, so as to show that it was a veritable sucking baby.) That will do. A woman, still young, and three children, all for 850 dollars. An advance, if you please, gentlemen. (A voice bids 860.) Thank you, sir, 860; any one bids more? (A second voice says, 870; and so on the bidding goes as far as 890 dollars, when it stops.) That won't do, gentlemen. I cannot take such a low price. (After a pause, addressing the mulatto): She may go down.' Down from the block the woman and her children were therefore conducted by the assistant, and, as if nothing had occurred, they calmly resumed their seats by the stove.

"The next lot brought forward was one of the men. The assistant beckoning to him with his hand, requested him to come behind a canvas screen, of two leaves, which was standing near the back window. The man placidly rose, and having been placed behind the screen, was ordered to take off his clothes, which he did without a word or look of remonstrance. About a dozen gentlemen crowded to the spot while the poor fellow was stripping himself, and as soon as he stood on the floor, bare from top to toe, a most rigorous scrutiny of his person was instituted. The clear black skin, back and front, was viewed all over for sores from disease; and there was no part of his body left unexamined. The man was told to open and shut his hands, asked if he could pick cotton, and every tooth in his head was scrupulously looked at. The investigation being at an end, he was ordered to dress himself; and having done so, was requested to walk to the block.

The ceremony of offering him for competition was gone through as before, but no one would bid. The other two men, after undergoing similar examinations behind the screen, were also put up, but with the same result. Nobody would bid for them, and they were all sent back to their seats. It seemed as if the company had conspired not to buy anything that day. Probably some imperfections had been detected in the personal qualities of the negroes. Be this as it may, the auctioneer, perhaps a little out of temper from his want of success, walked off to his desk, and the affair was so far at an end.

"'This way, gentlemen—this way!' was heard from a voice outside, and the company immediately hived off to the second establishment. At this office there was a young woman, and also a man, for sale. The woman was put up first at 500 dollars; and possessing some recommendable qualities, the bidding for her was run as high as 710 dollars, at which she was knocked down to a purchaser. The man, after the customary examination behind the screen, was put up at 700 dollars; but a small imperfection having been observed in his person, no one would bid for him; and he was ordered down.

"'This way, gentlemen, this way—down the street, if you please!' was now shouted by a person in the employment of the first firm, to whose office all very willingly adjourned—one migratory company, it will be perceived, serving all the slave-auctions in the place. In going in the crowd, I went to see what should be the fate of the man and boy, with whom I had already had some communication.

"There the pair, the two cousins, sat by the fire, just where I had left them an hour ago. The boy was put up first.

"'Come along, my man—jump up; there's a good boy!' said one of the partners, a bulky and respectable looking person, with a gold chain and bunch of seals; at the same time getting on the block. With alacrity the little fellow came forward, and, mounting the steps, stood by his side. The forms in front were filled by the company; and as I seated myself, I found that my old companion, Wide-awake, was close at hand, still chewing and spitting at a great rate.

"'Now, gentlemen,' said the auctioneer, putting his hand on the shoulder of the boy, 'here is a very fine boy, seven years of age, warranted sound—what do you say for him? I put him up at 500 dollars—500 dollars (speaking quick, his right hand raised up, and coming down on the open palm of his left)—500 dollars. Any one say more than 500 dollars? (560 is bid.) 560 dollars. Nonsense! Just look at him. See how high he is. (He draws the lot in front of him, and shows that the little fellow's head comes up to his breast.) You see he is a fine, tall, healthy boy. Look at his hands.'

"Several step forward, and cause the boy to open and shut his hands—the flexibility of the small fingers, black on the one side, and whitish on the other, being well looked to. The hands, and also the mouth, having given satisfaction, an advance is made to 570, then to 580 dollars.

"'Gentlemen, that is a very poor price for a boy of this size. (Addressing the lot)—Go down, my boy, and show them how you can run.

"The boy, seemingly happy to do as he was bid, went down from the block, and ran smartly across the floor several times; the eyes of every one in the room following him.

"'Now that will do. Get up again. (Boy mounts the block, the steps being rather deep for his short legs; but the auctioneer kindly lends him a hand.) Come, gentlemen, you see this is a first-rate lot. (590—600—610—620—630 dollars are bid.) I will sell him for 630 dollars. (Right hand coming down on left.) Last call. 630 dollars, once—630 dollars, twice. (A pause; hand sinks.) Gone!'

"The boy having descended, the man was desired to come forward; and after the usual scrutiny behind a screen, he took his place on the block.

"'Well, now, gentlemen,' said the auctioneer, 'here is a right prime lot. Look at this man; strong, healthy, able-bodied; could not be a better hand for field-work. He can drive a waggon or anything. What do you say for him? I offer the man at the low price of 800 dollars—he is well worth 1200 dollars. Come, make an advance, if you please. 800 dollars said for the man (a bid); thank you; 810 dollars—810 dollars—810 dollars (several bids)—820—830—850—860—going at 860—going. Gentlemen, this is far below his value. A strong-boned man, fit for any kind of heavy work. Just take a look at him. (Addressing the lot): Walk down. (Lot dismounts, and walks from one side of the shop to the other. When about to reascend the block, a gentleman, who is smoking a cigar, examines his mouth with his fingers. Lot resumes his place.) Pray, gentlemen, be quick (continues the auctioneer); I must sell him, and 860 dollars are only bid for the man—860 dollars. (A fresh run of bids to 945 dollars.) 945 dollars, once—945 dollars, twice (looking slowly round, to see if all were done), 945 dollars. Going—going—(hand drops)—gone!'

"Such were a forenoon's experiences in the slave-market of Richmond. Everything is described precisely as it occurred, without passion or prejudice. It would not have been difficult to be sentimental on a subject which appeals so strongly to the feelings, but I have preferred telling the simple truth. In a subsequent chapter I shall endeavour to offer some general views of slavery in its social and political relations."

APPENDIX (C.)

COST OF LABOUR IN THE BORDER STATES.

From a native Virginian, who has resided in New York:

"*To the Editor of the N. Y. Daily Times.*

"Sir—You will not object, I think, to receive an endorsement from a Southern man, of the statements contained in number seven of 'Letters on the Productions, Industry, and Resources of the Southern States' [by Mr. Olmsted], published in your issue on Thursday last * * *

"Where you would see one white labourer on a Northern farm, scores of blacks should appear on the Virginian plantation, *the best of them only performing each day one-fourth a white man's daily task, and all requiring an incessant watch to get even this small modicum of labour.* Yet they eat as much again as a white man, must have their two suits of clothes and shoes yearly, and although the heartiest, healthiest looking men and women anywhere on earth, actually lose for their owners or employers one-sixth their time on account of real or pretended sickness. Be assured, our model Virginia farmer has his hands full, and is not to be envied as a jolly fox-hunting idler, lording it over 'ranks of slaves in chains.' No, sir; he must be up by 'the dawn's early light,' and head the column, direct in person the commencing operations, urging, and coaxing; must praise and punish—but too glad to reward the meritorious, granting liberty (*i. e.* leave of absence) often to his own servant, that he dare not take himself, because he must not leave home for fear something will go wrong ere his return. Hence but too many give up, to overseers or other irresponsible persons, the care and management of their estates, rather than undergo such constant annoyance and confinement. Poor culture, scanty crops, and worn-out land, is the inevitable result; and yet, harassed and trammeled as they are, no one but a Southerner regards them with the slightest degree of compassion or even forbearance; and our good friends, the Abolitionists, would have 'all the rest of mankind' rank them with pirates and cutthroats. But my object in this communication is not to sympathize with nor ask sympathy on behalf of slaveholders. For, however sinning or sinned against, they seem quite able to take their own part, if molested; and are remarkably indifferent, withal, as to the opinions expressed by ignorant ranters concerning them.

"If I have the ability, my desire is to draw a parallel between the state and condition of Northern and Southern farmers and farming. The Northern farmer does undoubtedly experience a full share of those troubles and cares attendant even upon the most easy and favourable system of farming; but, sir, can he have any such responsibility as that resting upon the owner of from 50 to 300 ignorant, lazy negroes?

* * * * * *

"You must plough deep, follow up quickly, and sow with powerful fertilizers, attend closely to the growing crop, gather in rapidly before blight or mildew can come and destroy, says our Northern farmer. On a farm of three hundred acres, thus managed with five hands, two extra during harvest, I can raise thirty bushels of wheat to the acre. Now picture the condition of him South, and hear his answer. With from three to fifteen hundred acres of land, and a host of negroes great and small, his cares and troubles are without end. 'The hands,' able men and women, to say nothing of children, and old ones laid by from age or other infirmity, have wants innumerable. Some are sick, others pretend to be so, many obstinate, indolent, or fractious—each class requires different treatment; so that without mentioning the actual daily wants, as provisions, clothing, etc., etc., the poor man's time, and thoughts—indeed, every faculty of mind—must be exercised on behalf of those who have no minds of their own.

"His answer, then, to the Northern farmer is: 'I have not one hand on my place capable and willing to do the work you name.' They tell me that 'five of them could not perform the task required of one.' They have never been used to do it, and no amount of force or persuasion will induce them to try. Their task is so much per day; all over that I agree to pay them for, at the same rate I allow free labourers—but 'tis seldom they make extra time, except to get money enough to buy tobacco, rum, or sometimes fine clothes. Can it be wondered at that systematic farming, such as we see North and East, is unknown or not practised to any great degree South? The two systems will not harmonize.

"R. J. W."

From a native New Yorker, who has resided in Virginia:

"*To the Editor of the New York Daily Times.*

"I have read with deep interest the series of letters from the South, published in your columns. Circumstances have made me quite familiar with the field of your correspondent's investigation, much more familiar than he is at present, and yet I am happy to say, that his letters are more satisfactory than any I have ever seen relating to the South. It is now about ten years since, going from this State, I first became familiar with those facts in regard to the results of slave labour, etc., that your correspondent and his readers are so much surprised at. I have talked those subjects over as he is doing, with the planters along the shores of the Chesapeake, and on both sides of the James River, through the Tidewater, the middle and the mountainous districts east of the Blue Ridge, and in many of those rich counties in the Valley of Virginia. I may add that, subsequently, spending my winters at the South for my health, I have become well nigh as familiar with the States of North and South Carolina, and Georgia, as I am with Virginia. I have, therefore, almost of necessity, given not a little thought to the questions your correspondent is discussing.

"His statement, in regard to the comparative value of slave and free-labour, will surprise those who have given little or no attention to the subject. I wish to confirm his statements on this subject. In Eastern Virginia I have repeatedly been told that the task of one cord of wood a day, or five cords a week, rain or shine, is the general task, and one of the most profitable day's work that the slave does for his master. And this, it should be remembered, is generally pine wood, cut from trees as straight and beautiful as ever grew. The reason of this 'profitableness' is the fact that the labour requires so little mental effort. The grand secret of the difference between free and slave labour is, that the latter is without intelligence, and without motive. If the former, in Western New York, has a piece of work to perform, the first thought is, how it can be done with the least labour, and the most expeditiously. He thinks, he plans, before he commences, and while about his labour. His mind labours as much as his body, and this mental labour saves a vast deal of physical labour. Besides this, he is urged on by the strongest motives. He enjoys the products of his labour. The more intelligent and earnest his labours, the richer are his rewards. Slave labour is exactly the opposite of this. It is unintelligent labour—labour without thought—without plan—without motive. It is little more than brute force. To one who has not witnessed it, it is utterly inconceivable how little labour a slave, or a company of slaves, will accomplish in a given time. Their awkwardness, their slowness, the utter absence of all skill and ingenuity in accomplishing the work before them, are absolutely painful to one who has been accustomed to seeing work done with any sort of spirit and life. Often they spend hours in doing what, with a little thought, might be despatched in a few moments, or perhaps avoided altogether. This is a necessary result of employing labour which is without intelligence and without motive. I have often thought of a remark made to me by a planter, in New Kent County, Virginia. We were riding past a field where some of his hands were making a sort of wicker-work fence, peculiar to Eastern Virginia. 'There,' said he, in a decidedly fretted tone, 'those "boys" have been—— days in making that piece of fence.' I expressed my astonishment that they could have spent so much time, and yet have accomplished so very little. He assured me it was so—and after a slight pause, the tones of his voice entirely changed, said: 'Well, I believe they have done as well as I would in their circumstances!' And so it is. The slave is without motive, without inducement to exertion. His food, his clothing, and all his wants are supplied as they are, without care on his part, and when these are supplied he has nothing more to hope for. He can make no provision for old age, he can lay up nothing for his children, he has no voice at all in the disposal of the results of his earnings. What cares he whether his labour is productive or unproductive. His principal care seems to be to accomplish just as little as possible. I have said that the slaves were without ingenuity—I must qualify that remark. I have been amused and astonished at their exceeding ingenuity in avoiding and slighting the work that was required of them. It has often seemed to me that their principal mental efforts were in this direction, and I think your correspondent will find universal testimony that they have decided talent in this line.

"H. W. P."

In a volume entitled "Notes on Uncle Tom's Cabin; being a Logical Answer to its Allegations and Inferences against Slavery as an Institution," by the Rev. E. J. Stearns, of Maryland (much the most thorough review of that work made from the Southern stand-point), the author, who is a New-Englander by birth, shows, by an elaborate calculation, that in Maryland, the cost of a negro, at twenty-one years of age, has been, to the man who raised him, eight hundred dollars. Six *per cent.* interest on this cost, with one and three-quarters per cent. for life insurance, per annum, makes the lowest wages of a negro, under the most favourable circumstances, sixty-two dollars a year (or five dollars a month), *paid in advance*, in the shape of food and clothing. The author, whose object is to prove that the slaveholder is not guilty, as Mrs. Stowe intimates, of *stealing* the negroes' labour, proceeds, as follows, to show that he pays a great deal more for it than Mrs. Stowe's neighbours in New England do, for the labour they hire:—

"If now we add to this (what every New-Englander who has lived at the South *knows*), that Quashy does not do more than one-third, or, at the very utmost, one-half as much work as an able-bodied labourer on a farm at the North; and that, for this he receives, besides the five dollars above mentioned, his food, clothing, and shelter, with medical attendance and nursing when sick, and no deduction for lost time, even though he should be sick for years, while the 'farm-hand' at the North gets only ten or twelve dollars, and has to clothe himself out of it, and pay his own doctor's and nurse's bill in sickness, to say nothing of lost time, I think we shall come to the conclusion if there has been stealing anywhere, it has not been from Quashy."—P. 25.

"I recollect, the first time I saw Quashy at work in the field, I was struck by the lazy, listless manner in which he raised his hoe. It reminded me of the working-beam of the engine on the steam-boat that I had just landed from—fifteen strokes a minute; but there was this difference: that, whereas the working-beam kept steadily at it, Quashy, on the contrary, would stop about every five strokes and lean upon his hoe, and look around, apparently congratulating himself upon the amount of work he had accomplished.

"Mrs. Stowe may well call Quashy 'shiftless.' One of my father's hired men—who was with him seven years—did more work in that time than an average negro would do in his whole life. Nay, I myself have done more work in a day,—and followed it up, too—than I ever saw a negro do, and I was considered remarkably lazy with the plough or hoe."—P. 142.

APPENDIX (D.)

STATISTICS OF THE GEORGIA SEABOARD.

The notes here following are derived from a volume entitled "White's Statistics of Georgia," a large octavo of seven hundred pages, compiled and published in the State. A special section of the book is devoted to the condition of the trade of each county, while a comparison is also attempted to be given, from the personal observation of the compiler, of the comparative social, moral, and religious properties of the people. Thus, so far as the plan has been thoroughly executed, an estimate is presented, not only of the ordinary commercial demand of the citizens, but, so to speak, of the state of their intellectual and moral market.

The counties referred to by Mr. Gregg are in the second tier from the sea in South Carolina. I shall give statistics from Mr. White, and other authorities named in the note,* with regard to all the second tier counties of Georgia. What of good soil to be brought into cultivation, without a heavy expenditure at starting, there was originally in these counties begun to be first occupied by whites about 1740. It was not till nearly twenty years after this that slavery obtained the slightest footing in them, and it was not till about thirty years ago that they had begun to seriously deteriorate in production. There is yet some rich land upon the alluvial bottoms of the numerous rivers, which, rising above, pass through these counties toward the ocean; and here many wealthy planters still remain, owning a large number of slaves, and there has been recently a considerable increase of

* The population, following Mr. White, is given in round numbers, from the State Census of 1845; average personal estate, per family of citizens, reckoned from an official return, published in the "Soil of the South" (Columbus, Georgia, 1852, p. 210), the amount given for each county being divided by one-fifth the number of its population (for families). Observations on education and the character of the people, from "White's Statistics of Georgia" (generally in quotations). School, library, and church statistics, in figures from official United States Census, 1850.

production of some parts owing to the employment of capital in draining marshes, the riches of which have previously been considered impregnable.* In general, however, this whole range of country is now quite barren, and most of the land at present cultivated will not probably yield one-third as large a crop for the same expenditure of labour as would fair Mississippi cotton land. The slaves formerly owned here have therefore been very largely transferred westward, and the land they have worn out is left for the non-slaveholding whites to make the best of.

As an instructive contrast, I place in an adjoining column with the statistics of these counties those of the counties which bound each of them on the east. In these there is a much larger proportion of rich alluvial soil, and they contain the famous "sea island" cotton plantations, as well as the Georgian rice plantations. The valuable soil is still entirely possessed, as will be evident, by large planters and slave owners, the usual monopolizing effect of slavery being in this instance increased by the peculiar local insalubrity of the coast.

SECOND TIER COUNTIES.

Bullock County.—(The Central Railroad, the best conducted road in all the South, passes either through this county or close beside its northern boundary, for a distance of fifty miles. It is watered by the Ogeechee and Connauchee and a number of smaller rivers. On the larger rivers there is yet a considerable amount of productive land.)

COAST COUNTIES.

Bryan County, adjoining Bullock county, on the coast.

* The presence of these few planters, with their valuable human property, makes the average nominal wealth of each white family, at first sight, appear large. If, however, the slaves had been appraised at only $500 each, which would be low, they would alone amount in value in some counties to the sum assigned for the whole personal property of the citizens. This item is not, therefore, trustworthy, but, in comparing the coast and second tier counties, it serves to show the great difference in the average wealth of the citizens of each. A similar division of personal estate, as officially returned for the city of New York, would give $4,660 to each family.

SECOND TIER COUNTIES.

Population.—Whites, 2,000; slaves, 1,000. Average amount of property to each white family, $1, 570. State tax for each white family, $2.95.

Mr. White omits his usual statistics of trade. Both in this and the adjoining coast county of Bryan, the poor people, as well as the planters, are in the habit of dealing directly with Savannah, as described in "Seaboard Slave States," p. 414, and there are probably no established tradesmen in either.

The *soil* is described by Mr. White as generally poor, with some productive "hummock" and river tracts.

Education.—"No newspapers are taken, and few books read. The school fund was once sufficient to educate many poor children, but owing to bad management it has become exhausted." Thus says Mr. White. The census returns show, however, a public school expenditure of $150 per annum, and a private expenditure of $3,000, divided among fifteen schools, which is one for eighty square miles. This is so much better than usual, that, with Mr. White's remarks, I am inclined to think it an error.

COAST COUNTIES.

Population.—Whites, 1,000; slaves, 2,400. Average amount of property to each white family, $5,302 (fourfold what it is in Bullock county). State tax to each white family, $7.

No statistics of trade, again.

Soil.—"The soil, under the present system of culture, cannot, without rest and manure, be made to produce more than one half as much as when new." This appears to refer particularly to the rice plantations.

Education.—There is no academy, and there are no schools, except those supported by the "Poor School Fund" (a State provision for the children of indigent parents). "The children of the wealthy are either educated by private teachers or sent to school in the more favoured portions of the country; [the vicinity of Savannah, where there is a celebrated and well endowed academy, and of Liberty, where there are others, accounts for this;] the population is too sparse to furnish pupils enough to sustain a regular school" (large tracts of land being held by the planters, though wholly unpro-

SECOND TIER COUNTIES.

Character of the people.—"By industry and economy, they manage to supply their wants, which, however, are few. Many rely a great deal on game. * * * As far as temperance is concerned, they are behind the times. Whiskey has its votaries. Those who have attempted to show the citizens the folly and ill consequences of intemperance have been insulted and threatened. Even ministers of our holy religion have publicly denounced the motives and efforts of those who have attempted to form temperance societies."

Religion.—"The most numerous [sects] are the Anti-Missionary [hard shell?] Baptists." Ten church edifices; average value, $145. No Sunday school or other public libraries.

Tatnall County.

Population.—Whites, 2,000; slaves, 600. Average amount of property to each white family, $901.

Capital invested in trade, $4,200.

COAST COUNTIES.

ductive, to prevent the settlement of poor whites near their negroes, as one in this county informed me). According to the census returns, there were eight schools (one to twenty-five square miles) of all kinds, with an average of twelve pupils each. Total expenditure for each school, $38 per annum.

Character of the people.—No remarks.

Religion.—The county contains eleven church edifices; average value, $500. No Sunday school or other public libraries.

Liberty County.

Population.—Whites, 2,000; slaves, 6,000. Average amount of property to each white family, $6,330.

State tax to each white family, $10.

Capital invested in trade, $3,850.

SECOND TIER COUNTIES.

Soil.—" Light and sandy, except on the streams, which is stiff."

Education. — " Education is neglected." Eight public schools (1 to 148 square miles), with sixteen pupils each. Annual cost of maintenance of each school, $150. No other schools; no Sunday school or other libraries.

Character of the people.—" Sober, industrious and hospitable " (phrases applied to every county not specially noted as conspicuous for some vice or virtue of its inhabitants.)

Religion.—Sixteen church edifices, valued at $938 each. According to Mr. White, however, there are " about thirty churches " in the county.

Wayne County.

Population. — Whites, 930 ;

COAST COUNTIES.

Soil.—" The practice has been to wear out the virgin soils, and clear new lands. * * * Much waste land."

Education.—" Excellent schools are found. * * * And it is believed that a greater number of young men from Liberty county graduate from our *colleges* than from any other section of Georgia." There are five " academies," with an average of nineteen pupils each. Five public schools (1 to 160 square miles), maintained at an average expenditure of $15.40 per annum each. No libraries found in the census canvass of 1849. Mr. White states that the Medway and Newport Library Society had, in 1845, " about seven hundred volumes, in a very bad state of preservation." This library was established by some New England immigrants before the prohibition of slavery was annulled in the province. The early settlers of the county were chiefly from Massachusetts.

Character of the people.—" Generally upright and virtuous, and they are unsurpassed for the great attention paid to the duties of religion."

Religion.—Ten church edifices ; average value, $1,200.

McIntosh County, broadest on the sea.

Population.—Whites, 1,300 ;

SECOND TIER COUNTIES.

slaves, 350. Average amount of property for each white family, $898.

State tax, $1.23.

Capital invested in trade, $4,200.

Soil.—"Generally poor, barren pine land; when manured, will produce about twenty bushels of corn per acre."

Education.—"Few schools;" two academies (one Baptist, and the other Methodist, probably), with thirteen pupils between them. Four public schools (1 to 148 square miles), averaging ten pupils each; expense of maintenance not returned.

Character of the people.—"High for morality and hospitality;" "poor, but honest." At the seat of justice "are many beautiful pine hills, affording delightful summer residences to the wealthy planters of Glynn" (hence the academical advantages).

Religion.—Eight church edifices; average value, $240.

Ware County.—(About one fifth of this county is occupied by the Okefenokee Swamp.)

Population.—Whites, 2,000; slaves, 300. Average amount of personal property for each white family, $480.

COAST COUNTIES.

slaves, 4,400. Average amount of property for each white family, $7, 287, or eight times as much as in Wayne.

State tax, $2.77.

Capital invested in trade, $1,200.

Soil.—Poor turpentine pine land in the rear; on the Altamaha, "of inexhaustible fertility."

Education.—One academy, with thirty-eight scholars; four public schools, twelve and a half miles apart, averaging twenty pupils each. Expense of maintaining each school, $78 per annum. "The wealthier classes are highly educated; but, generally, little interest is felt in the subject of education."

Character of the people.—"Like all parts of Lower Georgia, the citizens of McIntosh are generally intelligent and hospitable."

Religion.—Twelve church edifices; average value, $1,041.

Camden County.—Much the largest part of this county, which is L shaped, with but one arm on the sea, is inland, and unfertile.

Population.—Whites, 3,000; slaves, 4,000. Average amount of personal property for each white family, $4,428.

SECOND TIER COUNTIES.	COAST COUNTIES.
State tax, $4.05. Stock in trade, $2,200.	State tax, $13. "Amount of business done at St. Mary's is about $30,000 per annum," nearly all in lumber, and done by New Englanders No other trade statistics.
Soil.—"Light and tolerably productive."	*Soil.*—"Of celebrated fertility."
Education.—"Very little interest is taken in the subject of education." No academies; six public schools (1 to 485 square miles), sixteen pupils each. Wages of teachers, etc., yearly, $41 each school. No Sunday school or other libraries.	*Education.*—No remarks on education or character by Mr. White. Four public schools (1 to 280 square miles), with seventeen pupils each, maintained at an average expenditure of $290 per annum. Two academies, with forty-five pupils. Five Sunday school libraries, with one hundred and ten volumes each.
Character of the people.—"The citizens are said to be hardy, industrious, and honest." "Much good might be done by the organization of temperance societies."	*Character of the people.*—No remarks.
Religion.—Fifteen church edifices, fourteen miles apart, each accommodating one hundred sitters, and valued at $56 each.	*Religion.*—Ten churches (five of which are in the town of St. Mary's, a beautiful and healthy village, resorted to by consumptives); average value, $850.

I have purposely omitted Effingham county in the above arrangement, because the adjoining coast county of Chatham contains the city of Savannah, an aggregate agency of northern and foreign merchants, through which is effected the commercial exchanges of a great extent of back country, the population of which can therefore afford no indication as to the point under consideration. Effingham, the county above Chatham, and one of the second tier, is worthy of notice, from some other important exceptional features of its constitution. Owing to the amount of rich soil in the county, along the Savannah river, there is a larger proportion of slaves to the whole population than is usual in the second tier, their number being sixteen hundred against only eighteen hundred whites; the non-slaveholders, however, appear to possess unusual privileges. There is an academy, with fifty pupils, which Mr. White describes as "a fine school." The public schools, eight in number, are less than eight miles apart, with an average attendance of sixteen pupils. Each school costs one hundred and twelve dollars a year. There are twenty-one churches, less than five miles apart, and valued at over twelve hundred dollars a-piece. Mr. White says that honesty and industry are leading characteristics of the people, who, notwithstanding the poverty of the soil, are generally in comfortable circumstances.

The reason of this is partially the close vicinity of Savannah, affording a cash market for a variety of productions and household manufactures, among which, as distinguishing the county from any other in the State, are mentioned fruits, silk, fishing lines, and cow-bells, "the latter," Mr. White is told, "superior to any manufactured in the North or in Europe." But an equally important reason for the better character and condition of the people is to be found in the fact that a majority of them * are descendants and heirs of the land of those very early settlers who most strenuously and to the last resisted the introduction of slaves into the colony, being convinced that, if permitted, it would, as they said in their memorials, "prove a scourge" to the poor people who were persuaded to petition for it.† It is most gratifying to perceive that all traces of the habits of industry, honesty, and manly self-reliance, in which they thus educated their children, are not wholly lost in the lapse of a century.

* "White's Statistics," p. 224.

† Hewitt, —; "Seaboard Slave States," p. 528.

INDEX.

LONDON: PRINTED BY WILLIAM CLOWES AND SONS, STAMFORD STREET.

RECENT AMERICAN BOOKS,

SELECTED FROM

LOW, SON AND CO.'S AMERICAN CATALOGUE.

IN HISTORY AND BIOGRAPHY.

I.

A HISTORY of the ORIGIN, FORMATION, and ADOPTION of the CONSTITUTION of the UNITED STATES of AMERICA, with Notices of its Principal Framers. By GEORGE TICKNOR CURTIS, Esq. . . . 2 vols. 8vo, cloth, 24*s.*

"A most carefully digested and well-written Constitutional History of the great Federal Republic of America."—*Examiner.*

"Mr. Curtis writes with dignity and vigour, and his work will be one of permanent interest."—*Athenæum.*

"An important and valuable contribution to Historical and Political Literature."—*Morning Chronicle.*

II.

A HISTORY of the UNITED STATES, from the Discovery of the American Continent. By GEORGE BANCROFT, Esq. . . Volumes 1 to 8, cloth, 5*l.*

III.

A HISTORY of the UNITED STATES of AMERICA. By RICHARD HILDRETH . . . . 6 vols. 8vo, cloth, 3*l.* 12*s.*

IV.

DIARY of the AMERICAN REVOLUTION, Collected from Newspapers and Original Documents. By F. MOORE . . . . 2 vols. 8vo, cloth, 30*s.*

V.

MEN and TIMES of the REVOLUTION; from 1777 to 1842; with Correspondence with Public Men, and Reminiscences and Incidents of the Revolution. Edited by WINSLOW C. WATSON . . . . 8vo, cloth, 10*s.* 6*d.*

VI.

LIFE and WRITINGS of GEORGE WASHINGTON. By JARED SPARKS . . . . 12 vols. 8vo, 4*l.* 16*s.*

VII.

LIFE of GEORGE WASHINGTON. By WASHINGTON IRVING. Illustrated . . . . 5 vols. imperial 8vo, 4*l.* 4*s.*

VIII.

LIFE of JOHN ADAMS, Second President of the United States; with Notes and Illustrations. By his Grandson, CHARLES F. ADAMS . . . . . . 14*s.*

IX.

THE LIFE of ANDREW JACKSON. By JAMES PARTON. 3 vols. royal 8vo, cloth, 48*s.*

X.

THE WORKS of DANIEL WEBSTER, Political and Literary; with a Biographical Memoir. By EDWARD EVERETT . . 6 vols. 8vo, cloth, 3*l.* 13*s.* 6*d.*

XI.

THE WRITINGS of THOMAS JEFFERSON. Published by the Order of the Joint Committee of Congress on Library, from the Original MSS. deposited in the Department of State . . . . 9 vols. 8vo, cloth, 6*l.* 6*s.*

XII.

THE LIFE and TIMES of AARON BURR, Lieut.-Colonel in the Army of the Revolution; Senator, Vice-President of the United States, &c. By J. PARTON. Crown 8vo, 10*s*. 6*d*.

XIII.

REMINISCENCES of RUFUS CHOATE, the Great American Advocate. By EDWARD G. PARKER . . . . Crown 8vo, cloth, 10*s*.

XIV.

THE LIFE and CORRESPONDENCE of JOHN A. QUITMAN, Major-General in the United States Army, and Governor of the ofState Mississippi. By J. F. H. CLAIBORNE . . . . 2 vols. crown 8vo, cloth, 16*s*.

XV.

LIFE of FREDERICK VON STEUBEN, Major-General in the Revolutionary Army; with Introduction. By GEORGE BANCROFT. Post 8vo, cloth, 10*s*. 6*d*.

XVI.

HOMES of AMERICAN STATESMEN; with Anecdotal, Personal, and Descriptive Sketches, by Various Writers. Illustrated in a very Superior style of Art . . . . Square 8vo, cloth extra, 16*s*.

XVII.

LOSSING'S MOUNT VERNON and its ASSOCIATIONS: Historical, Biographical, and Pictorial . . . . Cloth, extra, 18*s*.

XVIII.

THE MOUNT VERNON PAPERS. By EDWARD EVERETT. Crown 8vo, cloth, 8*s*. 6*d*.

XIX.

A HISTORY of AMERICAN PRIVATEERING and LETTERS of MARQUE; interspersed with Several Naval Battles between American and British Ships of War. By GEORGE COGGESHALL. Illustrated . . . . . . 8vo, cloth, 16*s*.

LAW, POLITICS, POLITICAL AND COMMERCIAL ECONOMY.

I.

A COURSE of LECTURES on the CONSTITUTIONAL JURISPRUDENCE of the UNITED STATES, delivered in Columbia College, New York. By A. W. DUER . . . . Crown 8vo, cloth, 10*s*. 6*d*.

II.

THE PRINCIPLES of POLITICAL ECONOMY applied to the Condition, the Resources, and Institutions of the American People. By FRANCIS BOWEN. 8vo, cloth, 14*s*.

III.

ELEMENTS of INTERNATIONAL LAW. By HENRY WHEATON, LL.D., with Last Corrections by the Author. Edited by WILLIAM BEACH LAWRENCE, Esq. 7th edition . . . . 8vo, cloth, 31*s*. 6*d*. (Just ready).

IV.

A HISTORY of the LAW of NATIONS in EUROPE and AMERICA. By HENRY WHEATON, LL.D. . . . . 8vo, cloth. 31*s*. 6*d*.

V.

THE LAWS of BUSINESS for BUSINESS MEN in all the STATES of the UNION: with Forms for Mercantile Instruments, Deeds, Leases, Wills, &c. By THEOPHILUS PARSONS, LL.D. . . . . 8vo, cloth, 16*s*.

VI.

THE ELEMENTS of MERCANTILE LAW. By THEOPHILUS PARSONS, LL.D. . . . . 8vo, cloth, 30*s*.

VII.

CHANCELLOR KENT'S COMMENTARIES on the LAWS of the UNITED STATES. 10th edition . . . . 4 vols. cloth 4*l.* 10*s.*

VIII.

A TREATISE on the LAW of DAMAGES. By THEODORE SEDGWICK. An entirely new edition . . . . 8vo, cloth, 31*s.* 6*d.*

IX.

JUSTICE STORY'S COMMENTARIES on the CONSTITUTION of the UNITED STATES . . . . 2 vols. 36*s.*

X.

JUSTICE STORY'S COMMENTARIES on the LAWS, viz., BAILMENTS—AGENCY—BILLS of EXCHANGE—PROMISSORY NOTES—PARTNERSHIP—and CONFLICTS of LAWS . . . . 6 vols. 8vo, cloth, each 28*s.*

EQUITY JURISPRUDENCE, 2 vols. 8vo, 63*s.*; and EQUITY PLEADINGS, 1 vol. 8vo, 31*s.* 6*d.*

XI.

W. W. STORY'S TREATISE on the LAW of CONTRACTS. 4th edition, greatly enlarged and revised . . . . 2 vols. 8vo, cloth, 63*s.*

XII.

PARSON'S TREATISE on the LAW of CONTRACTS. 2 vols. 8vo, 63*s.*

XIII.

HILLARD'S LAW of TORTS or PRIVATE WRONGS. 2 vols. 8vo, cloth, 56*s.*

XIV.

CUSHING'S ELEMENTS of the LAW and PRACTICE of LEGISLATIVE ASSEMBLIES . . . . 8vo, cloth, 25*s.*

XV.

DIGEST of the REPORTED DECISIONS of the SUPERIOR COURT and of the SUPREME COURT of ERRORS of the STATE of CONNECTICUT. By T. W. WATERMAN . . . . 8vo, calf, 2*l.* 2*s.*

XVI.

DIGEST of the DECISIONS of the COURTS of COMMON LAW and ADMIRALTY in the UNITED STATES. Vols. 1 to 6, 8vo, calf, 12*l.* 12*s.*, and vols. 7 to Annual Digest each The Annual Volumes contain the Equity, in addition to the Common Law and Admiralty, and vols. 11 and after embrace a Digest of English Law and Equity Report.

XVII.

DIGEST of the DECISIONS of the COURTS of EQUITY in the UNITED STATES. By JOHN P. PUTNAM . . . . . 2 vols. 8vo, calf, 3*l.* 10*s.*

XVIII.

DIGEST of the GENERAL LAWS of the UNITED STATES, with Notes of the Decisions and Dicta of the Supreme Courts of the Union upon their Construction. By JAMES DUNLOP . . . . . . 1 vol. royal 8vo, English law calf, 2*l.* 2*s.*

XIX.

A LAW DICTIONARY and GLOSSARY, containing full Definitions of the Principles of Common and Civil Law . . . . 2 vols. 8vo, sheep, 3*l.*

XX.

THE PATENT LAWS of the UNITED STATES; together with Rules and Proceedings in the Patent Office; also Hints to Inventors how to Obtain Letters-Patent in the United States and Europe, with Useful Legal Information to Inventors and Patentees . . . . 8vo, sewed, 6*s.* 6*d.*

XXI.

ENCYCLOPÆDIA of the TRADE and COMMERCE of the UNITED STATES. By J. B. DE BOW . . . . Thick 8vo, 3*l.* 3*s.*, reduced to 1*l.* 5*s.*, cloth.

XXII.

THE POLITICAL TEXT-BOOK or ENCYCLOPÆDIA. By W. M. CLURKEY . . . . 8vo, cloth, 20*s.*

XXIII.

OPPORTUNITIES for INDUSTRY; or, One Thousand Chances for Making Money. By EDWIN T. FREEDLEY, Esq. Author of a Practical Treatise on Business. . . . . 8vo, cloth, 6*s.*

XXIV.

THE IMPENDING CRISIS of the SOUTH, and how to meet it. By H. R. HELPER. Enlarged Edition . . . . Crown 8vo, cloth, 7*s.* 6*d.*

XXV.

THE AMERICAN ALMANACK and REPOSITORY of USEFUL KNOWLEDGE for the YEAR 1861 . . . . 8vo, 5*s.*

XXVI.

THE MERCHANT'S and BANKER'S ALMANACK for 1861. 8vo, cloth, 7*s.* 6*d.*

XXVII.

THE COTTON PLANTER'S MANUAL: being a Compilation of Facts from the Best Authorities on the Culture of Cotton. By J. A TURNER. Crown 8vo, cloth, 6*s.*

XXVIII.

THE ORDEAL of FREE LABOUR in the BRITISH WEST INDIES. By WILLIAM G. SEWELL . . . . Post 8vo, cloth, 7*s.* 6*d.*

XXIX.

MR. F. L. OLMSTED'S JOURNEYS and INVESTIGATIONS in the SLAVE STATES of AMERICA. An entirely New and Revised Edition of the three works, corrected to the Present Crisis. Complete in 2 vols. . . . 8vo (in the Press).

IN SCIENCE, LITERATURE, AND ART.

I.

THE ANNUAL of SCIENTIFIC DISCOVERY; or, YEAR-BOOK of FACTS in SCIENCE and ART in 1861. Edited by D. A. WELLS, A.M. Crown 8vo, cloth, 7*s.* 6*d.*

II.

A HISTORY of AMERICAN MANUFACTURES, from 1608 to 1860; with a Notice of the Important Inventions. By J. LEANDER BISHOP, M.D. 8vo, vol. 1. 14*s.*

III.

RAILWAY PRACTICE, EUROPEAN and AMERICAN; comprising the Economical Generation of Steam, including the Materials and Construction of Coal-burning Boilers, Combustion, the variable Blast, Vaporization, Circulation, Superheating, Supply and Heating, Feed-water, &c.; and the Adaptation of Wood and Coke-burning Engines to Coal-burning, and in Permanent Way, including Road-bed, Sleepers, Rails, Joint-fastenings, Street Railways, &c. By ALEXANDER L. HOLLEY, B.P. With 77 Plates, engraved by J. BIEN . . . . Folio, half morocco, 3*l.* 3*s.*

IV.

REPORTS of EXPERIMENTS on the STRENGTH and other PROPERTIES of METALS for CANNON; with a Description of the Machines for Testing, &c., &c. By Authority of the Secretary of War. With 25 Plates . . 4to, cloth, 50*s.*

V.

GENERAL M'CLELLAN'S REPORT of the CRIMEAN WAR, made to the U. S. Secretary at War (1857). . . . . 4to, cloth, maps, 38*s.*

LONDON: SAMPSON LOW, SON AND CO., ENGLISH, AMERICAN, AND COLONIAL BOOKSELLERS, 47, LUDGATE HILL, E.C.

VI.

VENTILATION in AMERICAN DWELLINGS, with a Series of Diagrams presenting Examples in Different Classes of Habitations. By D. B. REID, M.D. Illustrated . . . . 8vo, cloth, 12*s.*

VII.

CANADIAN NATURALIST and GEOLOGIST, and PROCEEDINGS of the NATURAL HISTORY SOCIETY of MONTREAL.
Vols. 1 to 5, 8vo, cloth, each 18*s.*, separate parts each 3*s.*

VIII.

CLASS-BOOK of BOTANY; being Outlines of the Structure, Physiology and Classification of Plants, with a Flora of the United States and Canada. By ALPHONSO WOOD, A.M. . . . . 8vo, half-bound, 12*s.*

IX.

ICHNOGRAPHS from the SANDSTONE of CONNECTICUT RIVER. By JAMES DEAN, M.D. 46 Plates, Imperial 4to. . . . . Cloth, 27*s.*

X.

THE BIRDS of NORTH AMERICA; the Descriptions of Species based chiefly on the Collections in the Museum of the Smithsonian Institution. By SPENCER F. BAIRD, with the co-operation of J. CASSIN and G. N. LAWRENCE. With an Atlas of 100 Coloured Plates . . . . 2 vols. 4to, cloth, 6*l.* 6*s.*

XI.

NATURAL HISTORY, for the use of Schools and Families. By W. HOOKER, D.D. . . . . Crown 8vo, cloth, 8*s.* 6*d.*

XII.

MANUAL of GEOLOGY, designed for the use of Colleges and Academies. By EBENEZER EMMONS. 2nd Edit. 8vo, Illustrated with Numerous Engravings . . . . half-bound, 7*s.* 6*d.*

XIII.

ARCHAIA; or, STUDIES of the COSMOGONY and NATURAL HISTORY of the HEBREW SCRIPTURES. By J. W. DAWSON, LL.D., F.G.S.
8vo, cloth, 7*s.* 6*d.*

XIV.

LECTURES on the ENGLISH LANGUAGE. By the Hon. G. P. MARSH, late U.S. Minister in Turkey . . . . 8vo, cloth, 16*s.*

XV.

A MANUAL of ENGLISH PRONUNCIATION and SPELLING; containing a Full Alphabetical Vocabulary of the Language; with a Preliminary Exposition of English Orthoepy and Orthography. By R. J. SOULE, A.M., and WILLIAM A. WHEELER, A.M. . . . . Crown 8vo (Boston, 1861), pp. 467, cloth, London, 7*s.*

XVI.

LIFE WITHOUT and LIFE WITHIN; or, Reviews, Narratives, Essays, and Poems. By Margaret Fuller Ossoli . . . . 8vo, cloth, 7*s.* 6*d.*

XVII.

ART STUDIES—The OLD MASTERS of ITALY. By James J. JARVIS, Esq., Author of "Art Hints," "Parisian Sights," &c. In 2 vols. medium 8vo, printed on toned paper, with 43 Engravings on copper, uniform style with KUGLER'S Works on Painting, edited by EASTLAKE . . . . 32*s.*

XVIII.

A DESCRIPTIVE CATALOGUE of OLD MASTERS. Collected by J. J. JARVIS . . . . 8vo, sewed, 2*s.*

XIX.

PAGES and PICTURES. From the Writings of J. F. COOPER. Illustrated from Original Drawings by F. O. C. DARLEY, &c. 40 Steel Engravings and 109 Woodcuts . . . . Half-bound morocco, 42*s.*

XX.

FOLK SONGS, with Sixty Original Illustrations and Facsimiles of Fifteen Famous Poems . . . . Royal 8vo, morocco, 52*s.* 6*d.*

XXI.

HOME BALLADS and POEMS. By J. C. WHITTIER. 12mo, cloth, 5*s.*

XXII.

POEMS, SACRED and SECULAR. By the Rev. W. CROSSWELL, D.D., with a Memoir by Rev. A. CLEVELAND COXE. Fcap. 8vo, cloth, antique, 6*s.*

XXIII.

THE MONEY KING, and other Poems. By J. G. SAXE. 12mo, cloth, 5*s.*

IN TRAVELS AND GEOGRAPHY.

I.

CANADA and HER RESOURCES. Two Prize Essays. By J. SHERIDAN HOGAN and ALEXANDER MORRIS, M.A. Second Edition, with Maps . . . . 8vo, cloth, 7*s.*

II.

CANADA, PAST, PRESENT, and FUTURE: a Topographical and Statistical Description of Canada West. By W. H. SMITH, Author of the *Canadian Gazetteer* . . . . 2 vols. 8vo, cloth, 24*s.*

III.

THE STATES OF CENTRAL AMERICA. By E. G. SQUIER, with Numerous Original Maps and Illustrations . . . . 18*s.*

IV.

NICARAGUA: its People, Scenery, Monuments, Resources, Constitution, and Proposed Canal; with One Hundred Original Maps and Illustrations. A Revised Edition. By E. G. SQUIER . . . . 8vo, cloth, London, 18*s.*

V.

BRAZIL and LA PLATA: the Personal Record of a Cruise. By C. S. STEWART, A.M., U.S.N. Illustrated . . . . Crown 8vo, cloth, 7*s.*

VI.

JAPAN EXPEDITION: Narrative of the Expedition of the American Squadron, 1852-3-4, under the Command of Commodore M. C. Perry. Vol I. The Narrative: with Maps, 80 Lithographs and 75 Woodcuts. Vol. II. 42 Plates. Vol. III. The Zodiacal Light . . . . 3 vols., royal 4to, cloth, 6*l.* 6*s.*

VII.

KANSAS: its INTERIOR and EXTERIOR LIFE. By SARA T. L. ROBINSON . . . . Crown 8vo, cloth, 6*s.* 6*d.*

VIII.

WOODS and WATERS; or, the Saranacs and Racket, with Map of the Route and Nine Illustrations on Wood. By ALFRED B. STUART. Crown 8vo, cloth, 7*s.* 6*d.*

IX.

WILD SPORTS of the SOUTH. By E. WHITEHEAD. Crown 8vo, cloth, 7*s.* 6*d.*

X.

A TRIP to CUBA. By Mrs. JULIA WARD HOWE. Crown 8vo, cloth, 5*s.*

XI.

A RUN THROUGH EUROPE. By ERASTUS C. BENEDICT. Crown 8vo, cloth, London, 8*s.* 6*d.*

XII.

NOTES of TRAVELS and STUDY in ITALY. By C. E. NORTON. 12mo, cloth, 5*s.*

IN CHEMISTRY, MEDICINE, AND SURGERY.

I.

ELEMENTS of CHEMICAL PHYSICS. With numerous Illustrations, by JOSIAH P. COOKE . . . . 8vo, cloth, 14s.

"As an introduction to Chemical Physics, this is by far the most comprehensive work in our language."—*Athenæum.*

II.

HUMAN PHYSIOLOGY, STATICAL and DYNAMICAL; or, the Conditions and Course of the Life of Man. By J. W. DRAPER. 2nd Edition (New York, 1858), Illustrated with nearly 300 Wood Engravings, pp. 649, London . . . . 25s.

III.

A TREATISE on the PRACTICE of MEDICINE. By GEORGE B. WOOD, M.D. . . . . 2 vols. 8vo, cloth, 1*l.* 16*s.*

IV.

THE DISPENSATORY of the UNITED STATES. By GEORGE B. WOOD and FRANKLIN BACHE . . . . 8vo, sheep, 1*l.* 12*s.*

V.

CLINICAL LECTURES on the DISEASES of WOMEN and CHILDREN. By GUNNING S. BEDFORD. 6th Edition, Revised and Enlarged. 8vo, cloth, 21*s.*

VI.

A PRACTICAL TREATISE on FRACTURES and DISLOCATIONS. By F. H. HAMILTON, M.D. . . . . 8vo, cloth, 25*s.*

VII.

A PRACTICAL TREATISE on the DISEASES of CHILDREN. By J. FORSYTH MEIGS, M.D. . . . . 8vo, 18*s.*

VIII.

CHEMICAL and PHARMACEUTICAL MANIPULATIONS. By C. C. MORFIT. Enlarged Edition, with Illustrations . . . Royal 8vo, cloth, 21*s.*

IX.

ELEMENTS of CHEMISTRY. By M. V. REGNAULT. 3rd Edition, greatly Improved . . . . 2 vols. 8vo, cloth, 36*s.*

X.

THE HISTORY of PROSTITUTION: its Extent, Causes, and Effects throughout the World. By WILLIAM W. SANGER, M.D. . . . . . . cloth, 16*s.*

XI.

DENTAL COSMOS: a Monthly Record of Dental Science. Each Number, 1*s.* 6*d.*

THEOLOGICAL WORKS.

I.

THOUGHTS on PREACHING; being Contributions to Homiletics. By JAMES W. ALEXANDER . . . . Crown 8vo, cloth, 7*s.* 6*d*

II.

PREACHERS and PREACHING. By Dr. N. MURRAY. Post 8vo, 6*s.*

III.

THE NATIONAL PREACHER: Original Sermons from Living Divines of the United States. With Portraits. Annual Volumes, each, post 8vo, cloth, 7*s.* 6*d.*

IV.

THE GOSPEL ACCORDING TO MATTHEW EXPLAINED. By JOSEPH A. ALEXANDER, D.D. . . . . Cloth, 6*s.* 6*d.*

V.

NOTES on the NEW TESTAMENT LITERATURE and ECCLESIASTICAL HISTORY. By Rev. J. A. ALEXANDER, D.D. . Crown 8vo, cloth, 6s.

VI.

FORTY YEARS' FAMILIAR LETTERS of JAMES W. ALEXANDER, D.D., constituting, with the Notes, a Memoir of his Life. 2 vols. post 8vo, cloth, 18s.

VII.

SERMONS. By JOSEPH ADDISON ALEXANDER. 2 vols. post 8vo, cloth, 16s.

VIII.

COMMENTARY on the EPISTLE to the HEBREWS. By MOSES STUART. Edited and Revised by R. D. C. ROBBINS. 4th Edition, 8vo, pp. 575, cloth, London . . . . 12s.

IX.

A CHURCH HISTORY of the FIRST THREE CENTURIES, from the 30th to the 323rd Year of the Christian Era. By MILO MAHAN. Crown 8vo, cloth, 9s.

X.

BIBLIOTHECA SACRA and BIBLICAL REPOSITORY. Edited by E. A. PARKE and S. H. TAYLOR . . . . Each Number 3s. 6d.

NEWSPAPERS AND PERIODICALS

Received by every Mail. The following S. L. & Co. *are the London agents for, and supply at the prices quoted :—*

	Per annum (including the U.S. postage). £	s.	d.
The New York Herald, daily	3	6	0
Ditto semi-weekly issue	2	0	0
Ditto weekly	1	0	0
The New York Times, daily	2	16	0
Ditto semi-weekly	1	5	0
Ditto weekly.	0	15	0
The New York Tribune, daily	3	0	0
Ditto semi-weekly	1	5	0
Ditto weekly	0	15	0
The New York Independent	0	18	0
Wilkes' Spirit of the Times	0	18	0
The New York Ledger	0	13	6
The Scientific American: a Journal of Practical Information in Art, Science, Mechanics, &c.	0	15	0
Ditto half annual Volumes (cloth)	0	12	0
North American Review, quarterly, each Number	0	6	0
Hunt's Merchant's Magazine, monthly, each Part	0	2	6
The Banker's Magazine, edited by J. S. Homans, jun., monthly, each Part	0	2	6
The American Publisher's Circular, weekly	0	10	6

*** *Now ready, price 2s. 6d., the American Catalogue of Original Works published from* 1800-1857, *with the prices at which they can be obtained in London, or if not in stock, procured to order.*

Supplemental List of Importations 1857-1860, *price* 6d.

Made in the USA
Coppell, TX
21 September 2020

38533964R00233